# Kant's *Groundwork of the Metaphysics of Morals*

**Critical Essays on the Classics**

General Editor: Steven M. Cahn

This new series is designed to introduce college students to major works of philosophical and political theory through the best critical essays on those works. The distinguished editors of each collection have selected essays for their scholarly excellence and their accessibility to students. Each collection is meant to serve as a companion to the work itself, providing a gateway into a deeper understanding of the text.

Descartes's *Meditations*: Critical Essays
  *edited by Vere Chappell*

Kant's *Groundwork on the Metaphysics of Morals*: Critical Essays
  *edited by Paul Guyer*

Mill's *On Liberty*: Critical Essays
  *edited by Gerald Dworkin*

Mill's *Utilitarianism*: Critical Essays
  *edited by David Lyons*

Plato's *Republic*: Critical Essays
  *edited by Richard Kraut*

# Kant's *Groundwork of the Metaphysics of Morals*

## *Critical Essays*

EDITED BY
PAUL GUYER

ROWMAN & LITTLEFIELD PUBLISHERS, INC.
*Lanham • Boulder • New York • Oxford*

ROWMAN & LITTLEFIELD PUBLISHERS, INC.

Published in the United States of America
by Rowman & Littlefield Publishers, Inc.
4720 Boston Way, Lanham, Maryland 20706

12 Hid's Copse Road
Cummor Hill, Oxford OX2 9JJ, England

British Library Cataloguing in Publication Information Available

**Library of Congress Cataloging-in-Publication Data**

Kan't Groundwork of the metaphysics of morals : critical essays /
    edited by Paul Guyer.
        p.   cm. — (Critical essays on the classics)
    Includes bibliographical references and index.
    ISBN 0-8476-8628-0 (hardcover : alk. paper). — ISBN 0-8476-8629-9
(pbk. : alk. paper)
    1. Kant, Immanuel, 1724–1804.   Grundlegung zur Metaphysik der
Sitten.   2. Ethics.   3. Ethics, Modern—18th century.   I. Guyer,
Paul, 1948–   .   II. Series.
B2766.Z7K36   1998
170—dc21                                                97-30157
                                                        CIP

ISBN 0-8476-8628-0 (cloth : alk. paper)
ISBN 0-8476-8629-9 (pbk. : alk. paper)

Printed in the United States of America

 ∞ ™ The paper used in this publication meets the minimum requirements of
American National Standard for Information Sciences—Permanence of Paper
for Printed Library Materials, ANSI Z39.48–1984.

# Contents

       *Barbara Herman*

**7**   Humanity As End in Itself                                    165
       *Allen Wood*

**8**   The Categorical Imperative                                   189
       *Thomas W. Pogge*

**9**   The Possibility of the Categorical Imperative                215
       *Paul Guyer*

**Part IV.  The Categorical Imperative and
the Freedom of the Will
(*Groundwork* III)**

**10**  Kant's Argument for the Rationality of Moral Conduct         249
       *Thomas E. Hill, Jr.*

**11**  Morality and Freedom: Kant's Reciprocity Thesis              273
       *Henry E. Allison*

**12**  The Deduction of the Moral Law: The Reasons for the
       Obscurity of the Final Section of Kant's *Groundwork of
       the Metaphysics of Morals*                                    303
       *Dieter Henrich*

       Bibliography                                                  343

       Index                                                         359

       About the Authors                                             367

# Abbreviations

PE      "Prize Essay" (1763)

*Prol*    *Prolegomena to Any Future Metaphysics*
           *(Prolegomena zu einer jeden künftigen Metaphysik,*
           1783)*

*G*      *Groundwork of the Metaphysics of Morals*
           *(Gundlegung der Metaphysik der Sitten,* 1785)*

*IUH*    *Idea for a Universal History from a Practical Point of View*
           *(Idee zu einer allgemeinen Geschichte in*
           *weltbürgerlicher Absicht,* 1785)*

*MFNS*  *Metaphysical Foundations of Natural Science*
           *(Metaphysische Anfangsgründe der Naturwissenschaft,*
           1789)*

*CPracR* *Critique of Practical Reason*
           *(Kritik der praktischen Vernunft,* 1788)*

*CJ*     *Critique of Judgment*
           *(Kritik der Urteilskraft,* 1790)*

*R*      *Reflexion*
           (handwritten notes of various dates)

*Rel*     *Religion within the Boundaries of Mere Reason*
           *(Religion innerhalb der Grenzen der bloßen Vernunft,*
           1793)*

*MM*    *Metaphysics of Morals*
           *(Metaphysik der Sitten,* 1797)*

*Anth*      *Anthropology from a Pragmatic Point of View*
                  *(Anthropologie in pragmatische Hinsicht,* 1798)

*DR*         *Doctrine of Right,* Part I of *Metaphysics of Morals*

*DV*         *Doctrine of Virtue,* Part II of *Metaphysics of Morals*

The *Critique of Pure Reason* (*Kritik der reinen Vernunft,* 1781 and 1787) is usually cited solely by reference to the pages of its first (A) and second (B) pages.

When used, the abbreviation "*Ak*" refers to *Kant's gesammelte Schriften*, edited by the Royal Prussian (later German) Academy of Sciences (Berlin: Georg Reimer, later Walter de Gruyter, 1900– ).

# Acknowledgments

J. B. Schneewind, "Natural Law, Skepticism, and Methods of Ethics," originally appeared in *Journal of the History of Ideas* (1991). Reprinted by permission of the author and publisher.

Nelson Potter, "The Argument of Kant's *Groundwork*, Chapter 1," originally published in *Canadian Journal of Philosophy*, SV 1, Part 1 (1974): 73–91. Reprinted by permission of the author and publisher.

Christine M. Korsgaard, "Kant's Analysis of Obligation: The Argument of *Groundwork* I," originally appeared in *The Monist* 72 (1989): 311–39. Copyright © 1989, *The Monist*, La Salle, Illinois 61301. Reprinted by permission of the author and publisher.

Tom Sorell, "Kant's Good Will and Our Good Nature," originally appeared in *Kant-Studien* 78 (1987): 87–101. Reprinted by permission of the author and Walter de Gruyter & Co.

Onora O'Neill, "Consistency in Action," originally appeared in *Universality and Morality: Essays on Ethical Universalizability,* ed. N. Potter and M. Timmons (Dordrecht: D. Reidel Publishing, 1985). Reprinted with kind permission from Kluwer Academic Publishers and the author.

Barbara Herman, "Mutual Aid and Respect for Persons," originally appeared in *Ethics* 94 (1984): 577–602. Reprinted by permission of the author and University of Chicago Press.

Allen Wood, "Humanity As End in Itself," originally appeared in *Proceedings of the Eighth International Kant Congress,* vol. 1, part 1 (Milwaukee: Marquette University Press, 1995), 301–19. Reprinted by permission of the author and publisher.

Thomas W. Pogge, "The Categorical Imperative," originally appeared in *Grundlegung der Metaphysik der Sitten: Ein kooperativer Kommentar*, ed. Ottfried Höffe (Frankfurt am Main: Vittorio Klostermann, 1989), 172–93. Reprinted by permission of the author and publisher.

Paul Guyer, "The Possibility of the Categorical Imperative," originally appeared in *Philosophical Review* 104 (1995): 353–85. Copyright 1995 Cornell University. Reprinted by permission of the author and publisher.

Thomas E. Hill, Jr., "Kant's Argument for the Rationality of Moral Conduct," originally appeared in *Pacific Philosophical Quarterly* 66 (1985): 3–23. Reprinted by permission of the author and publisher. The essay is reprinted in this volume as it appeared in Hill's *Dignity and Practical Reason in Kant's Moral Theory* (Ithaca, N.Y.: Cornell University Press, 1992).

Henry E. Allison, "Morality and Freedom: Kant's Reciprocity Thesis," originally appeared in *Philosophical Review* 95 (1986): 393–425. Copyright 1986 Cornell University. Reprinted here by permission of the author and publisher.

Dieter Henrich, "The Deduction of the Moral Law: The Reasons for the Obscurity of the Final Section of Kant's *Groundwork of the Metaphysics of Morals*," originally appeared in German in *Denken im Schatten des Nihilismus*, ed. Alexander Schwann (Darmstadt: Wissenschaftliche Buchgesellschaft, 1975), 55–110. Translated with permission of the author and publisher.

# Introduction

Immanuel Kant's *Groundwork of the Metaphysics of Morals* (*Grund-legung der Metaphysik der Sitten*) has remained one of the most important and influential works in modern moral philosophy since it was first published in 1785; its only possible peers are John Stuart Mill's two masterpieces *On Liberty* and *Utilitarianism*, published eight decades later. In the second half of the twentieth century, Kant's *Groundwork* has if anything been even more widely read than before, studied intensively by students in courses in moral philosophy at every level and providing the inspiration for some of the most creative work done by contemporary moral philosophers.

There are obvious reasons why the book enjoys and deserves its popularity: it provides impressive formulations of the most fundamental principle of morality; it provides concrete but controversial examples of virtuous human conduct and the application of the fundamental principle of morality that continues to supply material for fruitful discussion; and it offers a stirring image of the possibility of deriving rules for human conduct from the value of human freedom and autonomy itself that does not depend on a theological view of the world and the place of humanity in it although it is not incompatible with an enlightened theology. In this regard, the *Groundwork* can be regarded as the paradigmatic expression of the ideals of the European Enlightenment, ideals that many regard as having been irremediably undermined by the gloomy history of the twentieth century, but which are probably better regarded as not yet having had a real chance to prove themselves. The twentieth century's long nightmare of fascism and totalitarianism in all its forms did not undermine the validity of the ideals of the Enlightenment, although it may have shown how hard it is to realize them.

In spite of its importance and even a kind of popularity, the *Groundwork* is one of the most difficult to read and understand of the great works of Western philosophy. The book is mercifully short, but its arguments are often too obscure and the transitions between them too abrupt to be clear. Kant's formulations of the fundamental principle of morality are impressive, but it is by no means clear how they are meant to be related to each other nor exactly how they are to be applied. And while Kant clearly thought that he could make his views intuitive by including more examples than he did in his *Critique of Pure Reason* (1781), what he has to say about these examples—such as that a person who acts entirely out of sympathetic inclination to others displays no special moral worth in his actions and deserves no special praise— often seems thoroughly counterintuitive, thus standing in the way of comprehension and acceptance of his general principles rather than helping them gain a proper hearing.

Because of both its importance and its difficulty, Kant's *Groundwork* has received careful attention from some of the best moral philosophers and historical scholars currently working, and in the last couple of decades an immense body of helpful secondary literature about the *Groundwork* has been published. The purpose of the present volume is to introduce students and readers of Kant's work to some of the best of this literature, and in so doing to introduce them to some of the most important issues in the interpretation of the work and to some of the most helpful voices in its contemporary discussion. To accomplish these two goals, two principles have been adopted in the selection of the work here presented. First, following J. B. Schneewind's initial essay ("Natural Law, Skepticism, and Methods of Ethics"), which furnishes some of the key historical background for understanding Kant's aims in the *Groundwork*,[1] the rest of the essays presented each focus on one of the three sections of Kant's book and one or more issues raised in and by that section. These essays are grouped in the order of Kant's three sections, and as far as possible the order of the essays within these sections parallels the sequence of topics in Kant's own work. To that extent the essays can be used as a selective, collective commentary[2] as the reader reads through Kant's book. Second, to maximize readers' exposure to leading writers on Kant's ethics, only one article from each author represented here has been included, although many of these authors have published numerous articles and books that can be immensely helpful even to beginning students of the *Groundwork*. The authors' own notes as well as this volume's suggested readings will help readers to find further works by the authors represented here as well as valuable work by others that could not be presented here.

The essays that follow offer a great wealth of insight about Kant's *Groundwork*, about both its promises and its problems. So that readers can get to those papers as quickly as possible, this introduction will be kept short. What follows will be only a brief outline of the *Groundwork* and suggestions about how the papers included bear on the various issues of both interpretation and assessment that it raises.

## Title and Preface

The first question a reader might ask is just what Kant meant by the title *Groundwork of the Metaphysics of Morals*, or, in German, *Grundlegung der Metaphysik der Sitten*. The first part of the title has in the past been translated as *principle* or *foundations*.[3] But German has other words for those English terms, *Grundsatz* and *Grundlage* respectively, the first of which Kant frequently uses, which therefore makes the use of another word for the translation of *Grundlegung* preferable. In addition, the terms *principle* and *foundations* also lack the active connotation of the participle *Grundlegung*, which suggests something like laying the foundation or preparing the ground for something. To capture that connotation, one recent translator used the word *grounding* as a noun,[4] but that seems an unnecessary neologism. As do most of the authors in the collection, I have preferred the translation "Groundwork," used by H. J. Paton in his classical translation of the book from 1948,[5] which by incorporating the word "work" captures the active element of Kant's participle without mimicking its grammar. This term has also been used by Mary J. Gregor in her monumental new translation of all of Kant's writings in both moral and political philosophy.[6]

Why is it important to preserve this connotation? To answer this question already requires an interpretation of Kant's intentions. Clearly, Kant meant this book to enunciate the fundamental principle of morality and show something about how it is applied, at least enough to show that he has correctly formulated the principle. But if that were all he meant, he could have simply called the book *The Principle of Morality*, without using the peculiarly active term *Grundlegung*—nor, for that matter, would he have had to use the mysterious phrase *metaphysics of morals (Metaphysik der Sitten)* instead of just *morals (Sitten)* or *morality (Moralität)*. In fact, by making the title of his book complex in just the way he did—using the participle and inserting the word *metaphysics* into it—Kant seems to have meant to signal two different points about his aims. First, he clearly did not mean simply to formulate the principle of morality and illustrate its application, but also to show how that principle is rooted in and can be justified by irreducible features of human thought and action, in Kant's terms in practical reason and the freedom of the will. To provide the groundwork for a principle rather than just to state the principle is to prepare the way for the reception of the principle by grounding it in a certain conception of these most fundamental human faculties or capacities. Since a philosophical conception of these most fundamental faculties as the basis for morality can be called a "metaphysics of morals," then one thing that Kant meant by calling his work a "groundwork of the metaphysics of morals" is that it is a groundwork for the fundamental principle of morality *in* a metaphysics of morals, an argument for it that roots it in a particular philosophical account of the most fundamental of human capacities and their value. Kant indicated this aspect of his intentions by his use of the phrase *metaphysics of morals (Metaphysik der Sitten)* at several key places in his text (for example, *G*, 388–89 and 426).

However, there is something else that Kant meant by the phrase *metaphysics of morals.* During the two decades before he published the *Groundwork*, Kant had often expressed his intention to write a systematic moral philosophy, that is, a systematic enumeration of our obligations and duties, under the title of a "Metaphysics of Morals." Kant reiterated this intention in the preface to the *Groundwork*, making it clear that the present work was intended as a preparation for such a systematic treatise on duties. Finally, a dozen years after the publication of the *Groundwork*, Kant did at last publish a systematic account of what he had by then come to call our duties of right and of virtue (our duties and rights as members of polities and our duties just as human beings) under the title of the *Metaphysics of Morals* (1797). This work offers a systematic account of our duties and obligations based on the division of all of our duties to ourselves and to others into two classes, those that are coercively—juridically and politically— enforceable and those that are not, but can only be enforced by the application of our own consciences to our natural dispositions and inclinations. In publishing the *Groundwork of the Metaphysics of Morals* in 1785, Kant clearly intended to provide the introduction to such a work, although in the dozen years between 1785 and 1797 he ended up writing two additional critiques—the *Critique of Practical Reason* (1788) and the *Critique of Judgment* (1790)—as well as his major work on morality as the only possible basis for religion—*Religion within the Boundaries of Mere Reason* (1793)—none of which were foreseen at the time of the *Groundwork*, and all of which in various ways also introduce the eventual *Metaphysics of Morals*. When Kant finally did write the *Metaphysics of Morals*, the relation of both its foundation and its division of duties to the earlier *Groundwork of the Metaphysics of Morals* was by no means straightforward. Nevertheless, when he wrote the *Groundwork* Kant clearly intended it as a preparation for a work like the later *Metaphysics of Morals*, and this tells us something about how it must be understood.

In the preface to the *Groundwork*, Kant compares a metaphysics of morals to a metaphysics of nature, suggesting that the metaphysics of morals will be the pure or exclusively rational part of ethics, contrasted to an empirical part that might be called "practical anthropology," just as a metaphysics of nature must contain both a pure and an empirical part (*G*, 388). In the preface to the *Metaphysics of Morals*, however, Kant suggests that a work with such a title must include at least a certain amount of practical anthropology or empirical information about human beings, so that it can be seen what sorts of duties and obligations human beings applying the fundamental principle of morality in the general circumstances of human life must have, even though such a work can never amount to a complete empirical system or specification of all of our duties (*MM*, 6:205–6). In this second sense, a "metaphysics of morals" is not an entirely abstract foundation for moral theory, but rather a worked-out system of duties that takes account of at least some general features of the human condition as made known to us empirically rather than by reason alone (just as a metaphysics of nature turned out [in Kant's 1786 book *Metaphysical Foundations of Natural Science*] not to be entirely pure or a priori but rather to explicate the consequences of applying the pure principles of the understanding to the empirical concept of motion).

Thus the title of a *Groundwork of the Metaphysics of Morals* must be taken in a double sense. On the one hand, the task of such a work must be that of grounding a conception of the fundamental principle of morality in highly abstract concepts of reason and will, in abstraction from all details about the human situation except the minimal assumption that we have such a reason and such a will. In this sense, the work grounds the fundamental principle of morality *in* a metaphysical conception of the basis of morality, as Kant several times suggests. On the other hand, the work must also be a preparation *for* the metaphysics of morals in Kant's later sense, or at least begin to show how the most general principle of morality can give rise to a concrete system of obligations and duties when it is applied to the human condition considered in at least some of its particularity, that is, considering at least very general but still empirical facts about human beings such as that the kinds of ends we can freely choose to fulfill depend upon our being not pure wills but embodied creatures, that our ability to fulfill the ends we set for ourselves depends upon our mental and physical health as well as upon the development of skills and talents that require time and education, and perhaps a few other extremely general but still empirical presuppositions of this sort.

This in turn suggests that the *examples* that Kant offers in the course of the *Groundwork* also have a dual function. On the one hand, insofar as they play a part in suggesting the analysis of the fundamental principle of morality *in* a metaphysics of morals, they anchor Kant's account of the fundamental conceptions of reason and will themselves, which will in turn be used to ground the fundamental principle of morality, in intuitive and commonly accepted claims about human nature. On the other hand, as part of a preparation *for* a metaphysics of morals in Kant's later sense, the examples are there to confirm his account of the fundamental principle of morality not by looking back to its foundations but by looking forward to its application. Thus Kant appeals to examples both to ground his account of the fundamental principle of morality and to confirm it by showing that it will lead to a system of duties that we will all recognize, one that may well refine commonsense conceptions of our duties but will still be recognizable by common sense. This dual function is to some extent divided, with the first role of the examples more prominent in the *Groundwork*'s Section I and the second more prominent in Section II, but there is a risk of serious confusion in the discussion of Kant's examples if both of their roles are not recognized.

So much for the implications of Kant's title. We can now consider the brief remarks about the structure and method of the book that he makes in the Preface. Kant offers two different statements of his purpose, each of which must be kept in mind in all that follows. On the one hand, Kant suggests that the purpose of the *Groundwork* is purely theoretical, "nothing more than the search for and establishment of the *supreme principle of morality*, which constitutes by itself a business that in its purpose is complete and to be kept apart from every other moral investigation" (*G*, 392). The phrase "search for and establishment of" suggests that even from a purely theoretical point of view, the work has a twofold aim, being intended both to discover the proper formulation—or formulations—of this supreme principle of morality and to prove its validity. On the other hand, Kant also suggests that his project has a practical as well as a theoretical motivation: "A metaphysics of morals is therefore indispensably necessary, not merely because of a motive to speculation—for investigating the source of the practical principles that lie *a priori* in our reason—but also because morals themselves remain subject to all sorts of corruption as long as we are without that clue and supreme norm by which to appraise them correctly" (G, 389–90). A clear account of the fundamental principle of morality and a convincing proof not only that this principle is binding upon us but also that we are capable of living up to it is not a matter of interest solely to the philosopher, but is of practical importance to every human being as a means by which to counteract the natural human tendency to find ways to lighten the demands of morality even if at some level we also naturally acknowledge them. Only with both the clearest possible understanding of the principle of morality and a convincing proof that we can really do what it demands of us can we be fortified against the natural and inevitable temptations to escape or minimize its rigorous demands.

This dual purpose complicates Kant's arguments in the *Groundwork* and has profound implications for the development of his moral philosophy in his works subsequent to the *Groundwork*, especially the *Critique of Practical Reason* and *Religion within the Boundaries of Mere Reason*. Kant can appeal to common moral knowledge as the basis for the initial formulation of the fundamental principle of morality because it is part of his doctrine that no normal human being is simply unaware of this principle. However, the reality of human evil-doing is a fact, to put it mildly, but one that must be compatible with universal human knowledge of the fundamental principle of morality if Kant's entire theory is not to be undermined. Kant will steer his way through this dilemma by assuming that human evil-doing arises not from sheer ignorance of the moral law, but rather from the temptation to make exceptions for oneself, not to reject the moral law out of hand but to find loopholes in it (see *G*, 424). In the *Critique of Practical Reason*, Kant will expand upon the theme that every human being is aware of the content and force of the moral law, by means of what he comes to call the "fact of reason," and on some interpretations of this work he drops any attempt to give a metaphysical proof of the freedom of human beings to live up to the moral law in favor of a derivation of it directly from the fact of our awareness of our obligation under this law and the principle that "ought implies can," that is, that it is irrational to suppose that we have an obligation we cannot fulfill.[7] The *Religion* responds to this increased emphasis on the universality of our knowledge of the moral law by expanding upon the theme that wrong-doing always takes the form of excepting oneself from the moral law rather than either being ignorant of it or rejecting it wholesale, while also arguing that the possibility of choosing to do evil is part and parcel of the capacity to make free choices at all, thus part of the capacity to choose freely even what is right; it is in this sense that the possibility of evil is "radical" for human beings, or just as fundamental as the possibility of doing what is right. These developments may seem to lie in the future in the *Groundwork* but are to a considerable extent already implied by its dual assumptions that knowledge of the moral law is not only both common and natural but also subject to corruption. The argument of the book must thus find a way to build upon the first of these facts while giving us the tools to deal with the second.

This complexity of Kant's aims in the *Groundwork* is by no means hinted at in the statement about the method of the work with which Kant concludes the Preface. Here Kant just says: "I have adopted in this work the method that is, I believe, most suitable if one wants to proceed analytically from common cognition to the determination of its supreme principle, and in turn synthetically from the examination of this principle and its sources back to the common cognition in which we find it used" (*G*, 392). This statement suggests only part of what we need to understand the theoretical argument of the *Groundwork*. It implies that the book will proceed by first *analyzing* common-sense beliefs about morality in order to arrive at a "determination" of the supreme principle of morality, that is, presumably, a formulation of this principle that is implicit in but more determinate than common-sense moral beliefs, and that it will then confirm this formulation by turning "back to the common cognition in which we find it used," that is, presumably, by showing that the principle arrived at by the analysis of commonsense moral beliefs explains actual moral practices or particular moral judgments, which would be evidence that it is in fact the principle that underlies common moral beliefs.

This is certainly part of what Kant is up to in the *Groundwork*. In particular, as already suggested, this statement explains the difference between the role of Kant's examples in Section I and in Section II: the examples of virtuous persons in Section I, such as that of a formerly sympathetic person whose love of humanity has been dulled by his own misfortunes but who nevertheless manages to continue to act virtuously out of respect for duty itself (*G*, 398), are intended to help us properly formulate the supreme principle of morality, while the examples of the derivation of particular duties from what turn out to be several different formulations of the supreme principle of morality in Section II, the examples of the duties to refrain from suicide and false promises and to develop our own talents and practice beneficence toward others (*G*, 421–23 and 429–30), are clearly meant to confirm Kant's formulations of the principle by showing that they do give rise to commonly recognized duties and indeed to a commonly recognized classification of duties.

Nevertheless, even Kant's purely theoretical argument in the *Groundwork* is not confined to an appeal to common sense first for insight and then for confirmation. The division of the book that he announces immediately after the statement about its method that we have just considered makes this clear. Kant divides the book thus:

1. *First section:* Transition from common rational to philosophic moral cognition.

2. *Second section:* Transition from popular moral philosophy to metaphysics of morals.

3. *Third section:* Final step from metaphysics of morals to the critique of pure practical reason. (*G*, 392)

If the analysis of common sense for the formulation of the principle of morality and then a return to common sense for its confirmation were all that he had in mind, Kant might have described the first section as he does, but not the remaining ones. On that account there should only have been two sections, the first described as it is and a second that would constitute a transition back from "philosophic moral cognition" to "common moral practice" or something of the sort. In fact, Section II as it is written *does* include such a transition: returning to common moral practice to confirm the formulation of the supreme principle of morality is part of what Kant does in Section II. But it is by no means all that Kant does there. While doing this, Kant also *criticizes* not "common rational cognition" but, rather, "popular moral philosophy," arguing that the latter can only lead to a misconception of the fundamental principle of philosophy (the essays by J. B. Schneewind and Christine M. Korsgaard supply some of the background and details for this critique). Kant then turns to "metaphysics of morals" to provide a derivation and formulation of the moral law that is consistent with but more refined than the formulation that is derivable from "common moral cognition" and altogether superior to what might be suggested by "popular moral philosophy." Thus, the expression "metaphysics of morals" seems to bear both of its senses in the title of Section II: it seems to connote a derivation of the moral law itself from the concept of a rational being and the conditions of the possibility of rational willing, as well as a confirmation of the formulation of the moral law by showing that it gives rise to a recognizable system of duties, as Kant's remark about analysis and synthesis would lead us to expect.

Given this turn to fundamental metaphysics in Section II, Kant could have used the distinction between analytical and synthetical methods, which we have already used to describe the two different roles of examples in Sections I and II, in another way to describe the relation between those two sections. In his *Prolegomena to Any Future Metaphysics* (1783), Kant had said that this popular exposition of his theory of knowledge used the analytical method and the original *Critique of Pure Reason* the synthetical method (4:263–64), suggesting by this that a derivation of general principles of human knowledge from the assumption of the validity of particular scientific and mathematical claims, which is what he offers in the *Prolegomena*, is analytical in method, while a derivation of those same general principles from even more fundamental assumptions about the basic faculties of human thought and the structure of consciousness itself, which is what he offers in the first *Critique*, is synthetical in method. But that model cannot be carried over to the *Groundwork* without some modification (as Dieter Henrich argues in his essay), because Kant repeatedly states that *both* Sections I and II of the *Groundwork* are analytical in method, and that only Section III is synthetical; that is, he claims that his method does not become synthetical until he makes the final transition from "metaphysics of morals" to the "critique of pure practical reason." This is partly just misleading, since the confirmation of the correctness of Kant's formulations of the supreme principle of morality by showing that they give rise to a recognizable classification of duties, which is included in Section II, surely is properly described as synthetical rather than analytical in method. But Kant does not seem to mean to deny this in insisting that Section II is analytical in method and only Section III is synthetical. Instead, he seems to mean that there is a difference between deriving the supreme principle of morality from an analysis of certain basic assumptions about the nature of moral law and of rational but also willing beings in general—which is what he does in Section II—and showing that this analysis really applies to and indeed binds or obligates creatures like *us*—which seems to be at least part of what he is doing in Section III. Several of the essays included in this volume, especially those by Henry E. Allison and Dieter Henrich in part IV, try to explicate in some detail the difference between Kant's argumentative strategy in Sections II and III and to explain precisely what he is arguing in Section III.

But even these remarks about the complexity of Kant's theoretical method in the *Groundwork* do not fully explain why he even thought it necessary to write such a book. Kant precedes the methodological remarks we have thus far been considering with a statement that the necessity of working "out for once a pure moral philosophy, completely cleansed of everything that may be only empirical and that belongs to anthropology . . . is clear of itself from the common idea of duty and of moral laws." This is clear, he holds, because "everyone must grant that a law, if it is to hold morally, that is, as a ground of an obligation, must carry with it absolute necessity" (*G*, 389). Is common sense then completely nonproblematic and authoritative about the fundamental principle of morality, that is, sufficient to both lead to and confirm the formulation of such a principle? And is the role of philosophy, or of a metaphysics of morals in its first sense, then, purely theoretical? That is, is the *Groundwork* intended just to provide a philosophical explanation of the type Kant prefers for the unquestioned absolute necessity of moral law, an explanation tracing it back to some pure faculties of mind, which is of interest only to the philosopher? Such an interpretation would not seem to explain the importance of the *Groundwork* to Kant, nor its continuing interest to readers over two centuries. And it is not all that Kant has in mind.

As we have seen, Kant thinks that common sense, at least about morality, does possess great authority, and that it thus constitutes both a natural starting point for and a check on the philosophical discussion of the supreme principle of morality. But as we have also seen, Kant also thinks that the natural and common commitment to the fundamental principle of morality can easily be shaken. In the Preface, what Kant seems to have in mind is that our natural recognition of our obligation under the moral law can be corrupted by equally natural selfish temptations. In the main text, however, Kant might seem to suggest that our natural morality is liable to corruption by bad philosophy. But what Kant probably thinks is that bad moral philosophy is itself a product of our natural desire to evade moral responsibility, a form of rationalization we create in order to justify our evasions. If that is so, then his own improved moral philosophy is not meant just for our theoretical satisfaction but has the very practical aim of depriving us of the rationalization for our temptation to moral evasion that we can find in philosophy.

The first threat to our commitment to duty is reflected in popular moral philosophy's use of a merely empirical method, which by restricting its attention to what may most often be observed about actual human behavior is likely to confuse duty with an unmitigated pursuit of individual human happiness and thereby subvert our original commitment to duty by *hedonism* or the crudest form of consequentialism. Kant's fear of the threat of hedonism is part of what explains the rigidity of his distinction in the *Groundwork* between virtue and any concern for happiness, even though the doctrine of the "highest good" that he enunciates in each of his three *Critiques* recognizes that the relation between virtue and happiness is more intimate and complex than the *Groundwork* usually suggests.[8]

Second, the commonsense commitment to morality can be threatened by the common belief in *determinism*, the doctrine that every event, even human actions, is completely and inexorably determined by previous states of affairs, which may lead us to think that we cannot always perform our duty even if we know what it is and, thus, may weaken our commitment to what seems to be an unrealizable ideal of duty. An attempt to avert the practical rather than merely theoretical threat of determinism is a large part of Kant's concern in Section III of the *Groundwork*. Indeed, the fact that Kant recognizes two different sources for the corruption of moral common sense may even explain why the *Groundwork* has three sections instead of two, why it contains both a "metaphysics of morals" to distinguish the content of the fundamental principle of morality from any principle of morality that could be derived merely from empirical observation of human behavior in all its weakness (Section II) and a "critique of pure practical reason" to show that human beings are, in fact, always capable of living up to the exacting demands of this supreme principle in spite of the apparent threat of determinism (Section III). (The essay by Korsgaard, although it is about Kant's argument in Section I, prepares the way for such an interpretation of Kant's intentions in Section II, as does Schneewind's essay; all three essays in Part IV, that is, those by Thomas E. Hill, Jr., Allison and Henrich, focus at least in part on the issue of freedom from determinism in Section III.)

Reflection on Kant's few methodological comments in the Preface to the *Groundwork*, then, already suggests how many issues are at stake in the work and why Kant's exposition of his argument is unavoidably dense and often difficult to follow. Further discussion of methodological issues is best left to the essays in this volume. At this point, we can turn to a brief overview of Kant's main arguments in Sections I through III of the book.

## Section I

As its title, "Transition from common rational to philosophic moral cognition" (*G*, 393), may be taken to suggest, the primary purpose of Section I is to arrive at an initial formulation of the fundamental principle of morality by appealing to what Kant takes to be universally shared moral concepts and judgments that are supposed to show that everybody already assumes the validity of the principle he will identify, even if philosophy is needed to make the formulation of the principle more precise and rigorous as a first step toward constraining the natural tendency to evade its implications. Several of Kant's claims and examples, especially his examples of virtuous persons supposedly motivated by the fundamental principle of morality alone, have been intensely contested almost since the publication of the *Groundwork*. But in reflecting upon Kant's argument in this section, it is important to keep the role of these examples in perspective. They are supposed to lead us to accept Kant's initial formulation of the principle of morality, but they are not his whole argument for it. While it is part of Kant's view that the fundamental principle of morality is readily accessible to every human being, that need not be part of every moral philosophy, and it might be possible to establish Kant's fundamental principle of morality on other grounds even if his appeal to common sense is shaky. And even if an initial appeal to "common rational cognition" is held to be an indispensable foundation for any moral theory, perhaps analyses and examples of common moral beliefs and practices different from Kant's might still lead to the same general principle. So it is important not to get too caught up in the debates about Kant's examples and thereby loose sight of his goal.

Kant begins with several claims about the concept of a *good will*. He claims that a good will is the only thing that is unconditionally good, good in itself and under all circumstances. Other goods, gifts of nature such as strength, intelligence, and character traits such as courage, as well as gifts of fortune such as wealth and power, may be put to good or evil uses and, thus, are not intrinsically or unconditionally good; but a good will itself is incapable of being put to an evil use and is, thus, always good (*G*, 393–94). Further, Kant argues, a good will is not good because of any "proposed end" that it "effects or accomplishes," but solely because of the quality of the volition or intention that it expresses (*G*, 394). This claim raises difficult issues about the moral significance of ends or purposes that will pervade the first two sections of the work. Almost any moral theory could allow that in appraising the moral worth of particular human actions we must look to what the agent *intended* rather than to the state of affairs that may actually have *resulted* from that intention, because there's many a slip 'twixt spoon and mouth—even our most well-intended actions do not always turn out as we plan. But it would be compatible with that commonplace to infer that we should evaluate actions by their *intended* rather than *actual* outcomes; we don't have to immediately jump to the conclusion that the moral worth of actions and their agents have nothing to do with intended outcomes at all, as Kant seems to do. Further, while Kant may yet be able to make a case that the moral worth of actions and agents cannot depend upon what he will call *material* ends, goals of action the value of which depends entirely upon particular desires, it is not clear that this is the only kind of ends we can consider, thus that moral worth has nothing to do with ends at all. In fact, in the second section of the *Groundwork* Kant will introduce the idea of a *necessary end*, an object or state of affairs that is of unconditional value regardless of particular desires, and will suggest that the fundamental principle of morality is obligatory because abiding by it is the only way to attain the necessary ends of mankind or any conceivable rational agents (see Paul Guyer's essay, "The Possibility of the Categorical Imperative"). From the outset, then, Kant's puzzling statements that even common sense proves that morality has nothing to do with the value of human ends or purposes may have to be treated cautiously. Finally, Kant completes his initial discussion of the good will with an argument that if every natural human capability has some purpose that it is best suited for, then, since human reason does not seem to be particularly effective at producing *happiness*, the only alternative is that it is meant to produce nothing other than the good will (*G*, 395–96). This argument raises questions about the role of appeals to nature and especially to alleged purposes and intentions of nature in a moral theory that is supposed to be based on pure reason, as Kant has insisted from the outset that his theory is (*G*, 389).[9]

In the next part of Section I, Kant argues that the implications of this supposedly commonsense notion of good will can be further revealed by exploring the concept of *duty*, "which contains that of a good will though under certain limitations and hindrances, which, however, far from concealing it and making it unrecognizable, rather bring it out by contrast and make it shine forth all the more brightly" (*G*, 397). In the discussion of duty, Kant makes three claims: First, having a good will, the sole thing of unconditional moral worth, lies in acting not just in accord with but *from* duty (*G*, 397–98); second, "an action from duty has its moral worth *not in the purpose* to be attained by it but in the maxim in accordance with which it is decided upon" (*G*, 399); and third, a proposition that is supposed to follow from the previous ones, "duty is the necessity of an action from respect for law" (*G*, 400), or an action entirely motivated by recognition of the moral law. In other words, morally good action is action motivated by respect for duty itself, action from duty is action that regards not the ends but the lawful form of action, so morally good action is action motivated by respect for the lawful form of action. Kant's argument is then that the fundamental principle of morality must be one that is consistent with this conception of duty, thus one that is independent of any particular purpose or end an agent may have but at the same time is still capable of motivating a human being as a rational agent to action.

The culminating argument of Section I is that this constraint on the fundamental principle of morality, derived from common views about the concept of duty, is enough to entail what that principle must be: this conception of duty has excluded the possibility that any rule for action, or what Kant calls a "maxim" (see *G*, 401n), could be adopted as the principle of duty because of the value placed on some particular end that it should bring about, so the only alternative is that a maxim can be adopted as a guide to duty only because it conforms to the idea of a universally valid moral law as such. In Kant's words, "Since I have deprived the will of every impulse that could arise for it from obeying some law, nothing is left but the conformity of actions as such with universal law, which alone is to serve the will as its principle, that is, *I ought never to act except in such a way that I could also will that my maxim should become a universal law*" (*G*, 402). This principle, Kant claims, is implicit in common sense, even if common sense does not formulate it so precisely: "Thus, then, we have arrived, within the moral cognition of common human reason, at its principle, which it admittedly does not think so abstractly in a universal form, but which it actually has always before its eyes and uses as the norm for its appraisals" (*G*, 403–4). Kant will go on to argue in Section II that this principle actually presents itself to human beings in the form of a "categorical imperative," a principle that is *categorical* because it holds unconditionally, independently of whatever particular desires or inclinations we might happen to have, but that presents itself to us as an *imperative*, or a constraint, precisely because we do have particular desires and inclinations that might lead us to act otherwise than as the principle requires. By the "fundamental principle of morality," then, Kant means the most basic law of morality that would hold for any agent conceived as a rational being, no matter how abstractly that agent is conceived; by the "categorical imperative" he means this principle in the form in which it presents itself to creatures like us, who not only are rational beings but also have in our bodies and psyches sources of desire and inclination independent from pure reason and that may have to be constrained by pure reason.

Kant supports his claims that virtuous actions are those done from the motive of duty alone with several examples, some of which have proven noncontroversial but others of which have turned out to be quite controversial. Kant supports his claim that to have a good will and, thus, moral worth is to act *from* duty with the example of a shopkeeper who treats his customers fairly because, as we say, "honesty is the best policy" for earning a good reputation and therefore an extensive clientele; such a person is acting *in conformity* with duty but not *from* duty and therefore does nothing that is morally praiseworthy, although also nothing that is blameworthy (*G*, 397). This claim has not been challenged. But Kant goes on to support his further claim that to act from duty is to act out of respect for the moral law alone with several further examples: for instance, he says that a person who helps others simply out of feelings of sympathy displays no special moral worth or praiseworthiness, but that a person whose sympathy with others has been deadened by his own misfortunes but who still helps them out of his sense of duty and respect for the moral law does display moral worth in all its distinctness (*G*, 398). This example has proven highly controversial; indeed one can even say that it has outraged readers of Kant from the days of Friedrich Schiller and Arthur Schopenhauer, both of whom argued that sympathetic feeling plays just as large a role in our conception of the morally desirable personality as does commitment to abstract principles.[10]

In their essays, Nelson Potter ("The Argument of Kant's *Groundwork*, Chapter 1") and Christine M. Korsgaard ("Kant's Analysis of Obligation: The Argument of *Groundwork* I") focus on Kant's derivation of the fundamental principle of morality from his analysis of the concept of duty and are less concerned with the question of whether Kant's supposedly commonsense examples of virtuous and dutiful persons are consistent with a plausible moral psychology. To the extent that Kant's examples are meant as heuristic devices to introduce a formulation of the principle of morality that will then be both grounded in and extended by more purely philosophical considerations, by what Kant calls a turn to the metaphysics of morals (*G*, 412, 426–27) in the first of the senses we explained above, this approach is correct. But, as we saw earlier, it is also part of Kant's theory that moral philosophy and common sense must be consistent, because he believes that the moral law really is known by every human being, a position he would have difficulty maintaining if his conceptions of duty and moral worth were noticeably divergent from what most people believe.

In recent years, an extensive debate has grown up about just what Kant is claiming about morally praiseworthy motivation and about whether his position is plausible. Much of this discussion begins with a 1979 article by Richard Henson and a 1982 reply to it by Barbara Herman.[11] Because I have not wanted to focus the discussion of the issues raised by Section I too exclusively on the plausibility of Kant's conception of morally praiseworthy motivation, and also because these papers have been very widely cited and are readily accessible, I have chosen not to reprint these essays here, but have instead chosen to represent this debate with the less well-known essay by Tom Sorell, "Kant's Good Will and Our Good Nature," which gives a reliable account of this debate and stakes out an eminently reasonable position in it, namely, that the point in moral psychology that Kant is trying to make is that we should not see inclinations as motivations for action that are in *competition* with the principle of morality, but, rather, we should see inclinations as ineliminable elements of human psychology that are precisely what is to be *regulated* by our commitment to the fundamental principle of morality. In other words, these examples not only introduce the fundamental principle of morality by means of the argument cited above, which is analyzed in detail by both Potter and Korsgaard, but also prepare the way for the distinction between the fundamental principle of morality and its presentation to creatures like us as a categorical imperative that is central to the arguments of both Sections II and III of the *Groundwork*.

## Section II

The second section of the *Groundwork,* entitled "Transition from popular moral philosophy to metaphysics of morals," is the heart of the book, but it is also as complicated a stretch of argumentation as Kant ever wrote. The title might suggest that the point of the section is theoretical, that Kant simply aims to replace what is in his view theoretically inadequate moral philosophy with his own, improved moral philosophy. And certainly that is part of what he is trying to do. The final paragraph of Section I, however, begins with the striking statement that "There is something splendid about innocence, but what is bad about it, in turn, is that it cannot protect itself very well and is easily seduced" (*G*, 404–5). This suggests that the section that follows will also have the practical goal of showing how "innocence," that is, the sound insights of moral common sense on which Kant has based his analysis of duty in Section I, can be saved from "seduction." But what sort of seduction does Kant have in mind?

The professional philosopher might flatter himself that philosophy, even bad philosophy, has the power to seduce common sense; but perhaps philosophy, which, after all, cannot be pulled out of thin air but has to build on at least some assumptions of common sense, can itself be seduced by the natural inclination to try to evade what we all know to be true and right but also hard. Kant writes as if the faults of popular moral philosophy are due to empiricism, a poor choice of philosophical methodology for a moral philosophy that is to be unconditionally valid; but perhaps our natural tendency to evade the strict demands of morality invokes empiricism to try to put on a better face, to justify its own weakness precisely by limiting our belief about how we *ought* to behave by the inglorious facts about how we usually *do* behave. And if the empiricism in moral philosophy against which Kant argues is itself not the case but is, rather, only the expression of a natural human tendency to try to evade the demands of morality even though we all know what those demands are, then we should not think that saving innocence from seduction can be done once and for all just by replacing a poor philosophical foundation for morality with a better one. Rather, even armed with a sound moral philosophy, we will still face a lifelong struggle against our natural tendency to evade morality's strict requirements, which will surely find other forms of self-justification even if it is deprived of empiricism. Such a view would certainly be compatible with Kant's view about moral self-reform in the *Religion within the Boundaries of Mere Reason*, where he writes that even "If by a single and unalterable decision a human being reverses the supreme ground of his maxims by which he was an evil human being," still, "he is a good human being only in incessant laboring and becoming, i.e., he can hope—in view of the purity of the principle which he has adopted as the supreme maxim of his power of choice . . .—to find himself upon the good (though narrow) path of constant *progress* from bad to better" (*Rel*, 6:48).[12]

Kant begins the section by asserting that his appeal to the "common use of our practical reason" is not to be confused with treating morality "as a concept of experience," or as a form of empiricism. He charges empiricism, which might seem compassionate because of its "deep regret of the frailty and impurity of human nature," with undermining our moral idealism by denying the reality of the concept of duty and ascribing "everything to more or less refined self-love": it "uses reason, which should serve it for giving law, only to look after the interests of the inclinations" (*G*, 406).

Why does Kant make this harsh charge against an approach to ethics that has been advocated not by deviants but by personally noble and blameless human beings from Epicurus to Francis Hutcheson and David Hume? The answer is that it is not just a methodological mistake to try to ground moral theory on experience "when it is absolutely impossible by means of experience to make out with complete certainty a single case in which the maxim of an action otherwise in conformity with duty rested simply on moral grounds and on the representation of one's duty" (*G*, 407); rather, if you try to ground a moral theory on observation of how people actually do behave rather than on our innate knowledge of how we ought to behave, then you will end up sanctifying the hodge-podge of inclinations on which people often do act, a mixture of self-love and sympathetic feelings, or inclinations to one's own happiness as one presently imagines it and the happiness of some other persons who just happen to be near and dear to one. One will end up with principles advocating "now perfection, now happiness, here moral feeling, there fear of God, a bit of this and also a bit of that in a marvelous mixture" (*G*, 410). This might be considered the subversion of moral philosophy by the natural inclination to evade the demands of morality as well as the seduction of common moral understanding by bad philosophy.

In order to avoid these dangers, Kant argues that moral philosophy must use a metaphysical rather than empirical method. Such a metaphysical method must begin by "follow[ing] and present[ing] distinctly the practical faculty of reason, from its general rules of determination to the point where the concept of duty arises from it" (*G*, 412). In other words, the metaphysics of morals must begin with an analysis of the concept of rational action, and the main argument of Section II would appear to be intended as such an analysis. In fact, the analysis of the section will be more complicated than that, both because the concept being analyzed will be enriched along the way and because at key points Kant will once again appeal to commonly accepted examples of duty to confirm his analysis. In his theoretical writings, Kant argues that analysis always presupposes synthesis,[13] and the appeal to examples might be understood as Kant's attempt to confirm the results of his analysis of rational action by showing that it does fit with our common understanding of morality, where such an assertion is always synthetic.

The concept of rational agency that Kant proposes to analyze is the concept of "the capacity to act *in accordance with a representation* of laws," or the concept of a "will" that acts "in accordance with principles" (*G*, 412). A will can act in accordance with a principle that says that in order to achieve some particular end some particular means must be used. This is a "technical" principle, or a principle of "skill" (*G*, 415), telling us what technique has to be used to achieve a certain end. Even where the end involved is arbitrary, such a principle can seem like a constraint to us, because we may want the end but not want the means, and we may have to choose between our desire for the end and our aversion to the means; thus, even a rule of skill can present itself to us as an imperative. Such an imperative can also be called "hypothetical," because it is an imperative for us only on the hypothesis that we do desire the end for which it specifies the means

(*G*, 414). Second, a will can act in accordance with a more general principle that tells it that some particular action would be a means to happiness rather than to some more particular end. Here happiness is thought of as a general end, consisting in the satisfaction of all of our particular ends over our lifetimes rather than just the satisfaction of some particular end at some particular time. A prescription for happiness, or a "counsel of prudence" (*G*, 416), can certainly present itself to us as an imperative, because what we know is best for our happiness in the long run may well conflict with what we want in the short run. But it is still, in Kant's view, a hypothetical imperative, not because the desire for happiness is a merely natural end that we all do seem to have but might not necessarily have—rather, Kant says that this end "can be proposed surely and *a priori* in the case of every human being" (*G*, 415)—but apparently because it is a vague object of desire, that is, we do not really always know what will bring us happiness in the long run, but can at best form conjectures or hypotheses that this or that will satisfy us in the long run (*G*, 417–18). In any case, Kant holds that the goal of happiness, whether our own or that of others, cannot immediately and directly give rise to any absolutely necessary and unconditional principles of action for a rational agent, although he will later argue that, once we have adopted the fundamental principle of morality that he has already identified in Section I and is about to reintroduce into the present analysis as the categorical imperative, that principle itself can make the happiness of others and even the happiness of all including ourselves into a mandatory or necessary end of morality.[14]

Finally, Kant argues that if it is to be possible for a rational agent to act in accordance with our conception of morality, there must be a categorical rather than hypothetical imperative, an imperative that represents "an action as objectively necessary of itself, without reference to another end" on which its validity would be contingent (*G*, 414), Such an imperative would have to "do not with the matter of the action and what is to result from it, but with the form and the principle from which the action itself follows" (*G*, 416). Because the very idea of the categorical status or universal and necessary validity of such a principle of the will excludes the possibility that its adoption can depend upon the adoption of any particular, arbitrary end,

> When I think of a *categorical* imperative, I know at once what it contains. For, since the imperative contains, beyond the law, only the necessity that the maxim be in conformity with this law, while the law contains no

> condition to which it would be limited, nothing is left with which the
> maxim of action is to conform but the universality of a law as such. . . .
> There is, therefore, only a single categorical imperative and it is this: *act
> only in accordance with that maxim through which you can at the same
> time will that it become a universal law.* (*G*, 420–21)

This is Kant's first formulation of the fundamental principle of morality
as a categorical imperative in Section II of the *Groundwork*; the philosophical analysis of the possible kinds of principles in accordance with
which a rational agent could act has brought the argument to the same
place reached by the analysis of the commonsense notion of duty in
Section I.

At this point, of course, numerous questions arise. The first question
is about how this formulation of the fundamental principle of morality
is supposed to work: How are we supposed to be able to use it to
distinguish right from wrong, to determine what sorts of actions we
should not do and what sorts we may or should do? This question, in
turn, cannot be considered independently of a further question: How
does this formulation of the categorical imperative relate to the two,
three, or four formulations of the categorical imperative that Kant
states in the remainder of the section? Kant himself says there are three
formulations (*G*, 436), but some commentators count as many as five
(for discussions of this issue see the essays by Thomas W. Pogge, and
Paul Guyer in this volume). That question in turn divides into two
more: how do the derivations and justifications of the further formulations relate to this one, and how do the applications of the subsequent
formulations relate to the application of the initial one? Finally, there
are methodological or procedural questions: Kant has presented this
first formulation as the product of an *analysis* of the concept of a will
that is capable of acting in accordance with a law of reason, or an unconditional law; but how can such an analysis be shown to be binding
*for us*? How can we make the transition from a mere analysis to what
Kant calls a synthetic *a priori* proposition (see *G*, 420n and 444–45)
that asserts that the categorical imperative is not a mere possibility but
a principle that really binds us, without appealing to mere experience?

The question about how the categorical imperative is to be applied
is vexed by the fact that Kant offers several different formulations of it.
Immediately following the initial formulation, he claims that "Since the
universality of law in accordance with which effects take place constitutes what is properly called *nature* in the most general sense, . . . the

universal imperative of duty can also go as follows: *act as if the maxim of your action were to become by your will a* **universal law of nature**" (*G*, 421). Some interpreters have thought that the reference to nature in this reformulation introduces a fundamental new consideration into Kant's thought, a view that, in spite of what Kant says in deriving the categorical imperative, the morality of actions cannot be tested by formal considerations alone, but requires references to nature's purposes for us.[15] But most interpreters now reject that approach, arguing that Kant's rephrasing of his initial formula does not introduce any factual assumptions about how nature actually is, let alone any assumptions about purposes nature may have for us, but simply makes explicit the test that is already required by the initial formulation: in testing whether a maxim, or a proposed principle of action that recommends pursuing a certain kind of end in a certain kind of situation, is morally legitimate, we are to see whether we could in fact act on our proposed maxim if everyone else did too, or how it would be *if* our maxim were to become a law of nature, that is, a principle on which everyone in fact acted. This does not mean that we have to believe that our acting on a particular maxim would itself *cause* other persons to act on it, but simply asks whether we could reasonably act on our maxim *if* everyone else also did. As Onora O'Neill puts it in her essay, the question is whether in acting on a proposed maxim we could achieve "consistency in action."

Kant famously divides this question into two: in some cases, the necessary test is whether there is consistency in the *conception* of a maxim, or whether "a maxim [can] even be *thought* without contradiction"; in other cases, the question is not about the consistency of the conception of a particular proposed course of action, but whether it is possible "to *will* that [the] maxims be raised to the universality of a law of nature" (*G*, 424). Kant's idea is that in the first case, a proposed maxim will be internally inconsistent—and therefore incompatible with the concept of rational agency—if actually acting on that maxim would be incompatible with the universalization of the maxim. For instance, trying to obtain a loan by making a false promise to repay it would be an internally inconsistent or self-contradictory maxim of action, because *if* it were universalized, that is, *if* everyone were to act on it (and that fact was known), then (given how we assume that human beings would respond to this fact) nobody in his right mind would ever make a loan, and one's own initial proposal would thereby be frustrated. In other cases, a proposed course of action might not be internally incoherent—one could, for example, decide never to help other people in need without any logical contradiction—but the universalization of such a policy might nevertheless frustrate one's rational will in a more general way: as a rational agent, one *should* will that adequate means to whatever permissible ends one might someday formulate should be available, and by willing a course of action the universalization of which would entail that the help that one might sometime need would not be available—because everyone has adopted the policy of not helping others in need—one might be frustrating one's own capacity to act or will rationally.

By means of four examples (*G*, 421–23), Kant suggests that these two applications of the categorical imperative, giving rise to the two principles that we should avoid internal contradictions in our maxims and contradictions between our maxims and the general conditions for rational willing, are sufficient to cover all the kinds of moral duties commonly recognized. Narrow or perfect duties to ourselves and to others, for example the duty to ourselves to refrain from suicide and the duties to others to refrain from false promises, can be explained as duties to avoid internal contradictions in our maxims. Broad or imperfect duties to ourselves and others, that is, duties to adopt certain general goals and policies in our conduct, such as the duties to cultivate our talents or to help others in need, which cannot be mechanically translated into requirements to perform specific actions on specific occasions, can be explained as duties to avoid contradicting the general conditions of rational willing. (For example: it would be irrational if no human beings cultivated any talents, for then there would be all sorts of reasonable human ends that could not possibly be fulfilled; but that does not mean that I must, say, practice the violin now, because playing the violin might not be a reasonable talent for me to attempt to develop, or, even if it is, now might not be a good time to practice—there might be an emergency next door that I should be trying to remedy. Judgment is always needed in the execution of imperfect duties.) Although Kant's classification and explanation of the specific kinds of duties to ourselves and others that we have will be considerably refined in the *Metaphysics of Morals*, it is important for him to introduce at least examples of the main classes of duty in the *Groundwork of the Metaphysics of Morals* to show that his analysis of the philosophical concept of a rational agent has given rise to a formulation of the fundamental principle of morality that is consistent with common sense or with widely shared conceptions of what sorts of duties human beings actually have. In these examples, then, Kant departs from a purely analytical method and appeals, if not to mere experience, then to widely shared prephilosophical beliefs about morality in order to confirm the correctness of his analysis.[16]

From the time of Hegel,[16] Kant's first formulation of the categorical imperative as a principle requiring the "universalizability" of maxims has been charged with being empty: anyone can universalize any policy, it is objected, as long as he is single-minded enough.[17] For instance, a Nazi who believed that he should kill any Jew, gypsy, or homosexual that he can find would certainly also have believed that everyone should kill any Jew, gypsy, or homosexual that he can find, even for example, that Jews should kill other Jews and themselves. (This is not just a hypothetical, of course; the Nazi "final solution" quite intentionally included such policies as that of co-opting the *Judenrat*, the traditional Jewish organization for self-government and for representation of the community to the local Christian powers, into a police force that would help the Nazis in their deadly work, and of having Jews and their other victims dig their own graves. They thereby showed a certain kind of terrible consistency in their actions.) But, as a number of interpreters have shown in recent years—for example, Onora O'Neill, in the essay "Consistency in Action" reprinted here, but also in her groundbreaking book *Acting on Principle*,[18] and Christine M. Korsgaard, in her essay" "Kant's Formula of Universal Law"[19]—Kant does not mean that one can morally act on any policy that one would *oneself* be willing to see universalized but, rather, only on policies that could be truly universalized in the sense of being freely adopted by *all* who would be affected by them. Such a requirement obviously excludes the Nazi policy toward Jews, gypsies, and homosexuals.

In "Consistency in Action," Onora O'Neill gives a general account of how the requirement of universalizability does give rise to real constraints on our actions, and in her essay "Mutual Aid and Respect for Persons" Barbara Herman takes up the specific question of whether what Kant calls imperfect duties, such as the duty to adopt a general policy of helping others in need, can really be derived from the categorical imperative. But as the title of Herman's essay already suggests, it may often seem easier to see the concrete consequences of the categorical imperative by focusing on what Kant introduces as its second main formulation, the imperative *"So act that you use humanity, whether in your own person or in the person of any other, always at the same time as an end, never merely as a means"* (*G*, 429). As Kant's renewed discussion of his four examples of the main classes of duty suggests (*G*, 429–30), at least part of what is involved in treating others as ends rather than means is treating them in ways that they themselves could adopt as their own ends or purposes, that is, treating them in ways to which they could *freely consent*. This makes clear that the principle of universalizability has to be interpreted as a principle of universal consent: asking whether a principle can be universalized is not just asking whether *I* would like to see everyone acting upon it but whether *everyone* could agree to acting on it. (To apply this formulation of the categorical imperative to exclusively self-regarding actions, we have to ask whether proposed maxims of actions are ones that respect our own capacities to freely set and consent to the ends of our actions, not just in the circumstances at hand but over the whole course of our lives.) In his essay "Humanity As End in Itself," Allen Wood offers an especially instructive interpretation of this formulation of the categorical imperative and shows in detail how it can be applied to concrete moral issues.

The appeal to Kant's conception of humanity as an end in itself raises the question of how Kant's several formulations of the categorical imperative are related to each other. This question becomes more complicated when Kant introduces what he says is a third formulation, the principle that "A rational being must always regard himself as lawgiving in a kingdom of ends" (*G*, 434), but that he also breaks down into two different versions: what is sometimes called the formula of autonomy, the imperative "to act only *so that the will could regard itself as at the same time giving universal law through its maxim*," and the formula of the kingdom of ends, "that all maxims from one's own lawgiving are to harmonize into a possible kingdom of ends, as with a kingdom of nature" (*G*, 436). Kant makes conflicting statements about all these formulations, even on the very same page: on the one hand, he says that what he counts as the "three ways of representing the principle of morality are at bottom only so many formulae of the very same law," and on the other hand, he suggests that the formula of universality brings out only the *"form"* of virtuous action, the formula of humanity as an end in itself, its *"matter,"* its end or its object, and that only the formula of the kingdom of ends gives a *"complete determination"* of the principle (*G*, 436). This suggests that each of the main formulations of the categorical imperative makes a distinct and essential contribution to our understanding of the fundamental principle of morality and that we are not really in a position to understand and apply this principle until we have recognized all the formulations.

This vexed issue is studied in detail by Thomas W. Pogge ("The Categorical Imperative") and Paul Guyer ("The Possibility of the Categorical Imperative") in part III of this volume. These authors agree that each formulation makes an essential contribution to Kant's project but do not agree on just how the differences among the principles are to be understood. One important issue they discuss is the significance of the introduction of a necessary end for rational agents in the formula of humanity. Kant argues, presumably still as part of his analysis of the concept of a rational agent, that a rational agent necessarily acts with some end in view and, thus (in spite of his initial hostility to connecting the fundamental principle of morality to any end at all), that there must be some end or ends that are in fact compatible with the categorical imperative; otherwise a rational agent bound by that imperative would simply be incapable of acting (*G*, 427–28). But he suggests different models for bringing ends into the picture: in the later *Metaphysics of Morals*, he suggests that there must be certain ends (one's own perfection and the happiness of others) that can be seen as necessary once the categorical imperative has been adopted (6:385); in the *Groundwork*, however, he may mean that there must be some necessary end that makes it rational to adopt the categorical imperative in the first place, an end that would be "the ground of a possible categorical imperative." This end would be the value of "the human being and in general every rational being . . . as an end in itself, *not merely as a means* to be used by this or that will at its discretion" (*G*, 428). In other words, the point of adopting the principle of being able to universalize one's maxims would be that this is the only way to ensure that one will be treating both oneself and others as ends in themselves, agents who can always freely consent to how they are being treated. The question of just how these several arguments are to be understood is one of the main issues discussed in these two essays.

Another important issue discussed in these essays is how to understand the difference between the first formulation and the principle of autonomy, the principle that everyone must be treated as a legislator of universal law, when these two principles sound virtually identical. One possibility here is that Kant is introducing a motive for adopting the original principle of universalizability: by conceiving of oneself not just as *subject* to the requirement of universalizability but as *creating* that requirement by one's own legislative act, one conceives of oneself

as a free and autonomous agent, worthy of a kind of respect that nothing that is merely a subject of laws is. And by conceiving of others also
as self-legislators of the same law to which one is subject, one explains
the source of their dignity and thus explains why one must legislate
universalizability in the first place. Kant suggests something like this
toward the end of Section II, in what are among the most passionate
pages of the *Groundwork*, where his vision of the possible dignity of
human beings takes on its clearest form:

> Every rational being, as an end in itself, must be able to regard himself as
> also giving universal laws with respect to any law whatsoever to which he
> may be subject; for, it is just this fitness of his maxims for giving universal
> law that marks him out as an end in itself; it also follows that this dignity
> . . . he has over all merely natural beings brings with it that he must always
> take his maxims from the point of view of himself, and likewise every
> other rational being, as lawgiving beings (who for this reason are also
> called persons). (*G*, 438)

On this account the conception of human beings as autonomous legislators who are members of a kingdom of ends or a community of such
legislators would make the categorical imperative possible by introducing a conception of ourselves and our fellow human beings as objects
worthy of the special kind of respect that can only be shown through
adherence to the categorical imperative in either of its previous formulations. Again, this is an important issue discussed in the last two essays
of part III.

There is a certain sense in which these considerations already seem
to have gone beyond the mere analysis of the concept of a rational
being as a source of the categorical imperative that Kant promised at
the outset of Section II, by introducing a conception of human beings
that would make the adoption of the categorical imperative rational
and well motivated, and in that sense possible. At the same time, there
is another sense in which all this discussion still seems to present that
categorical imperative merely as a possibility: Kant may have presented
a rich conception of rational agency and its value that would make the
adoption of the categorical imperative by any such rational agent both
possible and necessary; but it might still remain to be shown that we
human beings really are capable of being such rational agents and thus
of being both bound by and motivated to accept the categorical imperative. The task of moving beyond a mere analysis of the concept of a

rational agent, whether thinly or thickly conceived, to showing that this concept applies to us, seems to be the task of Section III of the *Groundwork*.

## Section III

This section is entitled "Transition from metaphysics of morals to the critique of pure practical reason." By the "metaphysics of morals" with which Section II culminated, Kant first seemed to have in mind the derivation of the fundamental principle of morality from a metaphysical conception such as that of a rational agent, but then also the illustration and confirmation of the validity of that principle by showing that it gives rise to the kind of concrete system of duties for human beings later developed in more detail in the *Metaphysics of Morals*. By a "critique of pure practical reason," he seems to have had in mind an investigation into the nature of human reason as practical, or governing our actions, that would show that we really are free agents capable of acting in accordance with the conception of rational agency explored in the previous section. But while the metaphysics of morals in Section II seems complex but rewarding and uplifting, the critique of pure practical reason in Section III can seem obscure and vexing.

This is partly because Kant still seems to be working on two different projects in Section III. On the one hand, in spite of his promise to turn from analysis to synthesis in Section II, he seems to continue the "analytic" project of Section II, still trying to prove that the conception of free and rational agency really does give rise to the categorical imperative, or that a free and rational agent must act in accordance with that principle. On the other hand, he also seems to embark on the different, "synthetic" rather than "analytic," task of showing that we human beings really are free and rational agents, subject to all the conditions that being such agents entails. The second of these projects is immensely important to Kant: just as the previous project of showing that a rational agent can be moved to act out of respect for universal law rather than from a merely natural inclination toward its own (typically short-range) happiness can block one natural temptation to evade the strict demand of morality, so proving that we really do have the freedom to live in total conformity with the ideal of rational agency would deprive us of determinism as an excuse by which we can rationalize our inclination to evade the demands of moral responsibility.

Seeing Kant as still working on two distinct projects even in Section III of the *Groundwork* may help explain something that may otherwise appear confusing about the structure of this section. Kant seems to go over the same ground twice, once quickly and provisionally and then once at greater length and presumably conclusively. First he appears to argue that conceiving of ourselves as acting under "the idea of freedom" may be just as good as proving ourselves actually to possess freedom of the will, because any agent that even conceives of itself as free will have to adopt the same principles as one that actually is free (*G*, 448); but then he seems to worry that maybe this is not enough of an argument, indeed that it is a circular argument—that it derives our obligation to comply with the moral law from a freedom that we assume only because we already assume that we are obliged under the moral law (*G*, 450)—and to look for a more compelling way to prove our freedom. However, if we look at Kant as first trying to complete the argument of Section II by establishing one last time the analytical claim that a truly free agent can only maintain and preserve its freedom in action in accordance with the moral law, and only then as proceeding to argue for the synthetic proposition that we human beings really are free, then we can avoid this peculiar appearance of back-tracking.

Three essays on Section III of the *Groundwork* are included in part IV of this volume, and the difference between the first two, "Kant's Argument for the Rationality of Moral Conduct" by Thomas E. Hill, Jr., and "Morality and Freedom: Kant's Reciprocity Thesis" by Henry E. Allison, and the third, "The Deduction of the Moral Law: The Reasons for the Obscurity of the Final Section of Kant's *Groundwork of the Metaphysics of Morals*" by Dieter Henrich (here translated into English for the first time), suggest such an approach. Both Hill and Allison are concerned to argue that a truly free being really would conform its actions to the moral law, or, in Kant's terms, that genuine freedom has to be conceived in a positive and not merely a negative sense (*G*, 446), that is, as being bound by the moral law and not just free from determination by some other kind of factors. The argument is that a free being would be one that is not just impelled to act by whatever inclinations happen to occur to it but, rather, precisely one that determines which of its naturally occurring inclinations to act upon; but to attempt to decide which inclinations to act upon without a nonmaterial, formal law by means of which to do so would in fact be nothing but to allow oneself to be buffeted about by naturally occurring inclinations after all. But to argue this is still not to prove that *we* really are free, and thus capable of rising above the level of being buffeted about by natural inclinations, instead determining for ourselves by the use of a formal principle which inclinations we should act upon and which not. To establish this further, crucial point, Henrich argues, Kant tries to shift his ground into a "critique of pure practical reason," or an investigation of the faculty of reason that we actually have. In particular, he shows, Kant tries to argue that the distinction that we have to make between how things appear to us and how they really are, a distinction that Kant rather sanguinely supposes all will concede is necessary in order to understand the nature of knowledge quite independently of any concerns about action, requires us also to distinguish between how we appear to ourselves and how we really are. And we can only give any content to the latter conception of ourselves by conceiving of ourselves as being governed by laws of reason, in the inmost nature of our thoughts and also our actions (*G*, 451–52). Thus, a conception of ourselves that has to be adopted for reasons independent of any prior assumptions about our obligations under the moral law proves that we really are free agents, who must be governed by a law of reason, which has, in turn, been shown by the opening argument of Section III and all that has gone before to be equivalent to the moral law.

Kant's argument from the distinction between appearance and reality to the fact of our freedom has proven very controversial. Henrich sees it as foundering upon an unsubstantiated assumption that we actually have a will—what Kant suggests will be the middle term between being free and being rational (*G*, 454)—which smuggles the assumption of freedom back into the beginning of the argument. He thinks Kant was to some extent aware of this problem all along, and never really meant the *Groundwork* to provide what he calls a "strong" deduction of the moral law in the first place; rather, the *Groundwork* already anticipates the *Critique of Practical Reason*'s frank admission that we cannot deduce our obligation under the moral law from a prior, essentially theoretical, demonstration of the fact of our freedom but can only assume our freedom, as a postulate of pure practical reason, as a precondition of our sense of moral obligation that must be taken as rock-bottom—and, that, indeed, it could be argued, was the starting point of Kant's argument in Section I. Such a reading would be consistent with the idea that the point of the *Groundwork* is not to *prove* the fundamental principle of morality without any prior presuppositions but, rather, to refine our common conception of morality and indeed our common understanding of ourselves in such a way as to *preserve* our sound, pretheoretical understanding of morality while blocking our natural temptations to evade it. Others have taken different positions on this issue. In an important essay not included here, Karl Ameriks has argued that Kant really did mean to provide a metaphysically persuasive proof of the existence of human freedom in the *Groundwork* but then realized that his attempt was a failure and radically changed his strategy in the *Critique of Practical Reason*.[20] Henry E. Allison, on the contrary, has argued that Kant has a sound inference from the spontaneity of human reason in a theoretical context to freedom in a practical context, which he consistently maintains from the first *Critique* through the *Groundwork* and into the second *Critique*.[21] Since these works have been more readily accessible than Henrich's essay, and since in any case this issue remains unresolved, Henrich's essay, with its reflections on the difficulties and obscurities of Kant's general concept of a deduction as well as its specific discussions of the issue about the demonstrability of the freedom of the human will, has been presented here.

Aside from the question of its justifiability, Kant's suggestion that the moral law is actually the causal law that governs our behavior as we really are, a "causality in accordance with immutable laws but of a special kind" (*G*, 446), raises another kind of problem. This is what is sometimes called the "Sidgwick problem," in honor of the particularly sharp formulation given to it by the great Victorian moral philosopher Henry Sidgwick: If a free will is a will necessarily governed by the moral law, then a will that does not comply with the moral law must not be a free will at all, in which case a malefactor who acts in opposition to the moral law must not be accountable for his actions, because he must not have acted out of free will.[22] Kant clearly did not want this outcome, but wanted to attribute to human beings a *capacity* to choose freely between good and evil that would make them accountable for their actions; only this would prevent us from evading the moral obligations that we all know we have. The kind of argument for freedom that Kant employed in the *Critique of Practical Reason* clearly does not give rise to the Sidgwick problem: if freedom is inferred from our fundamental knowledge of our moral obligation, by the principle "ought implies can," all that follows is that we *can* live up to our moral obligations, not that we always *do*; thus, that we sometimes—or often—do *not* comply with requirements of morality throws no doubt on our initial inference that we *are* free and capable of doing so. Kant clearly emphasized this feature of his view about freedom in the *Religion*, where our capacity for evil is presented as radical in the sense that it is inseparable from our capacity to do what is right—what it is to be free is precisely to have the freedom to choose between right and wrong, even if it is only choosing rightly that can preserve our own freedom and that of others.[23] Whether one thinks that Kant already held this view in the *Groundwork* depends on what kind of argument for the existence of human freedom one thinks Kant makes in this work.

Clearly Kant wanted to put *some* distance between his argument for freedom in Section III of the *Groundwork* and an argument for freedom drawn solely from speculative metaphysics—what he seems to have cared about most is that the reader come away from the book persuaded of the nobility of freedom as a practical ideal rather than the irrefutability of freedom as a cognitive claim. Thus the penultimate paragraph of the book ends with these stirring words, with which this introduction can also conclude:

> The idea of a pure world of understanding as a whole of all intelligences, to which we ourselves belong as rational beings (though on the other side we are also members of the world of sense), remains always a useful and permitted idea for the sake of a rational belief, even if all knowledge stops at its boundary—useful and permitted for producing in us a lively interest in the moral law by means of the noble ideal of a universal kingdom of *ends in themselves* (rational beings) to which we can belong as members only when we carefully conduct ourselves in accordance with maxims of freedom as if they were laws of nature. (*G*, 462–63)

Above all, what Kant's *Groundwork of the Metaphysics of Morals* aims to do is put before us an image of the nobility of the life we can lead if we try to regulate our conduct by the fundamental principle of morality instead of acting out of self-interest and excusing our so acting by denying our own freedom.

## Notes

1. Schneewind furnishes much more extensive historical background for understanding Kant's ethics in two works, an anthology of sources entitled *Moral Philosophy from Montaigne to Kant*, 2 vol. (Cambridge, U.K.: Cambridge University Press, 1990), and a monumental work of interpretation, *The Invention of Autonomy* (Cambridge, U.K.: Cambridge University Press, 1998).

2. An earlier model for such a "cooperative" commentary, containing essays in German, English, and French, one of which is reprinted in the present

volume (the essay by Thomas W. Pogge), is Ottfried Höffe, ed., *Grundlegung der Metaphysik der Sitten: Ein kooperativer Kommentar* (Frankfurt am Main: Vittorio Klostermann, 1989).

3. *Fundamental Principles of the Metaphysics of Morals*, in *Kant's Critique of Practical Reason and Other Works on the Theory of Ethics*, tr. Thomas Kingsmill Abbott, 6th ed. (London: Longmans, Green, 1909), and *Foundations of the Metaphysics of Morals*, tr. Lewis White Beck (Indianapolis: Bobbs-Merrill, 1959).

4. Immanuel Kant, *Grounding for the Metaphysics of Morals*, James W. Ellington (Indianapolis: Hackett Publishing Co., 1981).

5. Immanuel Kant, *Groundwork of the Metaphysics of Morals*, tr. H. J. Paton (London: Hutchinson University Library, 1948).

6. Immanuel Kant, *Practical Philosophy*, tr. and ed. Mary J. Gregor, with a general introduction by Allen W. Wood (Cambridge, U.K.: Cambridge University Press, 1996).

7. The most detailed discussion of the *Critique of Practical Reason* remains Lewis White Beck, *A Commentary on Kant's Critique of Practical Reason* (Chicago: University of Chicago Press, 1960). The "fact of reason" doctrine is discussed in chapter 10.

8. On the "highest good," see *Critique of Pure Reason*, "The Canon of Pure Reason"; *Critique of Practical Reason*, the "Dialectic of Pure Practical Reason"; the *Critique of Judgment*, the "Methodology of Teleological Judgment"; *Religion within the Limits of Mere Reason*," preface to the first edition; and especially the 1793 essay "On the common saying: That may be correct in theory, but it is of no use in practice," Section I.

9. For an interpretation of Kant's argument in the *Groundwork* that makes the appeal to a teleological conception of nature central to it, see H. J. Paton, *The Categorical Imperative* (London: Hutchinson, 1947). While Paton's commentary (meant to accompany his translation) remains valuable in many ways, his central thesis is not widely accepted.

10. See the essay by Friedrich Schiller, "On Grace and Dignity" (1793), and the book by Arthur Schopenhauer, *On the Basis of Morality* (1841).

11. Richard Henson, "What Kant Might Have Said: Moral Worth and the Over-determination of Dutiful Action," *Philosophical Review* 88 (1979): 39–54, and Barbara Herman, "On the Value of Acting from the Motive of Duty," *Philosophical Review* 90 (1981): 359–82, reprinted in her *The Practice of Moral Judgment* (Cambridge, Mass.: Harvard University Press, 1993), chap. 1.

12. Translation from Immanuel Kant, *Religion and Rational Theology*, tr. and ed. Allen W. Wood and George Di Giovanni (Cambridge, U.K.: Cambridge University Press, 1996), p. 92.

13. *Critique of Pure Reason*, B 130.

14. See the "Doctrine of Virtue" in the *Metaphysics of Morals*, 6:387–88 and especially §27, 6L450–51. In the heat of his polemic against happiness, Kant often makes it sound as if happiness cannot be an object of moral action at all. This is not what he means, as is proven by his insistence in all three of his *Critiques* and in the *Religion* that the highest good, which *includes* happiness in a certain relation to virtue, is the ultimate object of morality and the basis

for the moral proof of the existence of God, which is in certain respects the culmination of Kant's entire theoretical and practical philosophy. But he does not mention this doctrine in the *Groundwork*—even though he had already mentioned it in the first edition of the *Critique of Pure Reason* published four years earlier—and thus the *Groundwork* can by no means be taken as a complete statement of Kant's moral philosophy.

15. See Paton, *The Categorical Imperative,* pp. 146–64.

16. See especially his early essay *Natural Law: The Scientific Ways of Treating Natural Law, Its Place in Moral Philosophy, and Its Relation to the Positive Sciences of Law* (1802–3), tr. T. M. Knox (Philadelphia: University of Pennsylvania Press, 1975).

17. For discussion of this charge, see Allen W. Wood, "The Emptiness of the Moral Will," *Monist* 72 (1989): 454–83, and *Hegel's Ethical Thought* (Cambridge, U.K.: Cambridge University Press, 1990), chap. 9.

18. Published under the name Onora Nell, *Acting on Principle* (New York: Columbia University Press, 1975).

19. Originally published in *Pacific Philosophical Quarterly* 66 (1985): 24–47, reprinted in her book *Creating the Kingdom of Ends* (Cambridge, U.K.: Cambridge University Press, 1996), pp. 77–105.

20. Karl Ameriks, "Kant's Deduction of Freedom and Morality," *Journal of the History of Philosophy* 19 (1981): 53–79; revised as chap. 6 of his *Kant's Theory of the Mind* (Oxford: Clarendon Press, 1982).

21. Henry E. Allison, *Kant's Theory of Freedom* (Cambridge, U.K.: Cambridge University Press, 1990).

22. See Henry Sidgwick, *The Methods of Ethics,* 7th ed. (London: Macmillan, 1907), appendix, "The Kantian Conception of Free Will," pp. 511–16. This appendix is reprinted, with some omissions, from *Mind* 13 (1888).

23. Kant does not explicitly formulate the famous premise "ought implies can" in the *Critique of Practical Reason* although he clearly assumes it; in the *Religion* he clearly does formulate it, as when he says that "Duty commands that [a human being] be good, and duty commands nothing but what we can do" (6:47), and "duty commands [a person] unconditionally: he *ought* to remain true to his resolve; and from this he rightly *concludes* that he must also be *able* to do it, and that his power of choice is therefore free" (6:49n; both translations from Wood and Di Giovanni, pp. 92, 94). The *Religion* is, as it were, the dark side of the *Critique of Practical Reason*, reminding us that the freedom to do evil is an inescapable concomitant of the capacity to freely do what is right; both works correct any impression that the *Groundwork* might have made that the fact of our freedom necessarily entails that we will always act in accordance with the moral law.

# Part I
# Historical Background

# 1

# Natural Law, Skepticism, and Methods of Ethics

## J. B. Schneewind

In the *Foundations of the Metaphysics of Morals* Kant presented a method for discovering what morality requires us to do in any situation and claimed that it is a method everyone can use. The method consists in testing one's maxim against the requirement stated in the formulations of the categorical imperative. There has been endless discussion of the adequacy of Kant's method in giving moral guidance, but there has been little effort to situate Kant's view of ethical method in its historical context. In this paper I try to do so.

I take the label "method of ethics" from the work of Henry Sidgwick. A method of ethics, he says, is any rational procedure by which we determine what it is right for an individual to do or what an individual ought to do.[1] Since the moralists I want to consider do not all think of morality as rational, I shall broaden the notion by saying that a method is any systematic or regular procedure, rational or not, by which we determine what morality requires.

Sidgwick does not say who the "we" are who make use of a method of ethics. Are "we" theorists or bystanders or members of a privileged social group who determine what others are to do? Or is a method something every normal adult uses, even if she is not aware of it as such and could not explicitly formulate it? If Sidgwick meant the latter, as I think he did, then it is worth noting that he simply took it for granted that everyone is in possession of some adequate method or other. I shall try to show that this now common position emerged from two opposed responses to modern natural law theory. One was an attempt to preserve its essential understanding of morality; the other was an effort to reject it and replace it with a quite different understanding. Kant, I suggest, worked out a remarkable synthesis of these two developments.

The "modern" theorists of natural law, Grotius and his followers, did not have a high opinion of the ability of the majority of people to steer their own moral course unaided. Although they had views on the proper methods to be used by a lawyer in deriving the laws of nature, they would not have accepted Sidgwick's assumption about the moral capacities of ordinary people. Hobbes took a step toward the Sidgwickian position by offering a formula "by which we may presently know, whether what we are doing be against the law of nature or not." It is summarized by the well-worn maxim, "Do not that to others, you would not have done to yourself,"[2] and Hobbes thought it could be used by even the simplest person.

The Hobbesian method is what I shall call "opaque." It points out a right act but does not let the agent see why the act is right. Hobbes does not even try to explain why the method succeeds in picking out acts which are made right by other features than the one the method uses.[3] Consequently, its users would have to take it on authority that it is a reliable method. There is not much of a departure here from the usual cavalier attitude of natural law theory toward ordinary people.

A number of followers of the natural lawyers were unhappy about this particular feature of their outlook. The reason for their concern was perhaps first voiced by Jean Barbeyrac. In the "Historical and Critical Account of the Science of Morality . . . ," which he prefixed in 1706 to his translation of Pufendorf, Barbeyrac gives us a reason for supposing that God must have made moral knowledge accessible to everyone. God has given us the ability to grasp "a vast number of mathematical truths," so he must have made us capable of "knowing, and establishing with the same evidence, the Maxims of Morality; in which are contained those Duties he indispensibly requires of us" and the performance of which, moreover, is the sole path to our happiness. God's goodness, he says, "will not permit us to doubt of this." And the fact that moral truths are easier to grasp than mathematical ones bears this out.[4]

Unless it is somewhere in his copious footnotes, Barbeyrac makes no positive suggestions about the method we should all use to become aware of what is required of us. But the suggestion that we must be able to know what is required of us because we will be held accountable for acting accordingly was taken up by others. Here is a statement of it by Heineccius, whose treatise on natural law, first published in Latin in 1737, was translated into English by George Turnbull in 1743:

> Every principle of science must be true, evident, and adequate; wherefore the principle of science, with respect to natural law . . . must be evident, and that not only in this sense, that it is intelligible to the literate; but universally, to the unlearned as well as the learned, all being equally under obligation to conform themselves to the law of nature . . . a too subtle principle of natural law is suspicious, since all are . . . without excuse, even the illiterate, and those who are strangers to subtle refined philosophy, if they offend against the law of nature.[5]

A position not unlike this was taken earlier by Bishop Butler. One of his central assertions is that of the full competence of the individual conscience. Philosophers have looked for some general rule which determines the rightness and wrongness of action, he says, and such inquiries are in some ways useful. Yet, he says, "let any plain honest man, before he engages in any course of action, ask himself, Is this I am going about right, or is it wrong? I do not in the least doubt, but that this question would be answered agreeably to truth and virtue, by almost any fair man in almost any circumstances."[6] Butler's point, indicated in his Preface, is that anyone who knowingly transgresses a law may justly be punished, even if he did not believe he would be punished. Hence a religious skeptic who refuses to do what he knows he ought will be as justly punished by God as a believer.[7] For Butler as for Heineccius, the universal availability of awareness of the requirements of morality is needed to defend the full accountability of each of us before God.

We find a similar line of argument in the *Guide to Rational Living* (1744) of Christian August Crusius, whose work Kant knew and in his early years admired.[8] Crusius teaches the universal availability of moral knowledge as a necessary consequence of God's justice. We must believe that God will reward the good and punish the wicked, and we cannot doubt that God is just. Hence we must all be equally able to know what we are to do in order to deserve well. The faculty through which we come to have this knowledge is conscience, which makes it unnecessary to argue and reason about what is right. Scholars who try to answer moral questions through ratiocination get nowhere, so if it were necessary to use their methods, "how would the unlearned get it all right? But now, since all men are subordinated to God's laws and will be judged according to them, it is easy to infer that he has created a shorter way to knowledge of them and made his will known in such a way that it can be accessible to everyone's knowledge."[9] "A moderate understanding soon becomes aware in the hardest and most complicated cases," he adds, "of what would be right or wrong . . ." (§136). The learned agree on what is right or wrong in particular cases, even though their theories never agree about why: happily theory does not matter.

Butler appeals to conscience as the faculty which explains our awareness of what to do but does not claim that conscience shows us what makes right acts right. The method he thinks available to everyone is opaque. Although we can all see that conscience was given us to be an authoritative guide, to ask why conscience guides us as it does is to ask God's reasons for requiring certain actions. We do not need to know these in order to act properly, and we could not understand them if they were told us.[10] Hence Butler notoriously fudges on the question of whether moral directives spring from reason or feeling.

Crusius does not fudge: he tells us rather that there are two methods of ethics. One of them rests on the fact that conscience does not provide us with abstract rules or principles. It acts through a feeling which both directs and motivates us. The feelings involve distinctive ideas which are innate in conscience and which present God's commands to us (§137). We can thus obtain sufficient guidance through what is plainly an opaque method of ethics, but a second method is also possible. To use it we must acquire clear knowledge of the essential perfections of God and man. Then we can infer what we are to do, using the principle that God wills us to do what conforms to these essential perfections (§171, 181). In showing us what we ought to do, this method, unlike the first, allows us to see why we ought to do it. Its results do not differ from those of the opaque method in which unclarified feelings direct us, but the latter method is, I shall say, "transparent."[11]

Butler's admirers Price and Reid transformed his position into one centering on a transparent method of ethics. They took awareness of what morality requires to be knowledge of moral principles or laws which everyone grasps intuitively. These laws show us not only what is right but also what makes right acts right. Price and Reid are concerned to counter Hume's denial that there is moral knowledge; they are equally determined to preserve the simplicity and thus the general availability of moral knowledge. As Reid says, "the path of duty is a plain path, which the upright in heart can rarely mistake. Such it must be, since every man is bound to walk in it . . . ," adding that even in difficult cases the person who tries hard to see what is right will be "inculpable in the sight of God and man."[12]

Butler, Crusius, Price, and Reid are not avowed natural law theorists like Barbeyrac and Heineccius, but they have positive affiliations with the theory.[13] Like Pufendorf, they take it that free will is indispensable for individual responsibility and for morality. Though opposed to voluntarism[14] they see morality as having divine sanction and as indicating God's will for us. In describing an incipient or full intuitional method available to everyone, all of them are trying to show how the morality of natural law looks to the agent who is innocent of philosophy. They are explaining how natural law can provide every free agent with reasons to act. Motivated by their strongly Protestant sense of individual accountability before God, these thinkers ignore the complex methods by which Grotius and Pufendorf thought we could derive knowledge of what we ought to do. Ordinary people could not use such methods and do not need them. Still less does society require that there be some people who do use those methods and then explain to others what their duties are. We can each just see for ourselves how we are to behave. Intuitionism here was thus an epistemology that did more than answer the theoretical question of how in principle there might be moral knowledge. By showing how everyone can have that knowledge, the intuitionist epistemology carried a moral and religious point—that only individual self-direction articulates a Christian understanding both of responsibility and of obedience to God.

I turn now to a second, perhaps surprising, source of ideas on ethical method—skepticism. Pyrrhonian skepticism was a major concern for philosophy in the seventeenth century and not least for moral philosophy.[15] The skeptic was not interested in problems of epistemology for their own sake. Like the Stoic and the Epicurean, he was in quest of the good life, and he found it only when his repeated failures to find knowledge of the good led him to abandon the search. Knowing nothing of what was good or bad, he was no longer agitated by changing beliefs about what to pursue or avoid, and this absence of agitation turned out to be the tranquility he had vainly sought. As Sextus says, "the man who determines nothing as to what is naturally good or bad neither shuns nor pursues anything eagerly; and in consequence he is unperturbed."[16]

If skepticism, like Stoicism and Epicureanism, is taken to be a way of life, the question naturally arises: can anyone live that way? Would not the skeptic fall over a cliff or burn himself in a fire if he had no convictions about the good and the bad?[17] To this commonly made objection there is a reply. The skeptic allows himself to be moved by "the appearances." He does not doubt that the cliff looks dangerous or that the fire feels hot, and these appearances lead him to stay away from both. The skeptic can live because he lives by the appearances. How are we to understand this?

Appearances, for the Pyrrhonist, are to be contrasted with beliefs about the way things are. The master skeptic has no such beliefs. He comes to this condition by working through a wide variety of arguments. In all of them he contrasts one way in which things look with another, one claim about moral good with another, or one claim about proper law with another; and he finds no way to decide which of these appearances is true. The skeptic does not deny that there is a truth about all these things but finds it inaccessible. He is left with nothing but the appearances—the way things seem to him.[18] When he says he has no beliefs, he means "beliefs about the truth of the matter." He does not say that assent is altogether impossible. He assents to appearances, but that kind of assent is not belief. Belief is assent making claims about how things really are; and belief is what the skeptic does not have.

What then is included under the term "appearances"? Not simply sense impressions but everything which the skeptic may be tempted to believe can count as an appearance. That the fire is hot, that I would be hurt if I fell off the cliff, that bigamy is wicked, that there is nothing certain—all of these are appearances. Being an appearance is, as Burnyeat puts it, "entirely independent of subject matter." The contents of the mind are not divided into sensory appearances and propositional beliefs. They are divided rather into subjective states claiming to reach truth about the way things are, and subjective states not making any such claim. Consequently, "the skeptic who adheres strictly to appearance is withdrawing to the safety of a position not open to challenge or inquiry. He may talk about anything under the sun—but only to note how it appears to him, not to say how it really is."[19] Nonetheless, so it appears to the skeptic, this suffices for the guidance of life and even for the attainment of tranquillity or what appears to be the good.

Montaigne's engagement with skepticism was a major force in the development of modern moral philosophy. Here I can note only one aspect of its importance. In his late essays Montaigne presents himself as having won through to a certain degree of stability in his life, and his account of how he has done so shows one kind of skeptical response to the appearances. After much reflection, Montaigne says, he has discovered within himself "a pattern all his own, a ruling pattern" (*une forme maistresse*), and anyone can make a similar discovery.[20] This is the pattern according to which he now lives (for the most part; he has relapses) and it provides all the guidance he needs. In finding the pattern Montaigne appeals only to his own experience. Within that experience he includes his reading of the classical writers. But what matters to him is his reactions to them, not any authority they have over him. "Men are diverse in inclination and strength," Montaigne says, "they must be led to their own good according to their nature and by diverse routes."[21] We cannot gain much from "foreign examples." We must rather "profit from the experience we have of ourselves, which is more familiar to us, and certainly sufficient to inform us of what we need."[22] Life presents him with appearances of good and ill, through books or through daily occurrences; and he accepts or rejects according to some pattern of his own, which he is eventually able to articulate. The *forme maîtresse* is Montaigne's own personal essence. It is not something modelled on an eternal or universal form.

Is it too much to call this a method of ethics? Montaigne does not claim that his particular ruling form holds for others, and it gives him no guidance for anything outside his private life. Nonetheless, he thinks that the way he has found his pattern may provide his readers with a useful model. Things or ways of living present themselves, through experience or through books, as attractive or admirable; Montaigne asks if he can go along with the way the appearances draw him, if he can incorporate them in himself in a steady mode of life. His question is not whether the views of the Stoics or the Epicureans are true or false; his question is whether he finds that his own enduring response is acceptance or rejection.

Montaigne thus forms his pattern from his purely personal responses to the way things appear to him. In his gloomier phase or mood he finds man a lowly and despicable being, dependent on God for anything he can do that is decent and upright. In the more affirmative mood that dominates the later essays, he finds himself emulating Socrates, who showed us how much human nature can do for itself. He particularly dismisses Socrates's claim to have been guided by the Delphic oracle or some mysterious inner voice. Socrates directed himself, Montaigne thinks, and he suggests that each of us can do what Socrates did. We can each have a skeptic's method of ethics.

Shaftesbury is rightly seen as having initiated a new movement in moral philosophy. I suggest that we look at his views about how we form moral judgments as an attempt to spell out a skeptical method of ethics.

In his *Inquiry Concerning Virtue or Merit* Shaftesbury draws a sharp distinction between two kinds of judgments we make about the goodness of active beings. Some creatures have passions and affections which lead them to act in ways that tend directly to bring about some good either to their possessor or to others. We call these creatures "good" when they bring about good because of such an inner impulse, rather than incidentally. But there is another kind of goodness which can only be attributed to beings able to reflect on the affections they find within themselves. Reflection, Shaftesbury says, gives rise to "another kind of affection towards those very affections themselves, which have been already felt, and are now become the subject of a new liking or dislike."[23] This new "liking or disliking" is moral approval and disapproval, and it is only beings capable of having this reflective feeling who can be virtuous or vicious.

The exact nature of the reflective moral facility is not clear in Shaftesbury. Sometimes it is treated as yielding a feeling, sometimes it is endowed with cognitive capacities. Sometimes it is said to discern the propriety in the relative strengths of first-order active impulses, and propriety is likened to harmonious beauty. But sometimes Shaftesbury speaks of the heart approving "what is just and right" and disapproving the contrary, as if the first-order affections possess moral properties to which the second order affection somehow responds (I.ii.iii, R I, 173). It is not necessary for the present purpose to decide which of these readings is sound. I am inclined to think that Shaftesbury's basic idea is that the reflective affection discerns the presence or absence of harmony or proportion or beauty—a moral beauty—in the relations among the various spontaneous affections, approves of them when it is present and of course disapproves when it is absent. He also seems to believe that this harmony is objectively there to be perceived, and the faculty of perceiving it he sometimes calls the moral sense.[24]

However the moral sense functions, it is quite clear that it is the spontaneous active affections or some balance among them which Shaftesbury takes as the intentional object of the reflective feeling. It is also evident that he believes that actions are thought of as right or wrong depending on the virtue of the affections which lead the agent to do them. Shaftesbury says:

> Whatsoever is done through any unequal affection is iniquitous, wicked and wrong. . . . For wrong is not such action as is barely the cause of harm . . . but when anything is done through insufficient or unequal affection (as when a son shows no concern for the safety of a father; or, where there is need of succor, prefers an indifferent person to him) this is of the nature of wrong.[25]

And the same is true of right actions: not barely their effects, but their being done because of affections of which the moral sense approves, constitutes them as right.

Shaftesbury thus presents at least the rudiments of what I shall classify as a "constitutive" method of ethics that is used by everyone. Reflecting on one's motives one finds oneself giving them a unique kind of approval or disapproval; in any particular situation one is to act from the approved motive or set of motives, and the act so motivated is the appropriate action. There is no other source of rightness or wrongness in actions. One's motives reflect one's beliefs about the world in which one is acting, and about its goods and ills. But the moral sense operates not on that world but on the appearances within oneself. Shaftesbury is saying that the moral agent lives by her own responses to the way things seem to her.[26]

Hutcheson[27] and Hume take the same position. In their work we come to two closely related versions of the skeptical method which are rather different from Shaftesbury's. The main difference as far as the working of the method itself is concerned is that Hutcheson and Hume see approval or disapproval as directed at particular active affections one by one, rather than at an overall balance of affections. Hutcheson holds that only one motive receives moral approval, while Hume sees several such motives receiving it.

In his *Inquiry Concerning Moral Good and Evil* Hutcheson—here following Cumberland and Pufendorf—distinguishes between the natural goodness we attribute to things we desire and the special kind of goodness we attribute to beings possessed of benevolence.[28] The latter, he says, is not reducible to the former and arises from a "distinct perception of beauty or excellence in the kind affections of rational agents."[29] Much of the *Inquiry* is devoted to showing first, that benevolence is a real and independent motive in humans and, second, that it and it alone receives the accolade of moral approbation, the deliverance of the moral sense.[30] Hutcheson also tells us that actions which are morally good or evil must always "flow from some affection toward sensitive natures; and whatever we call virtue or vice is either some such affection, or some action consequent upon it."[31] And in various other passages he makes clear his belief that the moral value of actions stems from the motives that lead to them, and not from the natural good or evil they themselves cause. Benevolent acts are morally good, on his view, because and insofar as they arise from benevolent affections. And the benevolent affections are themselves only morally good in virtue of the special feeling of moral approval they arouse. A constitutive method like Shaftesbury's is plainly being explained, though the details of its functioning are different.

The same is true of Hume's well-known view. He argues that the moral sense is the source of a special distinction between virtue and vice, which cannot be reduced to any "matter of fact" or "relation of ideas" distinction. He then claims that it is obvious "that when we praise any actions, we regard only the motives that produced them, and consider the actions as signs or indications of certain principles in the mind and temper. The external performance has no merit. We must look within to find the moral quality."[32] The distinction between natural and artificial virtues arises because of the difficulties Hume uncovers in finding appropriate motives for kinds of action which we all agree in approving. He must show both what motives lead directly to acts of justice, promise-keeping, and loyalty to country, and why we approve of the motives, in order to explain how such acts can be right.[33] For there is no source of rightness in action other than a motive which receives the felt approval of our moral faculty. Hume shows us how a special motive, a sense of duty, might arise when the usual motives are not present in us and when there may be some question as to whether we approve of it as we do of what it stands in for; but in other respects the method he shows us using is similar to that ascribed to us by Shaftesbury and by Hutcheson, and later by Adam Smith.[34]

In all these variants the skeptical method requires the agent to have acquaintance with, and to carry out operations by, what may be described as matters internal to the mind or self. The agent's own affections or passions, or the desires or feelings of others sympathetically represented in the spectator's own mind or breast, come under the scrutiny of a reflective internal feeling or are adjudged by some other process which does not appeal to anything outside the self. Of course some beliefs about external states of affairs—about circumstances and consequences—must be present, since they are embedded in the direct affections judged by the moral faculty. The accuracy of the embedded knowledge of consequences or circumstances is irrelevant to the judgment delivered by the moral faculty. What matters is the affective response of the agent to what she takes to be the nature or outcome of a proposed or desired course of action. That response is wholly internal, and it is the approval that gives the motive its specifically *moral* value.

What are we to make of the continued effort of the British moralists to show that some variant of what I have suggested is a skeptical method of ethics shows how it is that we make moral decisions? Several problems are addressed by or through it which were important in the discussions of the period. First, the skeptical method offered a special kind of reply to contemporary skepticism about moral knowledge. Second, it located the place of morality in the kind of morally neutral universe which Newtonian science presented. And finally it did both of these things in a way that carried with it a special attitude toward humans as moral agents.

According to the various versions of the method which I have discussed, an inner condition is judged by an inner faculty which everyone possesses, and neither of these is open to any variety of skeptical doubt. "Let us carry skepticism ever so far, let us doubt, if we can, of everything about us," Shaftesbury exclaims:

> we cannot doubt of what passes in ourselves. Our passions and affections are known to us. They are certain, whatever the objects may be on which they are employed. Nor is it of any concern to our argument how these exterior objects stand: whether they are realities or mere illusions; whether we wake or dream. . . .[35]

Moral skepticism, for the exponents of the skeptical method, is not refuted by arguments showing that we do know the moral realities of the universe. Nor is moral skepticism evaded by being insulated from real life and being ignored for practical purposes.[36] It is rather neutralized by accepting that all we have, in morality, are appearances, and by showing that the appearances suffice. The principle, I think, is clear, but it works out quite differently for the different versions of the skeptical method.

Shaftesbury has only partially accomplished the move. He has found a way to account for morality in terms of what is wholly internal. He has shown that belief in the existence of God, his commands, and his sanctions is not prior to the operation of the moral faculty, but if anything depends upon it. Skeptical doubts about religion therefore do not touch morality.[37] But because Shaftesbury thinks the moral sense is cognitive, he leaves room for doubts about its deliverances. He does even more; for though he thinks the moral sense operates non-inferentially, he thinks it can and indeed must be trained and educated in order to sharpen its sensibilities. But this obviously implies that an untrained moral sense may make mistakes, and if so the skeptical problem of how one can tell an accurate from an inaccurate appearance arises even within the internal realm.

In Hutcheson and Hume the neutralization of skepticism is fully accomplished. Their view implies that Shaftesbury need not have been burdened with a cognitive faculty vulnerable to skeptical doubts. All that is needed for moral guidance is an inner disposition and an inner emotional response to it. As I said in discussing the method generally, it is true that the inner disposition may form around or include beliefs about the external world. Hutcheson and Hume agreed that these beliefs may be erroneous and that such errors might lead to actions a virtuous person would not do. But the moral response is not a response to those beliefs. Thus these more radical exponents of the skeptical method do not try to handle skepticism by refuting it abstractly or by presenting moral knowledge; instead they say that knowledge of morality of the kind whose availability the skeptic doubts is not needed.

The non-cognitivist exponents of the skeptical method agree with the skeptic in thinking that living by the appearances will bring one the good life for oneself. But they go beyond the skeptic in what they claim for "appearances." They think that without an appeal to knowledge of anything external one can obtain more than a personally tranquil life. The new skeptical method points us toward decent social life. The classical skeptic contents himself with living in accordance with the manners and laws of the country where he finds himself (or with the way these appear to him), because the appearances tell him nothing beyond this about proper social order. Not necessarily so the new skeptic.

His method enables him to explain how a proper society would be constituted, as well as to achieve the good for himself. The skeptical method can therefore take over the whole domain claimed by the natural lawyers. The appearances can do more than Pyrrho thought.

In addition to its usefulness as a way of neutralizing skepticism, the skeptical method conveys an account of the place of morality in a physical universe. It does this because of the centrality within the method of ideas of agency. All of the exponents of the skeptical method were concerned to mark a distinction between actions and events or occurrences involving only inanimate objects. This concern arises understandably from a Newtonian view of matter. Even prior to Newton, Pufendorf had drawn a sharp distinction between physical and moral entities, leaving the material and extended universe value-neutral. Our moralists accepted this view of the material world, but not the strong doctrine of free will which Pufendorf used both to explain how moral entities arise and to distinguish human action from physical motion. Hume's opposition to any such view is well known; and Hutcheson treats morality in terms that suggest purely causal interactions among motives, the desire for approval, and action, without anywhere asserting that we possess freedom of the will. For these moralists the differences between a mere occurrence involving a human body and a human action is not that the latter is caused by a free will, while the former is not. It is rather that an action is caused by a desire. Since animals as well as humans can have desires, animals can properly be said to act. The scope of their agency is limited because there are some concepts animals cannot have and consequently some desires they cannot have (such as a desire for the general good). And of course since animals, on this view, cannot reflect on their desires and so can neither approve nor disapprove of them, they cannot be *moral* agents. Human agency differs from animal agency in its scope, and it differs more importantly because humans can have their initial desires influenced to some extent by a reflective desire—the desire to act or not to act on the spontaneous desires. This human capacity for a unique and complex form of agency is what makes possible the presence of morality in the world.

In providing a reply to skepticism and explaining the place of morality in a Newtonian universe, the skeptical method also carries a view about the importance and capacities of human beings. It shows that humans are not subservient to some external order, which they must discover and follow. According to our moralists, we have within ourselves a source of guidance which enables us to live together in ways we all accept as just and decent. The exponents of the skeptical method were opposing the dominant natural-law views of morality because, among other things, those positions carried with them a deeply Augustinian picture of man as a fallen creature unable to order his own affairs and desperately in need not only of guidance by external directives but of sanctions to induce compliance. For our moralists this is all wrong. Our possession of a method of ethics that is neither opaque nor transparent but constitutive shows that we create the moral order in which we live, and supply our own motives for compliance.

Should we consider Kant a follower of the British exponents of the skeptical method? Kant was concerned with skepticism,[38] and there is a general similarity between his idea of method and theirs. Both hold that an inner faculty (for Kant, our own practical reason) tests an inner motivation (for Kant, a maxim) on which an agent contemplates acting. Only approval of the latter by the former makes the act morally appropriate. More precisely, there are three respects in which Kant's method seems exactly like other versions of the skeptical method.

(1) A maxim incorporates what we know or believe about the basic features of the situation in which we are proposing to act, but whether it passes the test of the categorical imperative does not depend on its accuracy in mirroring that situation. It depends rather on the aim contained in the maxim, and that in turn depends on our long range motivations and on the ways in which we conceptualize these.[39] So the immediate object of the moral faculty for Kant as for the moralists of the skeptical method is our active dispositions.

(2) For most people most of the time, on Kant's view, maxims elicit approval or disapproval through arousing a feeling—the moral feeling of respect. While Kant plainly thinks that conscious use of a procedure of applying the categorical imperative is possible and beneficial,[40] his Rousseauian moral admiration for ordinary people leads him to think that everyone usually knows what maxims are proper without the formula, through the feeling that is the way in which practical reason shows itself immediately in us. Thus Kant's view of the phenomenology of moral experience is in this respect close to the British position.

(3) Our awareness of the categorical imperative does not reflect some knowledge of an independently existing moral standard. It shows rather our consciousness of ourselves as practical rational beings, imposing a condition on those of our motivations which spring from our

existence as needy and dependent beings. For Kant as for the exponents of the skeptical method, doubt about moral realities outside the agent is irrelevant to the agent's ability to reach a justified decision about what to do.

These points of agreement between Kant and the British moralists must be placed within the perspective of an important disagreement. For Kant as for the exponents of the skeptical method, agency is absolutely central to an understanding of the place of morality in the post-Galilean physical world. But Kant has an idea of agency which is radically at odds with theirs. His views are in fact in line with the views of the natural law theorists and their successors. As I have indicated, for the natural lawyers and their successors free will is central to our being the sort of agent who can be morally responsible. And Hutcheson and Hume, as I indicated earlier, reject that view. Kant's difference from the British moralists on this point is accompanied by other differences between his method and theirs.

Kant holds that our inner active dispositions—our desires and aversions—are as fully determined by temporally antecedent events as are the motions of physical objects. Consequently he does not think that an adequate idea of agency can be derived from the distinction between bodily motions caused by desires and those not so caused, but caused, say, by slipping on the ice. One route of causation is as fully determined as another, whether the route involves an inner detour or not. If I am not an agent when I push you because I slipped, I am not an agent when I push you just because I feel angry and want to. To be an agent I must be as free from determination by my desires as I am from determination by purely physical causes. In the *Groundwork* Kant says that we cannot prove that such freedom is impossible, and in Section III he tries to convince us that we must understand ourselves as possessing it. My concern here is not with these much-discussed points as such, but with their bearing on Kant's method.

We are agents, Kant holds, because we are free and can express our freedom in action. A desire may suggest an end or goal to us, but unless we accept the suggestion freely we will not act on it. Thus Kant rejects the view that we are passive in relation to our desires, and that we must understand ourselves as simply moved by them. Since Hutcheson and Hume accepted such a view—another similarity between their position and that of the Pyrrhonists—[41] Kant could not agree with their version of the skeptical method. On Kant's view, what happens when my moral faculty approves my acting on a specific maxim is not fully described by saying that a reflective motivating disposition reinforces a spontaneous disposition. It must also be said that I believe that action on my maxim is permitted. Only then will I freely allow my desire to set a goal, or, in other words, only then will I freely adopt the maxim suggested by the desire.

To preserve free will, then, Kant must be a cognitivist about morality, but his cognitivism differs from that of Shaftesbury in two important respects. Whereas Kant gives us a formula which articulates the principle on which the moral faculty works, Shaftesbury tells us something about what that faculty approves but does not try to state a rationale behind the approvals. Kant's formulations of the categorical imperative are of course designed to accomplish this. Moreover, Shaftesbury apparently believes that the moral sense perceives the presence or absence of a prior harmony or propriety in the relations among our first-order dispositions, and that approval and disapproval respond to this. But Kant does not think that our initial desires or the maxims arising from them have any normative properties that are independent of their relation to the moral law. In this he resembles Hutcheson and Hume. They hold that it is by being approved that a disposition acquires moral goodness, while for Kant a maxim obtains its moral status through its relation to the moral law. Its moral goodness or badness is not prior to that law but is an outcome of its operation.[42]

Like Kant, Hutcheson and Hume offer articulations of the principle behind the operation of the moral faculty. Hutcheson, for example, tells us that the moral faculty approves most basically of benevolence and that all other moral approval can be explained in terms of our approval of the desire for the good of others. When we see this, he thinks, we will understand the moral faculty. But this understanding is essentially a causal understanding. If Hutcheson is right, the philosopher can discover what features of dispositions cause moral approval, but neither he nor ordinary people need this knowledge in order to approve or to act rightly. The account of the method of ethics Hutcheson gives is first and foremost an account which is of theoretical interest, though he thinks his philosophy might help some people to avoid the specious errors of skepticism, which would tempt them into immorality. Roughly the same is true of the way in which Hume presents his results.[43] On this matter Kant departs from his British forerunners and, because of his different view of agency, views his formulations of the principle on which the moral faculty works as grounding a method which each agent can if necessary consciously use in making decisions in daily life. It does not merely formulate a principle which operates, so to speak, behind the agent's back, causing her to approve as she does. For Kant as for the intuitionists, a principle that gives reasons for action can be deliberately used for explicit guidance.

I have indicated that Kant's view of agency links him strongly with the natural lawyers, and there are other ways in which it is correct to see him as continuing their tradition. But he diverges from the tradition as well, as we can see by contrasting Kant's view with that of Crusius. Crusius combined a strong natural law theory of free agency with a quite novel distinction between two kinds of proposition about what we ought to do. One kind asserts that there are actions we ought to do as means to some end of ours; the other kind asserts that there are actions we ought to do regardless of any ends we happen to have. He identified morality with the obligations asserted in the second kind of proposition and argued that there is a separate moral motive generated by awareness of these obligations. Here is the first clear assertion of the distinction Kant made famous as that between hypothetical and categorical imperatives. Yet whatever Kant owed to Crusius, his own moral outlook is distinctive. The agreement on agency is compatible with basic ethical disagreement.

Crusius begins with a discussion of will, which he defines as "the power of a mind to act according to its ideas" (§2). The primacy of will in human life is made clear at the start. "All minds must have wills," Crusius argues, because if they did not, "they could not act according to their ideas, and these would then be useful neither to them nor to others but quite in vain" (§4). But God makes nothing in vain. Will is moreover a separate power of mind, not simply an aspect of the understanding. And it is free: it is compelled neither outwardly nor inwardly (§38), not even by the mind's perceptions of perfection and imperfection. Crusius holds that there is a general category of spontaneous causes of which the free will is an instance. Metaphysics show, he says, that "an action or activity must come between an effect and its efficient cause," but, he adds, "the series cannot extend to infinity." That is, if a cause is brought about by an action, that action itself may be an effect needing explanation; and then between its cause and itself there must be another action or activity. But this series cannot extend to infinity, and so, Crusius concludes, "one must come to first actions or basic activities, for which it is not necessary that another activity of an efficient cause precede, but which arise immediately out of the essence of an active basic power. . . . The freedom of the human will must be of this category" (§41).

If there is a clear approach here to a Kantian idea of what is distinctive about human agency, three further aspects of Crusius's view of will make the similarity all the more striking. First, Crusius holds that without free will there could be no imputation of actions and no responsibility. People would simply be efficient causes, like other causes in the natural world. There would therefore be no guilt or merit, no punishment or reward (§38, 40). Second, Crusius makes a sharp distinction between moral and non-moral approval or disapproval. The latter we bestow on things proportionately to their fitness to bring about various ends; the former is reserved exclusively for beings with free wills (§132, 161). Third, according to Crusius what the will does is to select from among the active desires in us one with which to "connect its efficacy" and so to bring us to act. The will is free precisely because it can connect itself with an active desire, or not do so, or connect itself with some other desire (§43). Desires are among the necessary conditions of human action, but they are not sufficient conditions. It takes will to generate action out of desire. And in Crusius's view the reason for which God gave us freedom of the will was to control the desires on which we act, so that we would freely act only from the appropriate ones (§46).

On methods of ethics, Crusius and Kant both hold, as I have indicated earlier, that we can be appropriately guided either by special moral feelings or by conscious application of principles. The feeling, for both, can be clarified and seen to arise from a cognitive grasp of basic moral principles, but agents can behave properly without knowing this. This and the other striking agreements between Crusius and Kant are however less important than a central disagreement. Crusius in effect rejects the constitutive feature of the skeptical method, that whatever we are led to do by an appropriately approved disposition is *eo ipso* right. Since Kant makes this central, he distances himself radically from Crusius despite the fact that their views of agency are very close.

The fundamental morally relevant fact of the human condition, for Crusius, is that we are totally dependent on God and therefore owe him obedience (§133, 137, 174). The dependence is reflected in the details of both of Crusius's methods. And the fact that every individual can use one of the methods pins down personal responsibility before God. No one can plead ignorance of duty, saying that someone more authoritative should have told him what to do. Crusius develops the new idea of an adequate individual method of ethics to reinforce a quite traditional position.

Kant's aim is of course different. His theory of agency as freedom showing itself through rational self-legislation is meant to show how we as moral agents can be independent of divine legislation. It enables us to understand morality, with its due weight, as a human creation. The exponents of the skeptical method all approach this belief, to a lesser or greater degree. Kant and the British thinkers agree in believing that the view does not open the way to treating morality as merely a matter of custom, or as having no more weight than manners. It does not allow us to become licentious hedonists or crude libertines. The view simply offers an account, free of theological and metaphysical obfuscation, of the morality we have at all times in our hearts, no matter how we may have violated it in our behavior or misunderstood it in our explanations. With the British moralists, Kant holds that we can live in accordance with an order we impose on ourselves as individuals, and that out of this individual order there can be generated a just and caring society. There is no need for Crusian dependence on God.

Like the British moralists Kant believed that a value-free Newtonian universe is the scene and carrier of our actions, and that only some distinctively human attribute can separate action in the morally relevant sense from morally neutral happening. But his theory of agency was not solely a solution to the metaphysical problem of how to spell out that distinction. It was at least as much a result of his search for a way to elaborate his outlook on morality. Both Kant and the British moralists wanted to show that humans are capable of self-governance in a strong sense, and therefore that certain forms of external social and political control are neither necessary nor morally permissible. Their ways of doing so were, as I have tried to indicate, deeply different. Yet Kant is an exponent of the skeptical method not only because his method shares many features with the ones proposed by the British moralists but also because he shares their outlook on morality itself.[44]

## Notes

1. Henry Sidgwick, *The Methods of Ethics* (1874; seventh ed., London, 1907), 1. For discussion see J. B. Schneewind, *Sidgwick's Ethics and Victorian Moral Philosophy* (Oxford, 1977), 198–204.

2. *De Cive* (in the English translation, *Philosophical Rudiments*), Ch. III,

§26; in Sir William Molesworth (ed.), *Thomas Hobbes: The English Works* (London, 1841), II, 44–45.

3. Richard Hooker, *Laws of an Ecclesiastical Polity* (London, 1594), I, viii, 2, distinguishes between the characteristics that make something good and those which only enable us to tell whether it is good or not, and says that he will operate with the second kind of characteristic.

4. Samuel Pufendorf, *Of the Law of Nature and of Nations*, tr. Basil Kennett (4th ed.), with Mr. Barbeyrac's Prefatory Discourse . . . (London, 1729), 3–4.

5. J. G. Heineccius, *A Methodical System of Natural Law*, tr. George Turnbull (London, 1743), I, LXVIII (I, 45–46).

6. Joseph Butler, *Sermons* (1726), III, 4, in J. H. Bernard (ed.), *The Works of Bishop Butler* (London, 1900), I, 53. Future references to Butler are to this edition.

7. *Sermons*, Preface, §27–30 (I, 12–13).

8. See Josef Schmucker, *Die Ursprünge der Ethik Kants* (Meisenheim, 1962), for a pioneering discussion of Kant's debt to the ethics of Crusius, which, however, does not discuss the question of methods of ethics.

9. Christian August Crusius, *Anweisung, Vernünftig zu Leben* (1744), ed. G. Tonelli (Hildesheim, 1969), §135. References to Crusius hereafter are given in the text. The translations are taken from the selections in J. B. Schneewind (ed.), *Moral Philosophy from Montaigne to Kant* (Cambridge, 1990), II, 569–84.

10. For Butler's doubts that we can understand God's plans for the world, see especially the note to Sermon XII, 31 (I, 167). Wendell O'Brien has drawn my attention to *Analogy*, II, I, 21, (II, 149–50), where Butler explains the difference between what is moral and what is positive in religion. "Moral *precepts* are precepts, the reasons of which we see: positive *precepts* are precepts, the reasons of which we do not see." The footnote to this passage may mean that this explanation of the difference applies outside religion as well as within it. If so, the passage raises a difficulty for my claim that in the *Sermons* at least Butler presents the method of ethics as what I am calling "opaque."

11. Like Crusius, Butler allows that there is a systematic or non-intuitional method of arriving at knowledge of the requirements of morality. Ethical inquiry, he says, might proceed either by investigating "the abstract relations of things"—he has Samuel Clarke in mind—or by examining human nature as a whole. He prefers the latter but says that "both lead to the same thing" (*Sermons*, Preface, §12 [I, 4]).

12. Thomas Reid, *Essays on the Active Powers*, V, I, the final paragraph; in the edition by Baruch A. Brody (Cambridge, 1969), 370. Price holds that while the basic principles of morals are obvious and evident, their application may often be quite difficult, and he suggests that men will often not get the answer a divine intelligence would get. But he nowhere suggests that there is any special class of humans exempt from these difficulties and therefore in a position to guide others. On the contrary, even the most depraved sinner knows the principles, and even the most conscientious of us may have to be content with sincere effort. See Richard Price, *Review of the Principal Questions in*

*Morals* (3rd ed., 1787), ed. D. D. Raphael (Oxford, 1948), 168–74, and the later discussion in Chapter VIII.

13. Natural law interests are evident in Reid's *Essays on the Active Powers* but he does not explicitly align himself with natural law theory there. See Knud Haakonssen (ed.), *Thomas Reid: Practical Ethics* (Princeton, 1990), for Reid's more overt affiliation with natural law thinking.

14. For Butler see, e.g., *Analogy*, II, viii, 11 (II, 264f.), where he asserts, as something of "utmost importance" which he believes, "the moral fitness and unfitness of actions, prior to all will whatever. . . . Indeed the principle of liberty, and that of moral fitness, so force themselves upon the mind, that moralists, the ancients as well as the moderns, have formed their language upon it." He goes on to explain that he has tried, for his polemical purposes, to avoid speaking as if he assumed these points, but he plainly accepts them. In the *Sermons* Butler argues for the authority of conscience by pointing out that it has special features which show that it was meant by our creator to direct our actions; the mode of argument here is common among modern natural law writers.

15. Richard H. Popkin, *The History of Scepticism from Erasmus to Spinoza* (Berkeley, 1979); Myles Burnyeat (ed.), *The Skeptical Tradition* (Berkeley, 1983), referred to as Burnyeat 1983, especially the essays by Burnyeat and Schmitt; Julia Annas and Jonathan Barnes (eds.), *The Modes of Scepticism* (Cambridge, 1985), with a useful bibliography. In what follows I am particularly indebted to Myles Burnyeat, "Can the Skeptic Live his Skepticism," *Doubt and Dogmatism: Studies in Hellenistic Epistemology*, ed. Malcolm Schofield, Myles Burnyeat, and Jonathan Barnes (Oxford, 1980); references to this article are to the reprint in Burnyeat 1983. See also two further articles by Myles Burnyeat, "The Skeptic in his Place and Time," Richard Rorty, J. B. Schneewind, and Quentin Skinner (eds.), *Philosophy in History* (Cambridge, 1984), 225–54, cited hereafter as "Burnyeat 1984"; and "Conflicting Appearances," *Proceedings of the British Academy,* LXV (Oxford, 1979), 69–111, which, however, does not discuss the points central to my concerns. Julia Annas, "Doing without Objective Values," M. Schofield and G. Striker (eds.), *The Norms of Nature* (Cambridge, 1986), 3–29, is also a valuable discussion. For skepticism as a concern of the natural law theorists, see Richard Tuck, "Grotius, Carneades, and Hobbes," *Grotiana*, N.S. 4 (1983), 43–62, and "Optics and Skeptics: the Philosophical Foundations of Hobbes's Political Thought," Edmund Leites (ed.), *Conscience and Casuistry in Early Modern Europe* (Cambridge, 1987).

16. Sextus Empiricus, *Outlines of Pyrrhonism*, tr. R. G. Bury (Cambridge, 1933), I, 25–28. Cf. Burnyeat 1984, 241–42.

17. For sources of these objections, see Burnyeat 1984, 248, n. 44.

18. The skeptic does not—to the best of my knowledge—raise any doubts about his ability to formulate in language the way things appear to him, or to communicate to others the way things appear to him.

19. Burnyeat, in Burnyeat 1983, 128.

20. *Essais, Oeuvres complètes*, ed. A. Thibaudet and M. Rat (Paris, 1962), III, 2 (esp. 785–89); tr. Donald Frame, *The Complete Essays of Montaigne* (Stanford, 1965), 613–15.

21. *Essais,* III, 12, (1029), Frame, 805.

22. *Essais,* III, 13, (1050), Frame, 821.

23. Shaftesbury, *Inquiry Concerning Virtue or Merit* (1711) I, ii, iii, John M. Robertson (ed.), *Characteristics of Men, Manners, Opinions, Times, etc.* (London, 1900), I, 251 (hereafter identified as Robertson).

24. e.g., *Inquiry,* I, iii, ii, in Robertson, I, 262. For his general view, see e.g., *Advice to an Author,* III, iii (Robertson, I, 227): "harmony is harmony by nature, let men judge ever so ridiculously of music. . . . 'Tis the same where life and manners are concerned. Virtue has the same fixed standard. The same numbers, harmony, and proportion will have place in morals, and are discoverable in the characters and affections of mankind. . . ."

25. *Inquiry*, I, ii, iii (Robertson, I, 253).

26. In some respects Butler shares the views of the exponents of the skeptical method. But his method is opaque, and he accepts a strong doctrine of free will. On both these points he is allied with the natural lawyers, not with Shaftesbury and his followers, who are opposing the natural law position.

27. In discussing Hutcheson I have in view only his earlier works, not the *Short Introduction to Moral Philosophy* or the *System of Moral Philosophy.*

28. The distinction between moral and natural good derives from Cumberland and Pufendorf, but Hutcheson makes it in his own way.

29. Francis Hutcheson, *An Inquiry into the Original of our Ideas of Beauty and Virtue* (1725; 4th ed., 1738), I, i (112).

30. David Fate Norton has argued that Hutcheson, and following him Hume, must be read as holding a cognitivist view of the moral sense: see his *David Hume: Common-sense Moralist, Sceptical Metaphysician* (Princeton, 1982), Ch. 2; his own articles listed in the bibliography to that volume; and his defense of his view in "Hutcheson's Moral Realism," *Journal of the History of Philosophy*, 23 (1985), 397–418. I find Norton's arguments unconvincing, but I cannot analyze them here.

31. *Inquiry*, II, i (132).

32. David Hume, *Treatise of Human Nature* (1739–40), III, I, i–ii, and III, II, i; ed. L. A. Selby-Bigge and Peter Nidditch (Oxford, 1978), 469–71, 477.

33. We are first of all aware of our own active dispositions, then of those of others. Hume does not seem to have any skeptical doubts about our ability to grasp the motives of others.

34. I think that Smith's *Theory of the Moral Sentiments* offers a complex version of the skeptical method as a solution to some problems arising from earlier versions of it, but I have not space here to spell out this claim.

35. *Inquiry*, Conclusion (Robertson I, 336–37).

36. Burnyeat 1984, 225–32.

37. That Shaftesbury aimed at just this result was recognized by Butler, who shared the aim and thought his own theory better able to attain it (*Sermons*, Pref. §26–27 [11–12]).

38. On Kant and skepticism generally, see Giorgio Tonelli, "Kant und die antiken Skeptiker," *Studien zu Kants philosophischer Entwicklung* (Hildescheim, 1967), arguing that for Kant skepticism would be understood in part at least as setting appearances against appearances.

39. On maxims see Rüdiger Bittner, "Maximen," *Akten des 4. Internationalen Kant-Kongresses* (Berlin, 1974), 485–91, and Otfried Höffe, "Kant's Kategorischer Imperative als Kriterium des Sittlichen," *Zeitschrift für Philosophische Forschung*, 31 (1977). See also Barbara Herman, "The Practice of Moral Judgement," *Journal of Philosophy*, 82 (1985), 391–413, reprinted in Barbara Herman, *The Practice of Moral Judgment* (Cambridge, Mass.: Harvard University Press, 1993), 73–93.

40. See, e.g., Immanuel Kant, *Critique of Practical Reason*, 8n.

41. As discussed by Burnyeat 1983 and by Annas, 22.

42. For a clear statement see *CPracR*, 62–63.

43. I am speaking here of the rhetoric in which their views are presented. Both of them have reformist aims: they want to change the morality they see widely accepted in their culture. But their strategy for doing this is to present their views as "scientific" in the way that Newton's were. They are giving us a science of how man is, with the unstated aim of changing how people are.

44. An early and quite different version of this paper was read to the Johns Hopkins departmental colloquium, from which I received useful criticism; at a conference at Oberlin in April, 1987, where Karl Ameriks commented on it; at Riverside in May, 1987; and at a Kant conference in Sigriswil, Switzerland, in June, 1987. I am grateful to Prof. Ameriks for his incisive criticisms in Oberlin, to Stephen Darwall for a lengthy set of extremely helpful comments, and to Thomas Pogge, whose observations about the earlier version helped me in rethinking it. I received additional helpful discussion when I presented this material at Princeton in March, 1990, and when a shorter version was read at Dartmouth to an NEH Summer Institute on Hume during the summer of 1990.

# Part II

# The Good Will and the Categorical Imperative (*Groundwork* I)

# 2

# The Argument of Kant's
# *Groundwork,* Chapter 1

*Nelson Potter*

## I

A great deal has been written about Kant's *Groundwork of the Meta-physics of Morals.*[1] But in those writings little attention has been devoted to analyzing the structure and argument of Chapter I of that work. The discussions of Chapter I that one finds in most of the commentaries on the *Groundwork* do little to uncover and set forth any overall structure or argument in the chapter.

But in fact Chapter I contains a sustained argument beginning with the first sentence and continuing through to the point where the principle of morality is stated toward the end of the chapter. When this argument is made apparent, it is also apparent that Chapter I has a definite role to play in the economy of the whole work. Chapter I establishes what the "supreme principle of morality" is by an analysis of the concept of moral goodness. Chapter II continues with an exposition, using technical philosophical terminology, of that same principle; and Chapter III, of course, aims to justify that principle.

Of the writers and commentators on Kant's ethics who have written about the *Groundwork*, Chapter I, some discern no argumentative structure to the chapter as a whole, while others do discern that there is an argument running through this chapter. Into the first category fall W. D. Ross and H. J. Paton. Into the latter category fall A. R. C. Duncan, T. C. Williams, and Robert Shope.[2] Duncan gives an excellent analysis of the structure and argument of Chapter I, and states that there is to be found in this chapter an argument like the one that will be pre-

sented in this paper (though he does not spell it out), beginning with
the concept of the good will and ending with a description of the moral
or practical principle upon which such a will is acting.[3] Duncan's attempt throughout his book to discern the structure, strategy, and argument of the *Groundwork*, makes it an extremely valuable book; we
shall later (in Part IV) discuss briefly his "critical" interpretation of the
*Groundwork* in relation to its first chapter. Williams also states that
there is an argument of the kind that Duncan mentions, but does not
give the details of the argument.[4] And, finally, Shope states a version of
the argument in his discussion, with the aim of showing that Kant's
attempts to derive the categorical imperative in its first formulation are
unsuccessful.

In this essay, I shall set forth my own account of the argument that
is to be found in the *Groundwork*, Chapter I, in Part II. Part III is a
further discussion of certain parts of that argument. I discuss two possible interpretations of the argument in Part IV. In Part V, I shall make a
few concluding remarks. Finally, there is an appendix in which Kant's
remarks on "respect" (*Achtung*) are discussed.


# II


I have set forth Kant's argument in nine propositions, and will comment on each one.

(1) A good will only has absolute worth.

This is the assertion with which the section begins; it is a point which
is explained at some length (*G*, 393–394). Kant gives little in the way
of argument for this proposition. He thus apparently takes it to be part
of our "ordinary rational knowledge of morality."[5] Kant regards this
section as an analysis of our common rational beliefs about morality,[6]
so perhaps he thinks that this first proposition is one which would be
accepted by any rational being when he is presented with it.

There are two questions which naturally arise concerning this proposition: (a) What is a "good will"? and (b) What is "absolute worth"? (a)
We can give no very definite answer to the first question, for the concept of "good will" is simply a concept which is to be analyzed, and as
a preanalytical concept it is bound to be vague and indefinite. In a
sense the whole of Chapter I is devoted to arriving at an answer to this

question. We could say of this preanalytic concept, however, that a good will is that in virtue of his possession of which one may be said to be a morally good person. (b) "Absolute worth" may be regarded as a worth outweighing any worth which is not absolute. Thus Kant is claiming that the worth of a good will is greater than the worth of any other kind of thing. Now since it will turn out that a good will is a moral will, and is the locus of moral value in persons, we could also express proposition (1) as a statement about moral value:

(1a)  Moral value always outweighs any other kind of value.

To express proposition (1) in this way is perhaps to anticipate later features of the argument of this section, but we note it now because we find that later Kant uses "moral value" and "absolute value" interchangeably.

(2)  A good will is not good because of what it effects or accomplishes. (*G*, 394)

This proposition is advanced by Kant at the beginning of the third paragraph of Chapter I. Whenever anything is good because of what it effects, it is good only in a derivative sense, i.e., good as a means. But the good will is not just good as a means; it is good in itself. It is good simply in virtue of being what it is. Proposition (2) follows from (1), for although it is true that a thing may be intrinsically good without being absolutely good, it would be impossible for something good only as a means to be absolutely good—for the goodness of the means would always be qualified by the goodness of the end. And if a good will is *also* good as a means, this is a fact distinct from and independent of the fact of its intrinsic goodness.

(3)  A human action is morally good if and only if it is done from duty. (*G*, 397–399)

Central to Chapter I of the *Groundwork* are "three propositions" concerning morality which Kant presents and explains. Kant tells us what his second and third propositions are, but he fails to tell us just what the first proposition is. Let us regard (3) as Kant's "first proposition."[7] The proposition states the conclusion of a rather lengthy discussion running from *G*, 397 to *G*, 399.

It seems that Kant thought that proposition (3) followed from proposition (1), though the way in which it follows is not obvious. The two important aspects of the transition from the one proposition to the other are the following: (a) the shift from the value of a good will, to the value of actions which are expressions of that will. For the purposes of the present argument Kant could analyze either the notion of a good will or the notion of a morally good action and get the same results. (b) The introduction of the concept of duty, as a concept central to the analysis of acts expressive of a good will in human beings. Kant introduces the concept of duty as follows:

> We will therefore take up the concept of duty, which includes that of a good will, exposed, however, to certain subjective limitations and obstacles. (*G*, 397)

That is, wherever we have dutiful action, there we have an action which is an expression of a good will, though the converse is not true. The concept of duty is applicable when, as with human beings, the dictates of a good will are or may be resisted by the agent's feelings and desires. We may note, however, that proposition (3) does follow from proposition (1) only if we are given an analysis of action from duty adequate to show that such actions and only such actions are expressive of a good will. We shall discuss Kant's account of action from duty in greater detail in Part III of this paper.

(4) To act from duty is to act, not with regard to the purpose to be attained by our action, but with regard only to the maxim in accordance with which it is decided upon.

This is Kant's "second proposition" (*G*, 399). It has been reworded slightly to bring it into closer relation to our proposition (3). The paragraph in which Kant states this proposition and attempts to justify it is worth quoting in full:

> Our second proposition is this: An action done from duty has its moral worth, *not in the purpose* to be attained by it, but in the maxim in accordance with which it is decided upon; it depends therefore, not on the realization of the object of the action, but solely on the principle of volition in accordance with which, irrespective of all objects of the faculty of desire, the action has been performed. That the purposes we may have in our actions, and also their effects considered as ends and motives of

the will, can give to actions no unconditioned and moral worth is clear
from what has gone before. Where then can this worth be found if we are
not to find it in the will's relation to the effect hoped for from the action?
It can be found nowhere but *in the principle of the will*, irrespective of
the ends which can be brought about by such an action; for between its
*a priori* principle, which is formal, and its *a posteriori* motive, which is
material, the will stands, so to speak, at a parting of the ways; and since it
must be determined by something, it will have to be determined by the
formal principle of volition when an action is done from duty, where, as
we have seen, every material principle is taken away from it. (*G*, 399–400)

The argument here is complex, and Kant is not entirely clear about
what he is arguing for, as we shall see. If action from duty is action
expressive of a good will, and hence is action good in itself (as the
good will is good in itself), then the goodness of the action can lie
neither in its actual or intended effect, for in that case, the action would
only be good as a means. (*Cf.* proposition (2).) But all actions undertaken for the purpose of fulfilling some desire are actions which are
good merely as means. So morally good action cannot be action which
is undertaken to fulfill a desire. But when our actions are morally good,
our will has been determined to action by *something*. What can it be
which determines the will to a morally good action, if it is not some
inclination? Kant's answer is that the basis of determination can be
found nowhere but in "the principle of the will." The will is then pic-
tured as choosing between "an *a priori* principle, which is formal, and
its *a posteriori* motive, which is material" (*G*, 400). Since the latter has
been ruled out as a candidate for what determines the will in morally
good action, it must be the case that in action from duty the will is
determined by "the formal principle of volition."

In proposition (4) we have one of the first mentions in Chapter I of
the *maxim* of an action. Kant offers a definition of "maxim" a page
later: "The subjective principle of willing."[8] The maxim is thus the general rule or policy of action a person is following when he performs an
action. It is "subjective" in that it holds only for the agent who has
adopted it. Kant contrasts "maxims" with practical laws (*G*, 400n) or
imperatives[9] both of which are *objective* practical principles. As "objective" they are binding for all rational agents, *will* be followed by a fully
rational will, and *ought* to be followed by an imperfectly rational being.
(See *G*, 412–413.)

It was said earlier that Kant seems not entirely clear in the last quoted paragraph about what he is arguing for. In fact, it seems that he is establishing two distinct propositions. The first is:

(4a) The moral value of an action is a quality of its *maxim*.

This proposition is consistently a part of Kant's moral doctrine. This part of Kant's doctrine is especially prominent in the *Religion* and the *Metaphysics of Morals*; in the former work, virtue is defined in terms of a perfectly general and formal maxim of action;[10] in the latter work, it is said that the duties of virtue arise from imperatives directed, not to actions (as in the *Doctrine of Right*); but to maxims of action.[11] Maxims are rules of action which are freely chosen by the agent. They are the "inner" rules which are followed in the performance of "outer" actions; it is for our choice of maxims that we are most directly responsible, for actions for which we are responsible are simply consequences of our having adopted a certain maxim.[12] At times it seems that Kant intends a definite contrast between actions and maxims of action,[13] and at other times it seems that we may speak indifferently of an action or its maxim.[14] In any case it is consistently a part of Kant's moral doctrine that we cannot tell the moral value of an action from its "outer" nature—we must look to its "inner" principle, i.e., its maxim.[15]

But there is another proposition for which it seems that Kant is arguing in the present paragraph. He wants to assert not only (4a), but he also wants to say that the maxim of action from duty is of a particular kind—it is a maxim which has been adopted, not because its adoption will lead to the fulfilment of some desire of ours, but solely in virtue of its "form." Thus we have:

(4b)   Action from duty is action done on the basis of a maxim which we have adopted, not because its adoption will fulfil desires of ours, but because of its form.

This proposition will be discussed more fully in Part III. Kant next sums up the results of the argument so far:[16]

Therefore nothing but the *idea of the law* in itself, *which admittedly is present only in a rational being*—so far as it, and not an expected result, is the ground determining the will—can constitute that pre-eminent good which we call moral, a good which is already present in the person acting on this idea and has not to be awaited merely from the result. (*G*, 401) and then he asks:

> But what kind of law can this be the thought of which, even without regard to the results expected from it, has to determine the will if this is to be called good absolutely and without qualification? (*G*, 402)

Kant replies to this question as follows:

> Since I have robbed the will of every inducement that might arise for it as a consequence of obeying any particular law, nothing is left but the conformity of actions to universal law as such, and this alone must serve the will as its principle. That is to say, I ought never to act except in such a way *that I can also will that my maxim should become a universal law.* Here bare conformity to law as such (without having as its base any law prescribing particular actions) is what serves the will as its principle, and must so serve it if duty is not to be everywhere an empty delusion and a chimerical concept. The ordinary reason of mankind also agrees with this completely in its practical judgments and always has the aforesaid principle before its eyes. (*G*, 402)

We may state Kant's argument in this passage as follows:

(5) This formal principle of volition (i.e., the principle of the adoption of maxims in virtue of their form) is simply the requirement that my action conform to universal law as such.

Kant believes that we must accept this proposition because a purely *formal* principle of volition could require nothing more.

(6) The essence of law is its universality.

This is obtained by an analysis of the concept of law, in Kant's view.

(7) Hence the moral law commands nothing but that I always act in such a way that I can will my maxim should become a universal law.

It may seem that proposition (7) either does not follow from (5) and (6), or that it does not express all that Kant thought that it did. But it is plain enough that Kant thought that a principle adequate to be a supreme principle of morality did follow from (5) and (6). Also, when

Kant introduces the first formulation of the categorical imperative in Chapter II, he writes that by merely considering the concept of a categorical imperative, we can know what it must contain:

> For since besides the law this imperative contains only the necessity that our maxim should conform to this law, while the law, as we have seen, contains no condition to limit it, there remains nothing over to which the maxim has to conform except the universality of a law as such. (*G*, 421)

It seems that Kant thinks that moral imperatives command simply that our actions be law-like in general. It is at least doubtful whether Kant really can deduce the moral imperative from the concept of the law by itself. Whether he can depends, among other things, on what the meaning of that moral imperative is; the question of what the categorical imperative means—and the related question of how it is to be applied[17]—are themselves much controverted topics. For this reason I shall not attempt to judge whether Kant's derivation here is successful.

We may now draw some inferences from the argument as a whole: Propositions (5) through (7) purport to be an analysis of the "formal principle of volition" which purports to show that this formal principle tells us to "always act in such a way that I can will my maxim should become a universal law" (from (7)). And (4b) said that *action from duty* is action on such a "formal principle of volition" (i.e., a principle which we adopt in virtue of its form). Thus, putting together (4b), and (5) through (7), we obtain:

(8) To act for the sake of duty is to act only on that maxim which can at the same time be willed as a universal law.

Now we also know, from propositions (1) through (3) that a will which acts for the sake of duty is a good will. We may therefore conclude, from (1) through (3) and from (8), that

(9) A good will is a will which always acts only on that maxim which can at the same time be willed as a universal law.

It is now clear that there is a continuous argument from the concept of a good will to the first formulation of the categorical imperative, and it is also apparent that Kant thought that there was. Thus we may say that although the nature of the moral law has not been sufficiently explained when its formulation is introduced in the first chapter, and although certain aspects of it have not been explained,[18] at least the fact that a maxim of a good will would always have the character of universalizability has been sufficiently established in the first section, and is taken by Kant to have been so established, through an analysis of concepts to be found in "ordinary rational knowledge of morality."[19]

*    *    *

This analysis of the argument of Section I of the *Groundwork* leaves out of account those parts of that section which are not a part of what I take to be the main argument of the section. These parts are three: (1) There is an unusual and not very convincing argument from considerations of natural teleology concerning the "function of practical reason" (*G*, 394–396). Kant argues that if men have the ability to apply reason to action, as they do, this practical use of reason could not have been given them for the purpose of furthering their happiness, but only for the purpose of bringing about the existence of a will good in itself. We shall not discuss this passage further. (2) Kant introduces the concept of respect (*Achtung*) for the law (*G*, 400). We shall take this passage up in the Appendix. (3) After we are given the formulation of the moral law (*G*, 402), the section concludes with a further exposition of the contrast between moral reasoning and prudential reasoning, and argues that a philosophical understanding of morality is necessary if men, in their ordinary practical thinking, are not to confound moral and prudential concerns—a confounding which leads to the destruction of morality. We will not need to discuss this passage further.

**III**

It seems that Kant's primary purpose in his discussion of his "first proposition" (*G*, 397–399) is to develop the distinction between action from duty and action merely in accord with duty. Kant does not develop criteria for distinguishing between actions done on the basis of different motives, i.e., criteria which would be useful in the everyday task of making certain kinds of moral judgments. Rather he is attempting to distinguish from one another the *concepts* of action from duty and action merely in accord with duty.

In considering actions from duty, we can first eliminate actions which are contrary to duty; in the case of such actions "the question does not even arise whether they could have been done for the sake of duty" (*G*, 397). It is also relatively easy to distinguish actions from duty from those which are done as a means to the fulfilment of some inclination, because for such actions we have no immediate inclination, and thus they are not performed because of any intrinsic characteristics of the action. The distinction between actions done *aus Pflicht* (from duty) and those not so done is hardest to make out where we compare dutiful actions to those which fulfil some *immediate inclination.*

Kant does not define "action from duty" before proceeding to discuss it—this is in accord with his belief concerning philosophical methodology that proper definitions can come only at the conclusion of a philosophical analysis, and not at the beginning.[20] But Kant seems to be assuming in this discussion that action from duty is action which is done for its own sake. It is reasonable that action from duty should be of this character, since if it were not the doing of an action for its own sake, it is hard to see how the action could be expressive of a will good in itself. We can see why Kant says that it is more difficult to draw the contrast between action from duty and action from immediate inclination—in both cases we are performing an action for its own sake. In attempting to draw the contrast between these latter two kinds of action Kant uses a number of examples:

Consider the obligation we have to preserve our own life. Since in normal circumstances we *want* to preserve our lives, the actions by which we do so have no moral value. It is only when the grounds of immediate inclination are taken away that the contrast between inclination and duty becomes clear. Only then, if we refrain from taking our own life, do we so refrain *from duty* (*G*, 397–398).

Again, people with a sympathetic temperament help others out of immediate inclination, but Kant says that such actions have no moral value. An inclination is in any case an inclination, though some inclinations are more fortunate, happy, beautiful, etc. than others. Actions done on the basis of immediate benevolent feelings possess no moral value, because the maxim of the action has "no moral content" (*G*, 398). Such actions are performed, not from duty, but from inclination. For the maxim of such an action to have moral content, Kant tells us, the action must be performed *aus Pflicht* and not *aus Neigung* (from inclination).[21]

Kant gives the example of the (at least indirect) duty of promoting our own happiness. We ought to try to achieve happiness because unhappiness leads to temptations to the transgression of duty. But it is only in certain special circumstances that actions whereby we promote our own happiness can possess moral value. These are cases where we are tempted by some immediate inclination to do what we know to be imprudent; in such a case, perhaps the motive of prudence is not sufficient to determine the will, and here perhaps the "law to further his happiness, not from inclination, but from duty" (*G*, 399) becomes relevant. For here it is the motive of duty that supplies the motivation that the principle of happiness does not supply.[22]

Kant also comments that the scriptural command to love our neighbour and even our enemy must be regarded as a command to practical love, and not a command to "pathological love"—for the latter kind of love, love from inclination, cannot be commanded. Here I think we find one of the philosophical motives for Kant's assigning moral value only to actions from duty—only action on such a basis could be commanded by a moral law. Given the fact that any action has some motivational basis, no action could be commanded by the moral law if we acted only from inclination. Note that we're not here commanded to act from duty; rather it is simply that no action from inclination can be demanded of us at all. Whenever we have a moral obligation it is presupposed that an adequate motivational basis for the required action will be forthcoming. But it is only in the case of action from duty that such a presupposition is justified for every case of a moral command. If the moral law commands us unconditionally, it cannot wait on any such presupposition's being justified in each case, for this in effect would be to make the command conditional, and thus not categorical. The justification of the possibility of moral commands must include the justification of the motivational presupposition and it is only in the case of action done from a motive of duty, i.e., only in cases where the action is done *as* a morally required action, that the moral quality of the action is to be found in its very motive.[23]

As Kant recounts these examples, he tells us that maxims of action from duty have "moral content" (*'sittliche Gehalt'*) (*G*, 398), while other maxims do not. What is it for a maxim to have "moral content"? We do not get any very complete answer to that question in Chapter I. But Kant begins to provide an answer to this question in his discussion of his "second proposition." First, we must remind ourselves that the moral value of any action is a quality of its maxim. Secondly, the maxims of actions having moral value are either themselves in some sense "formal," or are determined by a "formal principle of volition." (It is not clear from what Kant says here which is the better way to state this point.) "Form" is to be contrasted with "matter" here, and the "matter" of an action or maxim of action is, it seems, the purpose (*Absicht*) (*G*, 399) for which it is done, the *end* of the action. Elsewhere Kant identifies the "end" of an action, and the "matter" of a volition.[24] To refer to the "form" of a maxim, in contrast, is to refer to it simply as a principle of action, without reference to the ends which acting on such a principle will realize.

All action to which we are determined by some subjective end (inclination) is action whose maxim is without "moral content." That has been said in the discussion of the "first proposition." So the maxim of action from duty must be a maxim which is determined by no such end, or, which has no such "matter." But we must be determined to the action by something or other. The only other thing which could determine us to action would be some "formal" principle, i.e., a principle containing no reference to any end. If a maxim is a moral maxim having "moral content" it must be so in virtue of its form, for the "matter" of maxims has been excluded as a determining factor in action from duty, or, as Kant puts it, "every material principle is taken away from it (the will)" (*G*, 400). Thus the "moral content" of the morally good maxim must be the result of the presence or the influence of purely "formal" practical principles. Kant then tries to show, as we saw in the last part of this paper, that the "formal" principle in question must be the one that he will later call the categorical imperative.

In this discussion, the nature of the "moral content" of maxims, of "formal" principles, and other key concepts of Kant's argument remains somewhat vague and unclear. It is thus difficult to argue that Kant's argument here is sound. But I think that one attempt to show it to be unsound is not successful: Robert Shope[25] argues that Kant's derivation of the categorical imperative is not successful, and that Kant's argument in Chapter I of the *Groundwork*, even when it is supplemented by other of Kant's arguments from other places, is either a *non sequitur* or it has some doubtful premises. Shope gives an account of part of the argument of Chapter I,[26] and then writes of it:

> Now this line of reasoning only excludes incentives of the will which are, as Kant goes on to call them, *a posteriori* incentives, that is, purposes which some wills *happen* to have but which every will need not have, e.g., an object of inclination. If there are ends which it is objectively, morally necessary to have we might be able to claim that these provide *a priori*

incentives, and Kant has said nothing yet to rule out the possibility that the worth of an action derives from a maxim whose object, end, and purpose is such a morally necessary end. To preserve my life out of inclination, from an *a posteriori* incentive, is to have as my maxim "To preserve my life since I have an inclination to do so." To act from duty however, might be to have as my maxim merely "To preserve my life (regardless of inclination)." Kant so far has not proved that the latter kind of maxim cannot be the ultimate maxim of a good will acting to preserve the agent's life. . . .[27]

An argument from the *Critique of Practical Reason*[28] is introduced as a possible aid in overcoming Kant's embarrassment. That argument concludes (in Shope's formulation): "Therefore, if the idea of an object or material of the faculty of desire determines the will, the practical principle of the agent is not a moral law,"[29] Shope comments that if "object of the will" is to be understood in a broad sense, to mean any intended action," . . . then the argument depends on a dogmatic, metaphysical assumption about the will,"[30] *viz.*, that

. . . any decision which appears to aim ultimately at some object, such as keeping a promise, or making money from a deceitful promise, must really aim ultimately at getting pleasure or avoiding pain.[31]

But Kant would then be making the unsupported, dogmatic claim that the will, whether good or bad, can never determine itself to action merely by adopting a principle such as "To keep a promise (regardless of the pleasure or pain I get from doing so)" or such as "To make a deceitful promise when that will get me money."[32]

Nor, Shope thinks, is there any satisfactory way to patch up or improve Kant's argument so as to avoid this unsupported premise.

But Shope's account fails to consider one of Kant's arguments, an argument from Chapter II of the *Groundwork*, concerning the concept of autonomy. (See *G*, 432–433.) There Kant is introducing the concept of autonomy, and giving an account of the categorical imperative as the only possible autonomous moral principle. He contrasts it with other supposed moral principles by noting that all other moral principles presuppose an "object" of the will, which, though it is distinct from the will, must determine or move the will to act; to be thus determined to action by something outside oneself is to be acting heteronomously. "Object" here may again be understood in a broad sense, as including any intended action. Further, an important part of Kant's general epistemological theory says that objects, i.e., things existing independently of the knowing subject, can only be empirically connected with that subject.[33] Thus the motivation to pursue some "object," e.g., the keeping of a promise or the preserving of one's life for its own sake, will be merely empirical, and will not have the necessity that is a mark of a moral principle in Kant's view (what is your moral obligation *must* be done). This last point is a statement of Kant's argument in the second *Critique* (the one mentioned by Shope), without any reference to the ideas of "pleasure" or "pain." Kant's argument there may now be seen, not as resting on an arbitrary metaphysical assumption, but on (a) a plausible epistemological doctrine saying that causal-motivational connections between objects and the knowing subject are always only empirical, and (b) the Kantian metaethical point that moral principles have a character of necessity.

It might be said that since Kantian autonomy presupposes the *principle* of autonomy (i.e., the categorical imperative itself), to use it to show that the supreme principle of morality is that same principle in Kant's Chapter I is to beg the question. But, from the point of view of the present discussion, what the principle of autonomy is remains to be seen; for all we know it might be Shope's "Tell the truth for its own sake." Thus the autonomy argument is not question-begging; we are speaking of autonomy only in the sense of "freedom" or "self-determination."

Finally, we may mention a reason not found in Kant why Shope's "Don't tell lies" proposal need not worry the defender of Kant; that is the inherent implausibility of such a maxim. "Don't tell lies" just does not seem to be a moral absolute or most basic moral principle, as it would have to be if "Don't tell lies, for its own sake" is to be a maxim of action from duty. It needs justification, in terms of more general moral principles.

If we suppose that Shope had shown that Kant's arguments for the categorical imperative were not sound, and if we suppose that the alternative to the categorical imperative that Kant had failed to rule out were a significant and plausible alternative conception of morality, then Shope's criticisms would have done Kant's moral philosophy serious damage.

## IV

What conclusions may be drawn from the argument of Chapter I? We note that Kant begins with the concept of a good will, and by a continuous analysis of this concept, he ends with a statement of the moral law. It is not referred to here as a "categorical imperative," since neither term in that familiar Kantian phrase has yet been introduced. But the law that is given is substantially the same (there is some difference in wording) as the categorical imperative in its first formulation (*G*, 420). Now the categorical imperative, among other things, serves as a criterion of right action; but here we have that same principle introduced *via* an analysis of action from duty and of moral value. We could summarize the argument of this section as follows: We know that moral value is absolute, and that what we morally ought to do is to be discovered by an analysis of actions having moral value. Actions having moral value are one and all actions from duty. What, then, is the nature of action from duty? If we can come up with a description of the principles that are operative in action from duty, we will thereby come up with a criterion of right action, a criterion by the use of which we can determine what we ought to do. Now this statement of Kant's argument seems to support the following two theses about Kant's moral philosophy: (1) That Kant is basically a teleologist (holding to a kind of self-realization theory), since he makes the basis for the rightness of actions the degree to which they contribute to our self-realization or perfection.[34] (2) Kant in the *Groundwork* is not doing moral philosophy, as such, but is simply descriptively analyzing moral action. This view is advanced by A. R. C. Duncan.[35] However, what Kant says in Chapter I and our analysis of his argument do not support either of these views.

For (1) to gain support from this analysis, it would have to be assumed that the concept with which Kant begins in his exposition is the basic moral concept for him. But Kant has told us that his procedure will be "analytical" (*G*, 392)—he will begin with some commonly accepted truth (e.g., the absolute value of a good will, or, the necessary truth of mathematical propositions) and will analyze it to discover the principles on which it is based. If this is his procedure, we may expect more primitive concepts to appear at the end of the section, not at the beginning.

It may be that no one has ever held the view that Kant is a "teleologist" or "perfectionist" of this kind. Nevertheless this possible interpretation is interesting to consider because (a) the "perfectionist" view was an influential view in Kant's own time, and one that Kant actively opposed in his critical ethics and (b) there is a certain kind of truth in this "teleologist" or "perfectionist" interpretation. That is, it is true that actions in accord with duty and done from the motive of duty *are* expressive of the moral perfection of the agent; it is for this reason that the basic moral principle can be discovered by an analysis of the nature of morally good action, as Kant has done in Chapter I. Also, the concept of moral perfection, as an end or goal which it is morally obligatory to pursue, comes to occupy an important part of Kant's moral philosophy in *The Doctrine of Virtue*, the second half of Kant's *Metaphysics of Morals*.

Thesis (2) seems to be supported by the fact that, according to the present interpretation, Kant in Chapter I is simply descriptively analyzing the nature of moral action, thereby deriving a moral principle. Thus, within the scope of this chapter, at least, Kant's main aim seems to be purely descriptive and analytical. And perhaps the best way to discover the principle of right action is through a descriptive analysis of action from duty. But all of these facts are consistent with the claim that the *Groundwork* is a piece of ethical philosophy. If, for example, the formal principle arrived at in Chapter I is then used to derive particular moral obligations, where such derivation is one of Kant's major aims in the *Groundwork,* then Duncan's critical interpretation would be false. Thus the present account of Chapter I is consistent with either the truth or the falsity of Duncan's thesis, and does not either strongly confirm or disconfirm that thesis.

## V

I have shown that Chapter I of Kant's *Groundwork* contains a continuous argument by which Kant seeks to derive a statement of the "supreme principle of morality" from an analysis of the concept of moral goodness. This supreme principle of morality, which in Chapter II Kant calls the "categorical imperative," is the principle on which a morally good man acts. It is also a criterion of morally right action, as Kant's model application to show that it is wrong to make a false promise (*G*, 402) is designed to make clear. The connection between the categorical imperative as a criterion of right action and the categorical imperative as the principle on which a morally good man acts seems to be the following: To perform a morally good action (i.e., to act from duty rather than merely in accord with duty) is to do what is right for the reason that it is right. That is, when an action is done *from duty* the empirical beliefs and the moral principle which together yield an argument *justifying* a particular moral conclusion, e.g., that one shouldn't make false promises, are the beliefs and principles that *motivate* one to perform the action. It is for this reason that the categorical imperative can be used both to describe the motivation of the morally good man, and to serve as a moral test for determining what one ought to do.

## Appendix: *"Achtung"*

The third proposition, which we did not consider in the analysis of Chapter I with which this essay began, considers the nature of action from duty, *subjectively* regarded. It is as follows: "Duty is the necessity to act out of respect for the law" (*G*, 400). In his discussion of this proposition, Kant attempts to show that respect, though it is a feeling, is a feeling which is of a quite special sort, and hence that it is such that it is characteristically moral. Feelings have objects to which they are attached or directed. One can feel inclination, but not respect, for an object (or, we might add, a state of affairs) which is an effect of a possible action. Nor can inclination itself be an object of respect; at most it can be an object of approval or love.

> Only something which is conjoined with my will solely as a ground and never as an effect—something which does not serve my inclination, but outweighs it or at least leaves it entirely out of account in my choice (*Wahl*)—and therefore only bare law for its own sake, can be an object of respect and therewith a command. (*G*, 400)

Now if we can accept this account of *Achtung*, we can see that it would be a feeling closely connected with morality, for it has the following characteristics: (1) Its object is never an *effect* or object of the will, but a ground of the determination of the will. What is never an effect or object of the will must be purely formal in nature, and thus respect must be respect for "only bare law for its own sake" (*G*, 400). (2) Respect is an effect of the moral law, and not a cause of the law. In contrast, the feeling of hunger is, or may be, a cause of the adoption of a certain maxim of action. The feeling of moral respect does not function as a cause in this way, for if it did, to act out of respect for the law would be to act on the basis of a feeling or matter of the will (*G*, 401n). (3) This feeling is not produced by some outside influence, but is rather "*self-produced* by a rational concept, and therefore specifically distinct from feelings, [which are so produced,] all of which can be reduced to inclination of fear" (*G*, 401n).

Thus the feeling of respect is unique in its cause, its object, and its effects in action. It is not clear, however, what role the concept of respect plays in action having moral value, or in Kant's moral philosophy generally. From what is said in the present passage, it seems that respect does not enter into the maxims of actions from duty in the way that sensuous feelings enter into maxims which are sensuously determined. On the other hand, it seems that respect is at least a necessary concomitant of action from duty and of our awareness of the moral law.[36] If it is a consequence of the will's determination by the moral law, then it is an effect which arises only after a morally good maxim has been formed and adopted—it does not determine such a maxim, but is determined by it. From what Kant says later, it seems that it is a necessary element in our awareness that we do fall under the moral law, and that we are capable of acting from duty. I.e., unless the feeling of respect for the law were present in us, we might act from moral motives, but we could never be aware of being under obligation, or of the fact that pure practical reason does have an influence on our will.
      Kant writes,

> Now an action done from duty has to set aside altogether the influence of inclination, and along with inclination every object of the will; so there is nothing left able to determine the will except objectively the *law* and subjectively *pure respect* for this practical law, and therefore the maxim of obeying this law even to the detriment of all my inclinations. (*G*, 400)

This passage suggests that respect is simply the subjective side of the law itself, and that the subjective and objective side of the law are inseparable from one another in action from duty. Kant writes a bit later,

> Therefore nothing but the *representation (Vorstellung) of the law in itself, which admittedly is present only* in a rational being—so far as it, and not an expected result, is the ground determining the will—can constitute that pre-eminent good which we call moral, a good which is already present in the person acting on this idea and has not to be awaited merely from the result. (*G*, 401)

The representation of the law, then, like any other representation, has a side or aspect relating merely to the subject in his capacity of being affected and another side or aspect which does not have reference merely to the subject, but to conditions which are valid independently of any state of such a subject. These latter, or objective, features of a *Vorstellung*, are those which are universally valid, because they are expressions of reason itself. Now in spite of this necessary concomitance of the objective law and the subjective feeling of respect, the former is said to be the cause of the latter; they are concomitants in the *Vorstellung* of the law. If the effect of the law (respect) were not present, neither would there by any *Vorstellung* of the cause.

The feeling of respect is thus not a separate additional element in the maxims of actions from duty. It is rather a necessary concomitant of the representation of any such maxim, and plays no role in its formation.

Thus Kant's third proposition states the nature of duty from its subjective side, whereas the second proposition and its discussion gave a preliminary analysis of the nature of the will's determination to action in action from duty, objectively considered. It is with the objective nature of the moral law and the morally good will that the greatest interpretive difficulties remain. Kant's brief remarks about *Achtung* in Chapter I have set forth the essentials of his doctrine concerning morality's subjective side.

## Notes

1. References to the *Groundwork* will be given in the text in this form: (*G*, 402). The translations in the text are from Paton (*The Moral Law* [3rd ed.; London: Hutchinson University Library, 1956].) In some cases I have altered Paton's translation.

2. Paton, *The Categorical Imperative* (London: Hutchinson & Co., 1947). Ross, *Kant's Ethical Theory* (London: Oxford University Press, 1954). A. R. C. Duncan, *Practical Reason and Morality: A Study of Immanuel Kant's Foundations of the Metaphysics of Morals* (London: Thomas Nelson and Sons, Ltd., 1957). T. C. Williams, *The Concept of the Categorical Imperative* (London: Oxford University Press, 1968). Robert Shope, "Kant's Use and Derivation of the Categorical Imperative," pp. 253–291 in Robert Paul Wolff (ed.), *Foundations of the Metaphysics of Morals with Critical Essays* (Indianapolis: The Bobbs-Merrill Company, 1969).

3. See *op. cit.*, p. 52, and Chapter IV (pp. 57–74).

4. See *op. cit.*, pp. 1–4.

5. The title of Chapter I is "Passage from Ordinary Rational Knowledge of Morality to Philosophical."

6. Cf. *G*, beginning of Chapter II, 406.

7. (3) is similar to what Paton (*op. cit.*, pp. 18–19) takes to be the "first proposition." A. R. C. Duncan on p. 59 of *Practical Reason and Morality* re-

gards Kant's opening statement (our proposition (1)) as Kant's "first proposition." It makes no difference who is correct.

   8. *G*, 400n., cf. *G*, 421n.; *Critique of Practical Reason*, 18–19; *Metaphysics
of Morals*, VI, 225.

   9. See the *Critique of Practical Reason*, 18–19.

   10. *Religion Within the Limits of Reason Alone*, 6:32–36.

   11. *Metaphysics of Morals*, 6:388–389.

   12. Kant argues that an agent is responsible only for "a rule made by the
faculty of choice for the use of its freedom, that is, in a maxim." (*Religion*,
6:21.)

   13. For example, see *Metaphysics of Morals*, 6:388–389.

   14. The examples of the application of the categorical imperative in Chapter
II of the *Grundlegung* (*G*, 421ff.) seem to be this way.

   15. That emerges from the discussion of action from duty, *G*, 397ff. Also see
*G*, 407ff. and *Religion*, Book I, *passim*.

   16. We omit here a discussion of Kant's third proposition, "Duty is the necessity to act out of respect for the law" (*G*, 400). This proposition is discussed
in the Appendix.

   17. This point is discussed in my paper, "How to Apply the Categorical Imperative," *Philosophia* 5 (1975): 395–416.

   18. In particular, its imperatival nature and the fact that it commands unconditionally or categorically are to be explained in Chapter II. Also a number of
alternative formulations will be given of it there.

   19. It is thus surprising that Kant should say, as he does at *G*, 447, that "An
absolutely good will is one whose maxim can always have as its content itself
considered as a universal law" is *synthetic* a priori. Kant's argument in Chapter
I seems to show that it is analytic. This passage has caused some interpreters
of Kant much pain.

   20. See Lewis White-Beck, "Kant's Theory of Definition," in his *Studies in
the Philosophy of Kant* (New York: The Bobbs-Merrill Company, Inc., 1965).

   21. It may seem that here and elsewhere in this section I am adopting the
infamous Schiller interpretation of Kant, which held that "1. An action has no
moral worth if any inclination to do the action is present or if any pleasure
results from the satisfaction of this inclination; and 2. An action has no moral
worth if any satisfaction arises from the consciousness of doing one's duty"
(quotation from Paton, *op. cit.*, p. 48). But I think that all that Kant and I say
here (I am in this section aiming to give a close account of Kant's own words)
is that actions *motivated by* any kind of inclination have no moral worth. This
claim sometimes shades into the Schiller thesis if (1) it is noted that the presence of an inclination to do what is morally required likely prevents us from
*knowing* for certain whether the action in accord with duty has any moral
worth, or (2) if Kant puts forward his thesis, advanced throughout his critical
ethical works (see *Metaphysics of Morals*, 6:386) that our *inclination* to pursue our own happiness, under ordinary circumstances, at any rate, prevents us
from having an obligation to do that same thing. To make it quite clear that
the Schiller interpretation is a distorted version of the Kantian doctrine as a
whole, one needs to discuss the account of dispositions and the process of

building moral strength of will that constitutes moral perfection, points that Kant puts forth in *Religion within the Limits of Reason Alone*, and the *Metaphysics of Morals*. But to introduce these matters here is not appropriate to our present purposes.

22. Kant in later ethical works says that in such a case the actual duty is that of promoting our own moral character; avoiding unhappiness is simply a means to this obligatory end, and hence not obligatory in itself. See *Metaphysics of Morals*, 6: 387.

23. Kant's justification of the categorical imperative consists of showing that it is possible to act out of purely moral motives, i.e., of showing that an adequate moral basis for any morally required action is within the power of the agent. On this point, see the discussion of the question "How are all these imperatives possible?", *G*, 417–420, and the discussion of the "fact of pure reason," *Critique of Practical Reason*, 31ff.

24. See *G*, 436; *Critique of Practical Reason*, 26–27; *Metaphysics of Morals*, 6:384.

25. Shope, *op. cit.*

26. *Ibid.*, pp. 264–265.

27. *Ibid.*, p. 266.

28. *CPracR*, 21 ff.

29. *Op. cit.*, p. 268.

30. *Ibid.*, p. 269.

31. *Ibid.*

32. *Ibid.*, p. 270.

33. See both *G*, 432–433, and *Critique of Practical Reason*, 21ff.

34. John Silber sometimes seems to hold to this view in "The Ethical Significance of Kant's *Religion*," printed as an introduction to Kant's *Religion Within the Limits of Reason Alone*, trans. by T. M. Greene and H. H. Hudson (New York: Harper Torchbooks, 1960), pp. lxxix–cxxxiv. See especially p. lxxxv. Also Paton in *op. cit.*, p. 45, writes, "We have now completed the examination of Kant's starting point and found it in the absolute and unique goodness of a good will. This requires to be stressed, because as the argument advances we shall find ourselves talking a great deal more about duty than about goodness. Kant is so commonly regarded as the apostle of duty that if we are to get his doctrine in true perspective we must remember that for him goodness is fundamental; and there is no warrant for supposing that he even entertained the conception of a duty divorced from goodness."

35. In *Practical Reason and Morality* (op. cit).

36. Compare Kant's remarks on respect in the *Critique of Practical Reason*, Chapter III, and in the *Metaphysics of Morals*, 6:402–403.

# 3

# Kant's Analysis of Obligation: The Argument of *Groundwork* I

*Christine M. Korsgaard*

## I. The Normativity of Morality

One of the debates of recent moral philosophy concerns the question whether moral judgments express "internal" or "external" reasons.[1] According to internalists, if someone knows or accepts a moral judgment then she must have a motive for acting on it. The motive is part of the content of the judgment: the reason why the action is right is a reason *for doing it.* According to externalists, this is not necessarily so: there could be a case in which I understand both that and why it is right for me to do something, and yet have no motive *for doing it.* Since most of us believe that an action's being right is a reason for doing it, internalism seems more plausible. It captures one element of our sense that moral judgments have *normative* force: they are *motivating.* But some philosophers believe that internalism, if correct, would also impose a restriction on moral reasons. If moral reasons are to motivate, they must spring from an agent's personal desires and commitments.[2] This is unappealing, for unless the desires and commitments that motivate moral conduct are universal and inescapable, it cannot be required of everyone. And this leaves out the other element of our sense that moral judgments have normative force: they are *binding.* Some internalists, however, have argued that the force of internalism cuts the other way. If moral reasons must motivate, and I show you that an action is morally right, I have *ipso facto* provided you with a motive for doing it. Moral reasons motivate *because* they are perceived

51

as binding.[3] A good person, according to these internalists, does the right thing because it is the right thing, or acts from the motive of duty.

Many of the moves in the contemporary debate were anticipated in the debate between the rationalists and the sentimentalists of the eighteenth century. At the center of their dispute was the notion of *obligation*, a term they used primarily to refer to the *normativity* of duty. The term "obligation" is a source of confusion, because "an obligation" is sometimes used loosely as synonym for "a duty," a required action. But "obligation" refers not so much to the action as to the *requiredness* of the action, to its normative pull. We say that we *feel* obliged, or are *under* an obligation, to express our sense that the claims of morality are claims *on us*. The idea that moral conduct is obligatory, like the idea that moral judgments express internal reasons, is intended to capture both elements of the normativity of morality: its power both to motivate and to bind. And the eighteenth-century moralists, like contemporary internalists, ran into a difficulty when they tried to combine these two elements.

Rationalist moral philosophers criticized their opponents for not being able to explain how we are *bound* to do our duty. Samuel Clarke, for instance, levels this complaint against what he takes to be the view of Hobbes: that moral laws are the positive laws of a sovereign (possibly God) who has the power to enforce them. Either we are obliged to obey the sovereign, Clarke urges, in which case obligation is prior to positive law, or there is no real obligation at all.[4] According to later rationalists, sentimentalism is subject to the very same objection. The sentimentalist Francis Hutcheson, for example, believes that God has provided us with a moral sense which causes us to approve benevolence and deem it virtuous. But rationalists argue that providing us with a sense which endues certain motives with a moral quality is just a way for God to create morality by positive institution. Hutcheson admits as much, for he says that God could have given us a malice-approving moral sense had He so chosen. It is not because benevolence is obligatory in itself, but because God is benevolent, and approving benevolence is good for us, that God has caused us to approve it.[5] But the rationalist Richard Price complains that this makes morality a kind of illusion. We may indeed have moral "perceptions," but unless what we perceive is a rightness that is really *in* the action, the action is not really right, and so not really obligatory, after all. Price says that moral sense theory implies "That there being nothing intrinsically proper or improper, just or unjust; there is nothing *obligatory*. . . ."[6] The rightness of an action cannot be something extrinsic to it, projected onto it, like a secondary quality, by the operation of a sense. The action must be *intrinsically* obligatory if it is obligatory at all.

But sentimentalists, in turn, criticized rationalists for not being able to explain how we are *motivated* to do our duty. According to rationalists, rightness is a real property of an action or of the relation of an action to its situation, discerned by reason. But the bare grasp of a rational truth seems to have no motivational power. Hume famously complains:

> . . . men are often govern'd by their duties, and are deter'd from some actions by the opinion of injustice, and impell'd to others by that of obligation.
>
> Since morals, therefore, have an influence on the actions and affections, it follows, that they cannot be deriv'd from reason; and that because reason alone, as we have already prov'd, can never have any such influence.[7]

The problem was to find an account of obligation that combines the two elements of normativity: motivation and bindingness.

This problem was inherited by Kant. A form of rationalism was the dominant ethical theory in Germany, and Kant was a rationalist by training as well as by temperament. But he was also a great admirer of the British sentimentalists.[8] As early as the so-called Prize Essay, Kant identifies obligation (*Verbindlichkeit*) as the "primary concept" of ethics[9] (PE, 2:298). There, he argues that the project of moral philosophy is to show how there can be obligations, understood as unconditional "oughts" which both bind and motivate. It is easy to see how an action can be necessary to achieve a certain end, but for an unconditional "ought" the end itself must also be necessary (PE, 2:298–99). At this point in his career Kant endorses the Wolffian ethical principles "Do the most perfect possible by you" and "Do not do that which would hinder the greatest possible perfection realisable through you" as the "primary *formal ground* of all obligation" (PE, 2:299). But he levels against these principles a charge later to be leveled against his own view by Hegel: by themselves, they constitute an empty formalism, from which "no particularly definite obligation flows" (PE, 2:299). The content of morality, Kant speculates, must be determined by the operation of unanalyzable feelings. He praises Hutcheson's idea of the moral sense as a possible source for this content (PE, 2:300). But the Prize

Essay's discussion of ethics ends inconclusively. Kant says, ". . . it has still to be discovered in the first place whether the faculty of knowledge or feeling . . . exclusively decides the primary principles of practical philosophy" (PE, 2:300).

By Kant's critical period this uneasy alliance between rationalism and sentimentalism is over, and rationalism has won the day. The problem of obligation, like any philosophical problem, must be solved in two stages. Since the concepts of morality are concepts of pure reason, we must start with a metaphysical account showing how pure reason generates these concepts and so what they (analytically) contain. But the claim that a concept of pure reason applies to the world is always synthetic. Kant cannot, like earlier rationalists, simply insist that a rational moral order is intuited in the nature of things. Dogmatic metaphysics has no more place in ethics than in theoretical philosophy. So we must turn to a critical synthesis to show that the concepts of morality apply to that part of the world to which they purport to apply: to us. The first step, and the one I am concerned with in this paper, shows what obligation is, that is to say, what the concept of obligation contains. The second, or synthetical, step shows that the concept has application, that is, that we have obligations.[10]

In *Groundwork* II, Kant appears to think there is no difficulty about analyzing the concept of obligation. An obligation would be prescribed by a categorical imperative, and analyzing that idea leads us immediately to the Formula of Universal Law. Kant says:

> . . . we will first inquire whether *the mere concept* of a categorical imperative does not also furnish the formula containing the proposition which alone can be a categorical imperative. . . .
>
> . . . if I think of a categorical imperative, *I know immediately what it contains.* For since the imperative contains besides the law only the necessity that the maxim should accord with this law, while the law contains no condition to which it is restricted, there is nothing remaining in it except the universality of law as such to which the maxim of the action should conform. . . .
>
> There is, therefore, only one categorical imperative. It is: Act only according to that maxim by which you can at the same time will that it should become a universal law. (*G*, 420–21, my emphases)

In fact, the analysis given in these cryptic passages is almost identical to the argument of *Groundwork* I.

In this paper my aim is to show how Kant's analysis of obligation, contained in the argument of *Groundwork* I, provides a solution to the problem of obligation that emerged from the controversy between rationalism and sentimentalism. In Section 2, I explain in more detail how the very concept of obligation generates a dilemma which is central to that controversy. The argument of *Groundwork* I, which I reconstruct in Section 3, shows the way out of this dilemma, and in so doing shows what sort of thing an obligation must be.

## II. Hume's Dilemma

The argument of *Groundwork* I is an attempt to give what I shall call a "motivational analysis" of the concept of a right action, in order to discover what that concept applies to, that is, which actions are right.[11] A motivational analysis is one that defines or identifies right actions in terms of the motives from which they are done by a morally good person.[12] The starting point of Kant's analysis is that a morally good action is one done from the motive of duty, or, we might say, a right action is one that is done by a morally good person *because it is right.* If the analysis works, Kant's achievement is to argue from this feature of right actions to a substantive moral principle which identifies which actions are right. In order to appreciate the importance of this achievement, we must consider it in light of an argument of Hume's which purports to show that exactly this cannot be done. This argument gives rise to what I shall call "Hume's Dilemma."

In opposition to the thesis that the sense of duty is the only moral motive, Hume argues that "the first virtuous motive, which bestows a merit on any action, can never be a regard to the virtue of that action, but must be some other natural motive or principle."[13] He points out that when we praise an action, and regard it as virtuous, we do so because we suppose that it has a virtuous motive. And:

> To suppose, that the mere regard to the virtue of the action, may be the first motive, which produc'd the action, and render'd it virtuous, is to reason in a circle. Before we can have such a regard, the action must be really virtuous; and the virtue must be deriv'd from some virtuous motive: And consequently the virtuous motive must be different from the regard to the virtue of the action. A virtuous motive is requisite to render an action virtuous. An action must be virtuous, before we can have a regard to its virtue. Some virtuous motive, therefore, must be antecedent to that regard.[14]

This argument can be recast in terms of rightness. Suppose that a right action is essentially, or by definition, one prompted by a morally good motive. To know which actions are right we must know which motives are good. But if the only good motive is the sense of duty, then we do seem to get the kind of circle Hume describes here. I want to do what is right and ask you what that is. You tell me: right actions are those done just because they are right. How can I derive any content from this? The objection may be taken to be a version of the "empty formalism" objection, for the principle "do the right thing because it is the right thing" appears to be an empty formalism. According to Hume, I need prior information about which acts and virtuous or right before I can do them with regard to their virtue or rightness. This shows the need for a moral sense, which will enable us to pick out the virtuous motives which make actions right. And the moral sense must approve motives other than the motive of duty, in order to get some content into the system. This leaves us with a dilemma. If we retain the thesis that it is motives that essentially make actions right, it apparently must be motives other than a regard for rightness itself. On the other hand, if we are to retain the thesis that the primary motive of virtuous action is the motive of duty, we must have some way of identifying or defining right actions which does not depend on their motives.

Sentimentalists opted for the motivational analysis, but at a cost. On Hume and Hutcheson's view, what renders actions virtuous is our approval of the natural affections which motivate them, and these are, accordingly, the "first virtuous motives," in Hume's phrase, to morally right action. This leads to two problems, one concerning the fact of obligation, and the other concerning the sense of obligation or motive of duty. I have already mentioned the problem concerning the fact of obligation. The action is supposed to be right because we approve its motive. But we might, had we been given a differently constituted moral sense, have approved a different motive and so a different action. So the action is not *necessarily* right. But then it is hard to see how it can be obligatory. An obligatory action is one that is binding—one that it is necessary to do. But if the action is not necessarily right, how can it be necessary to do? Contemporary internalists make a similar objection to externalism. If the moral motive is simply a natural affection such as benevolence, we can really have no obligations. For how can there be an obligation to have the motive which gives us obligations? And how can we be obliged to perform the actions, unless we are obliged to have the motive that produces them? If it is not necessary to have the motive, it is not really necessary to perform the actions.[15] Behind both objections is the idea that the rightness of an action cannot be extrinsically conferred. If it is *necessary* for us to have a benevolence-approving moral sense or benevolent motives, this must be because benevolent action is intrinsically obligatory. If benevolent action is not intrinsically obligatory, then neither an arbitrarily implanted moral sense nor dispensable natural affections can make it so.

As these arguments suggest, the idea that we are in fact obliged is naturally associated with the idea that we should act from the motive of obligation. To be obliged to the performance of an action is to believe that it is a right action and to find *in that fact* a kind of motivational necessity: the action is called for or demanded by the situation, and that is the motive for doing it. And this brings us to the second problem. If the "first virtuous motives" are admirable natural motives, then the motive of obligation must play at best a secondary role.

Hutcheson, accordingly, dismisses most of what is said about obligation as "confused" and "obscure."[16] When we say someone is morally obliged to an action we mean only that the moral sense approves the action: that there is a *justifying* reason for it.[17] We are not talking about *exciting* or motivating reasons. The two parts of the normativity of morality, its power to bind, or justify, and its power to motivate, or excite, have separate sources. But, Hutcheson complains:

> Some farther perplex this subject by asserting, 'that the same reasons determining approbation ought also to excite to election.'[18]

Obviously he disagrees. A good action need not be motivated by the agent's approval of it. This does not mean that there are no actions to which we are motivated by moral approval. Hutcheson says:

> The prospect of the pleasure of self-approbation is indeed often a motive to choose one action rather than another; but this supposes the moral sense, or determination to approve, prior to the election.[19]

Hume's account of actions done from the motive of duty is similar:

> But may not the sense of morality or duty produce an action, without any other motive? I answer, It may: But this is no objection to the present doctrine. When any virtuous motive or principle is common in human nature, a person, who feels his heart devoid of that principle, may hate himself upon that account, and may perform the action without the mo-

tive, from a certain sense of duty, in order to acquire by practice, that virtuous principle, or at least, to disguise to himself, as much as possible, his want of it.[20]

In both accounts, the motive of obligation is reduced to a desire for self-approval. It is also reduced to a second-rate moral motive; action from spontaneous natural affection is more authentically virtuous.[21]

This is contrary to the widely-shared idea that obligation is central to moral experience, and that there are at least some actions which ought to be performed from the sense that they are obligatory. Now in our own century it has been argued that we should abandon these ideas about obligation. In her famous 1958 paper "Modern Moral Philosophy," Elizabeth Anscombe argued that the moral "ought" and "obligation" are specifically modern notions that classical philosophers like Aristotle did very well without. Anscombe claims that these ideas are naturally associated with a divine law conception of ethics, and, in the absence of that conception, lack sense.[22] Similar charges have been made more recently by Bernard Williams in the last chapter of his book *Ethics and the Limits of Philosophy.*[23] But Anscombe and, although to a lesser extent, also Williams, share an important assumption with their sentimentalist predecessors, for both tend to think that the primary force of saying that I am obliged to do something is that I will be judged, punished, blamed, or will blame myself, if I do not.[24] This emphasis is characteristic of sentimentalism, which constructs morality from the standpoint of the spectator or judge, taking the affections of approval and disapproval as the source of our most fundamental moral conceptions. For a sentimentalist, the idea of obligation can only arise by turning disapproval against the self.[25] For a rationalist, however, the focus on obligation comes from an agent-centered or deliberative perspective, not from that of the moral judge. The primary deliberative force of saying "I am obliged to do this" is not "I will blame myself if I do not" but "my judgment that it is right impels me to do this."[26] And this is at least related to an older thought, which *is* found in the classical philosophers. Aristotle's person of practical wisdom does the virtuous action for its own sake and *for the sake of the noble* (το χαλον).[27] He is moved to act by an ethical quality, a moral beauty and nobility, which he apprehends in the action. He does not merely act on some spontaneous natural affection which sideline judges applaud.[28] And this element of moral action—this feature of how it looks from the agent's point of view—essentially drops out of sentimentalism.

This had a great deal to do, I believe, with keeping ethical rationalism alive in the eighteenth century. On many points, Hutcheson and Hume's attacks on early rationalism were effective, and later rationalists, such as John Balguy and Richard Price, particularly admired Hutcheson.[29] But the idea of obligation and its connection to motivation was captured better by Clarke's ethical system than by either sentimentalist or Hobbesian views. In describing right actions as "fit to be done," "reasonable," and "proportionate," Clarke tries to capture the sense that right actions are called for or demanded by their situations, that they have a kind of rational necessity comparable to the necessity of demonstrable truth.[30] He argues that "the original *Obligation* of all . . . is the eternal *Reason* of Things"[31] and that the moral motive is the sense of this obligation:

> For the Judgment and Conscience of a Man's own Mind, concerning the Reasonableness and Fitness of the thing, that his Actions should be conformed to such or such a Rule or Law; is the truest and formallest *Obligation*; even more properly and strictly so, than any opinion whatsoever of the Authority of the Giver of a Law, or any Regard he may have to its Sanction by Rewards and Punishments.[32]

Increasingly, as the eighteenth century progresses, we find philosophers on both sides of the debate working to combine the best insights of sentimentalism with a more rationalistic account of obligation.[33]

But rationalism too has a cost, so long as Hume's argument is accepted. For Hume's argument makes it appear that the idea that the motive of duty is the primary motive to right action can be maintained only at the expense of the idea that right actions are defined essentially in terms of good motives. Instead, the rationalist must hold that rightness is in the nature of the actions required. As Price puts it:

> . . . all actions, undoubtedly, have a *nature.* That is, *some character* certainly belongs to them, and somewhat there is to be *truly* affirmed of them. This may be, that some of them are right, others wrong. But if this is not allowed; if no actions are, *in themselves*, either right or wrong, . . . it follows, that, in themselves, they are all indifferent.[34]

Since that is unacceptable, we must conclude that "right and wrong are real characters of *actions.*"[35] This, of course, removes any difficulty about doing actions with regard to their rightness. If the rightness is in the action, we can certainly do it for the sake of that rightness. But now the rationalist is saddled with the view that rightness is (to speak anachronistically) a non-natural property, inherent in the actions, and intuited by reason. In this way, rationalism seems to entangle us in a metaphysical moral realism, as well as an epistemological intuitionism, which are both unpalatable. This will in particular be an objection for Kant, since his project forbids the uncritical assumption that necessary principles may be found, by rational intuition, to hold in the nature of things. And, although the rationalists rejected the empiricist theory of reason from which it follows that reason cannot motivate, they had no account of *how* we can be motivated by rational truths to put in its place. The rationalists saw that obligation is only possible in one way: the perception of the bindingness of the right action must be what moves us. But instead of explaining how this is possible, they simply insisted that it is.[36] . . .

### III.  The Argument of *Groundwork* I

In the Preface to the *Groundwork*, Kant says that his method in the first part of the book will be "to proceed analytically from common knowledge to the determination of its supreme principle" (*G*, 392). Specifically, *Groundwork* I seeks the principle behind "common rational knowledge of morals" (*G*, 393). Because he is analyzing common knowledge, Kant starts from an idea which he expects the reader, once he recognizes it, to accept: that nothing is unconditionally valuable except a good will. Whenever we believe we have witnessed the exercise of such a will, we think we have seen an action that has a special kind of value: value that is independent of "what it effects or accomplishes," and so, unconditional (*G*, 394). In order to discover the principle of morality, or of unconditionally good action, we need to discover what principle a good will acts on.

The notion of duty includes that of a good will, since the notion of duty is the notion of a good will operating under "certain subjective restrictions and hindrances" (*G*, 397). Therefore, Kant proposes to look at cases in which we should say that a person acted "from duty" in order to discover the principle of action which characterizes a good will. He proceeds to distinguish three kinds of motivation. One may act from duty (do the right thing because it is the right thing), from direct inclination (perform an action because one enjoys it), or from indirect inclination (perform an action as a means to a further end). The first of Kant's four examples concerns a merchant who refrains from over-charging hapless customers because a good reputation helps business. This is an example of *indirect* inclination. We are unlikely to confuse such an action with an action from duty, Kant says,

> For it is easily decided whether an action in accordance with duty is per-formed from duty or for some selfish purpose. It is far more difficult to note this difference when the action is in accordance with duty and, in addition, the subject has a direct inclination to do it. (*G*, 397)[37]

The other three examples are meant to illustrate this point: in each of them, we consider an action that one ought to do from duty, but that one may also be naturally inclined to do. For instance, Kant says, there are persons

> . . . so sympathetically constituted that without any motive of vanity or selfishness they find an inner satisfaction in spreading joy, and rejoice in the contentment of others which they have made possible. (*G*, 398)

Actions done on this basis are "dutiful and amiable" and "deserve praise and encouragement," yet they do not evince the moral worth of the action done from duty (*G*, 398). To find the essence of duty and the good will, we must find the basis on which we distinguish these actions from those done from duty.

It is essential not to confuse the point of these examples with that of the honest merchant, who acts "neither from duty nor from direct inclination, but only for a selfish purpose" (*G*, 397). According to a familiar but misguided reading of these passages, Kant holds a crudely hedonistic theory about all motives other than moral ones: he thinks that all actions except moral ones are done for the sake of one's own pleasure, and so are all equally selfish and without moral worth. So understood, Kant means to emphasize the *similarity* of actions done from direct inclination to those done from indirect inclination: their purpose, like the honest merchant's, is fundamentally selfish. But what Kant clearly emphasizes here is the *difference* between direct and indi-rect inclination, and he says explicitly that the sympathetic person is "without any motive of vanity or selfishness" (*G*, 398). He praises such actions as amiable and even "dutiful" (*pflichtmäßig*), and compares them to actions arising from the inclination to honor, which he else-where describes as a "simulacrum" of morality (*IUH*, 8:26).[38] In fact, if we suppose that Kant holds a hedonistic theory of the *purpose* of all actions done from inclination, neither the distinction between direct and indirect inclination, nor (as I will show in a moment) the general argument of *Groundwork* I, makes much sense. Instead, Kant envisions the act of the sympathetic person as one done for its own sake. The pleasure a sympathetic person takes in helping is not an ulterior purpose, but is rather the reason why he makes *helping* his purpose.[39] Pleasure is not the purpose of his action, but the ground of the adoption of his purpose.

And the person who helps others from duty *also* does so for its own sake. The duty in question, as Kant makes clear elsewhere, is the duty to make the happiness of others one's *end* (*G*, 430; *DV*, 6:385, 388). It is because of this similarity of purpose that the sympathetic person's actions are characterized as "dutiful" despite their lack of moral worth. We may say, going beyond Kant, that sympathy is a simulacrum of morality because it is an impulse inspired by the humanity in others, just as honor is a simulacrum of morality because it is a motive to obey certain strict laws of conduct for their own sake.[40] So the difference between the sympathetically helpful person and the dutifully helpful person does not rest in their purpose, but must lie elsewhere. This leads Kant to his "second proposition," namely, "An action performed from duty does not have its moral worth in the purpose which is to be achieved through it but in the maxim by which it is determined" (*G*, 399).

To say that the worth of an action does not lie in its purpose, but in its maxim, is to say that its worth lies in the grounds on which the action along with its purpose has been chosen. Unfortunately, at this point in the argument Kant introduces the idea of a maxim with no preparation whatever—he simply says, in a footnote clumsily attached to its fifth usage, that a maxim is a "subjective principle of volition" (*G*, 400). In fact, the idea of a maxim is essential to Kant's solution of the problem of obligation.

According to Kant it follows from the fact that a rational being acts "under the idea of freedom" (*G*, 448) that she acts for a reason or on a principle which she must regard as voluntarily adopted. The point here has to do with the way a rational being must think of her actions when she is engaged in deliberation and choice. When you make a choice, you do not view yourself as simply impelled into it by desire or impulse. Instead, it is as if there were something over and above all of your desires, something that is you, and that decides which if any of your desires to gratify. You may of course *choose* to act on a desire, but that does not mean that you are impelled by it. It means you take this desire as a reason, or, in Kant's language, you make it your maxim to satisfy this desire. You may even choose to act on your strongest desire, but still that does not mean its strength is impelling you. It means that you are taking strength as a reason for choosing to satisfy one desire rather than another, making it your maxim to act on your strongest desire. Your maxim thus expresses what you take to be a reason for action; since reasons are derived from principles, or laws, it expresses your conception of a law.

Kant believes that all human action is purposive, and so that every maxim of action contains an end (See *G*, 427; *DV*, 6: 381, 384–85; *Rel* 6:4). A maxim of action will therefore usually have the form "I will do Action-A in order to achieve Purpose-P." You will only act on that maxim if you also make it your maxim "to achieve Purpose-P." Since this maxim too must be adopted for a reason there are reasons for having purposes, which are again expressed in maxims. Although Kant does not emphasize this, it is perhaps easiest to think of maxims as hierarchically organized: "I will do Action-A to achieve Purpose-P" is adopted on the basis of "I will achieve Purpose-P" (plus a relevant hypothetical imperative); "I will achieve Purpose-P" is in turn adopted on the basis of a further maxim that "I will make it my purpose to have the things that I desire" or whatever it might be.

Therefore, when Kant says that the difference between the sympathetic person and the dutiful person rests in their maxims, the contrast he has in mind is this: although the sympathetic person and the dutiful person both have the purpose of helping others, they have adopted this purpose on different grounds. The sympathetic person sees helping as something pleasant, and that is why he makes it his end. The morally worthy person sees helping as something called for, or necessary, and this is what motivates him to make it his end.[41]

A common complaint is that this suggests that a person who helps reluctantly and with a stiff upper lip is morally better than one who does so gladly and from spontaneous benevolence, and that this is both unintuitive and unattractive. This complaint, however, is based on a misunderstanding of Kant's point. There are three important things to remember. First, Kant makes it clear that the reason he contrasts cases of natural affection with cases where the motive of duty operates in the absence of natural affection is that the operation of the motive of duty is especially obvious in the latter kind of case. Despite the misunderstandings to which this strategy gives rise, the essential difference between the two people contrasted does not rest in whether the helping action is enjoyed. It rests in whether one helps only because of this enjoyment or because help is perceived as something it is necessary to give. Nothing prevents an action from being done from the motive of duty by someone in whom sympathy is also present. Actually, we must distinguish two cases here. There might be a person in whom sympathy serves as a supplementary or cooperating motive that provides needed support for the motive of duty. This person's motives are impure, in the sense developed in *Religion Within the Limits of Reason Alone*, and he would not, or not always, do the helping action when required if sympathy did not serve as a prop to duty (*Rel*, 6:24). This *does* decrease the person's moral worth. But another person in whom sympathy is present might be motivated entirely, or at least sufficiently, by the motive of duty, so that she would do the helping action even if sympathy were not present. This person has moral worth, yet her native sympathy will contribute to her enjoyment of the action.

However, a second point is even more important. Kant is talking here about the grounds on which a purpose is adopted and held. We must distinguish between the emotions, feelings, and desires which prompt us to *adopt* a purpose and those that *result from* the adoption of a purpose. Once you have adopted a purpose and become settled in its pursuit, certain emotions and feelings will naturally result. In particular, in ordinary circumstances the advancement of achievement of the purpose will make you happy, regardless of whether you adopted it originally from natural inclination or from duty. So a dutiful person, who after all really does value the happiness of others, will *therefore* take pleasure in making others happy.[42]

This is a point that Kant makes explicitly in his later ethical writings. For instance, in *The Metaphysical Principles of Virtue*, when Kant is explaining the duty of beneficence, he says:

> Beneficence is a duty. Whoever often exercises this and sees his beneficent purpose succeed comes at last really to love him whom he has benefited. When therefore it is said, "Thou shalt love they neighbor as thyself," this does not mean you should directly (at first) love and through this love (subsequently) benefit him; but rather, "Do good to your neighbor," and this beneficence will produce in you the love of mankind (as a readiness of inclination toward beneficence in general). (*DV*, 6:402)

Of course you may wonder why then the dutiful person in Kant's *Groundwork* example does not enjoy the helping action. Kant suggests two scenarios. In one, the action is done by someone whose mind "is clouded by a sorrow of his own which extinguished all sympathy with the lot of others" (*G*, 398). In the other, the person is "by temperament cold and indifferent to the sufferings of others, perhaps because he is provided with special gifts of patience and fortitude" (*G*, 398). The conditions of these persons make them incapable of deriving enjoyment from their helping actions. These are cases in which the motive of duty shines, according to Kant, because the advancement of the happiness of others is so clearly conceived as necessary rather than merely pleasant. But neither case suggests that in ordinary conditions a dutiful person will not have the emotions normally consequent upon the adoption of a purpose, including enjoyment of its successful pursuit, and joy in its realization.

Once this is accepted, the intuition behind the common complaint should collapse, and this is the third important point. The complaint is based on the usual misreading of the examples, in which the person who acts from duty is envisioned as someone who does not really have the happiness of others as his end. This is simply a mistake. Duty is not a different purpose, but a different ground for the adoption of a purpose. So Kant's idea here is captured better by saying that the sympathetic person's motive is *shallower* than the morally worthy person's: both want to help, but there is available a *further* stretch of motivating thought about helping which the merely sympathetic person has not engaged in.[43] This further stretch of thought concerns the sort of world which this would be if no one helped—or better, if no one perceived the need for help as a *reason* to help, or a *claim* on help. Such a world would be unacceptable because we regard our own needs as reasons why *we* should be helped (*G*, 423; *DV*, 6:453). Regarding my needs as normative for others, or, as Kant puts it, making myself an end for others, I must regard the needs of others as normative for me (*DV*, 6:393).[44] And this is to say that the needs of others are a law to me. So the morally worthy person helps because she believes that the needs of others make a claim on her and so that there is a normative demands, or a law, that she ought to help. This characterization of the point of the example brings us to Kant's third proposition, which is that "Duty is the necessity of an action executed from respect for law" (*G*, 400).

Now at this point it is essential to remember that what Kant is doing is a *motivational analysis* of the notion of duty or rightness. Kant is analyzing the good will, characterized as one that does what is right because it is right, in order to discover the principle of unconditionally good action.[45] The assumption behind such an analysis is that *the reason why a good-willed person does an action, and the reason why the action is right, are the same.* The good-willed person does the right thing because it is the right thing, so if we can discover why the good-willed person does it, we will have *ipso facto* discovered why it is the right thing. What the analysis reveals is that the reason why the good-willed person does the action is not merely because it serves this or that purpose, but because it is necessary—that is, it is a law—to perform such an action or to have such a purpose. The maxim of the action, or the maxim of the purpose, has what I shall call a "legal character": that is, it is normative, it has the capacity to express a demand made on us. Since the legal character of the maxim is what motivates the good-willed person, it is that, and nothing else, that makes the action or the purpose right. Kant's analysis identifies the rightness of the action *essentially* with the legal character of its maxim.

Now comes the critical step. It follows that the maxim must not get its legal character from anything outside of itself. For, if there were an outside source of legal character, then that source, rather than legal character itself, would be what makes the action right. Instead, the maxim's legal character must be intrinsic: it must have what I shall call a "lawlike form." This is why legal character, or *universality*, must be understood as lawlike form, that is, as a requirement of *universalizability*. Kant draws this conclusion this way:

> Since I have robbed the will of all impulses which could come to it from obedience to any law, nothing remains to serve as a principle of the will except universal conformity of its action to law as such. That is, I should never act in such a way that I could not also will that my maxim should be a universal law. Mere conformity to law as such (without assuming any particular law applicable to certain actions) serves as the principle of the will, and it must serve as such a principle if duty is not to be a vain delusion and chimerical concept. (*G*, 402)

The point is a delicate one. You might suppose, at first, that the legal character by which the good-willed person is motivated could come from something other than lawlike form of the maxim. For instance, you might suppose that the action is prescribed by some law whose grounds are independent of everything Kant has said here, and that the maxim could be "legal" in the sense that it conforms to this independent law. This is the possibility which Kant means to *block* in the above quotation when he adds the words "without assuming any particular law applicable to certain actions," and it is important to see why it is disallowed. Suppose that there were such a law, prescribing certain actions. I will call this the External Law. And suppose we say that the maxim gets its legal character not from its intrinsic lawlike form, but from the extrinsic fact that the action is prescribed by the External Law. Then we will have to ask why the External Law is a law before we have found the real reason why the action is right. That is to say, we will have to ask why the External Law is in force, why it is normative. Because obviously, the mere *grammatical* form of universality cannot make anything a law: a law must be normative. A law does not make a claim on me merely because it is addressed to me, or to some group that includes me. It must get its grip or hold on me, its capacity to bind me, from some intelligible source. But then the source of the External Law's normativity, rather than legal character of the maxim, will be what motivates the good-willed person. The reason why the External Law is in force, rather than the fact that the maxim has legal character, will be the good-willed person's motive, for it will be the real reason why the action is right. And this is contrary to Kant's analysis of the motive of duty.

An example will make this point clearer: Suppose that right actions were those commanded in laws laid down by God. According to Kant's analysis, the good-willed person does these actions because it is a law to do so. But why is it a law to do so? The answer is: because God so commands. Now, which of these two reasons is the reason why the good-willed person does the action, which is also the reason why the action is right? If the action is right because God commands it, it is not right because its maxim is intrinsically legal; and the reason why the good-willed person does it will not be grasp of its legal character, but response to divine command. This is contrary to Kant's analysis. The maxim of the action must be legal in itself, and this can only be because it has a lawlike form. The religious moralist may want to reply that the maxim's legal character, and the action's being divinely commanded, are the same thing. But its conformity to divine law can only make a maxim extrinsically, not intrinsically, legal. So the dilemma remains: If the person is moved by divine command, then legal character is not the motive, and the motive of duty is not at work. Since the legal character of a maxim and the divine commandedness of an action are not analytically the same thing, rightness must essentially lie in one of them or the other, and, according to the analysis, it must be the legal character of the maxim. And so this must be its intrinsic lawlike *form*. This argument will apply to any attempt to derive the legal character of a maxim from anything other than its intrinsic lawlike form: only legal character and lawlike form are *analytically* or essentially the same thing.[46]

Now that last argument may make it clear why the legal character of a maxim cannot come from an External Law. But the conclusion—that it must therefore come from lawlike form, as specified by the universalizability test—may seem much less obvious. Why, then, does Kant conclude that a maxim has *intrinsic* legal character only if it has what the universalizability test identifies as lawlike forms?[47] To understand this, we must keep in mind two points. The first I have already noticed. In order to be a law, it is not enough that a principle be grammatically universal. It must also be normative for the person who is to follow it: there must be some intelligible reason why it binds *that person*. The second point concerns the way the universalizability requirement functions. The requirement tells us that we must act in such a way that we can at the same time will our maxims as universal laws. If a maxim passes this test, the action is right in the broad sense—it is all right, permissible, not wrong. It is only if a maxim fails the test that we get a duty—the duty of doing the opposite of what the failed maxim says, or, more precisely, of adopting the opposite of what the maxim says as law. So a maxim of *duty* is not merely one that you *can* will as universal law, but one that you *must* will as universal law. And this means that the maxim is a law to which your own will commits you. But a maxim to which your own will commits you is *normative for you*. And this, to return to the first point, is what a principle must be in order to be a law for you—it must be *normative for you*.

Again an example will clarify the point. I will take Kant's easiest example, that of the lying promise (*G*, 422). A man in financial difficulties considers getting ready money on the strength of a lying promise that he will repay. His maxim is "I will make a lying promise, in order to get some ready money." He asks himself whether he could will his maxim to be at the same time a universal law. This means that he imagines a world in which everyone who needs money makes a lying promise and he imagines that, at the same time, he is part of this world, willing his maxim. His question is whether he can will this whole state of affairs.

Now his maxim is derived from a hypothetical imperative: "If you will to get some ready money, then make a lying promise." This hypothetical imperative, in turn, is derived from the rational principle that whoever wills an end wills the necessary means, together with the "causal" law that lying promises are a means to, or will cause, the possession of ready money (*G*, 417). However, in the world in which this maxim is universalized, this "causal" law does not hold. For if everyone in want of ready cash tried to make a lying promise, Kant says, "no one would believe what was promised to him but would only laugh at any such assertion as vain pretense" (*G*, 422). The man in the example cannot, at the same time, rationally will both acting on his maxim and a state of affairs which undermines the causal law from which the rationality of acting on his maxim is derived. A man who wills to use the institution of promising in pursuit of his end must will that the institution should work. And it does not work unless promises are generally made in good faith. So he *himself* is committed to willing the law that people should make their promises in good faith, so long as he wills this particular maxim. Therefore, he cannot rationally will to act on this maxim at the same time as he wills it as a law.[48]

The important thing to see here is that it is the man's own will that commits him to the law that promises should be made in good faith, if they are to be made at all. The argument is not that promising is generally a useful institution or that the rightness of keeping promises is written into the nature of things. The man is committed to the institution of promising by his own maxim because he wills to employ it as a means to his end. It is his own will, and nothing else, that makes it impossible for him to will the universality of lying promises. In this way the universalizability test shows us what principles our own maxims commit us to willing as laws. As Kant says, if the man does will the maxim, he cannot also be willing it as a law, but rather must be regarding himself as an exception (*G*, 424).[49]

Let me digress a moment. It is at this point in the argument that the objection Kant leveled against Wolff—the "empty formalism" objection—enters the picture as an objection against Kant himself. According to the objection, the Formula of Universal Law lacks content, since there are no restrictions on what we *can* will as a universal law, and therefore no implications about what we *must* so will. Now I hope that the example that I have just given will suggest that this objection is mistaken, and that there are laws to which our own wills do commit us. But it is also important to see what is wrong with one proposal for solving the emptiness problem sometimes made by those who, like Hegel, approve Kant's account of moral motivation but think that the Formula of Universal Law is empty. This proposal is that some external law or normative consideration can be imported into the system to solve the supposed emptiness problem and give content to our duties.[50]

This was Kant's own solution in the Prize Essay, where the judgments of the moral sense were brought in to give content to the obligations of which the principle "do that which is perfect" is the form. A variant of Kant's own argument in *Groundwork* I shows why this solution is disallowed. Either the action has its perfection in itself, or we are not doing it on account of its perfection, but on account of what gives it its perfection—in this case, the approval of the moral sense. The reason why the action is perfect, and the reason why a good person does it, must be exactly the same. The action's perfection cannot be extrinsically conferred by the moral sense, but must be intrinsic to the action itself. Content brought in from external normative sources violates Kant's analysis in the way we have seen.

We can now see a rather simpler way of making the argument against the External Law. Suppose, again, that the External Law is in force because it is the law of God's will. This is supposed to be what makes it normative. But how? God's will is only normative for me if it is the law of my own will to obey God's will. This is an old Hobbesian thought—that nothing can be a law for me unless I am bound to obey it, and nothing can bind me to obey it unless I have a motive for obeying it.[51] But Kant goes a step further than Hobbes. *Nothing* except my own will can make a law normative *for me.* Even the imposition of a sanction cannot bypass my will, for a reward or punishment only binds my will if I will to get the reward or avoid the punishment—that is, if I make it my maxim that my interest or preservation should be a law to me. Only those maxims shown to be necessary by the universalizability test— only those to which my own will commits me—are *intrinsically* normative. And this, as the traditionalists had argued all along, is what an obligation must be. Autonomy is the only possible source of intrinsic normativity, and so of obligation.

One result of this is that it shows that the British rationalists to some extent mistook their target. They opposed Hobbesianism, moral sense theory, and divine command theory, all on the grounds, as they thought, that these make morality a matter of positive law. But Kant's analysis shows that positivity is not the problem. A law in the nature of things, if it is understood as a theoretical or metaphysical principle that is external to the will, gives rise to exactly the same problem that divine law does.⁵² Laws in the nature of things can only make our maxims extrinsically, not intrinsically, normative. The problem with these theories is not that their laws are positive, but that their laws are not willed autonomously, and so are not intrinsically normative. But the Kantian laws of autonomy are positive laws: moral laws exist because *we* legislate them.

Another mistaken target, this time of British moral philosophy more generally, is the analyzability of moral concepts. Price and Hutcheson agree that moral ideas are fundamentally "simple," and can only be defined trivially by synonyms.⁵³ This idea is echoed in G. E. Moore's concern with the "naturalistic fallacy": because "pleasure" and "good", for instance, cannot be taken to mean the same thing, Moore concludes that "good" is a simple idea.⁵⁴ Ross, following Moore, makes a similar claim about "right."⁵⁵ The truth in these arguments is this: claims about, say, pleasure, or what maximizes pleasure, are not intrinsically normative, the way claims about the right and the good are. The normativity of an ethical concept cannot be derived from any non-ethical concept, so no ethical concept can be completely analyzed in terms of a natural or factual one. All of these philosophers conclude that normative concepts are unanalyzable. As a result, they think that our understanding of the normative concept does not enable us to pick out its objects, and that we must therefore have recourse to a sense or to a faculty of intuition that functions like a sense.

But Kant's analysis does not reduce the normative concept to a non-normative one; instead, it reduces normative content to normative form. What the analysis yields is that right actions are those whose maxims have lawlike form, which is the form of normativity itself. Provided that the categorical imperative procedure can be made to work, Kant's analysis does enable us to pick out the objects of the concept; that is, it enables us to identify our duties. We discover the content of morality by seeing which maxims have normative form.

Both perhaps the most fundamental mistake of the British moralists of both the eighteenth and twentieth centuries has been the acceptance of Hume's dilemma. For Hume's dilemma leaves us with an unfortunate choice. If the virtue of an action is conferred by its motive, then that motive cannot be the motive of obligation. The rationalists found this objectionable, both because it seems as if at least some actions really ought to be done from the motive of obligation, and because the fact of obligation seems to be dependent on the possibility of the motive. The rationalist saved obligation, but at the cost of locating morality in the metaphysical properties of actions, rather than in the motivational properties of people.

The argument of *Groundwork* I shows us we do not have to accept Hume's dilemma. For Kant shows that the premise of Hume's argument—that doing your duty from the motive of duty is an empty formalism—is false. An obligation, or an action done from the motive of duty, is one that the agent herself must will as a universal law. It is, in its very nature and essence, an action autonomously willed. To complete the argument, and show that obligations really exist, Kant needs only to show that human beings are capable of autonomous motivation: that is, that we can be motivated by those laws that we must will. If we are capable of giving laws to ourselves, then we have obligations.

## Notes

I would like to thank Charlotte Brown and the late Manley Thompson for their valuable assistance with this paper.

1. The contemporary debate began with W. D. Falk's " 'Ought' and Motivation" in his *Ought, Reasons, and Morality: The Collected Papers of W. D. Falk* (Ithaca: Cornell University Press, 1980), chapter 1. Among other important discussions are William Frankena, "Obligation and Motivation in Recent Moral Philosophy" in his *Perspectives on Morality: Essays of William K. Frankena* (Notre Dame: University of Notre Dame Press, 1976); Bernard Williams, "Internal and External Reasons" in his *Moral Luck* (Cambridge: Cambridge University Press, 1981), chapter 8; and Stephen Darwall, *Impartial Reason* (Ithaca: Cornell University Press, 1983). I discuss the subject in "Skepticism About Practical Reason," Chapter 11 in my *Creating the Kingdom of Ends* (Cambridge: Cambridge University Press, 1996).

2. See for instance Frankena, "Obligation and Motivation in Recent Moral Philosophy" and Williams, "Internal and External Reasons."

3. See for instance Nagel, *The Possibility of Altruism* and my "Skepticism about Practical Reason."

4. Samuel Clarke, *A Discourse Concerning the Unalterable Obligations of Natural Religion and the Truth and Certainty of the Christian Revelation: The Boyle Lectures 1705* in *The Works of Samuel Clarke* (London: J. and P. Knapton, 1738), pp. 609–10. Selections from the Boyle Lectures can be found in D. D. Raphael, ed., *The British Moralists 1650–1800* vol. I (Oxford: Oxford University Press, 1969), the passages cited are at pp. 194–96. Hereinafter this work will be cited as "Clarke" with page numbers from the Garland edition followed by those from the Raphael selections where available.

5. Francis Hutcheson, *Illustrations on the Moral Sense*, ed. Bernard Peach

(Cambridge, Mass.: Harvard University Press, 1971). This work is the second part of *An Essay on the Nature and Conduct of the Passions and Affections. With Illustrations on the Moral Sense.* Hereinafter this work will be cited as "Hutcheson's *Illustrations.*"

6. Richard Price, *A Review of the Principal Questions in Morals,* ed. D. D. Raphael (Oxford: Clarendon Press, 1948), p. 49. The *Review* was the first published in London in 1758 under the title *A Review of the Principal Questions and Difficulties in Morals.* Raphael's edition, which I have cited, is reprinted from the third edition of 1787. Selections from the *Review* can be found in D. D. Raphael, ed., *The British Moralists 1650–1800* vol. II, pp. 131–98; the passage cited is at p. 147. Hereinafter this work will be cited as "Price" with page numbers from Raphael's edition of the book followed by those from the selections in *British Moralists.*

7. David Hume, *A Treatise of Human Nature,* 2nd ed. Ed. L. A. Selby-Bigge and P. H. Nidditch (Oxford: Clarendon Press, 1978), p. 457. Hereinafter cited as "Hume's *Treatise.*"

8. For discussion see Paul Schilpp, *Kant's Pre-Critical Ethics* (Evanston: Northwestern University Press, 1938), ch. 3. Kant praises Hutcheson in the Prize Essay (see below), and in later works treats Hutcheson's view as representative of attempts to base morality on feeling. In his Introduction to Adam Smith's *Theory of Moral Sentiments,* ed. D. D. Raphael and A. L. Macfie (Indianapolis: Liberty Classics, 1982), D. D. Raphael describes a letter of 1771 from Marcus Herz to Kant in which Herz refers to Smith as "your favorite" (p. 31).

9. "So-called" because it was written for a prize offered in 1763 by the Berlin Academy. Kant did not actually win the prize, which went to Moses Mendelssohn. See Lewis White Beck, *Early German Philosophy: Kant and His Predecessors* (Cambridge, Mass.: Harvard University Press, 1969), pp. 441–42.

10. The two steps described correspond approximately to the metaphysical and transcendental deductions of the categories in the *Critique of Pure Reason;* although the relation between a metaphysical deduction of an *a priori* concept and its analysis is not perfectly clear. In any case the analysis of the concept of obligation, with which I am concerned here, will show that it is logically possible—that the idea contains no contradiction—while the synthesis will show how it is really possible, how it can apply to us. For the distinction between logical and real possibility, see *Critique of Pure Reason,* A 243–44/B 301–02 and A 596n/B 624n. The account of real possibility in these passages is given in terms of the possibility of experience and therefore does not apply to ethical concepts, but there must still be an analogue of it for ethical concepts if dogmatic rationalism in ethics is to be avoided.

11. For the most part, I will use "right" and "obligatory" to denote any action that is morally called for. The term "right" may be used more broadly, to include permissible actions, and Kant's analysis also explicates this notion, but my focus will be on required actions. Both "right" and "obligatory" can also be used more specifically, to refer actions called for by so-called perfect duties, or still more specifically to actions called for by justice. Some philosophers, for example Hume and Bernard Williams, believe that "right" and "obligatory" should only be used for one of these latter two classes of actions,

and at various points would find in this view grounds for objecting to the argument of this paper. I do not try to deal with the issue, but I do try to notice the points where it comes up. See nn13, 21, and 23.

12. Rightness is strictly speaking a property of acts, and any given act can be done from a variety of motives, good, bad, or indifferent. But right acts can be defined or identified in terms of motives even if they are not always done from those motives; they can be defined as the ones a person with good motives would do, or ones that good motives would prompt. The strategy is thought to be characteristic of virtue-centered ethical theories, but as I will show it is also Kant's.

13. Hume's *Treatise*, p. 478. This argument occurs at the beginning of the section in which justice is identified as an artificial virtue, and it is important to point out that its conclusion in a certain way only applies to the natural virtues. The "first motive" to justice turns out to be self-interest (492; 495), but this is neither an especially virtuous motive (492) nor is it the motive usually at work in agents performing just actions. Particular acts of justice taken separately are not necessarily in our interest (497). We approve of justice because sympathy makes us approve whatever is in the collective interest (499–500); we perform just actions, or restrain ourselves from unjust ones, because we approve of justice: that is, because justice is virtuous, and we value our own character (500–01; see also the *Enquiry Concerning the Principles of Morals*, ed. L. A. Selby-Bigge and P. H. Nidditch [Oxford: Clarendon Press, 1975], pp. 282–83). This is one sense in which justice is an "artificial" virtue. This point becomes important later in the argument; see n21.

14. Hume's *Treatise*, p. 478.

15. See for instance Nagel, *The Possibility of Altruism*, pp. 4–5.

16. Hutcheson's *Illustrations,* p. 130.

17. Hutcheson's *Illustrations,* pp. 121, 130.

18. Hutcheson's *Illustrations,* p. 139.

19. Hutcheson's *Illustrations,* p. 140. See also Hutcheson's *Inquiry Concerning the Original of Our Ideas of Virtue or Moral Good*, in D. D. Raphael, ed. *The British Moralists 1650–1800*, vol. I, p. 293.

20. Hume's *Treatise*, p. 479.

21. However, as I point out in n13, the motive of obligation *is* the usual motive at work in the case of *just* actions (and, when we are tempted, abstentions), and this is an important point in Hume's favor. Our belief that obligation should be the motive of just actions is much firmer than our belief that it should be the motive of those actions springing from what Hume would call the natural virtues, which we may regard as meritorious rather than required (See n11). It should be observed that in the passage in which he complains that rationalists cannot account for morality's power to motivate us, which I have quoted on p. 315, Hume is careful about this: he speaks specifically about just actions. Thus Hume could argue, against the point I am making here, that his system favors the operation of the motive of duty in exactly those cases in which we feel most sure that it should operate.

22. Reprinted in her *Ethics, Religion, and Politics: Collected Philosophical Papers of G. E. M. Anscombe, Volume III* (Minneapolis: University of Minnesota Press, 1981), pp. 26–42.

23. Williams wants us to recognize that obligations "form just one type of ethical consideration" (p. 196). Some actions are not obligatory but more or less than obligatory: admirable, or heroic, or simply what a person of good character would do (p. 179). Williams's view is similar to Hume's view that the motive of obligation is appropriate for one kind of moral consideration (that of justice) but not all (See n11, 14, 21). Williams regards attempts to treat all ethical claims as forms of obligation (by means of such devices as Ross's *prima facie* obligations, or imperfect duties, or general duties, or duties to oneself) as fundamentally misguided (pp.178–92). The point of such attempts, I believe, is not merely to impose an artificial orderliness on the moral terrain, nor to license blaming people who ignore certain ethical claims, but to explain how these claims have normative force for the agents who act on them. Williams does see that this is part of the motive for the idea of general or imperfect or *prima facie* obligations, but thinks that it is an error to suppose that all practical necessity, or normative force, springs from obligations (p. 196). Even if he is right, some account of the normative force of these claims is needed, as he would agree. See n26.

24. Anscombe says that the terms "should" and "ought" "have now acquired a special so-called 'moral' sense—i.e., a sense in which they imply some absolute verdict (like one of guilty/not guilty on a man) on what is described in the 'ought' sentences" ("Modern Moral Philosophy," p. 29; see also p. 32.) Williams says: ". . . once I am under the obligation, there is no escaping it, and the fact that a given agent would prefer not to be in this system [the morality system] or bound by its rules will not excuse him; nor will blaming him to be based on a misunderstanding. *Blame is the characteristic reaction of the morality system*" (*Ethics and the Limits of Philosophy*, p. 177; my emphasis). This seems to me wrong; the morality system Williams describes in the text is distinctly rationalistic, but the emphasis on blame, and on the general ideas of merit and demerit, is more characteristic of sentimentalist theories, for reasons I mention in the text. Kant notices the ways the duties of respect *restrict* our practices of blaming: he says that "the reproach of vice . . . must never burst out in complete contempt or deny the wrongdoer all moral worth, because on that hypothesis he could never be improved either—and this is incompatible with the idea of man, who as . . . a moral being can never lose all predisposition to good" (*DV*, 6:463). I discuss this attitude to blame in "Morality as Freedom," Chapter 6 in *Creating the Kingdom of Ends*.

25. This is most explicit in the theory of Adam Smith, who has more to say about moral motivation than Hume or Hutcheson, and who gives a more positive account of the role of the motive of duty. Smith says: "When our passive feelings are almost always so sordid and selfish, how comes it that our active principles should often be so generous and so noble? . . . It is not the soft power of humanity, it is not that feeble spark of benevolence which Nature has lighted up in the human heart, that is thus capable of counteracting the strongest impulses of self-love. It is a stronger power, a more forcible motive, which exerts itself upon such occasions. It is reason, principle, conscience, the inhabitant of the breast, *the man within, the great judge and arbiter of our conduct*" (*The Theory of Moral Sentiments*, p. 137; my emphasis). The "man

within," Smith's impartial spectator, develops by a process of internalization that begins with our judgment of the conduct of others. Sympathizing with others who in a similar way judge us turns our attention to our own conduct, and by this process we are led to the idea of an internal spectator whose judgment is the motive of duty (*The Theory of Moral Sentiments*, pp. 109–78).

26. To be fair, Williams also discusses this side of the idea of obligation, in the chapter cited and in "Practical Necessity" in his *Moral Luck*.

27. See for instance *Nicomachean Ethics* III.7 1115b11–14; III.12 1119b15; IV.1 1120a23; X.9 1179b30; and X.9 1180a6–8.

28. I discuss this in my "Aristotle on Function and Virtue," *History of Philosophy Quarterly* 3 (1986): 259–79. See especially 269–72. The point is related to the fact that ". . . it is not merely the state in accordance with the right rule, but the state that implies the *presence* of the right rule, that is virtue" (*Nicomachean Ethics* VI. 13 1144b27). There *is* a sense in which Aristotle's virtuous person acts *from* the right rule, although it is not the same sense that the rationalists had in mind.

29. Both Price's *Review* and John Balguy's *The Foundation of Moral Goodness: Or a Further Inquiry into the Original of Our Idea of Virtue* were written directly in response to Hutcheson's theory.

30. Clarke, pp. 596–97; 608–12/192–99.

31. Clarke, pp. 614/202.

32. Clarke, pp. 614/202. These passages are quoted with approval by Price (118) and Frankena ("Obligation and Motivation," p. 59).

33. On the one side, Price incorporated Hutcheson's idea of a moral sense into his rationalist theory (see Price, pp. 57–68/148–52). On the other side, Adam Smith developed an account of the genesis of the motive of duty, and gave it a prominent role, in a sentimentalist context (see n25, above). And Joseph Butler, while aspiring like the sentimentalists to explain morality in terms of human nature, argued that conscience is intrinsically authoritative and no sanction is needed for obeying it. See Joseph Butler, *Five Sermons Preached at the Rolls Chapel*, ed. Stephen Darwall (Indianapolis: Hackett Publishing Co., 1983), hereinafter cited as "Butler," pp. 11, 43.

34. Price, pp. 47–48, 146–47.

35. Price, pp. 15, 133.

36. Several pages on the twentieth-century British philosophor W. D. Ross are here omitted. These pages may be found in *Creating the Kingdom of Ends*, pp. 52–54.

37. Kant must mean that there is room for conceptual confusion in the case of direct inclination. If you perform a dutiful act that is also, for some people, pleasant in itself, we cannot tell whether you acted from duty or only from pleasure. But no one gives correct change just for the pleasure of it, so here we know that the action was either from duty or self-interest. But there is surely no way to tell about an actual honest action that happens to be in someone's interest that she *did it* from interest rather than duty.

38. In the passage cited Kant sounds negative about honor; he says that "The ideal of morality belongs to culture; its use for some simulacrum of morality in the love of honor and outward decorum constitutes mere civilization"

and that "Everything good that is not based on a morally good disposition . . . is nothing but pretense and glittering misery." But in another passage Kant speaks more leniently of honor. He is discussing the question whether the government has the right to punish two kinds of murderers: young officers who kill in duels, and unmarried mothers who kill their children to avoid disgrace. Rather surprisingly, Kant thinks there is reason to doubt whether these murderers may be punished, for he says that honor "is no delusion in these cases" and that "legislation itself . . . is responsible for the fact that incentives of honor among the people do not accord (subjectively) with the standards that are (objectively) appropriate to their purpose" (*DR*, 6:336–37). Kant is generally characterized as believing that duty and inclination are the only two kinds of motivation, but both of these passages suggest that he regards honor as something in between—a sort of proto-moral motive that precedes the genuine motive of duty in the education of the human species. I speculate that Kant means that the motive of honor approximates the motive of moral autonomy insofar as the person governed by it follows, for its own sake, a strict law of conduct which represents an ideal of character. Yet motives of honor fall short of the full-fledged moral motive because the laws of honor are not derived from autonomy itself. See n40, below.

39. See Andrews Reath, "Hedonism and Heteronomy" *Pacific Philosophical Quarterly* 70 (1989): 42–72.

40. Kant calls the sympathetic person a *"Menschenfreundes"* (*G*, 398): a friend to humanity. And sentimentalist moral philosophers thought of sympathy as a response we have to human beings as such (not just to those to whom we are particularly attached) in virtue of the universal human characteristics which make them similar to ourselves. Thus sympathy makes an end of humanity and so serves as a simulacrum of the Formula of Humanity just as honor serves as a simulacrum of the Formula of Universal Law.

41. After Butler wrote his famous Sermon XI on the consistency of benevolence with self-love, it was not uncommon for eighteenth-century philosophers to treat the principle of self-love as providing a method of choosing among various ends, all of which are valued for their own sakes. Butler argued that the pleasure we get from satisfying a desire presupposes, rather than explains, the desire: it is because we have the desire that we enjoy achieving its object (Butler, pp. 46–54). The principle of self-love selects among things, all of which we desire for their own sakes, on the basis of how much pleasure we will get from achieving them. Kant apparently did not read Butler, but Butler's picture of the operation of self-love was adopted both by Hume in the *Enquiry Concerning the Principles of Morals* (pp. 281–82; 301–02), and to some extent by Hutcheson in *Illustrations Upon the Moral Sense*. Kant uses the principle of self-love in this sense—as one way of choosing among things we desire for their own sakes—but sets the principle of duty up as rival to it—as another way of choosing our purposes.

42. It may seem as if I am guilty of a commonplace error in making these remarks: confusing pleasure with satisfaction or gratification. Once I've made up my mind to do or achieve something, I am of course gratified to see it done. But that point applies even to actions undertaken for the most purely

instrumental reasons, actions that are only means to other ends. The point I am making here is a different one, having to do with what it *means* to say that you have made something your purpose. My claim is that if you really succeed in making something your purpose, and so value it as an end, you will come to take pleasure in its successful pursuit. I explain this further in "Morality as Freedom," Chapter 6 in *Creating the Kingdom of Ends.*

43.  The same point is made by other rationalists. Price distinguishes rational from instinctive benevolence, and, like Kant, claims that instinctive benevolence is lovable but falls short of virtue (Price, pp. 190–91, 196–97). Balguy makes a similar comparison (Balguy, pp. 59–60). Ross says, "The conscientious attitude is one which *involves* the thought either of good or of pleasure for some one else, but it is *a more reflective attitude* than that in which we aim directly at the production of some good or some pleasure for another, since . . . we stop to think whether in all the circumstances the bringing of that good or pleasure into existence is what is really incumbent upon us. . . ." (Sir David Ross, *The Right and the Good* [Oxford: Clarendon Press, 1930], pp. 162–63; my emphasis).

44.  Nagel employs a similar argument in *The Possibility of Altruism*, pp. 82–84.

45.  I say this in spite of the fact that in the third section of the *Groundwork*, Kant says that the principle that "an absolutely good will is one whose maxim can always include itself as a universal law" is synthetic because "by analysis of the concept of an absolutely good will that property of the maxim cannot be found" (*G*, 447). I believe that this is a misstatement, or at least a poor way of putting the point. What is synthetic is that the moral law holds *for us*—that we are capable of having absolutely good wills. The statement that a good will is one whose maxim is universalizable is synthetic only if "good" is being used in a fully normative sense—to signify a demand on us.

46.  I formulated an earlier version of this argument in a comment on David Cummiskey's paper "Kant's Refutation of Consequentialism" at the American Philosophical Association meetings in April 1988, and I would like to thank Cummiskey for prompting me to do so.

47.  Perhaps it is worth saying a word about what it means to claim that a maxim has a "form." The "form" of a thing is ordinarily thought to rest in the relations among its parts, and the parts of a maxim of action (to take the simplest case) are the action to be performed and the purpose to be realized. The plausibility of Kant's thought that the rightness of a particular action rests in the form of its maxim can be seen intuitively by considering the following triples of maxims:

(A)  I will knock Alex down, in order to remove him from the path of an on-coming bullet.

(B)  I will knock Alex down, in order to relieve my temper.

(C)  I will punch a punching bag, in order to relieve my temper.

Or:

(A) I will avoid visiting my grandmother in the hospital, in order to avoid a contagion to which I am especially susceptible.

(B) I will avoid visiting my grandmother are in the hospital, in order to spare myself unpleasantness.

(C) I will avoid watching prime-time television, in order to spare myself unpleasantness.

In each set, maxims A and B concern the same act or omission, yet adopting maxim A is permissible or even good, while B is wrong. But this is not simply because of the purpose in maxim B, for maxim C contains the same purpose, yet it, once again, is permissible. What is wrong with the action whose maxim is B, then, does not rest either in the action that is performed or in the purpose for which it is performed, but in the relation between the two. And the relation between the two parts of the maxim is its form.

48. I explain my views about how the Formula of Universal Law should be applied more fully in "Kant's Formula of Universal Law," Chapter 3 in *Creating the Kingdom of Ends.*

49. It is essential to keep in mind that these considerations by themselves do not show why the action is irrational. All that this argument shows is why the maxim cannot be willed as a law—not why a rational being must only will maxims that can be willed as laws. For that part of the argument we need to take the further step described in the conclusion of this paper.

50. For instance, after praising and affirming Kant's conception of the autonomy of the will Hegel says ". . . still to adhere to the exclusively moral position, without making the transition to the conception of ethics, is to reduce this gain to an empty formalism . . . of course, material may be brought in from the outside and particular duties may be arrived at accordingly. . . ." *The Philosophy of Right* (Oxford: Clarendon Press, 1952), trans. T. M. Knox, pp. 89–90. I owe the reference to Daniel Brudney.

51. See especially *Leviathan*, Part I, ch. 14.

52. This may be especially hard to see, because the arguments that British rationalists use to show that moral laws are indeed laws of reason are similar to those that Kant uses to show that moral laws are laws we must rationally will. Strictly speaking, rationalists should not give arguments *for* moral laws, since they think these laws are self-evident. But Clarke, in particular, tries to impress this self-evidence upon his audience by appeal to arguments from the "Golden Rule," and arguments from this principle are similar to those from the categorical imperative. For instance, Clarke says that if we were not corrupt, "It would be as impossible that a Man, contrary to the eternal Reason of things, should desire to gain some small profit to Himself, by doing violence and damage to his Neighbor; as that he should be willing to be deprived of necessaries himself, to satisfy the unreasonable Covetousness or Ambition of another" (Clarke, pp. 619–20/208).

53. Price, p. 41/141; Hutcheson, *Inquiry Concerning the Original of Our Ideas of Virtue or Moral Good,* p. 305.

54. G. E. Moore, *Principia Ethica* (Cambridge: Cambridge University Press, 1971), pp. 5–17.

55. Ross, pp. 7–12.

# 4

# Kant's Good Will and Our Good Nature

*Tom Sorell*

How much does a man's moral worth owe to benevolent feelings, to an amiable temperament, or even to what is good in human nature? Kant's answer is that moral worth owes nothing to those things. Whether someone is good or evil depends on whether his will is good or evil, and to have a good will is to suit one's 'maxims' or practical principles to what Kant calls the 'principle of autonomy.' This is the principle that requires one to act only according to a maxim it is possible to will to hold as a universal law. A person's feelings or temperament may well inspire maxims that happen to be universalizable, and so maxims in keeping with the principle of autonomy, but to act according to these maxims is not to have adopted the principle of autonomy. At best, someone's feelings, temperament and the rest can get him to act *as if* he were under the sway of the principle. And that, Kant suggests, would be a remarkable accident, since feelings or temperament cannot be counted upon to produce good behaviour. There is something unreliable about benevolent impulses, and about the good in human nature. Those things can be no substitute for a good will.

Are such claims credible? It is one thing to denigrate bad inclinations and bad temperaments, but many suppose that Kant goes too far in withholding positive moral worth from even desirable feelings and dispositions. To judge by some of Kant's examples it looks as if it is morally better to do the right thing in defiance of a cold temperament than to do the right thing out of a settled kindness. Yet, intuitively at least, the consistently kind person is a more convincing moral exemplar than the man whose good deeds have to be thawed out. Kant may be right and intuition wrong about who is morally exemplary, but in the *Foundations of the Metaphysics of Morals*[1] and elsewhere, he claims that his account of moral worth can be *derived* from intuition (from "common reason"); so he cannot take lightly evidence of a break from intuition. His conception of moral worth seems to lack initial plausibility, and the question is whether that can be supplied.

Two recent articles suggest that it can be. Richard Henson[2] thinks that in the *Foundations* Kant's examples do invite counter-intuitive generalization, but he claims that Kant did better in the *Metaphysics of Morals.* According to Henson there are two Kantian understandings of moral worth. One of these gives attributions of moral rightness the force of battle citations: in saying that someone has done what's morally right one is commending the agent for resolving in favor of duty a conflict in himself between the motive of duty and other motives. This is the model Henson thinks is prevalent in the *Foundations.* A second conception of moral worth—drawn from the *Metaphysics of Morals*—suggests that to attribute rightness to actions is to commend the agent for being alive to the motive of duty, whatever else moves him. On this "fitness model" of attributions, duty can be one motive among others for doing the morally right thing. It can be one motive among others so long as it could have brought about the right action on its own.

In a later paper,[3] Barbara Herman agrees that Kant allowed for the overdetermination of right action, and she agrees that attention to the possibility of overdetermination helps to clear up some common misunderstandings of Kant. But she doubts that Kant had more than one conception of moral worth, and she denies that Kant's examples in the *Foundations* do sustain counter-intuitive generalization. Herman and Henson seem to me to be wrong about the importance of overdetermination,[4] and wrong as a result in their (different) interpretations of Kant. I want to urge a reading that is simpler than theirs, and that makes Kant's position seem more like the reconstruction of "common reason" it was intended to be. On the preferred reading Kant's good will and our good nature co-exist in a wholesome partnership: they seem independent but compatible.

## I

If any claim can be attributed uncontroversially to Kant's writings it is this one: for an act to have moral worth it must be done from duty.

That is virtually the formulation Beck's translation gives of the "first proposition of morality" in Section One of the *Foundations* (399). What the first proposition does not make clear is whether a morally right action must be done from duty alone. The first proposition thus raises the question—Henson's—of whether an act with moral worth can be backed by moral *and* non-moral motives. Henson gives the example of Kant's lecture appearances. These might have been prompted by more than one motive. Perhaps Kant was moved to lecture by the enjoyment of lecturing as well as by a recognition of a duty to communicate valuable ideas. If both motives were present, but if each would by itself have brought Kant to the podium, did Kant's coming to lecture possess, or did it lack, moral worth? Were Kant's account to permit moral worth to attach to the lecturing, then influences like expected enjoyment would not after all be the blemishes on moral motivation that Kant's text seems to suggest they are. The mere presence of such a motive would not be enough to deprive an act of moral rightness, provided the motive co-operated with the motive of duty to overdetermine the act.

Henson says, and Herman agrees, that Kant never pronounced on the moral status of overdetermined acts.[5] It seems that Henson and Herman are wrong about this, for Kant did realize, what is anyway pretty obvious, that the statute book can provide an extra-moral motive for a type of act morality enjoins. Thus, a legal prohibition on killing often co-exists with the moral one, and the penalty of death or a life sentence can serve as a motive for the omission of killing as much as the motive of duty.

Every piece of legislation creates a duty, Kant says, but only the

> legislation which makes an action a duty, and this duty at the same time a motive, is *ethical.* That legislation which does not include the motive-principle in the law, and consequently admits another motive than the idea of duty itself, is *juridical.* In respect of the latter, it is evident that the motives distinct from duty, to which it may refer, must be drawn from the subjective (pathological) influences of inclination and of aversion, determining the voluntary activity, and especially from the latter . . .[6]

Where ethical and juridical legislation prescribe or prohibit the same type of act, several questions arise about the worth of compliance with the prohibition or the prescription. First, does a law-abiding choice *thereby* have moral worth? Not necessarily: if I decide against killing

only because I fear I will be caught and sentenced to death or life im-
prisonment, my motive is not the idea of duty but aversion to the legal
penalty. Here my motive is broadly speaking prudential rather than
moral. But what if I both understand that killing is something I am
duty-bound to avoid, *and* shudder at the thought of the gallows or the
electric chair?

Kant considers the related but less vivid case of keeping one's promises. The obligation to keep your promises is a moral one he says, even
though (as he thinks) the law that creates the obligation is originally
jurisprudential rather than ethical.[7] So when it comes to choosing
whether or not to keep your promise, say by honouring a contract, you
have to reckon with the consideration that it is your duty to keep your
promises. Keeping contractual promises can also be known to be com-
pulsory at law. "In this case," Kant writes,

> ethics specially teaches that if the motive principle of external compulsion
> which juridical legislation connects with a duty is even let go, the idea of
> duty alone is sufficient of itself as a motive.[8]

I take it that Kant is here acknowledging the possibility of one kind
of overdetermination of a dutiful act. Keeping one's contractual promises is normally recommended by external compulsion *and* the idea of
duty, but in the absence of external compulsion the idea of duty is
alone sufficient as a motive. On the other hand, to the extent that the
obligation to keep promises arises from juridical rather than ethical
legislation, external compulsion alone is sufficient as a motive. So
where both motives are operative, keeping one's promises is a type of
thing one is overdetermined to do.

What does Kant mean by saying that the idea of duty is "sufficient of
itself as a motive"? He does not mean, I think, that the idea of duty
alone is enough to *make* you keep your promises. Were this what was
meant, Kant would have to regard additional but specifically legal incentives to promise-keeping as superfluous. And of course he does not
see them that way. For him legal sanctions and the idea of duty each
operate in a distinctive way to counteract the "subjective contingency"
of promise-keeping. The idea of duty takes away the subjective contingency as follows. In representing promise-keeping to yourself as a duty,
you thereby represent promise-keeping as necessary.[9] This means that
if you do not keep your promises you consciously act contrary to how
you think (how reason tells you) you must act. You act irrationally. It is

different where you think of promise-breaking as something carrying such-and-such penalties. In that case it is consciousness of the penalties, not consciousness of the content of the law, that makes promise-keeping seem necessary. The thought of the penalties bears on the prospects for the thinker of pleasure and pain. Accordingly, to be activated by the thought is to be activated by a non-moral interest, an interest extrinsic to an interest in duty.

But suppose that someone with an interest in duty is also aware of the penalties for breaking those promises that constitute contracts. That sort of case raises a version of Henson's question. Given that each of the pair of motives is alone sufficient, and given that the relevant promise is kept, is the promise-keeping merely right or is it morally right? I think Kant's answer can be inferred from the following passage:

> Ethics has no doubt its own particular duties—such as those toward oneself—but it has also duties in common with jurisprudence, only not under the same mode of *obligation* . . . [T]he peculiarity of ethical legislation is to enjoin the performance of certain actions merely because they are duties, and to make the principle of duty itself—whatever be its source or occasion—the *sole* sufficing motive of the activity of the will.[10]

If there are normally two sufficient motives for fulfilling a duty shared by ethics and jurisprudence, and if what is peculiarly ethical about the shared obligation is the injunction to make duty the sole sufficing motive, then ethics is in tension with overdetermination. It is as if a plurality of sufficient motives, or a mix of motives, contaminates rather than fortifies a policy of action. This runs counter to Henson's conjecture that in Kant a mix of sufficient motives might be permitted by ethics.

## II

On the interpretation I am putting forward, Kant does acknowledge the overdetermination of dutiful acts, but he thinks that overdetermination is out of keeping with what ethical legislation specially enjoins. I have drawn textual evidence from the *Metaphysics of Morals,* but support for my interpretation can also be found in the *Foundations.*

The following comments, from Section One, concern the "third proposition of morality" ("Duty is the necessity of an action executed from a respect for law"):

> . . . that which is connected with my will merely as a ground and not as a consequence, *that which does not serve my inclination but overpowers it or at least excludes it* from being considered in making a choice—in a word, law itself—can be the object of respect and thus a command. Now as *an act from duty wholly excludes the influence of inclination* and therewith every object of the will, nothing remains which can determine the will objectively except the law, and nothing subjectively except pure respect for this practical law. This subjective element is the maxim that I ought to follow such a law even if it thwarts all my inclinations (400; my emphasis).

The strong implication of this passage, especially of its second itali-cized portion, is that inclination has no part to play in the motivation of an act that is morally right. Inclination includes, in Henson's example of Kant's motives for lecturing, the enjoyment of lecturing. So if the enjoyment of lecturing is part of what gets Kant to appear at the po-dium, then appearing at the podium is dutiful without being done *from* duty. As the passage says, an act done from duty "wholly excludes the influence of inclination."

It may be thought that in the passage Kant is inconsistent about possible influences on acts done from duty. For he speaks of "the law itself" as something which "overpowers [my inclination] or at least excludes it from being considered," and it is hard to see how the law could overpower an inclination that was not a co-present influence on the act. If Kant's talk of an overpowering law is not metaphorical, it is natural to take the overpowered thing as a bad inclination, a motive that conflicts rather that co-operates with duty. What is at issue for Henson, however, is whether a co-operating inclination is an ethically permissible influence on the will. My guess is that when Kant disjoins the possibility of the law's overpowering inclination with the possibility of the law's at least excluding the consideration of inclination, he is reserving the latter possibility for the case where the inclination is co-operative. In any case, it is clear from the last two sentences of the passage that the motivation of a morally right action is very confined indeed. *Nothing but* pure respect remains to determine the will subjec-tively. It is hard to find room here for the co-operating subjective in-fluences that overdetermination of the will would require. Pure reverence for law is all that Kant seems to allow.

None of this would seem surprising, given Kant's frequent and loud insistence on the need for purity in moral theory.[11] The question is whether the demand for purity can be made plausible. Barbara Herman thinks the answer is "Yes," and she supposes that this answer gets support from a neglected line of thought Kant trails at several places in the *Foundations*. Herman asks, "Why is it not possible that . . . non-moral motives give dutiful actions moral worth?"[12] Kant's answer, as she formulates it, is this. "Non-moral motives may well lead to dutiful actions, and may do this with any degree of regularity desired. The problem is that the dutiful actions are the product of a fortuitous alignment of motives and circumstances. People who act according to duty from such motives may nonetheless remain morally indifferent."[13]

I agree that Kant recognizes dutiful actions done from non-moral motives. But he seems to deny that dutiful actions regularly come of non-moral motives. Thus, at 390 of the *Foundations* he says that

> though the unmoral ground may indeed now and then produce lawful actions, *more often* it brings forth unlawful ones (my emphasis).

The point seems to be repeated in the course of the famous passage (398) in which Kant denies that actions done from a kind and sympathetic temperament have moral worth. He compares the sympathetic gesture to an action arising from the inclination to honour. The sympathetic action, he says,

> is on a level with [actions arising from] other inclinations, such as the inclination to honour, which, if *fortunately* directed to what *in fact* accords with duty and is generally useful and thus honourable, deserve praise and encouragement but no esteem (my emphasis).

This passage coheres with 390, I think, only if its "fortunately" and its "in fact" are taken to signal the irregularity of the connection between the unmoral ground and the lawful action.

Herman chooses to give a different slant to the passage. According to her, Kant's "fortunately" is meant to indicate the possibility, however seldom fulfilled, of sympathy's leading to a wrong action. She gives the example of a person whose sympathetic temperament leads him to help someone with a heavy burden, someone who unbeknownst to the helper is a thief laden with stolen goods. What explains the possibility of this misguided helpfulness, Herman suggests, is that the person acting on an inclination to be helpful does not have, just in virtue of the inclination, a moral interest in helping. So it is fortunate if the urge to help is engaged in circumstances in which gratifying the urge will accord with duty: the urge to help might be engaged in the course of a robbery. To exclude that unwanted possibility one needs to require with Kant that duty itself (or a specifically moral interest) move an agent.

Herman's suggestion is appealing because it seems to make sense of Kant's claim that inclinations lead only accidentally to the good (411), while detaching that claim from the idea that inclinations do not regularly lead to the good. The idea is certainly plausible: inclinations can lead regularly to the good and yet also, if only occasionally, lead unwittingly to the bad because they operate indiscriminately: it is their possibly indiscriminate operation that makes it an accident that they lead to the good. The idea is plausible: is it a correct reading of Kant?

I suggest that it is not. It is true that Kant wants to confine the motives for morally right actions to those that lead non-accidentally to the good. It is true, too, that for Kant inclinations are not motives of this kind: they violate the 'no accident' principle. The problem is that more than one explication of the 'no accident' principle excludes the inclinations. Herman thinks that the right explication ought to meet two requirements. It should (i) "credit an action with moral worth only if its performance does not depend on an accident of circumstances," and it should (ii) "allow that failure in different circumstances does not require denial of moral worth to the original performance."[14]

It is doubtful that Kant accepts the second of these constraints. The explication of the 'no accident' principle *he* is after must make it possible to get a purchase on the idea of a good will. A good will is a will that is absolutely good, and "that will is absolutely good which *cannot* be bad . . ." (437; my emphasis). Kant has in mind a will which could under *no* circumstances form intentions that violated the principle of autonomy. But a will such as Herman describes *could,* if only exceptionally, form intentions whose realization constituted wrong-doing. To take Herman's example, such a will could form an intention which abetted a theft. If such an intention can be formed, its source must be excised from a Kantian good will. The reason is simple. If inclination were allowed to influence the good will, then the good will would intend the right thing only conditionally on the absence of e.g. thieves in need of help. And the good will is supposed to will right action unconditionally. It is not enough for Kant, though it may be enough for us, that a good will actually have good intentions. It must actually have good intentions *and* be unable to form bad ones. Herman's condition (ii), by contrast, respects the intuition that actually having good intentions and acting on them is enough.

It is hard to make Kant's conception of moral worth persuasive, if the conception is made to lean on Kant's idea of non-accidentally right action. Intuitively, it seems that a 'no accident' principle is met when what is actually willed is right, and when something wrong *would* not have been willed in relevant counterfactual situations. Kant's text suggests a "could" in place of the "would," and thereby demands more for moral worth than intuition does.

**III**

To see what is compelling in Kant's account, one has to turn attention away from the 'no accident principle,' and toward points that the over-determination issue pushes into the background. In this connection it pays to linger over the preface to the *Foundations*. There Kant singles out for further consideration a question about moral philosophy. He is concerned with whether the subject overlaps with what he calls "anthropology." He asks,

> Is it not of the utmost necessity to construct a pure moral philosophy which is completely freed from everything which may be only empirical and thus belong to anthropology? (398)

This demarcation question does not look like one that could be settled by 'common reason.' Yet Kant thinks that there is a route from common reason to a positive answer to the demarcation question. As emerges, he is thinking of the way ordinary moral struggle simulates the metaphilosophical boundary dispute:

> Man feels in himself a powerful counterpoise against all commands of duty which reason presents to him as so deserving of respect; this counterpoise is his needs and inclinations, the complete satisfaction of which he sums up under the name of happiness. Now reason issues inexorable commands without promising anything to the inclinations. It disregards, as it were, and holds in contempt those claims which are so impetuous and yet so plausible, and which will not allow themselves to be abolished by any command. From this a natural dialectic arises, i.e., a propensity to argue against the stern laws of duty and their validity, or at least to place their purity and strictness in doubt and, where possible, to make them

more accordant with our wishes and inclinations. This is equivalent to corrupting them in their very foundations and destroying their dignity—a thing which even common practical reason cannot ultimately call good (405).

According to this passage, one's ordinary thoughts about what one ought to do run back and forth between a respect for duty and a wish to indulge one's inclinations. Yet in the background of such to-ing and fro-ing is this reflection, that tempting and understandable as it is to succumb to inclination or to put its demands before those of duty, it is not good to do so. This reflection does seem to operate in moral struggle, as Kant says. And as Kant implies, the ordinary reflection seems to be the counterpart of a position in metaphilosophy, to the effect that morals must not be adulterated. Moral philosophy must not cash out its idea of duty in terms of inclination; otherwise it may endorse what common sense rightly finds repellent: the substitution of the demands of inclination for those of duty.

Kant's task in the body of the *Foundations* is to make precise and persuasive the thought that common reason shares with metaphilosophy. This is the thought that moral requirements are inescapable: there is nothing one can do to exempt oneself from them, or to diminish the need for a will to act upon them. A philosophical reconstruction of this thought would say what it is that *makes* moral requirements inescapable.

The inescapability must have something to do with the will; but if it had to do only with the human will there would be no explaining the bindingness of moral requirements on beings other than humans.[15] So however inescapability depends on the will, it had better depend on what the human will can have in common with the wills of other beings. It is plausible that the direction of the will toward happiness is constant across different kinds of beings. The trouble with the aim of happiness is that it is indefinite, so that it is a bad adjudicator in cases where one is drawn toward conflicting plans of action. The indefiniteness of the global aim of happiness can even encourage one to sacrifice long-term well being to a pleasure of the moment, and a pleasure of the moment may do an agent harm (cf. 399). It may be that happiness is an inescapable aim, but its inescapability does not make for the inescapability of morals. On the contrary, the indefiniteness of the idea of happiness may engender the thought, in cases of moral conflict, that there *is* no right thing to do, so that the way out of a conflict is to do what one pleases. This runs counter to the common sense thought that the way out of moral conflict should not be the way of self-indulgence.

The inescapability of the aim of happiness cannot underlie the inescapability of morals: what about the inescapability of inclination? Inclinations are presumably part of the endowment of any creatures with a natural constitution, human beings included. The inclinations are inescapable to the extent that human beings are beings in nature. Could that inescapability be at the bottom of the inescapability of morals? Not if inclinations suggest policies of action recognizably at odds with duty. And of course inclinations *can* prompt plans that conflict with morality. But Kant cannot make very much of this point, since the possibility of conflict with duty does not obviously attend all inclinations. There are good inclinations, such as the inclinations to honour, the inclination to do the kind thing, and the inclination of sympathy. Suppose *these* were sufficiently entrenched in agents to whom moral demands are addressed: couldn't the need to gratify those inclinations underlie the necessity of doing one's duty? Kant wants an answer in the negative. But a satisfactory such answer must not make good inclinations too much of a special case. There must be something about the need to satisfy a bad *or* good inclination, that is unlike the need to do one's duty: otherwise morals may depend on anthropology by depending on what is naturally benign in human beings.

What, then, distinguishes the need to satisfy an inclination—any inclination—from the need to do one's duty? Kant's answer is that the need to satisfy an inclination is pathological. It affects an agent by way of his brute feelings or sensations. To omit to satisfy an inclination is to experience sensory discomfort. But how far are we at the mercy of sensory discomfort? Are we bound to be moved to relieve such discomfort or to prevent it? We would be if, like the brutes, we were activated only pathologically. In that case the laws of empirical psychology, whatever they were, would ensure that the presence of inclinations culminated in action in accordance with them. But we are not quite like the brutes. We are capable of detachment in thought from our inclinations. That is, we are able to reflect on our inclinations and not just experience their pushes and pulls. When we reflect on them we can locate inclinations within a global system of causes and effects, i.e. nature. More particularly we can reflect on inclinations as contained in a system of psychological causes and effects peculiar to human beings. Under this aspect the demands of inclination can seem parochial, affecting only one kind of being among possibly many others (425, 442). They can seem more parochial still, since characteristic human inclinations (like sympathy; cf. 398) are not necessarily enjoyed by *every* human being. Again under the aspect of states in the causal nexus inclinations do not seem to make demands on us as *agents* (cf. 450): if we 'act' to satisfy them the course we follow is the course of nature. If morality is to apply universally and not merely generally, if it is to make demands on something that is genuinely a will, i.e. something that initiates effects and is not just subject to them, then morality cannot apply to us in virtue of our belonging to a particular natural kind, nor hence in virtue of our place in nature.

## IV

We have before us the basis for Kant's claim that a "completely isolated," i.e., pure or unmixed, metaphysics of morals is the "indispensable substrate of . . . theoretically sound and definite knowledge of duties" (410). But Kant goes further to claim that a pure metaphysics of morals

> is also a desideratum of the highest importance to the actual fulfilment of its precepts. For the pure conception of duty and of the moral law generally, with no admixture of empirical inducements, has an influence on the human heart so much more powerful than all other incentives which may be derived from the empirical field that reason, in the consciousness of its dignity, despises them and gradually becomes master over them. It has this influence only through reason, which whereby first realizes that it can of itself be practical. A mixed theory of morals which is put together both from the incentives of feelings and inclinations and from rational concepts must, on the other hand, make the mind vacillate between motives which cannot be brought under any principle and which can lead only accidentally to the good and often to the bad (410–411).

He is claiming that a mixed philosophy of morals is not only bad as theory but bad for practice: it countenances motives which, because they are incommensurable, encourage vacillation. If the vacillation has an outcome in right action, that is an accident. But neither vacillation nor accidentally right action is on the cards if one's motives are unmixed.

Kant amplifies this point about purity of motivation in a footnote concerning moral instruction (410n). He says that duties should only be represented to children by examples in which agents ignore any possible advantage and "the greatest temptations of need or allurement." Presumably examples that allowed e.g. benevolent inclinations to figure as motives would mislead the innocent. But how exactly? Why could not the kind or sympathetic gesture be held up as the sort of gesture children should strive to make second nature? Differently, why could not learning to take pleasure in doing right, be part of learning to do right? Kant seems to disregard an intuitively appealing account of moral development, familiar from Aristotle, according to which the cultivation of virtue depends on acquiring habits of acting, and acquiring the relevant habits is a matter of learning to co-ordinate perception and appetite in ways that make right action gratifying and wrong action repugnant.[16]

In matters of moral development Kant's views seem to be one-sided. Can reasons be found for his restricting morally exemplary action to action not "affected in the least by any foreign incentive" (410n), benevolent impulses and the pleasure of virtue included? One reason has already come before us. Not every being who is constrained to do right has, or is able to acquire, benevolent impulses. Again, not every being who is constrained to do right is able to take pleasure in doing right. So if benevolent impulses and expected pleasure are taken as reasons for doing right that reinforce the simple recognition of duty, some beings will have less reason to do right than others. The need to do right will be less potent for some creatures, with the result that morality will have one kind of authority over some finite beings, or most finite being, but not *all* finite beings. The universality of moral authority threatens to give way to mere generality.

What is more, a merely general morality can create arbitrary moral advantage. If, as Aristotle suggests, it is criterial of being morally virtuous that one feel pleasure and pain at the right things, then certain beings whom nature has not equipped with the basis for the relevant sensitivity, or certain beings whom circumstance has deprived of the relevant sensitivity, will count as morally defective on account of something quite outside their control. Symmetrically, beings who are fortunately endowed, or fortunately circumstanced, will win a moral advantage from a natural or circumstantial advantage. Morality, in Kant's view, must either prescind from circumstantial or constitutional luck, or else not be binding in the same way on everyone. That is why he tries to derive foundations for morality that neutralize the effects of "unfortunate fate" and the sometimes "niggardly provision of a step-motherly nature" (cf. 394).

There is a corresponding view of moral training: it must call upon resources everyone can command, and it must set up as an ideal a way of life or a type of endeavor as much within one being's reach as within another's. The ideal or virtuous life for finite beings such as ourselves is one of perpetual striving toward the model of holiness of will. Finite practical reason is asked

> to make sure of the unending progress of its maxims toward this model and of the constancy of the finite rational being in making continuous progress.[17]

And the enabling condition—what makes it possible for the ideal to be realized—is no more than the possession of finite practical reason. What every finite being is asked unconditionally to do, viz. strive for holiness, is something every finite being is unconditionally able to do. It is different in Aristotle. In the *Nicomachean Ethics* he says more than once that unless one's activities foster the right sort of habits from an early age, so that there is no question for the agent of not doing right, but only a question of how to do right, the study of how to become virtuous will be profitless.[18] A kind of circumstantial bad luck in one's youth can put the virtuous life out of one's reach.[19]

There is a difference between Kant and Aristotle over the range of (human) beings to whom virtue must be accessible. There is a difference between them, too, over the kind of person who most vividly exemplifies virtue. In Aristotle it seems to be the man who enjoys *megalopsychia*—greatness of soul, high-mindedness or magnanimity. "High-mindedness," Aristotle says, "is the crown, as it were, of the virtues: it magnifies them and it cannot exist without them."[20] The high-minded man goes in for "great and distinguished" actions. What he does is prompted by the desire for great honour, but he is moderate in the pursuit of the external marks of such honour, and shuns the accolades of anyone inferior to himself.[21] He is a sort of noble and heroic figure. Kant dismisses this stylish type as a character fit only for romancing. Anyone intent on promoting right conduct chooses the wrong example, defeats his purpose

> by setting actions called noble, magnanimous and meritorious as models for children with the aim of captivating them by infusing them with enthusiasm for such actions.[22]

The reason those actions are of the wrong type is two-fold.[23] On the one hand they give the novice too much to live up to, and so daunt rather than encourage him. On the other hand, they distract the novice from the sector of morality most likely to matter in ordinary life, namely the "observance of the commonest duty, and even the correct estimation of it." The same drawbacks attend the promotion of magnanimous acts "among the instructed and experienced portion of mankind."

The great-souled man may inspire admiration in the experienced and inexperienced alike, but admiration falls short of genuine moral feeling, which is respect for righteousness superior to one's own in a fellow human being, or, what amounts to the same, reverence for the law which the example of superior righteousness in a plain, fellow mortal puts before one.[24] The respect aroused by the genuinely exemplary man works a double effect. It both counteracts the morally complacent thought that one has strived for holiness as much as anyone can, and it encourages one to renew one's efforts. Kant chooses his exemplary man carefully: it is not someone whose merits are so large as to put off would-be imitators. It is simply a "humble, plain man in whom I perceive righteousness in a higher degree than I am conscious of in myself."[25]

Which figure—Aristotle's man of surpassing merit, or Kant's plain, righteous man—is the better suited to inspiring the rest of us to do right? Forced to a choice between the moral aristocrat and the moral peasant,[26] one might well opt for the latter on Kant's grounds—that he keeps our eyes fixed on ordinary moral demands, and that the feelings he inspires do not make us think it is impossible to live up to his example. The problem is that more than one moral theory can claim the unassuming do-gooder for its standard-bearer. The figure is open to appropriation by a neo-Aristotellan theory,[27] and also by a theory that, in a Humean vein, founds our capacities to recognize and to do right on the wide natural distribution of sympathetic impulses. If Kant's appropriation of this figure is to prevail over, say, Hume's, then we are owed an account of why the attractiveness of the moral peasant derives from his reflective obedience to moral law rather than to the good in his natural constitution.

Kant meets this demand, I think, by distinguishing between two kinds of attraction that the moral peasant can exert on us. He attracts in one way when assumed to be motivated by natural inclination; he attracts in another way when assumed to be under the discipline of law. The first kind of attraction is purely aesthetic; the second is moral. In the *Critique of Practical Reason,* Kant says,

> It is a very beautiful thing to do good to men because of love and a sympathetic good will, or to do justice because of a love of order.[28]

This must mean that disinterested pleasure comes of witnessing the loving or sympathetic gesture. What the action done from duty inspires in us, on the other hand, is respect, and

> Respect is so far from being a feeling of pleasure that one only reluctantly gives way to it. We seek to discover something that will lighten the burden of it for us, some fault to compensate us for the humiliation we suffer from such an example.[29]

Rather than being beautiful, an action that wrests respect from us is more like (but only *like*) something sublime: we are alternately attracted and repelled, not given positive pleasure.[30]

These remarks gesture toward a clear distinction between the attractions of a Kantian moral peasant and those of a Humean one. Both do the right thing. But one man's example humbles us, that is, undoes the self-esteem that can curtail our striving to make our wills good; the other, Humean exemplar allows us to indulge in pure spectatorship, and so gives us unwonted relief from the struggle against self-conceit. We are momentarily arrested by the charm of good nature but not goaded by its example. On the contrary, the example of good nature can actually encourage us to take it easy by encouraging us to think that nature itself sees to the development of the good will. The spectacle of good nature can seduce us into thinking that nature, by an endowment of sympathy or love, on its own gets us to will to do the right thing. Kant adverts to this danger at §83 of the *Critique of Practical Reason,* immediately after saying that it is beautiful to do good out of love or sympathy:

> It is a very beautiful thing to do good to men because of love and a sympathetic good will, or to do justice because of a love of order. But this is not the genuine moral maxim of our conduct, the maxim which is suitable to our position among rational beings as men, when we presume, like volunteers, to flout with proud conceit the thought of duty and, as independent of command, merely to will of our own good pleasure to do something to which we think we need no command. We stand under a

*discipline* of reason, and in all our maxims we must not forget our subjection to it, or withdraw anything from it, or by an egotistical illusion detract from the authority of the law. . . .

Kant does not need to deny the attractiveness of good nature. He can and does grant it aesthetic appeal, but not the sort of power over the will that genuine moral force can be expected to exert.

Intuition seems to bear Kant out. That the acts of the good-natured man are attractive, is undeniable. But what makes them attractive? The answer intuition delivers, I think, is that the acts are attractive because they are unstudied, unforced and regular, much as if a kind of warm mechanism produced them. But despite the attraction of right actions that come automatically, intuition seems to demand that the agent be responsible for them, that he control their production. We do not want the kind person's good turns to be the enactment of a complicated computer programme or of a deterministic law. We want a will to operate, and we want the will to be guided by something other than the wish to gratify impulses, even good impulses. These intuitions translate into constraints on what the *inside* of a moral agent must be like. Kant's moral agent and Hume's can both look the same on the outside: they can both present the same appearance of humble, even cheerful righteousness. But turned inside out they are quite different. In the Humean man the good of his good nature works through him. His reactions are the outcome of how he has been constituted. So his actions betoken subjection to the laws of human nature, not the subjection of wilful obedience. And it is wilful righteousness intuition demands. Without wanting to *see* effort and reflective obedience behind another's good turn, and without wishing to *feel* submission behind our own good turns, we seem to require it, or something like it, to be there.

In other words, intuition drives us toward a demand for a good will behind a good nature. To demand this is not to demand that the good will take the place of good naturedness. To the extent that good acts are acts of men, inclinations (good or bad) cannot but affect agents. As Kant says at 405 of the *Foundations,* there is no legislating away their influence. What there *is* scope for is the recognition by men that it would be better if their good choices were prompted by duty and not by inclination. This recognition by itself diminishes the influence of inclination. For if an agent is moved by something he would like not to move him, he is at any rate unwillingly at the mercy of the relevant impulse, and to that extent the impulse does not move him by way of his will. That is how "reason, in the consciousness of its dignity, despises [incentives other than duty] and gradually becomes master over them." Reason does not eradicate the influence of inclinations. At best it diminishes the influence of inclinations on the will, i. e., on the faculty for making conscious choices. A good will can, then, co-exist with a good nature; only it must operate independently. That is what makes it free.

## Notes

An earlier draft of this paper was read to the Philosophical Society at the University of East Anglia, in February 1982. I have been helped by comments made in the discussion.

1. Lewis White Beck, trans., (New York: Bobbs-Merrill, 1969). Page references are to the Akademie edition.

2. "What Kant Might Have Said: Moral Worth and the Overdetermination of Dutiful Action," *Philosophical Review* 88 (1979), 39–54. Hereafter "Henson."

3. "On the Value of Acting from the Motive of Duty," *Philosophical Review* 90 (1981), 359–382. Subsequent references are to "Herman."

4. Paton does something to encourage attention to the overdetermination issue in *The Moral Law,* (London: Hutchinson University Library, 1956; published in the USA as *The Groundwork of Metaphysics of Morals,* (New York: Harper Torchbooks, 1964)). Paton says that "Kant's doctrine would be absurd if it meant that the presence of a natural inclination to good actions (or even of a feeling of satisfaction in doing them) detracted from their moral worth" (p. 19). He goes on to say (ibid.) that the issue of whether the motive of inclination and the moral of duty can be co-present in the same 'moral action,' or whether they can support one another, is not "discussed at all" in the *Groundwork.* In general, the suggestion that the presence of an inclination could detract from moral worth is rebutted by Paton at rather greater length than its claimed "absurdity" would seem to warrant. Perhaps this is because the suggestion is not absurd after all. Take the thought that a feeling of satisfaction in doing right detracts from moral worth: this can be true if the feeling of satisfaction amounts to a kind of self-congratulation for the acuity of one's moral sense.

5. Henson, p. 43; Herman, p. 360.

6. *General Introduction to the Metaphysic of Morals,* W. Hastie, trans., section III, "The Division of a Metaphysic of Morals," Akademie ed., p. 219.

7. Ibid., Akademie ed., pp. 219–20.

8. Ibid., Akademie ed., p. 221.

9. Ibid., section IV, "General Preliminary Conceptions Defined and Explained," Akademie ed., p. 222.

10. Ibid., section III, fourth paragraph, Akademie ed., p. 220. The emphasis on "sole" is mine.

11. See e.g. the *Foundations,* 410 ff.; *Critique of Practical Reason,* 91–92; *General Introduction,* section II.

12. Herman, 363.

13. Ibid., 366.

14. Ibid., 369.

15. *Foundations,* 398: "Everyone must admit that a law, if it is to hold morally, i.e., as a ground of obligation, must imply absolute necessity; he must admit that the command, 'Thou shalt not lie', does not apply to men only, as if other rational beings had no need to observe it . . ."

16. *Nicomachean Ethics,* M. Ostwald, trans., (New York: Bobbs Merrill, 1962), 1104 b 4–13, esp. 1104 b 9–13: "For moral excellence is concerned with pleasure and pain; it is pleasure that makes us do base actions and pain that prevents us from doing noble actions. For that reason, as Plato says, men must be brought up from childhood to feel pleasure and pain at the proper things; for this is correct education."

17. *Critique of Practical Reason,* Beck, trans., 32. (Page references are to the Akademie edition.)

18. *Nicomachean Ethics,* 1095 a 2–11; 1095 b 4–8.

19. See Aristotle's *Politics,* 1331 b 30–1332 a 1.

20. *Nicomachean Ethics,* 1124 a 1.

21. On shunning the honours of his inferiors, see *ibid.,* 1124 a 9; on the "great and distinguished" actions, see 1124 b 25.

22. *Critique of Practical Reason,* 154; Kant makes the same point, without reference to children, at 85.

23. *Ibid.,* 157.

24. *Ibid.,* 77, 78.

25. *Ibid.,* 77.

26. It is arguable that the choice between Aristotle's morally exemplary figure and Kant's is not the choice between the *megalopsychos* and the unassuming do-gooder, but rather the choice between, in Aristotle's terms, the *sōphrōn* and the *enkratēs.* Aristotle can be read as making exemplary the *sōphrōn,* the man who "takes no pleasure in what he should not, and no excessive pleasure" in what most men naturally find pleasant (cf. *Nicomachean Ethics* 1110 a 13). The *sōphrōn* is someone for whom it is out of character to have bad appetites, someone whose morally right actions never occur against the background of a struggle against base impulses. In a sense he is a figure who, presumably through training, does not have to have the 'subjective contingency' taken out of doing the virtuous thing. He sees what it's right to do and is never tempted to do otherwise. Kant's morally exemplary figure on the other hand, is always trying to discipline his endeavours so as to bring them into line with the policies of a holy will. He is always waging a battle against a will that is not wholly good. So, it might be suggested, he is like Aristotle's *enkratēs,* the morally strong person who, though he feels the temptation to gratify base appetites, struggles against the temptation and wins. I doubt, however, that the *enkratēs* is the same type as Kant's morally exemplary man. Kant is not saying that to be

morally exemplary we have to overcome base appetites and strive to be continent: he is saying we must make choices independently of *any* appetites, bad or good. That is why he sometimes locates a will like the good will in a man who is reduced to "dead insensibility" (*Foundations,* 398), someone who neither takes pleasure in anything, nor feels pain at the distress of others. In general, the controlling conception of the morally exemplary man seems to be that of someone who is *both* able to get the better of his base appetites, and who *renounces* (cf. *Foundations,* 432) any helps to right action that are contingently present in his dispositions to act.

27. See Philippa Foot's treatment of two exemplary figures in section II of "Virtues and Vices," the first essay in *Virtues and Vices,* (Oxford: Blackwell, 1978), pp. 8–14, esp. pp. 12 ff. See also the quotation on pp. 4–5.

28. *Critique of Practical Reason,* 83.

29. *Ibid.,* 77.

30. See the *Critique of Judgment,* § 23.

## Part III

# The Categorical Imperative and Its Formulations (*Groundwork* II)

# 5

# Consistency in Action

*Onora O'Neill*

## Universality Tests in Autonomous and in Heteronomous Ethics

Many recent discussions of universality tests, particularly those in English, are concerned either with what everybody wants done or with what somebody (usually the agent; sometimes an anonymous moral spectator) wants done either by or to everybody. This is true of the universality tests proposed in Singer's Generalization Argument, in Hare's Universal Prescriptivism and generally of various formulations of Golden Rules as well as of Rule Utilitarianism. Since universality tests of these sorts all make moral acceptability in some way contingent upon what is *wanted* (or, more circumspectly expressed, upon what is preferred or found acceptable or promises the maximal utility), they all form part of moral theories that are *heteronomous,* in Kant's sense of that term. Such theories construe moral acceptability as contingent upon the natural phenomena of desire and inclination, rather than upon any intrinsic or formal features of agents or their intentions. If we rely on any of these proposed criteria of moral acceptability, there will be no types of act that would not be rendered morally acceptable by some change or changes in human desires.

By contrast Kant's proposed universality test, the Categorical Imperative, contains no reference either to what everybody wants done or to what somebody wants done either by or to everybody. Kant's first formulation of the Categorical Imperarive, the so-called Formula of Universal Law, runs:

> Act only on that maxim through which you can at the same time will that
> it should become a universal law. (*G,* 421)

We are invited here to consider that we *can* will or intend, what it is
*possible* or *consistent* for us to "will as a universal law" (not what we
*would* will or *would* find acceptable or *would want* as a universal law).
Since the principle contains no reference to what everybody or anybody wants, nor to anything that lies beyond the agent's own capacity
to will, it is part of a moral theory for agents who, in Kant's sense of
the term, act *autonomously.* The principle asserts that such agents
need only to impose a certain sort of consistency on their actions if
they are to avoid doing what is morally unacceptable. It proposes an
uncompromisingly rationalist foundation for ethics.

Nevertheless, Kant interpretation, particularly in English, is rich in
heteronomous readings of the Formula of Universal Law and in allegations that (despite claims to the contrary) it is impossible to derive
nontrivial, action-guiding applications of the Categorical Imperative
without introducing heteronomous considerations.[1] Textual objections
apart (and they would be overwhelming objections), such heteronomous readings of Kant's ethics discard what is most distinctive and
challenging in his ethical theory. These are the features of his theory
on which I intend to concentrate. I want to challenge the view that
Kantian ethics, and nonheteronomous ethical theories in general, must
be seen as either trivially empty or relying covertly on heteronomous
considerations in order to derive substantive conclusions. To do so I
shall try to articulate what seem to me to be the more important features of a universality test for agents who, in a certain sense of the
term, can act autonomously, that is, without being determined by their
natural desires and inclinations.

I shall take Kant's Formula of Universal Law as the canonical case of
such a universality test, and shall argue that it neither is trivially formalistic nor requires supplementing with heteronomous considerations if
it is to be action-guiding. However, my main concern here is not to
explicate Kant's discussion of his universality test, nor to assess the
difficulty or adequacy of his various moves. I shall say nothing about
his vindication of the Categorical Imperative, nor about his powerful
critique of heteronomy in ethics, nor about his conception of human
freedom. By setting aside these and other more strictly textual preoccu-
pations I hope to open the way for a discussion of some features of
universality tests for autonomous agents that have an interest that goes

far beyond a concern with reading Kant accurately. I hope to show that Kant's formula, taken in conjunction with a plausible set of requirements for rational action, yields strong and interesting ethical conclusions that do not depend on what either everybody or anybody wants, and hence that reason can indeed be practical.

Over the last twenty years theorists have shed considerable light on the underlying structure of heteronomous ethical theories (as well as on other, particularly economic and political, decisions) by drawing on studies of the formal aspects of decision making under various conditions that have been articulated in various models of rational choice. In such discussions it is generally taken for granted that rational choosing is in some way or other contingent upon a set of desires or preferences.[2] I shall suggest that a similar concentration on certain requirements of rationality that are not contingent upon desires or preferences can help to provide a clearer picture of the underlying structure and strength of an ethical theory for autonomous beings.

The sequence of argument is straightforward. The following section provides an explication of Kant's Formula of Universal Law and of some of the ways in which it affects the character of an ethic for autonomous beings. The section entitled "Inconsistency without universalizing" discusses some ways in which action can fall into inconsistency even when the question of universalizing is not raised. The three sections that follow show how requirements for rational intending can be conjoined with Kant's universality test to yield determinate ethical conclusions.

## Maxims and Moral Categories

The test that Kant's Formula of Universal Law proposes for the moral acceptability of acts has two aspects. In the first place it enjoins us to *act on a maxim;* secondly it restricts us to action on those maxims *through which we can will at the same time that they should be universal laws.* It is only the latter clause that introduces a universality test. However, for an understanding of the nature of this test it is essential in the first place to understand what Kant means by "acting on a maxim". For, contrary to appearances, this is not a trivial part of his criterion of morally acceptable action. Because a universality test for autonomous beings does not look at what is wanted, nor at the results of action, but merely demands that certain standards of consistency be observed in action, it has to work with a conception of action that has the sort of formal structure that can meet (or fail to meet) standards of consistency. Only those acts that embody or express syntactically structured principles or descriptions can be thought of as candidates either for consistency or for inconsistency. Mere reflexes or reactions, for example, cannot be thought of as consistent or inconsistent; nor can acts be considered merely instrumentally as means for producing certain outcomes. In requiring action on a maxim Kant is already insisting that whatever is morally assessable should have a certain formal structure.

A maxim, Kant tells us, is "a subjective principle of action"; it is "a principle on which the subject *acts*" (*G,* 421n; cf. 401n). A maxim is therefore the principle of action of a particular agent at a particular time; but it need not be "subjective" in the sense that it seeks to fulfill that particular agent's desires. In speaking of maxims as subjective principles Kant is not adopting any sort of heteronomous standard, but means to propose a standard against which the principles agents propose to act on, of whatever sort, may be tested. The Categorical Imperative provides a way of testing the moral acceptability of what we propose to do. It does not aim to generate plans of action for those who have none.

Although maxims are the principles of action of particular agents at particular times, one and the same principle might be adopted as a maxim by many agents at various times or by a given agent on numerous occasions. It is a corollary of Kant's conception of human freedom that we can adopt or discard maxims, including those maxims that refer to our desires.

On the other hand, acting on a maxim does not require explicit or conscious or complete formulation of that maxim. Even routine or thoughtless or indecisive action is action on *some* maxim. However, not all of the principles of action that a particular agent might exemplify at a given time would count as the agent's maxim. For principles of action need only incorporate *some* true description of an agent and *some* true description of the act and situation, whether these descriptions are vacuous and vague or brimming with detail. But an agent's maxim in a given act must incorporate just those descriptions of the agent, the act and the situation upon which the doing of the act depends.

An agent's maxim in a given act cannot, then, be equated simply with intentions. For an agent's intentions in performing a given act may refer to incidental aspects of the particular act and situation. For example, in making a new visitor feel welcome I may offer and make him or her some coffee. As I do so there will be innumerable aspects of my action that are intentional—the choice of mug, the addition of milk, the stirring—and there will also be numerous aspects of action that are "below the level of intention"—the gesture with which I hand the cup, the precise number of stirs and so on. But the various specific intentions with which I orchestrate the offer and preparation of coffee are all ancillary to an underlying principle. *Maxims are those underlying principles or intentions[3] by which we guide and control our more specific intentions.* In this particular example, had I lacked coffee I could have made my visitor welcome in other ways: The specific intention of offering and making coffee was subordinate to the maxim of making a visitor welcome. Had I had a quite different maxim—perhaps to make my visitor unwelcome—I would not in that context have acted on just those specific intentions. In another context, for example, in a society where an offer of coffee would be understood as we would understand an offer of hemlock, the same or similar specific intentions might have implemented a maxim of making unwelcome.

The fact that maxims are underlying or fundamental principles has important implications.[4] It means in the first place that it may not be easy to tell on which maxim a given act was performed. For example, a person who helps somebody else in a public place may have the underlying intention of being helpful—or alternatively the underlying intention of fostering a certain sort of good reputation. Since the helpful act might equally well be performed in furtherance of either underlying intention, there may be some doubt as to the agent's maxim. Merely asking an agent what his or her maxim is in such a situation may not settle the issue. The agent might be unsure. Both agents and others can work out that if the action would have been performed even if nobody had come to know of it, then the underlying principle would not have been to seek a certain sort of reputation. But an agent may after all be genuinely uncertain what his or her act would have been had he or she been faced with the possibility of helping, isolated from any effects on reputation. Isolation tests can settle such issues (*G*, 398–9; 407)—if we know their outcome; but since most such tests refer to counterfactual situations we often don't know that outcome with any great certainty. Further, isolation tests provide only a *negative* test of what an agent's maxim is not. Even those who have not adopted a maxim of seeking a good reputation may still be unsure whether they have adopted the maxim of helpfulness. They may perhaps wonder whether the underlying intention was not to preserve a certain sort of self-image or to bolster their sense of worth. Kant remarks on the opacity of the human heart and the difficulty of self-knowledge; he laments that for all we know there may never have been a truly loyal friend (*G,* 407–8; *DV,* 440; 445–6). And he does not view these as dispellable difficulties. Rather, these limits to human self-knowledge constitute the fundamental context of human action. Kant holds that we can know what it would be to try to act on a maxim of a certain sort, but can never be sure that what we do does not reflect further maxims that we disavow. However, the underlying intentions that guide our more specific intentions are not in principle undiscoverable. Even when not consciously formulated they can often be inferred with some assurance, if not certainty, as the principles and policies that our more specific intentions express and implement.

On a certain view of the purpose of a universality test, the fact that the maxim of a given action is neither observable nor always reliably inferable would be a most serious objection. For it would appear to render the outcome of any application of a universality test of dubious moral importance—since we might mistakenly have applied the test to a principle other than the agent's maxim. Further, even if the maxim had been correctly formulated, whether by the agent or by others, the maxim itself might reflect mistaken beliefs or self-deception in the agent, or the agent's act might fail to live up to its maxim. How then could any test applied to the agent's maxim be expected to classify acts into moral categories such as the right and the forbidden? For these categories apply to the outward and observable aspects of action. It is after all common enough for us to think of acts that are at least outwardly right (perhaps even obligatory) as nevertheless reflecting dubious intentions (I aim to kill an innocent, but mistakenly incapacitate the tiger who is about to maul him), and of acts whose intentions are impeccable as issuing tragically in wrong action (I aim for the tiger but dispatch the innocent).

The answer Kant gives to this problem is plain. It is that rightness and wrongness and the other "categories of right" standardly used in appraisal of outward features of action are *not* the fundamental forms of moral acceptability and unacceptability that he takes the Categorical Imperative to be able to discriminate.[5] Since the locus of application of Kant's universality test (and perhaps of any nonheteronomous universality test) is agents' fundamental principles or intentions, the moral distinction that it can draw is in the first place an intentional moral distinction, namely that between acts that have and those that lack moral worth. In an application of the Categorical Imperative to an agent's maxim we ask whether the underlying intention with which the agent acts or proposes to act—the intention that guides and controls other more specific intentions—is consistently universalizable; if it is, according to Kant, we at least know that the action will not be morally unworthy, and will not be a violation of duty.

The fact that Kant is primarily concerned with judgments of moral worth is easily forgotten, perhaps because he speaks of the Categorical Imperative as a test of *duty,* while we often tend to think of duty as confined to the *outward* aspects of action. It is quite usual for us to think of principled action as combining both duty and moral worthiness, which we regard as separate matters (e.g., showing scrupulous respect for others), or alternatively as revealing a moral worthiness that goes beyond all duty (e.g., gratuitous kindness that we think of as supererogatory). Correspondingly, it is quite usual for us to think of unprincipled action as in any case morally unworthy but still, in some cases, within the bounds of duty (e.g., the case of a could-be poisoner who mistakenly administers a life-saving drug). This is quite foreign to Kant's way of thinking, which sees the *central* case of duty as that of action that has moral worth, and regards as *derivative* that which accords merely in external respects with morally worthy action. On Kant's view the would-be poisoner who inadvertently saves life has violated a duty by acting in a morally unworthy way.

By taking an agent's fundamental or underlying principle or intention as the point of application of his universality test Kant avoids one of the difficulties most frequently raised about universality tests, namely that it seems easy enough to formulate *some* principle of action for any act, indeed possibly one that incorporates one of the agent's intentions, which can meet the criterion of any universality test, whatever the act. Notoriously some Nazi war criminals claimed that they were only "doing their job" or only "obeying orders"—which are after all not apparently morally unworthy activities. The disingenuousness of the claim that such acts were not morally unworthy lies in the fact that these Nazis were not only obeying orders, and indeed that in many cases their specific intentions were ancillary to more fundamental intentions *or principles* that might indeed have revealed moral unworthiness in the agent. (Such fundamental intentions or principles might range from "I'll do whatever I'm told to so long as it doesn't endanger me" to a fundamental maxim of genocide.) The fact that we can formulate *some* universalizable surface intention for any action by selecting among the agent's various surface intentions is no embarrassment to a universality test that is intended to apply to agents' maxims, and offers a solution to the problem of relevant descriptions.

It is equally irrelevant to a universality test that applies to maxims that we may be able to find some nonuniversalizable intentions among the more specific intentions with which an agent implements and fills out any maxim. If in welcoming my visitor with a cup of coffee I intentionally select a particular cup, my specific intention clearly cannot be universally acted on. The very particularity of the world means that there will always be aspects of action, including intentional aspects, that could not be universally adopted or intended. Kant's universality test, however, as we shall see, construes moral worth as contingent not on the universalizability or otherwise of an agent's specific intentions but on the universalizability of an agent's fundamental or underlying intention or principle.[6]

For Kant, then, the Categorical Imperative provides a criterion in the first place for duties to act on underlying intentions or principles that are morally worthy. It is only as a second and derivative part of his ethical theory that he proposes that the Categorical Imperative also provides a test of the outward wrongness and rightness of acts of specific sorts. He proposes in the *Groundwork* that acts that accord in outward respects with acts done on morally worthy maxims of action should be seen as being "in conformity with" or "in accord with" duty. The claim that we can provide a *general* account of which specific actions conform to the outward expressions of morally worthy maxims is highly controversial. We have already noted that there are many ways in which ancillary intentions may be devised in undertaking action on a given maxim, and there may be no single specific intention that is indispensable in all circumstances for action on a given maxim. Hence it is not generally clear what outward conformity conforms to. Kant appears to accept that the notion of outward conformity to duty is empty in many cases of duties of virtue, which are not sufficiently determinate for any particular more specific intentions to be singled out as required. He speaks of such duties as being "of wide requirement." But he also speaks of duties of narrow or strict requirement, and includes among these duties of justice and certain duties of respect to ourselves and to others.[7] Hence he takes it that there could in principle be a merely outward conformity to these strict or "perfect" duties.

Whether this claim is justified depends on the success of his demonstration that the underlying maxims of justice and respect have determinate specific implications for all possible human conditions. If they do not, then there will be no wholly general account of the requirements of justice and respect for all possible situations. It is then at any rate not obvious that we can derive a standard for the outward rightness of acts from a standard for the moral worth of underlying intentions or principles. This is a major problem that I intend to set on one side in order to explore the implications of a universality test that applies to underlying intentions or principles and therefore aims, at least primarily, at a test of the moral worth rather than the outward rightness of actions.

The fact that Kant's universality test focuses on maxims, and so on the moral worth of action, implies that it is a test that agents must seek to apply to their own proposals for action. This is not, however, because agents are in a wholly privileged epistemological position with respect to their own underlying intentions. No doubt others may often have some difficulty even in discerning all of an agent's surface intentions, and may be quite unsure about the underlying intention. But Kant does not regard the agents' vantage points as affording infallible insight into their own intentions—self-consciousness is not transparent—and would not deny that on occasion others might arrive at a more accurate appreciation of an agent's underlying intention or principle than the agent could reach.

The reason why a universality test in a nonheteronomous ethical theory is primarily one for the use of agents rather than of moral spectators is that it is only an agent who can adopt, modify or discard maxims. Although a test of the outward moral status of acts might be of most use and importance to third parties (legislators, judges, educators—those of us who pass judgment on others), because it may be possible (or indeed necessary) to prevent or deter or praise or punish in order to elicit or foster outward action of a certain sort, it is difficult if not impossible for outward regulation or pressure to change an agent's maxim. Surface conformity can be exacted; intentional conformity is more elusive (*DV,* 6:380–1). Precisely because we are considering what a universality test for autonomous beings must be like, we must recognize that the test is one that we can propose but not impose upon moral agents.

## Inconsistency Without Universalizing

This account of acting on a maxim shows at least how action can be construed in a way that makes consistency and inconsistency possible, and provides some grounds for thinking that a focus on maxims may avoid some of the difficulties that have arisen in attempts to apply universality tests unrestrictedly to principles of action of all sorts. This opens the way for showing how action on a nonuniversalizable maxim is inconsistent and for considering whether such inconsistency constitutes a criterion of moral unworthiness. Before dealing with these topics it will be useful to run over some of the many ways in which action on a maxim may reveal inconsistency even when universalizing is not brought into the picture.

It is of course true that any act that is performed is possible, taken in itself. But it does not follow that the intentions that are enacted are mutually consistent. There are two sorts of possibilities here: In the first place there may be an internal inconsistency within an agent's maxim; in the second place there may be contradictions between the various specific intentions an agent adopts in pursuit of that maxim, or between some of these specific intentions and the agent's maxim. These two sorts of contradiction correspond closely to the two types of contradictions that Kant thinks may arise when attempts to universalize maxims fail, and that he characterizes as involving, respectively, "contradictions in conception" and "contradictions in the will" (*G,* 424). Since I am also interested in charting the inconsistencies that can arise independently of attempts to universalize, as well as those that arise when universalizing fails, I shall use the rather similar labels *conceptual inconsistency* and *volitional inconsistency* to distinguish these two types of incoherence in action. A consideration of the different types of incoherence that maxims may display even when the question of universalizability is not raised provides a useful guide to the types of incoherence that nonuniversalizable maxims display.

A maxim of action may in the first place be incoherent simply because it expresses an impossible aspiration. An agent's maxim might be said to involve a conceptual inconsistency if the underlying intention was, for example, both to be successful and to be unworldly, or alternatively, to be both popular and reclusive, or both to care for others and always to put his or her own advantage first, or both to be frank with everybody and to be a loyal friend or associate, or both to keep a distance from others and to have intimate personal relationships. Agents whose underlying maxims incorporate such conceptual inconsistencies do not, of course, succeed in performing impossible acts; rather, the pattern of their actions appears to pull in opposite directions and to be in various ways self-defeating. At its extreme we may regard such underlying incoherence in a person's maxim, and consequent fragmentation of the person's action, as tragic or pathological (and perhaps both), since there is no way in which he or she can successfully enact the underlying intention. In other cases we may think of the pattern of action that results from underlying conceptual incoherence as showing no more than ambivalence or presenting conflicting signals to others, who are consequently at a loss about what they should expect or do, finding themselves in a "double bind."

However, not all cases of disjointed action constitute evidence of an internally inconsistent maxim. For it may well be that somebody adopts some accommodation of the potentially inconsistent aspects of an underlying intention. For example, somebody may adopt the maxim of being competitive and successful in public and professional life but of disregarding such considerations in private life; or of being obedient and deferential to superiors but overbearing and exacting with all others. Provided such persons can keep the two spheres of action separated, their underlying intentions can be internally consistent. Hence one cannot infer an inconsistency in someone's underlying intentions merely from the fact that he or she exhibits tendencies in opposing directions. For these tendencies may reflect a coherent underlying intention to respond or act differently in different types of context or with different groups of people. A nonuniversalizable maxim embodies a conceptual contradiction only if it *aims* at achieving mutually incompatible objectives and so cannot under any circumstances be acted on with success.

A focus on maxims that embody contradictions in conception pays no attention to the fact that maxims are not merely principles that we can conceive (or entertain, or even wish) but principles that we *will* or intend, that is to say, principles that we adopt as *principles of action.* Conceptual contradictions can be identified even in principles of action that are never adopted or acted upon. But a second and rather different type of incoherence is exhibited in some attempts to will maxims whose realization can be quite coherently envisaged. Willing, after all, is not just a matter of wishing that something were the case, but involves committing oneself to doing something to bring that situation about when opportunity is there and recognized. Kant expressed this point by insisting that rationality requires that whoever wills some end wills the necessary means insofar as these are available.

> Who wills the end, wills (so far as reason has decisive influence on his actions) also the means which are indispensably necessary and in his power. So far as willing is concerned, this proposition is analytic: for in my willing of an object as an effect there is already conceived the causality of myself as an acting cause—that is, the use of means; and from the concept of willing an end the imperative merely extracts the concept of actions nessary to this end. (*G*, 417)

This amounts to saying that to will some end without willing whatever means are indispensable for that end, insofar as they are available, is, even when the end itself involves no conceptual inconsistency, to involve oneself in a volitional inconsistency. It is to embrace at least one specific intention that, far from being guided by the underlying intention or principle, is inconsistent with that intention or principle.

Kant, however, explicitly formulates only *one* of the principles that must be observed by an agent who is not to fall into volitional inconsistency. The Principle of Hypothetical Imperatives, as expressed in the passage just quoted, requires that agents intend any indispensable means for whatever they fundamentally intend. Conformity with this requirement of coherent intending would be quite compatible with intending no means to whatever is fundamentally intended whenever there is no specific act that is indispensable for action on the underlying intention. Further reflection on the idea of intending the means suggests that there is a *family* of Principles of Rational Intending, of which the Principle of Hypothetical Imperatives is just one, though perhaps the most important one. The following list of further Principles of Rational Intending that coherent intending (as opposed to mere wishing or contemplating) apparently requires agents to observe may not be complete, but is sufficient to generate a variety of interesting conclusions.

First, it is a requirement of rationality not merely to intend all *indispensable* or *necessary* means to that which is fundamentally intended but also to intend some *sufficient* means to what is fundamentally intended. If it were not, I could coherently intend to eat an adequate diet, yet not intend to eat food of any specific sort on the grounds that no specific sort of food is indispensable in an adequate diet.

Second, it is a requirement of rationality not merely to intend all necessary and some sufficient means to what is fundamentally intended but also to seek to make such means available when they are not. If it were not, I could coherently claim to intend to help bring about a social revolution but do absolutely nothing, on the grounds that there is no revolutionary situation at present, settling instead for rhetoric and gesture rather than politics. But if I do this, I at most wish for, and do not intend to help to bring about, a social revolution.

Third, it is a requirement of rationality not merely to intend all necessary and some sufficient means to whatever is fundamentally intended but also to intend all necessary and some sufficient *components* of whatever is fundamentally intended. If it were not, I could coherently claim to intend to be kind to someone to whom, despite opportunity, I show no kindness in word, gesture or deed, merely because acting kindly is not the sort of thing that requires us to take means to an end, but the sort of thing that requires that we act in some of the ways that are *constitutive* of kindness.[8]

Fourth, it is a requirement of rationality that the various specific intentions we actually adopt in acting on a given maxim in a certain context be mutually consistent. If it were not, I could coherently claim to be generous to all my friends by giving to each the exclusive use of all my possessions.

Fifth, it is a requirement of rationality that the foreseeable results of the specific intentions adopted in acting on a given underlying intention be consistent with the underlying intention. If it were not, I could coherently claim to be concerned for the well-being of a child for whom I refuse an evidently life-saving operation, on the grounds that my specific intention—perhaps to shield the child from the hurt and trauma of the operation—is itself aimed at the child's well-being. But where such shielding foreseeably has the further consequence of endangering the child's life, it is clearly an intention that undercuts the very maxim that supposedly guides it.

There may well be yet further principles that fully coherent sets of intentions must observe, and possibly some of the principles listed above need elaboration or qualification. The point, however, is to reveal that once we see action as issuing from a complex web of intentions, many of which are guided by and ancillary to certain more fundamental intentions or principles under particular conditions, the business of intending coherently and avoiding volitional inconsistency becomes a demanding and complex affair.

Reflection on the various Principles of Rational Intending reveals a great deal about the connections between surface and underlying intentions to which a rational being must aspire. Underlying intentions to a considerable extent express the larger and longer-term goals, policies and aspirations of a life. But if these goals, policies and aspirations are willed (and not merely wished for), they must be connected with some set of surface intentions that express commitment to acts that, in the actual context in which agents find themselves, provide either the means to or some components of any underlying intentions, or at least take them in the direction of being able to form such intentions, without at any point committing them to acts whose performance would undercut their underlying intentions. Wherever such coherence is absent we find an example of intending that, despite the conceptual coherence of the agent's maxim, is volitionally incoherent. In some cases we may think the deficiency cognitive—agents fail despite available information to appreciate what they need to do if they are indeed to act on their maxims (they may be stupid or thoughtless or calculate poorly). In other cases we might think of the deficiency as primarily volitional: agents fail to intend what is needed if they are to will their maxims and not merely to wish for them to be realized. Each of these types of failure in rationality subdivides into many different sorts of cases. It follows that there are very many different ways in which agents whose intentions are not to be volitionally inconsistent may have to consider their intentions.

Perhaps the most difficult of the various requirements of coherent willing is the last, the demand that agents not adopt specific intentions that in a given context may undercut their own maxims. There are many cases in which agents can reach relatively clear specific intentions about how they will implement or instance their maxims, yet the acts they select, though indeed selected as a means to or component of their underlying intentions, backfire. It is fairly common for agents to adopt surface intentions that, when enacted, foreseeably will produce results that defeat their own deeper intentions. Defensive measures generate counterattack; attempts to do something particularly well result in botched performances; decisive success in battle is revealed as Pyrrhic victory. It is perhaps unclear how long a view of the likely results of their action agents must take for us not to think action that leads to results incompatible with its underlying intention is irrational. But at the least the standard and foreseeable results of an action should not undercut the underlying intention if we are to think of an agent as acting rationally. Somebody who claims to intend no harm to others, and specifically merely intends to share a friendly evening's drinking and to drive others home afterward, but who then decides on serious drinking and so cannot safely drive, cannot plausibly claim to intend merely the exuberant drinking and bonhomie and not the foreseeable drunkenness and inability to drive safely. Given standard information, such a set of intentions is volitionally incoherent. For it is a normal and foreseeable result of exuberant drinking that the drinker is incapable of driving safely. One who intends the drinking also (given normal intelligence and experience) intends the drunkenness; and hence cannot coherently also intend to drive others home if the underlying intention is to harm nobody.[9]

This brief consideration of various ways in which agents' intentions may fail to be consistent shows that achieving consistency in action is a difficult matter even if we do not introduce any universality test. Intentions may be either conceptually or volitionally incoherent. The demand that the acts we perform reflect conceptually and volitionally coherent sets of intentions therefore constitutes a powerful constraint on all practical reasoning. This conclusion provides some reason for thinking that when these demands for consistency are extended in the way in which the second aspect of Kant's Formula of Universal Law requires, we should expect to see patterns of reasoning that, far from being ineffective or trivial, generate powerful and interesting results.

## Inconsistency in Universalizing

The intuitive idea behind the thought that a universality test can provide a criterion of moral acceptability may be expressed quite simply as the thought that if we are to act as morally worthy beings, we should not single ourselves out for special consideration or treatment. Hence whatever we propose for ourselves should be possible (note: not "desired" or "wanted"—but at least *possible*) for all others. Kant expresses this commonplace thought (it is, of course, not his argument for the Categorical Imperative) by suggesting that what goes wrong when we adopt a nonuniversalizable maxim is that we treat ourselves as special:

> whenever we transgress a duty, we find that we in fact do not will that our maxim should become a universal law—since this is impossible for us—but rather that its opposite, should remain a law universally: we only

take the liberty of making an *exception* to it for ourselves (or even just
for this once) . . . (*G*, 424)

It is evident from this understanding of the Formula of Universal Law
that the notion of a plurality of interacting agents is already implicit in
the Formula of Universal Law. It is not the case that Kant introduces
these notions into his ethics only with the Formula of the Kingdom of
Ends, which would imply that the various formulations of the Categorical Imperative could not be in any way equivalent. To universalize is
from the start to consider whether what one proposes for oneself
*could* be done by others. This seems to many too meager a foundation
for ethics but not in itself an implausible constraint on any adequate
ethical theory.

Clearly enough, whatever cannot be consistently intended even for
oneself also cannot be consistently intended for all others. The types
of cases shown to be conceptually or volitionally inconsistent by the
methods discussed in the previous section are a fortiori nonuniversalizable. This raises the interesting question whether one should think of
certain types of cognitive and volitional failure as themselves morally
unworthy. However, I shall leave this question aside in order to focus
on the types of failure in consistent intending that are *peculiar* to the
adoption of nonuniversalizable intentions.

I shall therefore assume from now on that we are considering cases
of maxims that are in themselves not conceptually incoherent, and of
sets of underlying and surface intentions that are not themselves volitionally inconsistent. The task is to pinpoint the ways in which inconsistency emerges in some attempts to universalize such internally
consistent intentions. The second part of Kant's Formula of Universal
Law enjoins action only on maxims that the agent can at the same time
will as universal laws. He suggests that we can imagine this hypothetical
willing by working out what it would be like "if the maxim of your
action were to become through your will a universal law of nature."[10]
To universalize maxims agents must satisfy themselves that they can
both adopt the maxim and simultaneously will that others do so. In
determining whether they can do so they may find that they are de-
feated by either of the two types of contradiction that, as we have already seen, can afflict action even when universalizing is not under
consideration. Kant's own account of these two types of incoherence,
either of which defeats universalizability, is as follows:

We must *be able to will* that a maxim of our action should become a universal law—this is the general canon for all moral judgement of action. Some actions are so constituted that their maxim cannot even be *conceived* as a universal law of nature without contradiction, let alone be *willed* as what *ought* to become one. In the case of others we do not find this inner impossibility, but it is still impossible to *will* that their maxim should be raised to the universality of a law of nature, because such a will would contradict itself. (*G,* 424)

Kant also asserts that those maxims that when universalized lead to conceptual contradiction are the ones that strict or perfect duty requires us to avoid, whereas those that when universalized are conceptually coherent but not coherently willable are opposed only to wider or imperfect duties.[11] Since we probably lack both rigorous criteria and firm intuitions of the boundaries between perfect and imperfect duties, it is hard to evaluate this claim. However, it is remarkably easy to display contradictions that arise in attempts to universalize maxims that we might think of as clear cases of violations of duties of justice and self-respect, which Kant groups together as perfect duties; and it is also easy to show how contradictions emerge in attempts to universalize maxims that appear to exemplify clear violations of duties of beneficence and self-development, which Kant groups together as imperfect duties. By running through a largish number of such examples I hope to show how groundless is the belief that universality tests need supplementing with heteronomous considerations if they are to be action-guiding.

### Contradictions in Conception

A maxim that may lead to contradictions in conception when we attempt to universalize it often does not contain any conceptual contradiction if we merely adopt the maxim. For example, there is no contradiction involved in adopting the maxim of becoming a slave. But this maxim has as its universalized counterpart—the maxim we must attempt to "will as a universal law"—the maxim of everybody becoming a slave.[12] But if everybody became a slave, there would be nobody with property rights, hence no slaveholders, and hence nobody could become a slave.[13] Consider alternatively a maxim of becoming a slaveholder. Its universalized counterpart would be the maxim of everybody becoming a slaveholder. But if everybody became a slaveholder, then everybody would have some property rights; hence nobody could be a slave; hence there could be no slaveholders. Action on either of the nonuniversalizable maxims of becoming a slave or becoming a slaveholder would reveal moral unworthiness: It could be undertaken only by one who makes of himself or herself a special case.

Contradictions in conception can also be shown to arise in attempts to universalize maxims of deception and coercion. The maxim of coercing another has as its universalized counterpart the maxim that all coerce others; but if all coerce others, including those who are coercing them, then each party both complies with others' wills (being coerced) and simultaneously does not comply with others but rather (as coercer) exacts their compliance. A maxim of coercion cannot coherently be universalized and reveals moral unworthiness. By contrast, a maxim of coordination can be consistently universalized. A maxim of deceiving others as convenient has as its universalized counterpart the maxim that everyone will deceive others as convenient. But if everyone were to deceive others as convenient, then there would be no trust or reliance on others' acts of communication; hence nobody could be deceived; hence nobody could deceive others as convenient.

An argument of the same type can be applied to the maxim that is perhaps the most fundamental for a universality test, namely the maxim of abrogating judgment. One whose maxim it is to defer to the judgment and decisions of others—to choose heteronomy[14]—adopts a maxim whose universalized counterpart is that everyone defer to the judgments and decisions of others. But if everyone defers to the judgments and decisions of others, then there are no decisions to provide the starting point for deferring in judgment; hence it cannot be the case that everybody defers in judgment. Decisions can never be reached when everyone merely affirms, "I agree." A maxim of "elective heteronomy" cannot consistently be universalized.

Interpreters of Kant have traditionally made heavier weather of the contradiction in conception test than these short arguments suggest is necessary. There have perhaps been two reasons why. One is clearly that Kant's own examples of applications of the Categorical Imperative are more complex and convoluted than these short arguments suggest.[15] But even if detailed analysis of these examples is necessary for an evaluation of Kant's theory, it is clarifying to see whether a contradiction in conception test works when liberated from the need to accommodate Kant's particular discussion of examples.

But a second reason why the contradiction in conception test has seemed problematic to many of Kant's commentators is perhaps of greater importance for present concerns. It is that whereas many would grant that we can detect contradictions in attempts to universalize maxims simply of slaveholding or coercing or deceiving or deference, they would point out that no contradiction emerges if we seek to universalize more circumspect maxims, such as "I will hold slaves if I am in a position of sufficient power" or "I will deceive when it suits me and I can probably get away with it" or "I will defer in judgment to those I either admire or fear." Still less do contradictions emerge when we aim to universalize highly specific intentions of deception or deference, such as "I will steal from Woolworths when I can get away with it" or "I will do whatever my parish priest tells me to do."

However, the force of this objection to the claim that the contradiction in conception test can have significant moral implications is undercut when we remember that this is a test that applies to agents' maxims, that is, to their underlying or fundamental intentions or principles, and that as a corollary it is a test of moral worth. For what will be decisive is what an agent's fundamental intention or principle in doing a given act really is. What counts is whether the expression of falsehood expresses a fundamental attempt to deceive, or whether agreement with another (in itself innocent enough) expresses a fundamental refusal to judge or think for oneself. For an agent cannot truthfully claim that an underlying intent, plan or principle was of a very specific sort unless the organization of other, less fundamental, intentions reveals that it really was subject to those restrictions. Precisely because the Categorical Imperative formulates a universality test that applies to *maxims,* and not just to any intention, it is not rebutted by the fact that relatively specific intentions often can be universalized without conceptual contradiction. Conversely, further evidence for the interpretation of the notion of a maxim presented in the section entitled "Maxims and moral categories" is that it leads to an account of the Categorical Imperative that is neither powerless nor counterintuitive. However, for the same reason (that it applies to maxims and not to intentions of all sorts) the Categorical Imperative can most plausibly be construed as a test of moral worth rather than of outward rightness, and must always be applied with awareness that we lack certainty about what an agent's maxim is in a given case. This is a relatively slight difficulty when we are assessing our own proposed maxims of action, since we at least can do no better than to probe and test the maxim on which we propose to act (but even here we have no guarantee against self-deception). But it means that we will always remain to some extent unsure about our assessment of others' acts. Kant after all insists that we do not even know whether there *ever* has been a truly morally worthy act. But that is something we do not need to know in order to try to perform such acts. Self-deception may cloud our knowledge of our own maxims; but we are not powerless in self-guidance.

## Contradictions in the Will

Just as there are maxims that display no conceptual incoherence until attempts are made to universalize them, so there are maxims that exhibit no conceptual incoherence even when universalized, but that are shown to be volitionally inconsistent when attempts are made to universalize them. Such maxims cannot be "willed as universal laws"; attempts to do so fail in one way or another to meet the standards of rationality specified by the group of principles that I have termed Principles of Rational Intending. For to will a maxim is, after all, not just to conceive the realization of an underlying intention; that requires no more than speculation or wishing. Willing requires also the adoption of more specific intentions that are guided by, and chosen (in the light of the agent's beliefs) to realize, the underlying intention, or, if that is impossible, as appropriate moves toward a situation in which such specific intentions might be adopted. Whoever wills a maxim also adopts more specific intentions as means to or constituents of realizing that underlying intention, and is also committed to the foreseeable results of acting on these more specific intentions. Since intending a maxim commits the agent to such a variety of other intentions, there are various different patterns of argument that reveal that certain maxims cannot be willed as universal laws without contradiction.

Clearly the most comprehensive way in which a maxim may fail to be willable as a universal law is if its universal counterpart is inconsistent with the specific intentions that would be necessary for its own realization. Universalizing such a maxim would violate the Principle of Hypothetical Imperatives. The point is well illustrated by a Kantian example.[16] If I seek to will a maxim of nonbeneficence as a universal law, my underlying intention is not to help others when they need it, and its universalized counterpart is that nobody help others when they need it. But if everybody denies help to others when they need it, then those who need help will not be helped, and in particular I will not myself be helped when I need it. But if I am committed to the standards of rational willing that constitute the various Principles of Rational Intending, then I am committed to willing some means to any end to which I am committed, and these must include willing that if I am in need of help and therefore not able to achieve my ends without help, I be given some appropriate help. In trying to universalize a maxim of nonbeneficence I find myself committed simultaneously to willing that I not be helped when I need it and that I be helped when I need it. This contradiction, however, differs from the conceptual contradictions that emerge in attempts to universalize maxims such as those considered in the last section. A world of nonbenevolent persons is conceivable without contradiction. Arguments that reveal contradictions in the will depend crucially upon the role of the various Principles of Rational Intending—in this case on the Principle of Hypothetical Imperatives—in constraining the choice of specific intentions to a set that will implement all underlying intentions. It is only because *intending* a maxim of nonbeneficence as a universal law requires commitment to that very absence of help when needed, to which all rational intending requires assent, that nonbeneficence cannot coherently be universalized.

A second Kantian example,[17] which provides an argument to volitional incoherence, is a maxim of neglecting to develop any talents. A world of beings who develop no talents contains no conceptual incoherence. The maxim of an individual who decides to develop no talents, though imprudent, reveals no volitional inconsistency. For it is always possible that others fend for the imprudent, who will then find means available for at least some action. (It is not a fundamental requirement of practical reason that there should be means available to whatever projects agents adopt, but only that they should not have ruled out all action.) However, an attempt to universalize a maxim of neglecting talents commits one to a world in which no talents have been developed, and so to a situation in which necessary means are lacking not just for some but for any sort of complex action. An agent who fails to will the development, in self or others, of whatever minimal range of talents is required and sufficient for a range of action, is committed to internally inconsistent sets of intentions. Such agents intend both that action be possible and that it be undercut by neglect to develop even a minimal range of talents that would leave some possibility of action. This argument shows nothing about the development of talents that may be required or sufficient for any *specific* projects, but only points to the inconsistency of failing to foster such talents as are needed and sufficient for action of some sort or other. It is an argument that invokes not only the Principle of Hypothetical Imperatives but also the requirement that rational beings intend some set of means sufficient for the realization of their underlying intentions or principles.

These two examples of arguments that reveal volitional inconsistencies show only that it is morally unworthy to adopt maxims either of systematic nonbeneficence or of systematic neglect of talents. The duties that they ground are relatively indeterminate duties of virtue. The first of these arguments does not specify whom it is morally worthy to help, to what extent, in what ways or at what cost, but only that it would be morally unworthy to adopt an underlying intention of nonbeneficence. Similarly, the second argument does not establish which talents it would be morally worthy to develop, in whom, to what extent or at what cost, but only that it would be morally unworthy to adopt an underlying intention of making no effort to develop any talents. The person who adopts a maxim either of nonbeneficence or of nondevelopment of talents cannot coherently universalize the maxim, but must either make an exception of himself or herself, and intend, unworthily, to be a free rider on others' beneficence and talents, or be committed to some specific intentions that are inconsistent with those required for action on the maxim.

Another example of a maxim that cannot consistently be willed as a universal law is the maxim of refusing to accept help when it is needed. The universalized counterpart of this underlying intention would be the intention that everyone refuse to accept help when it is needed. But rational beings cannot consistently commit themselves to intending that all forgo a means that, if ever they are in need of help, will be indispensable for them to act at all.

A further example of a nonuniversalizable maxim is provided by a maxim of ingratitude, whose universalized counterpart is that nobody show or express gratitude for favors received. In a world of non-self-sufficient beings a universal maxim of ingratitude would require the systematic neglect of an important means for ensuring that help is forthcoming for those who need help if they are to realize their intentions. Hence in such a world nobody could coherently claim to will that those in need of help be helped. Yet we have already seen that to will that all in need of help be refused help is volitionally inconsistent. Hence, willing a maxim of ingratitude also involves a commitment to a set of intentions not all of which can be consistently universalized. The volitional inconsistency that overtakes would-be universalizers of this maxim arises in two stages: The trouble with ingratitude is that, practiced universally, it undercuts beneficence; the trouble with nonbeneficence is that it cannot be universally practiced by beings who have at least some maxims, yet (lacking self-sufficiency) cannot guarantee that their own resources will provide means sufficient for at least some of their projects.

The hinge of all these arguments is that human beings (since they are adopters of maxims) have at least some maxims or projects, which (since they are not self-sufficient) they cannot always realize unaided, and so must (since they are rational) intend to draw on the assistance of others, and so must (if they universalize) intend to develop and foster a world that will lend to all some support of others' beneficence and talents. Such arguments can reveal the volitional inconsistencies involved in trying to universalize maxims of entirely neglecting the social virtues—beneficence, solidarity, gratitude, sociability and the like—for beings who are rational yet not always able to achieve what they intend unaided. It follows from this point that the social virtues are very differently construed in Kantian and in heteronomous ethics. An ethical theory for nonheteronomous agents sees the social virtues as morally required, not because they are desired or liked but because they are necessary requirements for action in a being who is not self-sufficient. The content of the social virtues in this framework cannot be spelled out in terms of the provision of determinate goods or services or the meeting of certain set needs or the satisfaction of a determinate set of desires. Rather, the content of these virtues will always depend on the various underlying maxims and projects, both individual and collaborative, to which agents commit themselves. What will constitute beneficence or kindness or care for others will depend in great part on how others intend to act.

## Contradictions in the Will and Further Results

The patterns of argument that can be used to show underlying antisocial intentions morally unworthy make use of various Principles of Rational Intending in addition to the Principle of Hypothetical Imperatives. In particular they draw on the requirements that rational agents intend not merely necessary but also sufficient means to or components of their underlying intentions or maxims, and that they also intend whatever means are indirectly required and sufficient to make possible the adoption of such specific intentions. However, the particular features of the fifth Principle of Rational Intending—the Principle of Intending the Further Results—have not yet been displayed. Attempts to evade this Principle of Rational Intending lead to a peculiar sort of volitional inconsistency.

Good examples of arguments that rely on this principle can be developed by considering cases of maxims that, when universalized, produce what are frequently referred to as "unintended consequences." For example, I can adopt the underlying intention of improving my economic well-being, and the specific intention of doing so by competing effectively with others. The maxim of my action can be consistently universalized: There is no conceptual contradiction in intending everyone's economic position to improve. The specific intention of adopting competitive strategies is not inconsistent with the maxim to which it is ancillary; nor is universal action on competitive strategies inconsistent with universal economic advance (that indeed is what the invisible hand is often presumed to achieve). But if an agent intends his or her own economic advance to be achieved solely by competitive strategies, this nexus of intentions cannot consistently be willed as universal law, because the further results of universal competitive activity, by itself, are inconsistent with universal economic advance. If everyone seeks to advance by these (and no other) methods, the result will not put everybody ahead economically. A maxim of economic progress combined with the specific intention of achieving progress merely by competitive strategies cannot be universalized, any more than the intention of looking over the heads of a crowd can be universally achieved by everyone in the crowd standing on tiptoes.[18] On the other hand, a maxim of seeking economic advance by means of increased production can be consistently universalized. It is merely the particular specific intention of advancing economically by competitive strategies alone that leads to volitional inconsistency when universalized. Competitive means are inherently effective only for some: Competitions must have losers as well as winners. Hence, though it can be consistent to seek individual economic advance solely by competitive methods, this strategy cannot consistently be universalized. Once we consider what it would be to intend the consequences of universal competition—the usually *unintended* consequences—we can see that there is an inconsistency not between universal competitive activity and universal economic progress, but between the *further results of intending only universal com-*

*petitive activity and universal economic progress.* Economic progress and competitive activity might each of them consistently be universal; indeed, it is possible for them to coexist within a certain society. (Capitalist economies do experience periods of general economic growth.) Nevertheless, there is a volitional inconsistency in seeking to achieve universal economic growth *solely by way* of universal adoption of competitive strategies.

This argument does not show that either the intention to advance economically or the intention to act competitively cannot be universalized, but only that the composite intention of pursuing economic advance solely by competitive tactics cannot be universalized. It does not suggest that either competition or economic progress is morally unworthy, but only that an attempt to achieve economic progress solely by competitive methods and without aiming at any productive contribution is not universalizable and so is morally unworthy.

Similarly, there is no inconsistency in an intention to engage in competitive activities of other sorts (e.g., games and sports). But if such competition is ancillary to an underlying intention to win, then the overall intention is not universalizable. Competitive games must have losers. If winning is not the overriding aim in such activities, if they are played for their own sake, the activity is consistently universalizable. But to play competitively with the fundamental intention of winning is to adopt an intention that makes of one's own case a necessary exception.

## Conclusions

The interest of a Kantian universality test is that it aims to ground an ethical theory on notions of consistency and rationality rather than upon considerations of desire and preference. Kant's universality test meets many of the conditions that any such universality test must meet. In particular it focuses on features of action that are appropriate candidates for assessments of coherence and incoherence, namely the maxims or fundamental intentions that agents may adopt and the web of more specific ancillary intentions that they must adopt in a given context if their commitment to a maxim is genuine. Although Kant alludes specifically to conceptual inconsistencies and to those volitional inconsistencies that are attributable to nonobservance of the Principle of Hypothetical Imperatives in attempts to universalize intentions, there is in addition a larger variety of types of volitional inconsistency that agents who seek to subject their maxims to a universality test (and so not to make an exception of their own case) must avoid. A universality test applied to maxims and their ancillary, more specific, intentions can be action-guiding in many ways without invoking any heteronomous considerations.

However, precisely because it applies to intentions or principles, a universality test of this sort cannot generally provide a test of the rightness or wrongness of the specific outward aspects of action. It is, at least primarily, and perhaps solely, a test of the inner moral worth of acts. It tells us what we ought to avoid if we are not to act in ways that we can know are in principle not possible for all others. Such a test is primarily of use to agents in guiding their own moral deliberations, and can only be used most intuitively in assessing the moral worth of others' action, where we are often sure only about specific outward aspects of action and not about the maxim. This point will not be of great importance if we do not think it important whether an ethical theory enables us to pass judgment on the moral worth of others' acts. But specific outward aspects of others' action are unavoidably of public concern. The considerations discussed here do not reveal whether or not these can be judged right or wrong by Kant's theory. Kant no doubt thought that it was possible to derive specific principles of justice from the Formula of Universal Law; but the success of this derivation and of his grounding of *Rechtslehre* is beyond the scope of this chapter.

The universality test discussed here is, above all, a test of the mutual consistency of (sets of) intentions and universalized intentions or principles. It operates by showing some sets of proposed intentions to be mutually inconsistent. It does not thereby generally single out action on any one set of specific intentions as morally required. On the contrary, the ways in which maxims can be enacted or realized by means of acts performed on specific intentions must vary with situation, tradition and culture. The specific acts by which we can show or fail to show loyalty to a friend or respect to another or justice in our dealings with the world will always reflect specific ways of living and thinking and particular situations and relationships. What reason can provide is a way of discovering whether we are choosing to act in ways (however culturally specific) that we do not in principle preclude for others. The "formal" character of the Categorical Imperative does not entail either that it has no substantive ethical implications or that it can select a unique code of conduct as morally worthy for all times and places.

Rather than presenting a dismal choice between triviality and implausible rigorism, a universality test can provide a rational foundation for ethics and maintain a serious respect for the diversity of content of distinct ethical practices and traditions.

## Notes

1. Heteronomous readings of Kant's ethics include Schopenhauer's in *On the Basis of Morality,* but are most common in introductory works in ethics. Recent examples include William K. Frankena, *Ethics* (Englewood Cliffs: Prentice-Hall, 1963), p. 25; Gilbert Harman, *The Nature of Morality* (New York: Oxford University Press, 1977), p. 73; and D. D. Raphael, *Moral Philosophy* (Oxford: Oxford University Press, 1981), p. 76. Allegations that Kant, despite his intentions, must invoke heteronomous considerations if he is to reach substantive conclusions can notoriously be found in J. S. Mill's *Utilitarianism,* but are also now more common in more general discussions of Kant's ethics. Examples include C. D. Broad, *Five Types of Ethical Theory* (Totowa, N.J.: Littlefield Adams, 1965), p. 130; and Marcus Singer, *Generalization in Ethics* (New York: Alfred Knopf, 1961), p. 262.

2. Even such a wide-ranging and reflective discussion of rational choice theory as Jon Elster's in *Ulysses and the Sirens* (Cambridge: Cambridge University Press, 1979) discusses no nonheteronomous conceptions or aspects of rational choice.

3. I would not now use the term *intention* here, or as I used it throughout this essay. Replacing it with *(underlying) practical principle* allows the same points to be made in more general form, and makes it easier to stress the extent to which maxims, unlike certain intentions, can be hidden from those whose maxims they are.

4. However, the claim that maxims are underlying or fundamental intentions or principles should not be collapsed into the claim, which Kant makes in *Religion within the Limits of Reason Alone,* that for any agent (rather than "for any act") at a given time there is one fundamental maxim, to which all other principles that we might think maxims are ancillary.

5. See *G,* 397–8: "the concept of *duty,* which includes that of a good will. . . ." The persistence of the view that Kant is primarily concerned with right action perhaps reflects the modern conception that duty *must* be a matter of externals more than it reflects the Kantian texts. Cf. Onora Nell (O'Neill), *Acting on Principle* (New York: Columbia University Press, 1975).

6. The points mentioned in this and the preceding paragraphs suggest why a focus on maxims may make it possible to bypass a variety of problems said to plague universality tests when applied to principles that are "too general" or "too specific"; these problems include invertibility, reiterability, moral indeterminacy, empty formalism and the generation of trivial and counterintuitive results. See Singer, *Generalization in Ethics;* and Nell (O'Neill), *Acting on Principle.*

7. Kant does not then see all acts that are specifically required by strict or perfect duties as matters of justice. Some duties of virtue also have (limited) strict requirements, such as refraining from mockery or detraction or otherwise damaging others' self-respect. These are indispensable elements of any way of enacting maxims of respect. *Cf. DV*, 6:421ff. and 463ff.; Nell (O'Neill), *Acting on Principle,* pp. 52–8; and Barbara Herman, "Mutual Aid and Respect for Persons," in this volume, chapter 6.

8. Kant's discussions of duties of virtue in any case suggest that he would count the necessary constituents or components of an end, and not merely the instrumentally necessary acts, as means to that end.

9. The fifth requirement of rational intending clearly deals with the very nexus of intentions on which discussions of the Doctrine of Double Effect focus. That doctrine claims that agents are not responsible for harm that foreseeably results from action undertaken with dutiful intentions, provided that the harm is not disproportionate, is regretted, and would have been avoided had there been a less harmful set of specific intentions that would have implemented the same maxim in that situation. (The surgeon foresees, and regrets, the pain unavoidably inflicted by a lifesaving procedure.) Although the Doctrine of Double Effect holds that agents are not to be held responsible for such action, it allows that they do, if "obliquely" rather than "directly," intend it. It is compatible with the Doctrine of Double Effect to insist that an agent whose oblique intention foreseeably undercuts the action for the sake of which what is directly intended is done, acts irrationally. Where the fundamental intention is so undercut by a supposedly ancillary aspect of action, proportionality is violated, and the attribution of the fundamental intentions may be called in question.

10. This is the so-called Formula of the Law of Nature. Cf. *G,* 421, and also 436: "maxims must be chosen as if they had to hold as universal laws of nature"; see also *MM,* 6:225: "Act according to a maxim which can, at the same time, be valid as a universal law." In this discussion I leave aside all consideration of the relationships between different formulations of the Categorical Imperative, and in particular the differences between those versions that are stated "for finite rational beings" (typics) and those that are formulated in ways that make them relevant strictly to the human condition. These topics have been much discussed in the literature: H. J. Paton, *The Categorical Imperative* (London: Hutchinson, 1947); John Kemp, *The Philosophy of Kant* (Oxford: Oxford University Press, 1968); Robrt Paul Wolff, *The Autonomy of Reason* (New York: Harpers, 1973); Bruce Aune, *Kant's Theory of Morals* (Princeton: Princeton University Press, 1979). See also chapters 8 and 9 below.

11. *G,* 424; *MM,* 4, Introduction; *DV,* 6, esp. 389.

12. For further discussion of the notion of the universalized counterpart of a maxim see Nell (O'Neill), *Acting on Principle,* pp. 61–3.

13. For an application of the Formula of Universal Law to the example of slavery see Leslie A. Mulholland, "Kant: On Willing Maxims to Become Laws of Nature" *Dialogue* 18 (1978): 92–105.

14. To see why Kant thinks the abrogation of autonomy would be the most fundamental of failings see his *What Is Enlightenment?* and Barry Clarke's dis-

cussion of "elective heteronomy" in "Beyond the Banality of Evil," *British Journal of Political Science* 10 (1980): 17–39.

15. See the various works of commentary listed in note 10 above; Jonathan Harrison, "Kant's Examples of the First Formulation of the Categorical Imperative," in R. P. Wolff, ed., *Foundations of the Metaphysics of Morals: Text and Critical Essays* (Indianapolis: Bobbs-Merrill, 1969), pp. 208–29; and John Kemp, "Kant's Examples of the Categorical Imperative," in *ibid.,* pp. 230–44.

16. Cf. *DV,* 6:447–64, for Kant's discussions of love and social virtues.

17. Cf. *DV,* 6:443–7, for discussion of the duty not to neglect to develop talents (the "duty to seek one's own perfection"). "Talents" here are to be understood not as any particularly unusual accomplishments, but as any human powers that (unlike natural gifts) we can choose either to cultivate or to neglect. Kant tends to think the most important talents are second-order ones (e.g., self-mastery, self-knowledge) and that we can do little to develop these in others. Both restrictions seem to me unnecessary. See Onora O'Neill, *Faces of Hunger: An Essay on Poverty, Development and Justice* (London: George Allen and Unwin, 1986), Chap. 8, for development of these thoughts.

18. See F. Hirsch, *The Social Limits to Growth* (Cambridge, Mass.: Harvard University Press, 1976).

# 6

# Mutual Aid and Respect for Persons

## Barbara Herman

> Yet a fourth is himself flourishing, but he sees others who have to struggle with great hardships (and who he could easily help); and he thinks: What does it matter to me? Let every one be as happy as Heaven wills or as he can make himself; I won't deprive him of anything; I won't even envy him; only I have no wish to contribute anything to his well-being or to his support in distress! Now admittedly if such an attitude were a universal law of nature, mankind could get on perfectly well—better no doubt than if everybody prates about sympathy and good will, and even takes pain, on occasions to practice them, but on the other hand cheats where he can, traffics in human rights, or violates them in other ways. But although it is possible that a universal law of nature could subsist in harmony with this maxim, yet it is impossible to will that such a principle should hold everywhere as a law of nature. For a will which decided in this way would be in conflict with itself, since many a situation might arise in which the man needed love and sympathy from others, and in which, by such a law of nature sprung from his own will, he would rob himself of all hope of the help he wants for himself. (*G*, 423)

It is surely no crude mistake of reading to interpret this passage as making some kind of prudential appeal in arguing for a duty of beneficence and as depending in its conclusion on the contingent, empirical fact about human agents that they may encounter situations in which they need the help of others. Such reading underlies the belief of some of Kant's most serious critics (Schopenhauer and Sidgwick, for example) that this argument is peculiarly well suited to reveal deep inconsistencies in Kant's claims about morality. It is, after all, a central claim

of the *Groundwork* that no categorical imperative can have a prudential foundation (or else it could not be a principle of duty); and it is our
rational, rather than our empirical, nature that is to be the ground of
moral duty. I do not think the accounts of these critics (and those of
many friendly commentators as well) have taken seriously enough the
idea that the sense in which Kant holds that impermissible acts are
irrational is not to be captured by considerations of a prudential nature.

In offering another interpretation of the *Groundwork* argument for
beneficence, I hope to make some progress in describing the sense
of rationality that Kant conceives to be connected with morality. The
reconstruction of the argument is guided by two methodological constraints. Since the argument takes place within a procedure for moral
judgment, and procedures of moral judgment provide moral instruction to agents using them beyond their rulings of permissibility, there
are grounds for rejecting an interpretation of the argument for beneficence if the way in which the argument proceeds teaches a moral lesson alien to the spirit of Kant's project. Second, the Categorical
Imperative (CI) procedure is used to establish moral requirements. It
also is to guide sincere moral agents in assessing actions and policies
whose moral permissibility is uncertain. Given this double function,
it is reasonable to expect that the casuistry of beneficence (how we
determine what we must do in particular cases) will be informed by
those considerations used to establish that there is a duty of beneficence. Casuistry should not be separated from the main line of moral
argument.

Let me turn now to the argument for beneficence, as it is presented
in the *Groundwork,* as the fourth example of the employment of the
Categorical Imperative.

I

It will help to begin by recalling the role the examples play in the argument of the *Groundwork.*[1] At the point of their introduction, Kant has
just produced the formula of the CI: "Act only on that maxim through
which you can at the same time will that it should become a universal
law" (*G*, 421). What he then must demonstrate is that the CI is a moral
principle: the CI must be able to judge an appropriate range of test
cases correctly. This will show that it correlates well with our considered moral judgments. But Kant also believes that the CI is the princi-

ple embedded in ordinary moral judgment, and correlation is not enough to show that it is. For this we must look to the detail of the examples—what is revealed by the CI procedure to be at work in the logic or rationale of impermissible maxims.

There is now fairly general agreement about the formal mechanics of the CI procedure of judgment.[2] The agent is to cast his maxim of action in universal form and then to examine what would follow if that universalized maxim were to become a law of human nature. That is, the agent constructs a hypothetical world that has all the features of the world as it is except for the addition of the universalized maxim as a law of its nature. An action is judged impermissible either if its maxim cannot be conceived as a law of nature without contradiction or if it is impossible for an agent to will that his maxim should become a law of nature without his will contradicting itself (see *G*, 424).

The *Groundwork* argument for a duty of beneficence takes the case of a man "himself flourishing" who is aware both that there are others who have "great hardships" and that "he could easily help." Only he would be indifferent: whatever he may feel,[3] he wishes to live so 'hat "every one be as happy as Heaven wills or as he can make himself." He has no wish to contribute to the well-being of others or to their support in distress. Kant's comment that "if such an attitude were a universal law of nature, mankind could get on perfectly well," irony aside, implies that there is no difficulty (contradiction) in conceiving the maxim of nonbeneficence ("to never help anyone") as a law of nature. A world just like this one except for the addition of a law of nonbeneficence would be a possible world; universal nonbeneficence is a possible natural law. (Something is not a possible natural law if it is impossible for everything subject to it to act according to it. It is possible for everyone to act nonbeneficiently.)

It is not possible, however, "to *will* that such a principle should hold everywhere as a law of nature." This is so because "a will which decided in this way would be in conflict with itself, since many a situation might arise in which the man needed love and sympathy from others, and in which, by such a law of nature sprung from his own will, he would rob himself of all hope of the help he wants for himself" (*G*, 423). The most obvious reading of this places the supposed contradiction in will in a self-produced (if hypothetical) failure of prudential reasoning. The procedure requires the agent to imagine that his maxim of nonbeneficence has become a universal law of (human) nature through his willing of it (for himself). He would thereby have created a world in which no one could help anyone. Yet in the hypothetical world, as in this world, he might come to need help and want to be aided. Then he would have willed a world in which he was the cause of his being unable to get the help he wanted. Here is the supposed contradiction in will: he would be willing both that the world be such that no one could help anyone and that he be helped.[4]

There is no specifically moral element in this demonstration of a contradiction in will. Suppose I adopt a policy of never saving any money. And suppose I also know that many situations may arise in which I will want something that (as a matter of contingent fact) will require my having saved money. When this comes to pass, my general policy of not saving will then stand in the way of my getting what I want. This is often enough to ground a charge of imprudence, and, to the extent that I could foresee this state of affairs, I have acted irrationally. As both the general policy and the want that requires savings are expressions of my will, it is not implausible to describe my will as in conflict with itself.[5]

I escape such ordinary conflict in two different ways. Knowing that I will want something I can have only if I save, either I may give up my general policy of never saving, or I may adopt the attitude toward future wants that require savings that it is tolerable for them to be unfulfilled. Other things equal, I will have acted rationally if I adopt either course.

So, similarly, we might expect the conflict of will in the nonbeneficence example to be resolvable either by abandoning the general policy of never helping anyone or by adopting the attitude toward needed help that it is a tolerable unfulfilled desire.[6] Of course, if the general policy is abandoned, the argument is over: the agent will have rejected nonbeneficence. But so long as it is open to the agent to maintain his nonbeneficent policy on condition that he give up the possibility of help, it is not necessary to reject nonbeneficence. The problem then appears to be: can the argument in the example be construed in a way that makes it impossible for a rational agent to adopt the strategy of being willing to forgo help in order to keep his maxim of nonbeneficence?

So, we might think, the agent needs to be reminded of his vulnerability. (He is, we are told, a flourishing individual, not someone struggling with great hardships or routinely needing assistance; such an individual might not find it difficult to be convinced that he is self-sufficient.) We let the examples turn a bit melodramatic: we ask him to imagine himself lying in the road about to be run over by a truck. Someone could easily help him escape certain horrible death. How could he not want help? Thinking of this, can he now decide that such a desire for help will not be satisfied? Surely he would want to live more than he wants to abide by a policy of never helping anyone. That, after all, was a policy based on no more than the desire not to be bothered by the needs of others. So, if he would want help in that case (and would be unwilling to forgo help for the sake of his policy of nonbeneficence) and since in the hypothetical world of universal nonbeneficence he would be robbed of that help by an act of his own will, he is then forced, insofar as he is rational, to resolve the conflict by abandoning the maxim of nonbeneficence. Prudence seems to require it.

But if the reasoning is prudential, then it would also be appropriate to consider the likelihood of situations arising when he would prefer help more than he prefers the benefits of his policy of nonbeneficence. This is Sidgwick's argument: "Even granting that everyone, in the actual moment of distress, must necessarily wish for the assistance of others: still a strong man, after balancing the chances of life, may easily think that he and such as he have more to gain, on the whole, by the general adoption of the egoistic maxim; benevolence being likely to bring more trouble than profit."[7] Indeed, any person well situated in life and of a sufficiently self-disciplined temper might have good reason to feel that the price of increased security in having the help of others available (in this world or in the hypothetical world of the CI procedure) is too high. The risk of accident with no one helping is one he can bear. Everyone must die sometime, and so on. To salvage the argument for beneficence then, it must be possible to show that such considerations cannot legitimately be introduced. As we have so far interpreted the argument, there seems to be no way to exclude them and so no way to show that people willing to tolerate risk have a duty to help others, if they would prefer not to help.

Moreover, this line of reasoning would show that not all who have a duty of beneficence are obliged to the same degree. Since attitudes toward security and the felt onerousness of beneficence will vary from person to person, this argument will yield a strong duty of beneficence for some (low-risk tolerators) and a decreasingly stringent duty of beneficence for those who have greater tolerance for risks. (And what of those who find risks not only tolerable but desirable or exciting?)

It is not just these consequences that are disturbing. The form of the argument urges our thinking about the duty of beneficence as a kind of (hypothetical) insurance policy. In the hypothetical world, prudence indicates rejection of the maxim of nonbeneficence in order to secure aid for oneself, as needed, in the future. The moral question seems to turn on the "premium"—how much protection you would lose if you do not want to pay in the currency of beneficence. (There is no obligation to do everything necessary to save one's life.) But how one comes to understand why we have the duties we do is part of how one learns what morality is about. The CI procedure tells an agent that what would happen were his maxim to be a universal law of nature matters in a way that will make a moral differnce. So if the salient question in the procedure is, "Would this harm or benefit you? Would it put you at risk or enhance your chances for the satisfaction of desires?" it would then be reasonable for an agent to conclude that it is his well-being that turns the moral argument—albeit his well-being in hypothetical circumstances. And since use of the procedure contributes to an agent's understanding of his place in a moral scheme, the role of the prudential elements must lead him to think that the satisfaction of his desires is significant in deriving duties. To center moral deliberation on a strategy for even hypothetical self-protection provides a lesson one would not have expected Kant to endorse.

One way out of this impasses is to use an interpretive strategy suggested by John Rawls.[8] He locates the difficulty in the argument for beneficence in the use made by the judging agent of those contingent facts of his life (his strength, fortune, health, and so on) that support the rationality of his risking a world of nonbeneficence. As Rawls holds, on what he argues are Kantian grounds, that such facts about persons are morally irrelevant in determining duties, he would amend the CI procedure by introducing a veil of ignorance, to eliminate differences in judgment produced by different risks and attitudes toward risk. By putting contraints on information, the veil of ignorance allows one to use the form of ordinary prudential reasoning to get moral results from the CI procedure.[9] Without the information necessary to assess one's chances of needing the help of others, it is no longer rational to risk the frustration of such need for the sake of the benefits to be had in not having to help others. Supplementing the Kantian procedure with the veil of ignorance has the effect of making everyone conservative about risk taking. The duty of beneficence would then apply to all persons and apply to them all equally. So Sidgwick's strong man would be answered.

The Rawlsian strategy produces the desired moral results because the veil of ignorance excludes distinctive personal information in a way that makes each person function (as he judges) as a kind of representative person. What the Rawlsian strategy fails to capture is a critical element in the Kantian conception of moral judgment. For Kant, the embeddedness of the person in the particular is the natural and necessary starting point of moral judgment. Rawls's strategy is drawn from the context of the "original position," where agents have no moral knowledge (apart from strictly formal matters) and are to decide together on the duties, obligations, and principles by which they will live. The Kantian moral agent, if the standard examples can be taken as a guide, comes to need a procedure for moral judgment when he is tempted to make an exception for himself from known moral precepts. It is because he believes that his particular circumstances are special that he concludes that he is morally entitled to act in ways others may not.[10] He will not be shown that he is wrong by being told that all features distinguishing him from others are morally irrelevant. If, as Kant suggests, those who are not evil are drawn to moral error through the sincere conviction that they may make an exception to the moral law for themselves to the advantage of inclination—he says we pretend the exceptions are "inconsiderable or apparently forced on us" (*G*, 424)—then a procedure of moral judgment will be more effective to the degree that it allows agents to bring their sense of their distinctiveness in and then shows them that it is not enough to justify excepting themselves.[11]

There is confirmation for this view in the fact that the CI procedure does not assess actions directly but, rather, assesses them through their maxims: actions *as they are willed* by the agent. As it expresses his conception of what he is doing and why, his maxim must be based on the kind of information the Rawlsian restriction is designed to eliminate. In the case at hand, the choice of a policy of nonbeneficence follows from the agent's assessment of his fortunate situation. In asking whether this choice is permissible, he wants, in a sense, to know why his special circumstances should not give him moral title to refrain from involvement in the welfare of others. That, to him, is the morally relevant background to his adoption of his maxim. Given his reasons for adopting this maxim, we may fairly conclude that he would not choose nonbeneficence if he were someone likely to need the help of others. He is not without feeling for consistency and reciprocity. The CI procedure amended in a Rawlsian way does not explain (within the Kantian framework) the moral error in his reasoning.

Still the difficulty with allowing this information in remains, compromising the generality of results yielded by the CI procedure.


## II


If the problem is not to be dealt with by restricting the information allowed into the procedure, the remaining aspect of the argument that bears reexamination is the appeal of prudence. We have been assuming that Kant's idea of a contradiction in will is accurately represented by errors in prudential reasoning, translated into conflicting willings by the device of the CI procedure. Here I want to argue that, although a contradiction in will is an expression of irrational willing, it is not in virtue of prudential considerations that it is so.

Let me begin by suggesting an alternative reading of the last sentence of the opening quotation, taking its point to be the ubiquity (inescapability) of the possibility of needing help. That is, for any end, it is not possible for an agent to guarantee in advance that he can pursue his end successfully without the help of others. I will argue that this is enough to demonstrate a contradiction in will (supposing one has already willed a law of universal nonbeneficence) if either of two conditions holds: (1) that there are ends that the agent wants to realize more than he could hope to benefit from nonbeneficence and that he cannot bring about unaided or (2) that there are ends that it is not possible for any rational agent to forgo (ends that are in some sense necessary ends).

I view the CI procedure as being designed to draw our attention to those features of our condition—as rational agents in this world and as members of a community of persons—that serve as the conditions of our willings. In part because we are moved by moral considerations (we may at times be bad; we are not often evil), we are drawn to use the surface logic of moral reasoning (its requirements of impartiality, consistency, and so on) to support the belief that we may on occasion be morally justified in acting as others would not be. It is just this sense of specialness that underlies the belief of the strong man that it would be possible, even reasonable, to live without the help of others. The CI procedure is to show that, for any of us, the availability of the help of others is not something it can be rational to forgo. It is this limit on what it can be rational to will that the strong man needs to be shown.

In willing an end, an agent conceives of himself as "an acting cause"—that is, as using means (*G,* 417). The willing of means to an adopted end is not, then, some separate and contingent act of willing. As we will an end we are, in that act of will, committing ourselves to will the necessary means, so long as we do not abandon the end. The things that are means for us are of three kinds: ourselves (as we have abilities and skills), things (both animate and inanimate), and other persons (given their capacities, as end setters, to take our ends as their own). The argument to a contradiction in will asks, in effect, whether it could be rational for a human being to renounce irrevocably the resource (means) of the help of others. That one will need (be unable to act for some particular end without) the help of others is something that may or may not come to pass. It depends on the nature of one's ends, the availability of resources (who has what), one's skill, strength, and so forth. Most important, it depends on how things happen to work out—the nature of the impersonal forces, the actions of others, and the like, that intersect with one's life. (There is a limit to "making one's own luck.") The extent to which one's skills are adequate to one's needs and projects, the extent to which the things one needs are plentiful or ready to hand, and the extent to which the help of others will be necessary for the successful pursuit of any given end—all of these involve contingencies that are not within our power.

Now the question is: why, knowing this, can't the strong man commit himself to abandon any end he discovers he cannot pursue without help? This is a kind of negative stoicism, and such a policy will describe for him a distinctive way of life. He must practice self-discipline, learning to withhold his will from desires, however strong or attractive they may be, that he cannot fulfill by his own unaided efforts. His stoical end serves as a limiting condition on his pursuit of all other ends and is thus acknowledged as of greater value (at the limit) than any other end. But with all this, a stoical strong man cannot escape the logic of his agency. It is always possible, however strong his commitment to living without the help of others is, that he will be tempted to abandon that end—tempted to reassess the priority he has given to his independence. First, there is room for temptation where there is need for discipline and strength. We have to imagine no more than an attachment to some other end strong enough to allow for the possibility that he will be tempted to forgo his stoical end and accept help for its sake. Second, whether the conditions of life he encounters are gentle or overwhelm his strength of will is not itself something he can control. It is also then possible that he will need help in resisting that temptation (perhaps someone just to distract him for a moment, to get his mind off the question, so that he will be able to regroup and sustain his discipline). If he rejects the possibility of help here, he will no longer be able to guarantee that he will abandon any end that he discovers he cannot pursue without help. So long as temptation is an open possibility for him, the stoical man cannot (rationally, given his commitment to a stoical end) withdraw from all possibility of help from others.[12] The point of the stoic example is to dramatize a very general fact: even with the focus of one's life directed at independence from others, at the limit, this may not be a goal one can pursue unaided.[13]

The stoic succumbs to the argument against his maxim of nonbeneficence because he has an end he is committed to—his independence. But what of a "wanton" with respect to ends: someone who does not care whether any of his particular ends are realized and so seems to be attached to nothing that would require him to accept the help of others? The argument against him will go through only if there are ends that he (and so we) cannot forgo for which the help of others may be needed.

We are not like the wanton since there are ends that we may be unwilling to forgo because of their value to us—because of the sense or meaning their pursuit gives to our lives. (The stoic represents an extreme form of attachment to a single end.) We are like the wanton since even ends that we may be unwilling to give up can be given up nonetheless. Ends, however, that are necessary to sustain oneself as a rational being cannot (on rational grounds) be given up. Insofar as one has ends at all, one has already willed the continued exercise of one's agency as a rational being. The ends that must be realized if a person is to function (or continue to function) as a rational, end-setting agent come from what Kant calls the "true needs" of human agents.[14] They are the conditions of our "power to set an end" that is the "characteristic of humanity" (*DV*, 6:392). The ends set to meet our true needs are like all other ends—we cannot guarantee that we can realize them unaided. But in contrast to all other ends, we cannot on rational grounds forgo them for the sake of other contingent ends. Willing universal nonbeneficence conflicts with what, as dependent rational beings, we must will, if we will anything at all.[15]

If we are asked to imagine a life independent of things (objects) to be used as means, we cannot do so, for our existence depends on them straightforwardly. The adequacy of our skills to our needs is a contingent state of affairs. The very bounty of nature and ease of life that might make us feel we will never have to place new demands on ourselves are not of our making or within our control. Thus it would not be rational to "freeze" our skills if we could not also control our circumstances.[16] This is parallel to the idea that I mean to capture in saying that, unless one could guarantee in advance that one will not require the help of others as means to ends one could not forgo, it would not be rational to will universal nonbeneficence. It is a fact of our nature as rational beings that we cannot guarantee that we shall always be capable of realizing our ends unaided, as it is a fact of our nature that we need things and skills to pursue our ends. If what we lack is some thing, we cannot call on that object to serve our need; nor can we obtain new skills and abilities at will. But we can call on the skills and resources of others to supplement our own.

The willing of a world of nonbeneficence thus conflicts with the practical consequences of the conditions of human rationality: the natural limitations of our powers as agents. This does not involve questions of risk and thus of prudence. The natural limits of our powers as agents set the conditions of rational willing within which prudential calculations are made. It is because these limits are not transcended by good fortune that considerations of risk and likelihood are not relevant.[17] Because we are dependent rational beings with true needs, we are constrained to act in certain ways (toward outselves and toward others). Thus the argument to defeat the maxim of nonbeneficence goes through: the world of universal nonbeneficence is not a world that it is rational for any human agent to choose. And since differences among persons with regard to their neediness, strength, and so on, do not affect the argument, the duty of beneficence that emerges is of the same degree or stringency for all persons.

One might worry that the reasoning used to defeat the maxim of nonbeneficence could be employed to show that we have an implausibly strong duty of beneficence: a duty to sacrifice ourselves when that is necessary to help another in need. Suppose I consider adopting a maxim of nonsacrificial beneficence (I will help others, but not when that requires great sacrifice). I imagine a world where no one can put himself at great risk or endure great cost in order to help. Can I guarantee that I will never need help that requires sacrifice? Obviously not. Then the CI test seems to require that I reject my maxim of nonsacrificial beneficence and accept a duty of helping others at all costs.[18] Quite apart from ordinary moral objections to such a duty, it is one Kant says we do not, and morally could not, have (*DV,* 6:452).

But we need to go carefully here. The response to the nonbeneficent person turned on the claim that no human being can guarantee his never needing help that it would be irrational of him to forgo. To arrive at a duty of sacrificial beneficence, it must be that I cannot guarantee that I will not need help that requires sacrifice. And of course I cannot make that guarantee. But in the first case it is the willing of a law of universal nonbeneficence that deprives one of what one needs. In the case of nonsacrificial beneficence, it is not what is willed but the contingent unavailability of resources that raises the issue of sacrifice. When I need help that requires sacrifice, I do not need a sacrifice. (It is quite a separate issue whether, if what I need is a sacrifice, I have any claim on help at all.) Suppose I need a complete set of new organs to stay alive: that could require the sacrifice of a life for my needs. In the imagined world of universal nonbeneficence I would be denied help. But were technology different, there might be artificial organs, and my need might be met easily. Someone may starve unless he is given food. In circumstances of plenty, his need can be met with no sacrifice. In times of famine, to feed one might require the sacrifice of another. So whether I can get the help I need (in this world or in the imagined world of nonsacrificial beneficence) depends on the accidents of circumstances (resources) which make it the case that the satisfaction of my need requires sacrifice. This is not a function of my willing. The maxim of nonsacrificial beneficence therefore does not generate a contradiction in will.

But couldn't the same argument be made about needed help? When one has a need he is not able to meet, it is not help that he needs but whatever it is that he lacks. If I am hungry and unable to get food that another could bring me, his help is just the contingently available means to what I need—which is food. So there is a sense in which needing the help of others is as much a contingent feature of my circumstances of need as needing help that requires sacrifice. (I do not have control over whether I will have needs I cannot meet or over whether help can provide what I lack.) Looked at this way, the help of another is a resource for me, as a long stick might be if what separated me from food was the limit of my reach. What makes the help of others more than just a contingently available resource is the fact that only another person (or rational being) can act for me, in response to my need, in answer to my call for help. Objects and animals cannot respond to need as such, nor can they take my ends as their own. It is the potential of others to act for my needs that it is irrational to forgo: it can stand in the place of my agency.

Now it may seem that willing any maxim to be a universal law creates the possibility of conflict with other ends or maxims, and thus the risk of not being able to satisfy ends that are true needs. Someone could reasonably adopt the maxim, "To set aside 10 percent of my income for my children's education." But this maxim, considered as a universal law, might deprive the agent of just those resources required to meet his true needs at some future time. Would it therefore be impermissible to adopt such a maxim of saving? Worse still, suppose a rich person adopts, as a positive maxim of beneficence, "To help others with true needs when doing so does not threaten my own true needs." As before, willing as a universal law a maxim that calls for the expenditure of resources creates a potential risk to one's own true needs. (Suppose he thinks: if I give resources to others, then I might not be able to afford some expensive medical treatment necessary to save my life in the future. Since I cannot now guarantee that I will never need such treatment to meet my true needs, it cannot be rational to will universal beneficence!) Would the rich person then have no duty of beneficence?

The maxims of saving and of positive beneficence do not generate any such contradiction in will. In the case of the rich man, it is not his willing of positive beneficence that causes trouble in the hypothetical world but the contingent possibility that his beneficence will absorb resources he could conceivably require later to meet true needs. With the stoic or the wanton, it is a function of what each wills (given life in a community of rational persons) that, within the hypothetical world, he will be denied help. But the rich man will not be denied help as a function of what he wills when he wills positive beneficence. What he may come to need is some sort of medical treatment; his giving away resources to meet the true needs of others does not interfere with his getting that. What may interfere is the costliness of the treatment. But costliness is a contingent fact of circumstances, on a par with the unavailability of a spare kidney machine. The stoic, as a result of his willing, cannot get help. The rich man may or may not get his medical treatment: that will depend on its cost, his resources, and the helpfulness of others. The maxim of saving poses no additional difficulties.

Only if we were required to do everything possible to minimize risks to our true needs would the maxims of saving and positive beneficence generate contradictions in will. But we cannot be required to do that. Suppose we were. Then the rich man could do nothing that involved true-need-independent expenditure of resources—including the most ordinary use of his resources for pleasure. The maxims of the rich man and saver involve use of resources. The use of any resource creates the risk that some future need may not be met. That is why questions of tradeoffs are appropriate. The stoic and the wanton would permanently alienate one of the three general categories of resources available to persons to meet their needs. This is not irrational because the risk involved in the loss of all possible help is greater than any possible benefits. That is a matter of circumstantial prudential reasoning. It is irrational because a person cannot both forgo any of the general conditions of successful agency and guarantee no contradiction in will insofar as he wills other ends: a condition of rationality set by the CI procedure.

The reasoning that showed why we do not have to adopt a maxim of sacrificial beneficence can also be used to explain why a maxim of exclusively self-interested helping will be rejected (as will any such restricted maxim of the form "To help only those with characteristic $c$ or in conditions $d$" where the restrictions mark preferences, prejudices, and the like). Since one cannot control whether one has needs that may require help, so, the argument of the CI procedure will show, it is not consistent with one's rationality to restrict in advance the nature of the help available. One may be lucky and never need help that is not also in the interests of others to give. But the moral status of this possible state of affairs is just the same as that of needing any kind of help at all. Its coming to pass or not is not a possible object of human willing. I cannot make it that the help I may require satisfies some condition decided on earlier. This does not mean that it is impermissible to provide self-interested help. What is rejected is a policy of never helping unless doing so is in one's interest.

Something needs to be said now about the central place in this construal of Kant's argument of contingent, empirical facts about human beings: their dependency and their true needs. When Kant speaks of excluding empirical considerations from morality, he has two related things in mind. First, the foundation of morality is to be nonempirical. This involves a thesis about the nonempirical status of reason and an argument that it is only if morality is a function of reason that its unconditional claim on us is valid. Second, each of us is subject to moral requirements independent of any contingent, empirical ends we may happen to have. (This is the thesis that morality is not a system of hypothetical imperatives.) Kant does not need to argue (nor does he) that the content of morality is to be determined without regard to the empirical nature of things.[19]

Nonetheless one may feel, for moral reasons, that the role of dependency in the argument introduces a disturbing element. It was an important result of the argument for beneficence that among dependent, vulnerable rational beings capable of mutual aid, variations in such things as risk tolerance, or resources, do not affect the application or stringency of the duty of beneficence. But suppose there are rational beings who are not vulnerable and dependent (call them angels); the argument for beneficence could not require them to reject a maxim of nonbeneficence toward human beings. (We suppose that they are in a position to intervene in human affairs.) Angels could will a world in which no one is able to help since they cannot need help. Would they then have no duty of beneficence toward human beings? Should not all rational beings have the same duties?

All rational beings are subject to the same fundamental practical principle—the Categorical Imperative. This is all that follows merely from the fact of their rationality.[20] Not all rational beings will have the same duties. The duties they have (that is, what follows if they apply the CI to their maxims) vary as their natures vary. For example, human beings are said to have no duty to promote their own well-being (happiness) because each of us naturally desires his own happiness (*DV,* 6:386). Suppose that there were rational beings who had no such natural desire, say, natural self-sacrificers. Such beings might have to be enjoined (morally) to care for themselves, perhaps on grounds suggested by Kant's argument against the neglect of one's talents. (This reasoning would also apply to human beings bent on self-neglect or servility.) So the mere fact that angels might not have the same duty of beneficence that we do should not in itself pose a problem.

What is troubling about the possibility that angels would not have a duty to help us is that their not having such a duty seems to stem from the fact that they do not need our help. This looks to be just the sort of consideration that the new interpretation of the beneficence example was to block. But for angels it is not a contingent fact about them (there is no appeal to strength, wealth, and such) that leads them not to need help. They can guarantee that they will never be compelled to want help in the pursuit of ends that they rationally cannot abandon. That is defining of their species of rational being. So we might say that the dependency interpretation of the argument for beneficence makes use of species-relative constraints on reasoning: if you are such and such a kind of rational being, you cannot rationally will a world in which beings like yourself act (as a function of natural law) as you propose. The procedure of moral judgment shows something about what a certain sort of rational being can rationally will.[21]

The dependency argument against a policy of indifference, then, does not simply yield a duty to help others. It defines a *community* of mutual aid for dependent beings.[22] Membership in the community is established as much by vulnerability (and the possibility of being helped) as by rationality (and the capacity to help).[23] It may well be that this is not the sole duty to help others that we have. Other arguments might yield duties with different requirements, different scope (some of which might apply to angels as well). In this case it is the fact of dependency—that we are, equally, dependent (again, not that we are equally dependent)—that is the ground of the duty to help. I may not be indifferent to others not because I would thereby risk the loss of needed help (this is not a duty of fairness or reciprocity) but because I cannot escape our shared condition of dependency. The claim of each of us on the resources of the others is equal. The argument that defeats the maxim of nonbeneficence leads, positively, to a duty of mutual aid.

Membership in the community of mutual aid is more inclusive than it may first appear. Those we are unable to help can still belong to our community of mutual aid and so be obliged to help us. Imagine a race of rational dependent beings, capable of helping us, yet outside the reach of any help we have to offer. Perhaps they live too far away; perhaps we do not possess food that would nourish them; and so on. But that someone may be unable (as it happens) to be helped is the way things are among us as well. Our need for help is no guarantee that the help we need will be available or possible. Membership in the community of mutual aid gives one's need a valid *claim* on the resources of the community. The claim does not (necessarily) fail to be acknowledged when left unmet. So long as there is no ultimately unbridgeable barrier to mutual help between us and this other race—so long as it is not true that nothing we could ever do, in any possible circumstances, could be of help to them, while they continue to be able to help us[24]—their inclusion in the community will stand.

Likewise, a rational being with needs counts as a possible provider of help even though, at any given time, he is not able to provide help. Membership does not depend on one's usefulness. All that is necessary is that one be the sort of being who could—given the desire, the opportunity, and so on—provide help. So a normal adult who through illness or other disability is not able to provide help has an undiminished claim on the community's helping resources. We do not pass in and out of the community in cycles of sleep; nor are we exiled when lack of skill or resources or knowledge make us unable to help. Membership in the community is strictly a matter of one's status as a dependent rational being.

It is tempting to wonder whether a parallel line of reasoning could be used to extend the scope of the argument to include babies and future generations. The idea would be to treat the fact of being contemporaries as arbitrary with respect to membership in the community of mutual aid. Since it is not the possibility of another's being of use to me that is the ground of his claim on my help, but our both being dependent beings, capable in principle of providing help, we might regard an infant as one whose present inability to help will be overcome in the passage of time. In time, he will come to have the necessary resources to provide help, as his now "dormant" physical and rational capacities come into use. Of course, problems with this sort of argument abound and are familiar in questions of the moral status of the fetus. Still, given Kant's deep silence on the question of the moral status of children, it is of interest to follow out elements in his argument that might bear on the question.[25]

That future generations might have a claim of mutual aid (despite the fact that they will never be able to provide help for those who look to their needs) would not mean that they have an equal claim on current resources. As we shall see when we investigate the casuistry of mutual aid, a valid claim requires that one's needs be considered, not that they be met.

No parallel considerations emerge for animal-human mutual aid. We may have duties of kindness to all sentient beings, but if we do it will be for reasons different from those appealed to in the argument for mutual aid. Animals are not, strictly speaking, capable of providing help, although they may of course do things that are helpful to us. This seems to be recognized in the fact that, apart from considerations of training and discipline, we do not believe that we have any claim on an animal's help. This is not because animals are privileged or selfish or dumb. Rather, I think we suppose they are not capable of recognizing human needs as such or of conceiving of themselves as agents of help. It is these capacities that are called on by the duty of mutual aid. (Those rational capacities necessary to be able to act under the conception of meeting another's need are, in Kant's view, just those that make one a moral agent, subject to moral requirements.)

## III

If the CI procedure shows that it is impermissible to adopt the maxim, "To never help anyone," it follows that we must adopt its contradictory, "To help some others sometimes."[26] This is the maxim that describes our positive duty of mutual aid. But this maxim, as it stands, is not much of a guide to action. It does not tell us whom to help, or in what circumstances, or when we may permissibly refrain from helping. Nor does it offer a way of determining when our efforts fall short of what mutual aid requires.[27]

By contrast, when the maxim of the deceitful promise is rejected (see *G,* 422,), we know exactly what we may not do: we may not make a deceitful promise when that is necessary to extricate ourselves from financial difficulties.[28] But we do not thereby get a positive duty based on this maxim's rejection. One would get a duty to truth in promising ("Never make a deceitful promise") only if no maxim that involves not telling the truth in a promise can pass through the CI procedure. What maxims we may (permissibly) act on, in the circumstances prompting the deceitful promise maxim, are not indicated by the procedure. And it is appropriate that it be unclear what one is to do on discovering that a proposed course of action is blocked by considerations of duty. Other courses of reasoning, other proposals for action, need to be introduced and in turn examined by the CI procedure.

Part of the difficulty with the maxim of mutual aid is that it is not directly a maxim of action at all. There is no action properly described as "sometimes helping someone." One might call such a maxim a general policy maxim, in that it expresses an agent's intention to act, in general, in a certain sort of way.[29] General policy maxims stand toward specific maxims of action as their principle. So when someone fails to help because he does not, as a matter of principle, want to help those in need, we conclude that he is acting on (or out of) a maxim of nonbeneficence (a maxim contrary to mutual aid) and therefore impermissibly. This gives us enough to begin the casuistry of mutual aid.

Suppose someone acts on the maxims, "To ignore requests for charitable donations." The no-donations maxim (as stated) would not fail the CI procedures. One can will a world in which no one does (because no one can) make charitable donations without a contradiction in will, for there is nothing we must will that is not possible in a world with no charitable institutions. Is this policy then permissible?

For the purposes of moral assessment, the no-donations maxim is incomplete. Compare the following:

1. To refuse requests for charitable donations because charitable institutions are likely to be corrupt and wasteful. (Something one disapproves of.)

2. To refuse requests for charitable donations because it is better to help as one can in a more personal way. (Something one wants to do.)

3. To refuse requests for charitable donations because making such donations leads to helping those in need. (Something one does not want to do.)

The relevant differences involve the ends that bring the agent to refuse to make charitable donations. Though people acting on the three maxims behave in the same way (none gives charitable donations), there is good sense in saying they are not doing the same thing. They act on or from different principles, and the moral quality of their actions is judged differently in light of the different principles their actions instantiate. A maxim like 3 above will be judged impermissible because it is an instance of the general policy maxim, "To never help anyone." Maxims 1 and 2 raise no similar moral difficulty because their general policy maxims are permissible (let us suppose). Knowing what is behind a maxim's adoption is therefore essential to its assessment by the CI procedure. It is through the general policy maxim that the morally distinctive aspect of each is revealed. It is not the refusal to give but the purpose of principle of indifference it serves that is impermissible.

How, in general, to determine a maxim's principle is a technical matter in the theory of maxims that we cannot investigate now. What I want to argue here is that, for the purpose of practical judgment, attending to elements in the argument which defeat the maxim of general indifference can help determine if nonbeneficence is the principle behind particular maxims of not giving help.

Although the duty of mutual aid allows one not to help sometimes, in the normal course of things someone who acknowledges the duty will in fact give help. One cannot have the opportunity and the ability to help, never help, and yet claim to have (to live by) a policy of sometimes helping others. We call this hypocrisy.

Now suppose someone is in a position to give life-saving help with little cost to himself. He is just a passerby, with no special relation to the person in need. He knows it is wrong never to help anyone, and so he does, sometimes, help. This time he would rather not. But from the fact that the duty of mutual aid does not require us to promote the well-being of others on every occasion, it should not follow that we are free to refuse help to a person in distress on such grounds. The action we are considering seems to epitomize the spirit of indifference to others. How can an understanding of the argument for mutual aid help us here?

Suppose someone passes by a serious request for aid with the thought, "I helped someone yesterday." The agent acknowledges that the duty of mutual aid applies when he registers that help is needed, his would serve, and that some excuse, or excusing idea, needs to be brought forward to justify his passing by. We want to say that someone who passes by with such an excuse cannot have adopted the required maxim of mutual aid (as the principle of his maxims of action), even though he seems to accept the idea of sometimes helping someone.

Someone who monitors the frequency of his beneficent acts perhaps holds the belief that the satisfaction of the duty of mutual aid involves taking a (fair?) share of the burden of helping others; that the "sometimes" in the principle of the duty is a numerical notion—like a quota. The argument of the CI procedure shows where this belief mistakes what mutual aid requires. In requiring that we recognize one another as equal members of a community of mutual aid, we are brought to acknowledge the claim on us of others' needs. The rejection of the maxim of nonbeneficence is a rejection of indifference to others. We may not be required to help in all cases, but we may not be indifferent to the claim of need.

The fact of having done a good deed yesterday cannot weigh against that claim. If the cost of giving aid in this case is negligible,[30] there is nothing in the agent's excuse that legitimately stands between the need of the other and the help he can give. To acknowledge the claim of the other's need is just to take his need as a reason to offer help. So unless one has a morally relevant reason why one need not help, the valid claim is sufficient. Someone who rejects the claim on his help because he believes his beneficence quota has been met has failed to take the duty of mutual aid as the principle of his helping maxims.

There is a striking consequence of this. It may be my lot that people needing help are frequently in my path. If it turns out that I am often in a convenient position to help, then I must. I do exactly what I ought to do, and so no special moral merit is earned. I am no more virtuous than someone genuinely prepared to help whose encounters with those needing help are less frequent.[31] What counts, morally, is the willingness to take need as a reason to give aid. There is a parallel feature of mutual aid on the receiving side. If it is someone's misfortune to need help frequently (suppose through no fault but through bad luck and the like), he does not use up his stock of mutual aid and has a claim on the help of others that is undiminished by his past withdrawals.[32]

Morally relevant reasons for refraining from help will be those that have weight when placed against the claim of need on one's help. Suppose helping is something one would rather not (in a given case) do; or suppose it poses a minor but real inconvenience. Do these count as legitimate reasons to refrain from helping someone in distress? One way to proceed is to look further at what I have called "the claim of need." There are two issues here. First, what are the sorts of needs that are relevant to the duty of mutual aid? Surely I may not claim aid for every end I have that I cannot pursue without help. Second, when are the costs of giving aid sufficient to justify a refusal of help? When we know what the argument for the relevant class of needs is, we will know why some reasons for refraining from help do not have moral weight.

The duty of mutual aid has its ground in the facts that we are dependent beings and beings with ends that it is not rational for us to forgo: ends set by "true needs" whose satisfaction is a necessary condition for the exercise of rationality. As we are rational agents, we set ends. We are able to formulate and act from a conception of the good. If to set ends is to put oneself to the realization of more or less complex goals and projects, one respects one's humanity in oneself by developing those capacities needed to realize a wide variety of ends (*DV*, 6:392). Thus an imperfect rational being must acknowledge the obligatoriness of developing his powers and talents: they are necessary conditions of the possible expression of his rationality. As a person's true needs are those that must be met if he is to function (or continue to function) as a rational, end-setting agent, respecting the humanity of others involves acknowledging the duty of mutual aid: one must be prepared to support the conditions of the rationality of others (their capacity to set and act for ends) when they are unable to do so without help. The duty to develop (not neglect) one's talents and the duty of mutual aid are thus duties of respect for persons.

The ground of the duty of mutual aid then reveals its moral point. The good it looks to is the preservation and support of persons in their activity as rational agents. The needs for which a person may make a claim under the duty of mutual aid are those that cannot be left unmet if he is to continue in his activity as a rational agent.[33] Thus we may refrain from helping only if such action would place our own rational activity in jeopardy. Excuses that look to the ordinary difficulties encountered when help is given or that look to other helping actions recently done to get the agent off the hook therefore provide good evidence that the principle of the agent's particular maxims in the circumstances where help is needed is not that of mutual aid.

We are not obliged to help everyone, or everyone we can, because the point of the duty of mutual aid is to sustain dependent beings in the (permissible) activity of their lives. If giving aid undermines the life activity of the giver, the point of mutual aid is not achieved. (It is a duty of mutual aid, not sacrifice.) The requirements of beneficence do not interfere with what is necessary for one to continue to live a human life; they also do not protect all that one may find necessary to live as one wants. We are required to acknowledge both the claim of true need on our aid and the moral weight of that need against the claims of our own interested desires.

It is possible that a person will be called on frequently to give aid and that each time his help is needed no serious sacrifice is required. Yet the cumulative effect on his life may be such that the frequency does undermine his pursuit of his life. It is not clear to me that this affects what he is to do when help is needed again. For although his well-being is compromised over time, what he is being asked to do in a given case is not the cause. I think it is appropriate to look at such a scenario as one of moral misfortune—in much the same sense of misfortune that one would find in a series of physical accidents hindering one's legitimate pursuit of happiness. As there are historical and physical limitations on what one may expect to be able to do, so there may be moral ones—undeserved, compassion-provoking, but not changing what one is morally required to do. We might hope that the cumulative effects of past helpings would have moral weight in determining who among several possible helpers should be the one to give help, but the argument for mutual aid does not show that this is so.

In general, looking to the point of a duty lays the ground for explicating intuitions about relative stringency, setting the framework for a casuistry of excuses. Compare the Kantian arguments against deception. Kant takes the point of fidelity or nondeception to be centrally involved with sustaining what he calls "the dignity of man as a rational being" (*DV,* 6:429–30). The argument against deception is that it subverts the natural function of one's rational faculties. Therefore, excusing one's proposed deception on the grounds that honesty will jeopardize one's projects or goals (that one "needs to" deceive) will be judged impermissible because the loss of well-being is less grave than the subversion of one's rationality. What is at stake is respect for oneself as a rational being.[34] This manner of argument seems to fit well with Kant's belief that apparent conflicts of duties are to be resolved by looking to the stronger "ground" of obligation (*MM,* 6:224).

## IV

If each person, in adopting the general policy maxim of mutual aid, is to be prepared to help those in need except when the degree of sacrifice is too great, this will generate a lack of uniformity in what is required of different people in similar situations of meeting need: the cost of helping will not be the same for all persons. But in fulfillment of the duty of mutual aid, the difficulties of one's own situation are relevant in determining what one must do. This is not true for all duties. Such difficulties are irrelevant in determining whether one may deceive for self-interest, betray a trust, and so on. The facts of one's situation that are relevant differ for different kinds of duties. In a given set of circumstances it is morally appropriate that the duty of mutual aid should oblige only some people to give aid.

But different people will put different value on the cost of their helping act. And different people will decide differently about which of their needs cannot be sacrificed. How is this to be dealt with? The duty of mutual aid does require some sacrifice. We are not to help only when it costs us little or nothing. On the other hand, we do not need to help when the cost undermines our lives, and each person must judge when that is so. There can be no simple rule that will guarantee correct judgments. This is why training in casuistry is an essential part of a moral education, for when it is not taught we are more likely to require simple principles that cannot do justice to particular cases. But if we suppose that knowing how to assess one's needs is something that can be taught (to know what one may permissibly ask for as well as what one may legitimately protect), then we may expect sincere and reasonable people, with a proper attachment to their own lives and a commitment to doing what is right, to weigh fairly the cost of the helping act against the gravity of the need it will meet.

Differences in circumstances and needs do not weigh at all in the argument for the duty of mutual aid. Since we are all dependent rational beings, we are all equally obliged by the duty of mutual aid. One should not confuse the uniformity of obligation (where all of a kind of rational being must have the same obligations) with the uniformity of what one is obliged to do (which will vary with the kind of circumstances picked out as morally relevant by the duty).

If true needs set the content of the duty of mutual aid, not all (not even many) of our normal helping actions fall within the scope of mutual aid. We loan money so that pleasures do not need to be postponed; we stop and give directions; we lend a hand. These are all helping acts that (normally) are not responses to true needs. Are they actions we have a duty to do? Surely it is a good thing that people help each other. But since not everything that would be good to do is something that we are morally obliged to do, it may be that most helping actions are not matters of duty. Given the argument for the duty of mutual aid, there are two possibilities here. Either, on most occasions where we are asked for (or are in a position to) help, it is permissible not to help, or there is some other argument to a duty of aid that would cover these cases.

There are passages in the *Groundwork* and in the *Doctrine of Virtue* that suggest this stronger version of a duty of beneficence. We are to take the ends of others as our ends, to further them as we can (*G,* 430). We are to take the happiness of others as an obligatory end (*DV,* 6:387–8). It would then seem that we may limit our helping activity only when it would put us in the position of needing help ourselves, or when helping would prevent our doing something else we had a duty to do, or when we disapprove of the pursuits we are to lend a hand in promoting (*DV,* 6:388, 454). Otherwise, wherever we can help we must.

There are considerable grounds for skepticism about such a duty. It involves a radical conception of a community of need and action in which it does not seem to matter whose end an end is. All one would need to know is that a person has an end, that he is unable to realize it unaided, and that one is in a position to help. Although it is hard to avoid seeing Kant's words as implying such a duty, it is implausible in its own right and at odds with deeper features of Kantian ethics.

First, it makes no distinction between ends that an agent could easily give up on discovering that he could not realize them without aid (going to a movie on a day I am short of cash) and ends that an agent cannot rationally abandon (true needs). Both sorts of ends would have an equal claim on others. Second, the duty neglects the way in which it matters how a desire is satisfied: from what source, by whose agency. That is, the radical community of aid that such a duty describes would not be supportive of the expression of rational agency in one's life. The duty would thus be at odds with a moral conception that stressed the development of capacities for responsible choice and effective action: the practical expressions of autonomy.

There is a way of making good sense of what Kant says. One might view the idea of taking another's ends as my own not in the sense that I should be prepared to act in his place (I act for him; I get for him what he wants when he cannot) but, rather, in the sense that I support his status as a pursuer of ends, so that I am prepared to do what is necessary to help him maintain that status. We might say "I help him pursue-his-ends" and not "I help him in the pursuit of his ends." This interpretation acknowledges the other as a rational, autonomous agent in a way that the "community of ends" interpretation does not. It leads me to view the well-being of another as something more than the (passive) satisfaction of his desires. What I support is the other's active and successful pursuit of his self-defined goals. I promote another's well-being or happiness by supporting the conditions for his pursuit of ends. That is, what I have a duty to do is to contribute to the meeting of his true needs when that is not within his power. On this interpretation, then, in taking another's ends as my own or his happiness as an obligatory end, I acknowledge him as a member of the community of mutual aid.

If, within the Kantian system, the duty of mutual aid is the only duty directing us to help others, there remain reasons to offer help for less than true needs and moral reasons to encourage an attitude of helpfulness in oneself and others. Although general helpfulness (or kindness) shares with the duty of mutual aid a willingness to take the need of another as a reason for action, it is the expression of a distinct attitude toward other persons. The helpful person is willing to set aside or delay his own pursuits to ease the way for someone else. He views the other as, in a sense, a fellow pursuer of happiness. In that, they are equals. Yet it is appropriate for him to weigh costs. While it matters to him that others succeed in their (permissible) endeavors, the demands of his own pursuits need to be met. The helpful person has an interest in the well-being of others. It is this interest that makes the need of another an occasion for his acting. This is unlike the circumstances of mutual aid where the true need of another has a claim, independent of interest, on one's help.

So, if someone needs help changing a tire, a helpful person, in the absence of pressing demands of his own, will help. There is no moral requirement that he do so: it is not impermissible not to help. If, however, the person who needs this help is in great distress (someone on the way to the hospital, an elderly person who cannot tolerate exposure to bad weather), it is no longer an act of kindness but a duty to help. When if help is not given, a life will be in jeopardy or gravely diminished, then changing a tire is addressing someone's true need. It is not the action (its strenuousness, and so on) but the nature of the need to be met that determines whether it is an occasion where helping is required of us.

I am not saying that kindness and benevolence are without moral structure or content (they are not "mere inclinations"). The claim is rather that they have a different moral structure, one that parallels the difference between interests and true needs. The difference is most readily seen in the nature of the excusing conditions each allows for refraining from giving help. According to the casuistry of mutual aid, when the true needs of another constitute a claim on one's help, it does not count as a reason to justify not responding that one gave yesterday or that the price in terms of sacrificed interests (not sacrificed true needs) is high. The casuistry of benevolence accepts these as excusing considerations. When someone's life is at stake, benevolence might have us see that the cost of helping is outweighed by the gravity of the need. Mutual aid, by contrast, instructs that, if one's own true needs are not at risk, one is simply to help as one can. The needs of the other do not outweigh the losses that will be involved in giving help. The losses have no moral weight in such cases. Consequently, one might expect the casuistry of gratitude and indebtedness to be significantly different for help required by the duty of mutual aid from that called for by benevolence. This is part of what is involved in distinguishing a duty of mutual aid from benevolence. They are different moral requirements, fulfilling different moral roles. A complete Kantian account of the morality of helping should contain them both.

Nothing is required of a helpful or kind person as such. But what it is to be such a person involves a readiness to take someone's need as a reason for helping. It is an active attitude, leading one to be engaged with the lives and projects of others. We call this sort of attitude a virtue and praise (value) those who become truly helpful persons. Although the duty of mutual aid and the virtue of kindness present different moral requirements, it may be that both need to be present for the exemplary exercise of either. Although true needs usually speak for themselves, one may turn away or become preoccupied with activities insulated from encounters with others who have such needs. A kind person maintains a sense of connectedness with others, an a priori acknowledgment, as it were, that he may be of use. Kant says: "Thus it is our duty: not to avoid places where we shall find the poor who lack the most basic essentials, but rather to seek them out; not to shun the sick-rooms or debtor's prisons in order to avoid the painful sympathetic feelings that we cannot guard against" (*DV,* 6:457). Kindness, on the other hand, may need to be supplemented by the clarity about what the moral point of helpfulness is that can be derived from attention to the duty of mutual aid. Our good-heartedness is to be tempered by the moral need for self-development and struggle in others. So we should not meddle and we should be wary of impulses to paternalism, not because they may bring more harm than good (as they may) but because they go against the grain of the respectful help we are morally required to give.

There should be no suggestion here that these remarks complete the casuistry of mutual aid. I take it as barely begun. What I have hoped to demonstrate is the power of the argument for the duty of mutual aid to guide reflections on fundamental casuistical questions.

## Notes

1. The argument showing the impermissibility of nonbeneficence is one example; the others argue against suicide, deceitful promising, and neglect of talents.

2. Here I do not explicitly challenge the agreement. But the method of argument I use—especially in sections II and III—suggests that moral judgment is not best understood as an iterated sequence of passes through the CI procedure. In Chapter 7 of *The Practice of Moral Judgment* (Cambridge,

Mass.: Harvard University Press, 1993), I argue for the shift in understanding of the role of the CI procedure in moral judgment that is implicit in this chapter.

3. It is not a necessary feature of the example that the man be cold—only that he wants to refrain from any involvement in the well-being of others. The "any" here is quite thorough, for he also wishes not to envy others when they are well-off.

4. Throughout Kant's argument there is the (reasonable) assumption that, if you want something, then, other things equal, it is irrational to act in ways that prevent your getting what you want. On the connection between needing help, wanting it, and willing that one be helped, I will have more to say later.

5. The "contradiction" arises in the ordinary case from the effects, over time, of holding to a general policy of not saving. Under the CI procedure, these conditions are simulated by the supposition that the intended maxim becomes a universal law of action. In the first case, I place irrational constraints on my future actions through commitment to a general policy. In the beneficence example, the constraints are there through the inaction of others, imagined to come about through my willing of a policy of nonbeneficence.

6. In Kant's terminology we would describe the resolution of the conflict as either abandoning the policy or giving up the end of wanting help. To adopt $x$ as an end is to set oneself to bring about $x$. To give up $x$ as an end is to forgo $x$ (not to act to bring about $x$ or, when necessary, to act to prevent $x$ from coming about). It does not follow from giving up $x$ as an end that one no longer has a desire for $x$. Adopting the attitude toward $x$ that it is a tolerable unfulfilled desire is a way of giving up $x$ as an end.

7. Henry Sidgwick, *The Methods of Ethics,* 7th ed., (New York: Dover Publications, 1966), p. 389n.

8. This account is drawn from Rawls's lectures on Kant's ethics at Harvard in 1977 and from a written version of those lectures that he generously made available to his students. Since at some points I introduce elements based on interpretive conjecture, Rawls might not endorse the views that I attribute to him. Yet the account I give seems to me "Rawlsian" in spirit and, in any case, worthy of examination since it provides such a tempting amendment to Kant's argument.

9. Rawls finds a textual support for such a move in the "Typic of Pure Practical Judgment" (*Critique of Practical Reason,* 68–72).

10. See *G,* 424. Moreover, given the structure of the CI procedure for moral judgment, unless the agent is able to formulate his maxim in a way that includes the relevant moral precept—in a way that uses his moral knowledge—it would be remarkable if the proposed action were described in a way that captured its morally problematic features.

11. It does not follow from the fact that the agent needs to see that his particular circumstances do not warrant an exception from a rule of duty that the assessment of his maxim must be through a procedure allowing him to take his point of view. An impartial procedure could show that as well. I am arguing only that a procedure that does allow him to maintain his point of view would be more effective (a practical argument) and that such a procedure provides a more natural reading of the passages in which Kant sets out the procedures of judgment of the first formulation of the CI.

12. It seems to me a strength of Kant's argument that we are pushed to the edge of what we can imagine to find a potential exception to the CI procedure. To force the stoic example further, to deny that the stoic will form attachments or pursue projects in a way that will make him vulnerable (only) to temptation is to save his independence by sacrificing the idea of his having a life. Bernard Williams uses this sort of strategy in his Humean counter to the possibility of a complete egoism. See his "Egoism and Altruism," in *Problems of the Self* (Cambridge: Cambridge University Press, 1973). I can imagine someone forgoing ends for the sake of some project or commitment. Then it seems to me that I can imagine someone being prepared to forgo all ends for the sake of stoical independence. But from the fact that I can imagine someone lifting something I am not strong enough to lift, it does not follow that I can imagine someone lifting my house, although I can picture it (form an image).

13. Stephen Engstrom, in "Herman on Mutual Aid," *Ethics* 96:2 (1986), 346–349, has argued that this analysis mistakes the nature of the stoic's end. He suggests that the end belongs to a class of ends that are "personal in the sense that the possibility of assistance from others is ruled out by the nature of the end itself." If someone wants to solve a difficult geometry problem, his "chances of doing so will be ruined by someone who, says, gives [him] hints that makes the problem easy to solve." There appears to be nothing irrational in refusing help for such personal ends. This misses the strangeness of the stoic's end. There is nothing irrational in accepting all kinds of support while working on the geometry problem: a glass of juice, some quiet, a pad of paper. Having a personal end does not remove one from the normal network of social support. Yet it is from just this network that the stoic seeks independence. This fact, and not the fact that the end is personal, accounts for his double bind. Further, personal ends fit within a framework of other ends and projects. Part of the structure of a personal end will (typically, not necessarily) include provision for failure: it may make sense, given other ends, to get help if the problem proves to be too hard (though it can also make sense, given other ends, to hold that if *this* problem resits one's efforts, one should abandon the project). Because the stoic's end is regulative with respect to all his other ends, he cannot accept help, but he can have no *reason* to reject help if he thereby abandons his stoical end.

14. This term is introduced in *DV*, 6:393. Rawls also appeals to "true needs" to explain which ends a person, behind a veil of ignorance, would agree to have covered by a duty of beneficence.

15. It does not follow from this that we may never will self-sacrificially or choose to forgo help (suppose the only help available involved impermissible action). It is only within the fiction of the CI procedure that forgoing all help produces a contradiction in will.

16. This is of course the ground of the argument against neglect of talents in the third *Groundwork* example.

17. This seems to me a significantly different acknowledgment from the realization, behind a veil of ignorance, that without knowledge of one's personal strengths and fortune it is not rational to risk nonbeneficence.

18. A better way of evaluating the maxim of nonsacrificial beneficence is

through the agent's justifying reasons. An argument that shows the impermissibility of a maxim of nonbeneficence tout court sets a moral presumption the more restricted maxim must rebut. We then ask whether the exclusion of sacrificial acts is out of respect for the conditions of our agency or instead expresses a desire not to give when it hurts. This method of judgment and deliberation is argued for in Chapter 7 of *The Practice of Moral Judgment*; it also explains the practice of section III of this chapter.

19. A clear argument for this can be found in Allen Buchanan, "Categorical Imperatives and Moral Principles," Chapter 7 in this volume.

20. Being subject to the CI does not even entail obligation. Only imperfectly rational beings are under moral constraint.

21. One might argue in a slightly different way here. The contradiction-in-will test depends on an agent's appreciating what he must will, given his nature, under the assumption that his maxim is to become a universal law of nature. A rational being with a different nature might require a different kind of test to show it its duties. That is, from the fact that a course of reasoning does not generate a duty for angels, it might not follow that angels have no such duty. The CI procedure might not represent an exhaustive procedure of judgment for all rational beings. Its usefulness, and its validity, might be tied to the nature of the being using it. Kant discusses the constraints imposed on the procedure of moral judgment by features of the human imagination in the second *Critique*'s "Typic of Pure Practical Judgment."

22. In *DV*, 6:453 Kant concludes that the argument for beneficence compels us to regard one another as "fellow-men—that is, rational beings with needs, united by nature in one dwelling place for the purpose of helping one another."

23. Schopenhauer argued (1) that Kant's argument for beneficence has an egoistic foundation because we are moved to reject nonbeneficence in order to ensure the satisfaction of our natural inclinations and needs, and (2) that the CI procedure itself therefore depends on conditions derived from our inclinations, which Kant holds that we, as rational beings, must want to overcome. See *On the Basis of Ethics* (1840), trans. E. F. J. Payne (New York: Liberal Arts Press, 1965), pt. 2, no. 7, pp. 89–92. The dependency interpretation, however, works from the practical conditions of human rationality, which are a function not of inclination but of the natural limitations of our powers as agents. There need be nothing egoistic in the content of the maxims which generate a contradiction in will. A rational, perfectly altruistic human being would be equally subject to the duty of mutual aid for the same reason, and in response to the same facts about his human nature, that apply in the ordinary case.

24. If there were in principle no way one could help, it is not clear to me in what sense the need of the other could establish a claim. When as a matter of fact one cannot help, there is a sense of how things could be otherwise. If the help can in principle go only one way, we might have to imagine something like one-way causality. I suppose this is the nature of a relation to God. His acts are, of course, miracles. There is nothing in principle we could do that could be of help. (None of our actions could reach God: he is not within the realm of our effects; but then he is also not a dependent being.) It may be a feature

of God's goodness that he will acknowledge human need, but his doing so would not follow from any acknowledgment of shared dependency.

25. Considerations extending the argument to infants would not take account of defective rational beings. In those cases, the inability to help cannot be seen as a function of naturally transient circumstances. Perhaps the model here should be innocent loss of resources.

26. That is, it would not be permissible to fail to adopt this maxim. That would not prevent one from having a more extensive maxim of mutual aid: the rejection of "Never help anyone" sets a minimal maxim of mutual aid.

27. There are always such issues for duties of wide obligation, as Kant calls them: they leave room for choice. The question is of what sort. In this section, I sketch a casuistry for mutual aid based on the fact that the argument for the duty establishes a claim of need.

Kant offers two suggestions about imperfect duties worth noting. The first relies on the *Groundwork* division of duties: perfect duties differ from imperfect duties in that the former allow "no exception for the sake of inclination" (*G*, 421n). This seems very un-Kantian. Why should any sort of duty allow exceptions for inclination? Could one refrain from helping A because of fondness for B? May one withhold help because one is inclined to do something else? It does not follow from the fact that I may make exception for *some* inclination that the grounds for excepting an inclination are arbitrary; but the *Groundwork* division of duties gives no guidance. A second interpretation of the choice that attends duties of wide obligation marks the fact that they are duties to adopt an end: "if the law can prescribe only the maxims of actions, not actions themselves, this indicates that it leaves a play-room *(latitudo)* for free choice in following (observing) the law, i.e. that the law cannot specify what and how much one's actions should do toward the obligatory end.—But a wide duty is not to be taken as a permission to make exceptions to the maxim of actions, but only as a permission to limit one maxim of duty by another (e.g. love of one's neighbor in general by love of one's parents)—a permission that actually widens the field for the practice of virtue" (*DV*, 6:390). That is, "latitude of duty" allows exception for inclinations (love of parents) only when they are taken up into a more restricted maxim of duty. There is room for judgment, but judgment constrained by a complex array of moral requirements.

28. Or, if we follow Allen Wood's interpretation, the argument for the second example yields the more general result that we may not use deceitful promises as means in promoting our self-interest. See "Kant on False Promises," in *Proceedings of the Third International Kant Congress*, ed. L. W. Beck (Dordrecht: D. Reidel, 1972), pp. 614–619.

29. Although all maxims are general in form ("To do *x*, in circumstances *y*, in order to *z*"), a maxim of action need involve no commitment or intention to act in similar ways in similar circumstances.

30. It does matter if helping turns out to be costly, disrupting one's life and basic projects; but that is not relevant to the case at hand.

31. There is a fuller argument for this nonquantitative model of virtue in Chapter 2, section II, of *The Practice of Moral Judgment.*

32. This sort of case is complicated when the needy person requires con-

stant help from the same source. Then we are inclined to think that a relationship of dependency has formed, which might well alter what each might legitimately expect from the other. How such cases are to be understood will figure importantly in the full casuistry of mutual aid, but they must not be taken up at the outset, when the relevant reasons in deliberations about mutual aid are being laid out.

33. It might seem that the stoic had grounds drawn from the argument against his maxim of nonbeneficence to claim aid for his end of independence. But that argument showed he could not guarantee that he could act unaided for any end, even his end of independence from aid. It establishes the inescapability of the condition of dependency. The duty of mutual aid follows as there are ends that cannot be abandoned (true needs). The stoic remains free to abandon his stoical end.

34. This suggests an interesting contrast with the duty of promise keeping. I would think that this duty would be less stringent in the face of serious misfortune. Let us conjecture that the good this duty looks to is the security of mutual expectations. If keeping a promise would endanger one's life (or the conditions for the exercise of one's rationality), it would be reasonable to see that fact as sufficient to excuse breaking it. Moreover, if keeping the promise would involve such loss, one might suppose the duty of mutual aid would require the promisee to release the promisor from his obligation. (It is, after all, a duty to help where we can.) Of course it might be relevant to consider whether the promisee was the only one in a position to help and the release from the promise the only way to avert the loss. However this worked out, the purpose here in pursuing these speculations is to emphasize the role the point of a duty plays in determining the duty's scope and stringency.

# 7

# Humanity As End in Itself

*Allen Wood*

This paper will discuss Kant's second formulation of the moral law in the *Groundwork*, the "formula of humanity as end in itself":

> FH: "Act so that you use humanity, in your own person as well as in that of another, always also as an end and never only as a means" (*G*, 429).[1]

Most people associate Kantian ethics most closely not with FH but with the "formula of universal law":

> FUL: "Act only according to a maxim by which you can at the same time will that it should be a universal law" (*G*, 421).

But there are several reasons for emphasizing FH. First, there are notorious problems, arising from the criticism of Hegel and others, with FUL as a procedure for moral reasoning. For those who are sympathetic to the criticisms of FUL (and I am among them), it is worth looking closely at FH to see if we cannot do better by Kantian ethics if we associate it with FH. Secondly, the idea of human dignity which grounds FH is in any case the Kantian principle which arguably has the greatest resonance with our culture's moral consciousness. This idea even has the greatest universal appeal, since it seems to ground the human rights in terms of which decent people everywhere frame both their protests against obvious wrongs and their ideals of a better world. Thirdly, it is to FH which Kant himself nearly always appeals in the *Metaphysics of Morals* when he derives particular ethical duties.[2] FH is also the only formulation of the *moral* principle Kant ever invokes in relation to the *right* of human beings, which makes FH uniquely pertinent to issues of political right and international law, including the final end of perpetual peace (*G*, 430; *MM*, 6:236, 238, 239, 270, 278, 295). Finally, FH has much to teach us about Kantian ethical theory itself. For (in contrast to common misunderstandings of that theory) it presents ethics as based on an *end*, whose character, however, clearly distinguishes Kant's theory from all forms of consequentialism.

FH strikes many people as high-sounding but too abstract to yield determinate moral prescriptions, and hence just as "formal" and empty as FUL. People wonder what it means to claim that human beings are "ends in themselves," and whether Kant has any good argument for according them this special moral status (whatever it may turn out to be). These worries are not entirely without substance, but I think they are due partly to a failure to understand some of the value conceptions employed in FH and the meaning of claims Kant employs in its defense. These are the matters on which I hope to shed some light.

In this paper I will try to do three things. First, I will try to say something about what FH means, by discussing the different value conceptions involved in it and their relation both to FH and to one another. Second, I will examine Kant's derivation of FH in the *Groundwork*, his argument that humanity does have the value FH attributes to it, of being an end in itself. Finally, I will try to say something about how FH is to be interpreted and applied.

## 1. What Is an 'End in Itself'?

FH is introduced by way of an inquiry into the possibility of a will's conforming itself to a categorical imperative or practical law. It is supposed to address a question to which many of Kant's critics think he has no good answer: namely, *why*—for what reason or motive, or in the name of what value—should we obey categorical imperatives? FH formulates the moral law in terms of the value which provides the kind of ground or reason which could motivate a rational being to act on a categorical imperative. In other words, FH provides the content of what Kant described in the First Section of the *Groundwork* as the motive of duty—an idea which many have found objectionably cold, empty and forbidding. It may make that idea more attractive to realize that for Kant, to act from duty means to act out of esteem for the worth of humanity in someone's person as an end in itself. We then see that when Kant regards the cold-hearted man who helps others from duty as more deserving of esteem than the warm-hearted person who helps them from sympathy, he is not saying that it is bad to care about people and good only to follow abstract rules. Instead, he is saying that it is better to care about people because we recognize them as beings with worth and dignity, who have a genuine claim on our concern, than because we just happen to like them or because in our present mood helping them makes us feel good.

Kant distinguishes two types of grounds on which a will may act: subjective grounds, based on empirical desire for an object, and an objective ground, which is also an end, but one given by reason alone and valid for all rational beings. A subjective ground is called an "incentive" (*Triebfeder*), while an objective ground is called a "motive" (*Bewegungsgrund*) (*G*, 427–428). The most striking thing Kant says here is that a motive must always be an end (*Zweck*). This might seem to contradict what he says elsewhere. In the *Critique of Practical Reason*, for instance, Kant distinguishes between "formal principles" of the will, whose determining ground consists solely in the "legislative form" of the agent's maxim, and "material principles," whose determining ground is the end of the action. Formal principles alone, Kant says, can be practical laws; material principles are all empirical, fall under the principle of one's own happiness, and are opposed to the determination of the will by reason alone (*CPracR*, 5:21–22).

Yet on closer inspection there is no real disagreement between the two texts. The *Groundwork* draws the same distinction between "formal" and "material" principles, characterizing material principles as based on "incentives," and formal principles as based on motives (*G*, 427). When the second *Critique* says that the ground of a formal principle is the "legislative form of the maxim," that is "the mere form of giving universal law" (5:27), the *Groundwork* merely tells us that this form, when it motivates us, constitutes a certain distinctive kind of end. If it surprises us that Kant should have characterized the legislative form or the motive duty as an *end*, we should investigate further to see why he does so.

Light is shed on this question by something Kant argued twenty years earlier in his prize essay, *Inquiry Concerning the Distinctness of the Principles of Natural Theology and Morals* (1764).

No specifically determinate obligation flows from [any formal grounds of obligation] unless they are combined with indemonstrable material principles of practical cognition. . . . They cannot be called obligations as long as they are not subordinated to an end which is necessary in itself (2:298–299).

To those who think of Kant's ethical theory as "deontological" in the sense that it is a theory which regards moral principles as binding independent of any end served in following them, it should be enlightening to find Kant explicitly rejecting any such position, and to realize that it is this rejection which lies behind the *Groundwork's* argument that a rational will can be motivated to obey a categorical imperative only by a distinctive kind of end.

Kant begins with a hypothetical account of the kind of value he ascribes to humanity or rational nature.

> Suppose, however, that there were something *whose existence in itself* had an absolute worth, which, as *end in itself* could be the ground of determinate laws; then in it and it alone would lie the ground of a possible categorical imperative, i.e. a practical law (*G*, 4:428).

Here Kant invokes three distinct value conceptions.

*First*, there is the conception of an *end in itself* or *objective* end, whose worth, as the ground of categorical imperatives, is *unconditional*, independent of desire and valid for all rational beings, a "motive" constraining the will through its own faculty of reason. The opposite of an end in itself is therefore a *relative end*, whose worth is relative to, conditioned by and dependent on the subjective constitution of each particular rational being, and hence varying contingently from one such being to another. This sort of end would be only an "incentive" and could ground only hypothetical imperatives (*G*, 428).

*Second*, Kant introduces the concept of an *existent* end, or, as Kant also calls it, a *self-sufficient* end (*G*, 437). Kant opposes this sort of end to an *end to be effected*, that is, some thing or state of affairs which does not yet exist, but is to be brought about through an agent's causality (*G*, 437). An existent end, by contrast, is something that already exists, and whose "existence is in itself an end," having worth as something to be esteemed, preserved and furthered. This concept perhaps requires a bit of discussion, because people are often tempted to think that the concept of an end is nothing but the concept of a not yet existent object or state of affairs to be brought about. Until this prejudice is overcome, the idea of an existent end may appear nonsensical, self-contradictory, or at least peculiar and suspicious. But it is nothing of the kind.

An end is anything *for the sake of which* we act (or refrain from acting). Or, what I think amounts to the same thing, an end is something whose value provides some kind of terminus in a chain of reasons for an action. These descriptions fit ends to be effected, since when we build a house, our action is for the sake of bringing the house into being, and the house's value to us is the reason why we build. But they also fit existing things or states of affairs, for whose sake we act. My self-preservation as an existent end, because I cross the street at the crosswalk (rather than charging out into traffic) for the sake of preserving my life, and the value I place on my life is my reason for crossing the street in the way I do; of people who drive recklessly or put themselves in needless danger we say that they place less value on their lives than most of us do.

Other kinds of existent ends often play a role in our actions. When people bow their heads or doff their hats to their country's flag or to a religious object, they may have no end to be effected, except perhaps the successful performance of the gesture of veneration itself. But they certainly do act for an end, namely, the value of the revered object. It is for the sake of this value that they perform the act of respect or reverence. Finally, when I build a house for myself and my family I build not only for the sake of the value of the house but also for *my* sake and that of my family; in fact, I value the house as our dwelling only because I place value on myself, my spouse and my children. The existence of the house is an end to be effected, but we are the existent ends for whose sake the producible end is pursued.

Kant's theory maintains that to act morally is always to act for the sake of the value of humanity in a person. FH is based, in other words, on the worth of humanity regarded as an existent end, that is, as an object of respect, esteem or veneration. From the standpoint of FH, all conduct is regarded fundamentally from the standpoint of what it *expresses* about the agent's valuation of humanity. Morally good conduct is that which expresses respect for humanity as an existent end, while bad conduct is bad because it expresses disrespect (or lack of respect) for this value.

But what is it to value, respect or esteem the value of humanity? We will be misled here if we think of "valuing," "respecting" and "esteeming" merely as subjective attitudes or states of mind, and interpret FH as commanding only that we put ourselves in such inner states. If I make a promise to you which I don't intend to keep, then I am treating humanity in your person with disrespect, no matter what subjective attitude I may have or what inner state I may be in. On the other hand, in dealing honestly with you, I treat you with respect in that dealing even if I do so only from self-interested motives and will cease treating you with respect as soon as it ceases to serve my self-interest. The actions commanded by FH are those which express respect for humanity, whatever the subject's feelings toward humanity may be. Of course Kantian ethics is not indifferent to what motivates the respect or disrespect shown to humanity. An action which expresses a respect the agent does not feel accords with duty, but it has no moral worth because it is not produced by the motive of duty, which is the worth of humanity as an existent end in itself.

Kant famously insists that practical philosophy must not begin with an end or object of reason and attempt to derive the moral law from that, but must instead begin with the law or principle of reason and through it determine the object or end of practical reason, or the good (*CPracR*, 5:58). He insists that determination of the will by its objects always results in heteronomy of the will (*G*, 440). In such claims, he appears always to have in mind an end to be produced (e.g. the highest good or *summum bonum*), as something to be "obtained" through conduct which follows the law (*CPracR*, 5:108). He is mainly concerned to reject the view that moral principles may be based on the representation of a future object or state of affairs, such as happiness or well-being, the representation of which gives pleasure and stimulates the will to actualize the object of the representation (*CPracR*, 5:22–26, 58–62). Kant does not mean to deny that conformity to the law itself must be motivated by a value; on the contrary, he claims that *only* a certain existent end is capable of determining the will to follow the moral law (*G*, 427). This end, the worth of humanity as end in itself, does not undermine autonomy simply because, as we shall see presently, its value is necessarily connected with autonomy. The worth of humanity as an end in itself (in our own person) may even be seen as the value which grounds autonomy itself, from the standpoint of our *motivation* to act autonomously.[3]

The *third* value conception we need to consider is that of an *end with absolute worth* or (as Kant also says) *dignity*, something whose value cannot be compared to, traded off against, or compensated for or replaced by any other value (*G*, 434). This is to be contrasted with an end with only relative worth or *price*, whose value can be measured against the value of something else and can be rationally sacrificed to obtain something else of equivalent or greater worth. It is this absolute worth in our own person, and specifically in our rational capacity to set ends and make laws, which provides the motive for obeying the laws we give ourselves through reason. That is the sense in which even autonomy itself is grounded on the worth of humanity as an end in itself.

Now let us consider these three value conceptions in relation to each other and to the value attributed to humanity in FH. Kant's position is that there is only one thing, namely humanity or rational nature, which satisfies the concept of end in itself; and humanity is in fact also an existent (or self-sufficient) end having absolute worth or dignity. As far as these three value conceptions themselves are concerned, however, there is no reason the three value properties would have to be found together. There is no contradiction in supposing that an end in itself might be an end to be produced: that is, that there should be some thing or future state of affairs which we have an objective reason to produce independently of any contingent desire for it. An end in itself might also be an end with only relative worth or price. In that case, rational deliberation would be able to weigh objective ends against the ends which depend on our desires, and a certain amount of what is objectively valuable might be rationally traded away to get a greater amount of what is subjectively valuable. Conversely, we sometimes do things for the sake of non-human animals, regarding them as existent ends, even though they are not (at least in Kant's view) ends in themselves and do not have absolute worth. Moreover, an end having absolute worth could be both a relative end and an end to be effected. This would happen, for instance, if there were an object of inclination to whose satisfaction we gave absolute priority over everything else in our scheme of values.

Therefore, Kant's attribution of all three value properties to humanity or rational nature is not a conceptual claim about these value properties. It is instead a substantive value claim about that which in fact possesses the property of being an objective end or end in itself, namely humanity. The claim is that humanity is an end in itself whose objective value takes the form of its being an existent or self-sufficient end which has dignity or absolute worth.

What does Kant mean by 'humanity' when he says it is an end in itself? The term refers to the capacity to set ends and choose means to them (*G*, 437). It is being used interchangeably with 'rational nature.'

For this reason, FH in no way contradicts Kant's frequent assertions that the moral law is independent of empirical anthropology. FH also does not privilege the members of our own species over other possible rational beings, and involves no preference toward members of our own species just because it is ours (and therefore is not a form of "speciesism," in Peter Singer's sense). "Humanity" is one of the three "original predispositions" belonging to our nature, falling midway between 'animality' and (3) 'personality' (*Rel*, 6:26). The predisposition to humanity includes the "technical predisposition," which includes all our learned skills and deliberative abilities used for arbitrary ends, and the "pragmatic predisposition," which is the basis of our ability to compare our contingent ends and organize them into a systematic whole, which is called 'happiness' (*Anth*, 7:322–324; *CJ*, 5:426–427). Humanity, therefore, refers to the capacity to set ends in general, to select means to them, and to weigh and combine them into a conception of our overall well-being.

"Personality" is the rational capacity to respect the moral law and to act having duty or the moral law as a sole sufficient motive of the will; it is the basis of moral accountability, and what makes it possible for us to have a good will (*Rel*, 6:27–28). Personality therefore seems to be a 'higher' predisposition than 'humanity.' For this reason, it may puzzle us that Kant regards 'humanity' rather than 'personality' as the end in itself. But Kant does not regard personality as distinct from humanity. The rational capacity to set and organize ends necessarily involves the capacity to make comparative judgments of value and therefore an (at least implicit) awareness of standards of value. The foundation of all such standards, if Kant is right, is the dignity of rational nature itself. Therefore, any being which has humanity will have the capacity to recognize the worth of humanity, and will therefore have personality as well. In fact, Kant specifically links the *dignity* (absolute worth) of rational nature (as distinct from its status as an end in itself) to its capacity to be morally self-legislative, thus to personality rather than to humanity (*G*, 437–440). So the designation of humanity as an end in itself is not meant to imply that personality has any lesser value than humanity.

The point of characterizing the end in itself as humanity rather than as personality is simply to emphasize that this end is rational nature, in all its functions and not merely in its moral function. This follows directly from Kant's argument that the end in itself must ground categorical imperatives. For since such imperatives must be necessarily binding on all rational beings, the end which grounds them cannot have merely contingent or even doubtful existence, as it would if it were present only in the good will or the virtuous person. A morality grounded on the principle that only virtuous people have worth could not issue categorical imperatives capable of determining the will.[4]

## 2. Kant's Argument for the Formula of Humanity

Let us now turn to Kant's derivation of FH, which is also his argument that humanity is the sole end in itself. This argument has four steps, which I will separate and number for the sake of perspicuity.

> The ground of [the moral principle] is: *Rational nature exists as end in itself.*
>
> [1] This is how the human being necessarily represents its own existence; to this extent, therefore, it is a *subjective* principle of human actions.
>
> But [2] every other rational being also represents its existence consequent to precisely the same rational ground which is valid for me;
>
> [3] therefore, it is at the same time an *objective* principle, from which, as a supreme practical ground, all laws of the will must be able to be derived.
>
> [4] The practical imperative will therefore be the following: *Act so that you use humanity in your own person, as well as in the person of every other, always at the same time as end, never merely as a means"* (G, 429).

In this argument, (1) and (2) may appear to be independent premises, though as we shall see, (2) is best understood as grounded on (1). In (3) Kant infers that rational nature as an end in itself provides an objective principle, and (4) formulates that principle. The main difficulties with the argument concern the interpretation of (1). (1) evidently harmonizes with Kant's view that propositions of ultimate good are indemonstrable and can be argued for only by appealing to what is already somehow acknowledged or presupposed to be of ultimate value. Thus (1) involves Kant's anticipation of Mill's idea that principles of ultimate value are indemonstrable, though they can be argued for rationally and even 'proven' in a looser sense of 'proof,' by showing that what the principle takes to be valuable is already, "in theory and in practice, acknowledged to be an end."[5]

Beyond this, however, (1) is difficult to interpret. At first reading it looks like merely a universal empirical generalization about the worth people subjectively attribute to their existence. So regarded, it would clearly be false since in fact people sometimes do think of their own existence as lacking in value. Even if it were a true empirical generaliza-tion, it could not sustain Kant's claim that every rational being *neces-sarily* represents its existence as an end in itself. Nor, finally, could (1) on this reading be put together with premise (2) to yield the argu-ment's conclusion, since a mere subjective representation of my exis-tence as an end in itself would not provide any *rational ground* for representing the existence of *every other* rational being in the same way. It is only the existence of such a ground which could justify the objective principle whose existence is inferred in (3) and finally formu-lated in (4).

But these considerations may make it possible for us to reconstruct how (1) would have to be taken if Kant's argument is to work. (1) would have to mean that necessarily, rational beings *subjectively* repre-sent their existence in some way which brings to light an *objective* ground for regarding them as ends in themselves.[6] (1) therefore means that whenever a human being sets an end for itself through reason, it thereby necessarily represents itself (if only obscurely or inexplicitly) as having some property which makes it an end in itself, thus providing all rational beings with an objective ground for respecting its absolute worth. In the *Groundwork* Kant identifies this feature as the capacity to set ends, and says that the worth of rational nature as an end in itself can be inferred from the fact that it is the subject of all possible ends.

> Rational nature is distinguished from others in that it sets an end for
> itself. . . . It is that which must never be acted against and which must
> never be valued merely as a means but in every volition also as an end.
> Now this end can never be other than the subject of all possible ends
> themselves (*G*, 437).[7]

Christine Korsgaard is on the right track in suggesting that Kant be-gins from the value we place on the ends we set, and infers (by means of a "regress on conditions") that this value is grounded in the rational nature of the being who set the end. She claims that rational nature therefore possesses a "value-conferring status" in relation to the ends it sets. Because humanity or rational nature is the source of all such value, it is regarded as absolutely and unconditionally valuable, and an end in itself.[8] Crucial to this line of reasoning is the idea that when we set an end we attribute to it *objective* value or goodness. Goodness, whether moral nor nonmoral, is objective value in the sense that the good is represented by reason as practically necessary (as either means or end) and hence as an object of will for all rational beings (*G*, 412). The fact that every end we set is represented by us as good therefore entails that it is represented by us as having a rational claim on the will of every rational being. The idea here is *not* that all goodness is only subjective (because it depends on the choice of the being who sets the end and considers it good), but on the contrary, that rational choice of ends is the act through which objective goodness enters the world, and the fact that rational nature serves as this source of all value is supposed to imply that it has objective value as an end in itself.

It might prove illuminating to consider Kant's conception of objective value in light of J. L. Mackie's contention that "objective goodness" is a "queer" property because it has to be "objectively prescriptive."[9] Mackie is operating within the options standardly available within twentieth century analytical metaethics. He is supposing that either goodness exists only relative to desire (it is only "subjective") or else it is real out there in the world (as something "objective"). In the latter case, goodness is either something which necessarily provides reasons for action (if we hold what is called "internalism") or else such reasons must be added contingently to it (as "externalism" maintains). In the latter case, the good gives us reasons to act only if along with it there is contingently present in us some desire or attitude disposing us toward the good (which once again reduces the authority of the good to something merely subjective). The good has genuine practical authority, therefore, only if internalism is accepted. But then real goodness must be a property out there in the world which somehow of itself tells us what we must do—it must be Mackie's "queer" property of being "objectively prescriptive".

The options canvassed so far, however, do not include any Kant would find attractive. Kant maintains that goodness is indeed objectively prescriptive, but not because there is some queer property out there in the world which imposes itself prescriptively on the will (thus violating its autonomy). Kant instead locates the good's objective prescriptivity in precisely the sort of thing which might naturally have been thought to prescribe: namely, the rational will itself. It says that the objectivity of a will's prescriptions comes from its rational capacity to make objective laws and set ends having objective value. The source of all such value is therefore nothing except the value of the rational will itself. Rational volition is what makes it the case that other things are good (i.e. that they make objective claims on human beings). Rational volition can do this only if it is presupposed that the worth of rational nature is that which makes such claims necessarily and unconditionally. In other words, the autonomy of the will can be reconciled with the objectivity of value only if the sole object of value which is not legislated to be such by the will is the absolute value of the legislating will itself as the single necessary ground of all objective value.

Kant's argument for FH depends on an inference from the premise that the objective goodness of all ends is grounded in rational nature to the conclusion that rational nature itself is objectively good or an end in itself. We might balk at this inference on the ground that if Y is something valuable and X is its source, it does not in general follow that X is something valuable, still less that it is objectively valuable or an end in itself. Sometimes in such cases we don't consider X itself good at all, but merely tolerate it as a necessary evil required to procure Y. So even if we grant that the rational will is the source of all objective values, it does not seem to follow that it is valuable, still less that it is absolutely valuable.

But this objection misses the point, because in Kant's argument rational nature is not being viewed as the source of good things (of their existence, for example), but rather as the source of their goodness itself, of the very fact that they are good, indeed, of the fact that anything at all is good. The right parallel here is rather with our attitude toward an authority as a source of recommendations or commands. It makes sense for us to take someone's advice or prescription as authoritative only to the extent that we respect and esteem the authority itself as their ground. Hence we have reason to regard as good the ends we ourselves set only to the extent that we (at least implicitly) respect and esteem our own rational nature as that which sets them.

More generally, if something is good only through being made the object of rational choice, then the capacity to make such choices is the sole authority over goodness, or as Kant puts it, "the subject of all possible ends." If rational nature is the prescriptive source of all objective goodness, then it must be the most fundamental object of esteem or respect, since if it is not respected as objectively good, then nothing else can be regarded as objectively good. Rational nature is therefore the only thing which could answer to the concept of an objective end or end in itself.

In the Second Section of the *Groundwork*, Kant has provisionally assumed that there is a categorical imperative. He has argued that if there is such an imperative, then the possibility of its determining the will depends on there being an objective end or end in itself. Thus if, as we have just seen, rational nature is the only thing which could answer to the conception of such an end, then Kant is entitled to conclude that rational nature, and it alone, is an end in itself.

### 3. Applying the Formula of Universal Law

This will have to suffice as a discussion of Kant's argument for FH. I now turn to the question of interpreting and applying FH in moral deliberation. It was said earlier that to many people FH seems a highly abstract principle from which determinate moral conclusions would be hard to derive. Now it is time to consider the reasons why FH gives this impression, and to what extent it is accurate.

FH involves a kind of moral appeal which is unfamiliar in philosophical theories of morality. Consequentialist theories represent the fulfillment of our duties as bringing about desirable states of affairs; deontological ones (including Kant's own theory, to the extent that we consider only formulas such as FUL) represent it as obedience to an obligatory rule or commandment. FH, however, bases duties on the *worth* of something—on the dignity of rational nature as an end in itself. This is not a rule or principle to be obeyed, but a value which grounds moral rules, providing an objective rational motive for obeying them. But it is not a value in the sense of a desired object to be brought about through obeying moral principles. It is something existing, whose value is to be respected in our actions. What FH demands of our actions is not that they *pursue* some good result or *obey* some obligatory rule but rather that they *express* due respect for the worth of humanity. Since FH identifies the end in itself which is the objective determining ground of the will which acts from duty, it even presents the expression of respect for humanity as *the fundamental reason* why we should conform to moral laws and pursue moral ends.

In ordinary life people often do things in order to show respect or reverence for someone or something. Often they behave politely toward others, thank them or congratulate them in order to manifest respect, gratitude or esteem. Earlier I mentioned saluting the flag or bowing one's head as ways of honoring one's country or venerating a religious object. Yet if we think only of these examples, the motives

involved in expressing respect or esteem may seem suited only to matters of etiquette or ritual, and therefore an unlikely ground for a comprehensive rational morality. But if we think that expressive reasons for
acting are restricted in this way, we are badly misled. For in fact every
action which is done for a reason, as distinct from being merely a response to an impulse, is based on regarding something as valuable.
The performance of such an action is always an expression of respect
or esteem for that value, and this expressive reason for performing the
action is even the ground of all the other reasons we have for performing it.

From this standpoint even our furtherance of a producible end is
fundamentally a piece of *expressive* behavior, since it demonstrates or
exhibits how much we value the object pursued. We care about someone's good only to the extent that we value that good, and we value it
only insofar as we think of the *person* as *worth* caring about. This is
true even about our concern for our own good. When I choose to
satisfy a desire (as distinct from merely reacting to an instinctive impulse) I do so because I judge the desire to be *worth* satisfying, and
this in turn expresses a judgment about my own worth. When people
consider themselves worthless, they tend not to care very much about
their ends, and even their own happiness may not matter very much
to them. This pathology expresses a piece of consequent reasoning,
though if Kant is right its premise is necessarily false, since their humanity always has absolute worth.

Conversely, the basic reason why it is wrong to harm people, or to
fail to help them, is that we thereby show that we place too little value
on them. Consider California's Proposition 187, which intends to deny
education, health care and other basic social services to undocumented
immigrants. Ignoring for the moment issues of legality and right, what
is so morally repugnant about the attitude of those who proposed,
supported and voted for this reprehensible measure?[10] It is not merely
that they have done something which will cause human suffering. For
the thought of such suffering, by itself, makes us only sad, not indig-
nant. Likewise, what makes their conduct blamable is not their "lack of
compassion." For in many cases they may feel sincerely sorry for those
whom Proposition 187 will hurt. Their contention is only that they have
a right to deny social services to immigrants, and that, regrettably, the
state can no longer provide these services to undocumented immigrants.

However, even if we grant that everything they say here is true, there is still something outrageous about their conduct, which no decent person can fail to perceive. (Even they themselves cannot have failed to perceive it. This is why such a measure could pass only in a political season in which a sizeable proportion of the voting electorate was seized by a fanatical paroxysm of fear, hate and blind rancor, which turned them with aggressive perversity against every impulse in themselves belonging to reason, decency or humanity.) Proposition 187 says, in effect, that the State of California does not consider undocumented immigrants valuable enough as human beings that those around them are required to meet their basic needs for education and medical treatment. No doubt the supporters of Proposition 187 meant to say to these people that they should go back where they came from. And perhaps this message, nasty as it sounds, is one which they not only have the right to convey but which it might be morally permissible for them to want to convey. However, the problem with Proposition 187 is that it conveys this message in such a way as to express contempt for the humanity of the immigrants. No one can fail to be aware that humanity in their person is not being treated as an end in itself.[11]

But exactly how do we determine that Proposition 187 expresses this contempt for humanity? More generally, how do we know when any sort of conduct treats, or fails to treat, humanity as an end in itself? Let us consider a couple of Kant's own examples. He alleges that suicide is always wrong because it involves disposing of a person (a being with absolute worth), merely as a means to some discretionary end, such as maintaining a tolerable condition up to the end of life (*G*, 429). Kant regards suicide as "degrading to the humanity in one's own person" (*MM*, 6:422–423). Our duty not to make promises we do not intend to keep is based on the fact that the making of such a promise uses those we deceive merely as means, "without considering that, as rational beings, they must always at the same time be esteemed as ends" (*G*, 430). When we violate these narrow or perfect duties, we have done something which fails to show respect or esteem for humanity or rational nature. Our wide or imperfect duties are based on the fact that proper esteem for rational nature requires us to bring our actions into "agreement" with the existent end of humanity, by setting ends which harmonize with those of rational nature, even if the precise manner and extent of their pursuit is optional. Kant uses this consideration to argue that we must make it our end to develop our talents (since rational nature is honored by putting these at its disposal for use in pursuing its optional ends) and to help others when they need it (since we honor their capacity to set these ends by helping to further them) (*G*, 430; cf. *MM* 6:445).

Every argument from FH depends on an intermediate premise, logically independent of FH itself, which tells us what the action expresses or fails to express concerning the worth of humanity in someone's person. Kant's argument about suicide, for example, is:

1. FH: One must always respect humanity as an end in itself in one's own person as well as in the person of another.

2. The act of suicide always fails to respect humanity in one's own person as an end in itself.

3. Therefore, one must never commit suicide.

One cannot reach the conclusion (3) from (1) without (2), or some similar premise connecting FH with suicide. But (2) is logically independent of FH, as we can easily see from the fact that it is possible to reject (3) simply because one rejects (2). For example, some people think that it is demeaning to human dignity for a person afflicted with a horrid and debilitating disease to live on in an agonized and subhuman condition. They might view the suicide of someone faced with this prospect as an act which positively respects the worth of humanity in one's own person. To accept FH, therefore, clearly does not commit one to accepting all the conclusions (about the immorality of suicide, for instance, or lying) that Kant himself would want to derive from it. For two people who equally accept FH may disagree over propositions such as (2), which purport to tell us what certain kinds of actions express regarding the worth of humanity.

Fewer of us will quarrel with Kant's conclusion in the case of the false promise. For coercive or deceptive actions often obviously violate FH because they adopt a means to an end which positively prevents the other person from rationally sharing the end. The use of such a means deliberately circumvents or frustrates the rational agency of the person coerced or deceived in a way which displays obvious contempt or disrespect for the value of that agency.

1. FH: One must always respect humanity as end in itself in one's own person as well as in the person of another.

2'. A false promise, because its end cannot be shared by the person to whom the promise is made, frustrates that person's agency and so fails to respect the other's humanity as an end in itself.

3'. Therefore, one must not make false promises.

(2') plays the same role in this argument as (2) did in the argument about suicide. It connects the nature of the action to FH by establishing that action as one which fails to respect humanity as an end in itself.

We may be tempted in the case of (2'), as we probably were not in the case of (2), to think that it follows directly from FH itself or is even part of the very meaning of FH. But this temptation should be resisted. For although (2) may be more controversial than (2'), it is still possible without contradiction to affirm FH while denying (2'). There are actions which frustrate or restrict someone's agency: for example, having an end that cannot be shared by the patient and nevertheless do not fail to respect the patient's humanity.[12] There are significant controversies, for instance, over the circumstances under which paternalistic interference with someone's agency might be permissible in the name of the worth of humanity, in order to prevent them from harming their own rational capacities or doing things which they will later regard as dishonoring their humanity. It is implausible to assume that the right answer on these issues can always be found right in FH itself. It is those who assume this who naturally infer that the meaning of FH is so flexible and disputable that no moral conclusions could be rationally drawn from it except those imported into it by an interpretation so vulnerable to controversy that FH itself is useless in the context of moral debate. People who understand FH in this way cannot be blamed for regarding it as high-sounding but virtually empty of content.

A more plausible way to look at the matter, however, is to insist that the meaning of FH is quite clear and determinate, because the concept of humanity as an existent end in itself possessed of dignity is clear and determinate. The application of FH is sometimes unclear or controversial, however, because every use of FH in moral deliberation requires an intermediate premise, logically independent of FH, which does the work of (2) or (2'), and in many cases there are legitimate questions about which acts express respect or disrespect for humanity. Controversies surrounding these intermediate premises constitute a legitimate reason for viewing FH as incapable, by itself, of settling the legitimate moral issues to which we might expect to apply it.

But it is all too easy to take such suspicions farther than is warranted. It would be entirely mistaken to claim, for example, that FH is empty or formalistic, settling nothing as regards the content of morality but leaving all the substantive moral issues still to be decided. For, in the first place, it is FH alone that serves as a *moral* principle in the above arguments for (3) and (3'). If (2) and (2') are independently necessary to derive these conclusions, it is even more obvious that the conclusions cannot be derived without FH, which alone gives moral significance to the fact that certain actions treat humanity with respect or disrespect.

Secondly, that FH is a contentful principle is attested by the fact that it is itself far from being undisputed. It says that rational nature is the highest value, that it is an absolute value for which none other can be substituted, and hence implies that all rational beings are of equal value, whether they are wise or foolish, useful or useless, even whether they are morally good or bad. FH is denied by all those who think rationality does not make human beings worth more than animals, or who believe some rational beings are worth more than others, or who hold the value of rational nature to be less than absolute. A principle as controversial as FH cannot be regarded as trivial or empty of moral content.

Finally, although every application of FH requires an intermediate premise logically independent of it, it is nevertheless true that FH itself is not entirely neutral regarding such premises. For what any such premise tells us is something about what it is to value rational nature, and that value is just what FH asserts. A premise such as (2') is easier to defend than a premise such as (2), because the direct frustration of a rational being's agency is more intimately related to rational nature than a rational being's termination of its life-processes, and hence a more direct and obvious expression of disrespect for rational nature. (2) in turn is easier to defend than the analogous premises in some of Kant's other arguments from FH, such as those which depend on the claim that we always dishonor our humanity when we enjoy sexual pleasure for its own sake (*MM*, 6:424–425).

Our concept of rational nature itself is a corrigible, hence variable one. That is why there is also variability, from person to person, or society to society, in what we take to show respect for rational nature. But we do have a certain amount of knowledge about rational nature, and this guides our judgments about what is valuable about it, and hence how respect for this value should be expressed. There is no algorithm or decision procedure leading from such knowledge and such judgments to intermediate premises which do the work of (2) and (2'), but because rational capacities themselves are something real about which knowledge is possible, the defense of such premises need not be merely a matter of incommensurable intuitions or irrational prejudices.

Therefore, there is after all a grain of truth in the temptation to treat intermediate premises such as (2) and (2') as part of the very meaning of FH. For FH itself, if taken seriously, can help to shape how people think, feel and perceive the various ways humanity is treated. Since FH holds that all rational beings have absolute worth, it implies that they all have *equal* worth. Of course it doesn't follow from this that all rational beings deserve *identical* treatment in any particular respect. Premises specifying how respect for human dignity is to be expressed, and which aspects of people are relevant to this, can be used to reconcile FH with all sorts of social, political and economic inequality. Kant himself regards FH as compatible with some inequalities which would today be regarded as abominable or at least controversial, such as the exclusion of the vast majority of society from the right to vote or hold political office, and the authority of the male heads of households over wives, children and servants within families.

Yet when a social order treats some people better and some worse in ways that they themselves regard as essential to their self-worth, there is a presumption, based on FH itself, that this social order fails to respect the humanity of those who receive worse treatment. As more people come to regard political participation as an essential function of their rational agency, it becomes harder to regard exclusion from it as anything but an expression of disrespect for the humanity of those excluded. Any such egalitarian presumption might be rebutted, of course, by showing that greater equality in one area could be achieved only at the cost of more fundamental failures to respect humanity in other areas—as defenders of economic inequality do, for example, when they argue that greater economic equality would require unacceptable restrictions on external freedom. But if we take FH seriously, we ought to be discontented with trade-offs when they concern matters essential to human self-worth and willing to adjust our views about what respect for humanity requires in order to give the equal absolute worth of every human being its due. For example, when untrammeled external freedoms in the economic sphere lead to large inequalities in wealth and status between human beings which are degrading to those placed in an inferior position, this should make us reluctant to regard the respect for economic liberty as vital to respect for humanity, and willing to see this liberty curtailed in the interests of human dignity. In short, there is in FH itself a powerful tendency toward the relentless expansion of human equality in all areas of life that matter to human self-worth.

## Notes

1. In this paper, Kant's writings will be cited according to the *Akademie Ausgabe* by volume:page number.

2. Kant glosses Ulpian's principle of natural right, *honeste vive*, as "asserting one's worth as a human being in relation to others, a duty expressed by the saying: 'Do not make yourself a mere means for others but be at the same time an end for them'" (*MM*, 6:237). The innate right to freedom is said to "belong to every human being in virtue of his humanity" (*MM*, 6:237). There are fourteen ethical duties explicitly enumerated by Kant. Of these, only (1) the duty of beneficence to others is grounded on FUL (*MM*, 6:389, 451, 453). Nine of the remaining thirteen are explicitly based on FH, and the other four are based on it by implication. The emphasis on FH is strongest in the case of duties to oneself. (2) The duty against suicide is based on the fact that disposing of oneself as a mere means to some discretionary end is debasing humanity in one's person (*MM*, 6:423); (3) the duty against carnal self-degradation on the fact that it "violates humanity in one's own person" (*MM* 6:425); (4) that against drunkenness on the fact that the drunkard is "like a mere animal," and cannot be "treated as a human being" (*MM*, 6:427). (5) Lying "violates the dignity of humanity in one's own person" (*MM*, 6:429) and (6) the self-respect opposed to servility is a duty "with reference to the dignity of humanity within us" (*MM*, 6:436). (7) The human being's duty to develop our natural perfection is one "he owes himself (as a rational being)" because it is "bound up with the end of humanity in our own person" (*MM*, 6:444, 392). (8) Violation of the duty of gratitude is "a rejection of one's own humanity" (*MM*, 6:454) based on "pride in the dignity of humanity in one's own person" (*MM*, 6:459), while (9) the duty to sympathize with others holds insofar as "the human being is regarded not merely as a rational being but as an animal endowed with reason" (*MM*, 6:456). (10) All duties of respect to others are grounded on "the dignity in other human beings" (*MM*, 6:462). There is no explicit appeal to any formula in the case of four duties: (11) our duty to ourselves not to be avaricious (*MM* 6:432), (12) our duty as self-judge (*MM*, 6:437–440), (13) our duty to increase our moral perfection (*MM* 6:446–447), or (14) our duty to ourselves regarding non-rational beings (*MM*, 6:442–443). But (12)–(14) are all duties relating to our acting from the motive of duty, which (as we have just seen) is explicitly grounded on our dignity as rational beings; and (11) our duty to avoid avarice is defended on the ground that it impairs our rational nature in respect of the

use of money (self-impairment is also used as the basis for (4).) Reference to FH also grounds Kant's discussion of five of the six enumerated vices opposed to duties to others: envy, ingratitude, arrogance, defamation, ridicule (*MM*, 6:458–461, 465–467); no explicit appeal to any formula occurs regarding the vice of malice (*MM*, 6:460).

3. I am grateful to Thomas Hill, Jr. for pressing me to clarify this point.

4. The same considerations tell us how Kant's theory should deal with the fact that humanity or rational nature apparently comes in degrees and also that there are borderline cases of it. A categorical imperative or practical law either has an objective ground or it does not, so the existence of an end in itself cannot be a matter of degree. Every being with the capacity to set ends according to reason is therefore equally an end in itself, irrespective of how well or badly it may exercise this capacity. By the same token, Kant's theory implies that if some members of our biological species lack 'humanity' in this sense, whether temporarily or permanently, then not every member of our species is an end in itself. It seems evident that young children and people whose rational capacities are severely impaired simply do not have the capacity to set ends according to reason. On Kant's theory, therefore, they have to count as nonpersons and are not ends in themselves. By itself, however, this does not entail that they should not be treated, as far as possible, as we treat persons, but only requires that additional arguments need to be given for treating them as persons. Most such human beings either have been rational agents at one time or can be expected to become rational agents in the normal course of things. Respect for the worth of humanity does not entail precisely the same respect for beings whose humanity is merely potential, or actual only in the past, or temporarily absent, but it may have some implications just the same. Even human beings who have never been and will never be rational agents are often bound to actual persons by the same emotional ties that other persons are, and the concern that others have for them may be indiscernible from that which they have for other persons. Kant's view implies that such ties and concern are not morally required, but where it exists, the theory entails that it has moral consequences, since respect for the humanity of those who have this concern requires us to share their morally permissible ends. It is a complex question how we should treat various beings (human or non-human, born or unborn) who lack 'humanity' in the strict Kantian sense but for whom moral claims can still be made in the name of humanity. Kantian moral theory sheds light on such problems by placing them in a theoretical context, but it would be a misunderstanding to think that it can or should pretend to a simple or neat solution of them. The Kantian position, admittedly controversial, is that such moral problems should be settled solely by reference to the absolute worth of humanity or rational nature as an end in itself. Mere sentience, for example, considered apart from the worth of rational nature, is not a basis for moral status. But it does not follow that there could not be indirect reasons, grounded in the value of rational nature, for giving moral weight to the pleasures and pains of non-rational creatures (*MM*, 6:442–443).

5. John Stuart Mill, *Utilitarianism*, ed. George Sher (Indianapolis: Hackett, 1979), pp. 4–5, 34–40.

6. That Kant believes something like this is indicated in his essay *Conjectural Beginning of Human History*, where he provides an imaginary account of how human beings first left the path of animal instinct and began to use reason to set ends. One result of this, Kant says, is that the human being "came to understand, albeit only obscurely, that he is the true end of nature," and made "the claim to be an end in itself, estimated as such by every other, and to be used by none merely as a means to other ends" (*MM*, 8:114).

7. A similar thought is expressed in the *Critique of Judgment* where the status of rational beings as the ultimate end of nature is inferred from their capacity to conceive of ends and organize them into a system: "The human being is the ultimate end of creation here on earth because he is the only being on earth who can form a concept of ends and use reason to turn an aggregate of purposively structured things into a system of ends" (*CPracR*, 5:427).

8. Korsgaard, "Kant's Formula of Humanity," *Kant-Studien* 77 (1986), pp. 194–197.

9. John L. Mackie, *Ethics: Inventing Right and Wrong* (New York: Penguin, 1977), pp. 26–27.

10. We need to distinguish the question whether Proposition 187 is constitutional (that is, in conformity with the Constitution of the State of California and with the United States Constitution), from the further question whether it is consistent with natural right. But even supposing (what is far from evident) that Proposition 187 is not objectionable on either of these grounds, we may still ask whether those who support it and vote for it are performing actions which are *morally* objectionable because they thereby fail to treat humanity in the person of the undocumented immigrants as an end in itself having dignity or absolute worth. It is only this last question that I am concerned with in the present discussion. It is worth focusing on this sort of question because in political discussions in states with a liberal ethos there is often a peculiar tendency to infer from the premise that we have the right to do something (for example, to agitate for a certain change in laws, or to vote for it) that it is morally permissible for us to do these things—as though anyone who points out to us that we are violating a moral duty in using our political rights in a certain way is trying to deprive us of those rights. The point that seems to me obvious is that even granting that the voters of California were acting within their rights in passing Proposition 187, they were behaving shamefully and blamably in doing so. Further, it is an extremely harmful feature of our political culture that it should confuse the rightful with the morally permissible in this way. For on the one hand, it encourages people to think that when they morally disapprove of something (some type of sexual behavior, for example), then what they disapprove of is a fit object of legal coercion, or at least that there can be no right (subject to legal protection) to engage in it. Conversely, if they held themselves morally accountable for their political behavior (for the way they vote, for instance) then measures such as Proposition 187 would stand no chance of passage and the issue of whether it is constitutional or something the state has a right to do would never arise. Kant might sometimes seem to be taking issue with this last point, when he suggests that moral beneficence might be superfluous from the standpoint of human welfare, and that all that

is needed for maximal human well-being is that people merely respect one another's rights (*G*, 4:423; *MM*, 6:452, 458). But it is noteworthy that in such contexts Kant also occasionally insists that existing differences in wealth, for example, are contrary to right, resulting from a "general injustice" in the social system of distribution (27:416, 20:140–141). (I am grateful to Professor Roman Hruschka for pressing me to clarify this point.)

11. Another source of offense is that those who would deny education and social services to immigrants ignore the positive contribution they make to society (the work they do, the taxes they pay, and so on). This one-sided portrayal of immigrants is also a denial of their humanity, since in effect it views them solely as objects to be exploited and not as people whose activities have value and whose needs ought to be satisfied. But from the standpoint of FH, it is objectionable to argue that immigrants should be eligible for social services only because they make an economic contribution to society, as if others have reason to satisfy their needs only if they pay for it. For the dignity of humanity is not conditional on one's ability to pay. Kant would point out that each of us owes it to the worth of humanity in our person not to be dependent solely on the charity of others, since such dependence is humiliating and degrading, and amounts to a form of servility (*MM*, 6:436). But from the converse standpoint, of those who have it in their power to meet the needs of others, it is wrong to withhold help from those dependent on it or to treat them in a humiliating fashion because they need it. On the contrary, benefactors must try to show those they help that they are honored that the recipients should accept it— which they always are, since the recipients are beings having absolute worth (*MM*, 6:453).

12. Kant himself would cite an act of just punishment as an example of this, since he maintains that it is impossible to will one's own punishment and yet that just punishment respects the dignity of humanity in the person of the criminal (*CPracR*, 5:37–38; *MM*, 6:331–337).

# 8

# The Categorical Imperative

## *Thomas W. Pogge*

This essay attempts a unified interpretation of the categorical imperative based on Formulas I, Ia, II, and IIIa.[1] Kant wants these formulas to be equivalent (*G*, 436), and I take this not as an *assertion* (as if each formula had an entirely clear meaning on its own), but as a *prescription*: The subsidiary formulas make distinctive contributions to the clarification and specification of the categorical imperative—they gradually enrich its meaning, until at last its full import can be understood.[2] And once fully understood, the categorical imperative can then be read back into each of these formulas so as to make them equivalent as Kant demands.

## 1. Universalizability

The categorical imperative applies in the first instance to maxims. These are subjective (intentional) principles of volition/action (*G*, 400n, 420n), i.e. fairly general personal policies. A maxim envisages—perhaps conditional upon certain situational or subjective circumstances—a specific course of conduct (action or inaction) aiming at some object(ive) or material end (*G*, 427f.). A maxim is then an ordered triplet consisting of a type of circumstances **S**, a type of conduct **C**, and a type of material end **E: M** $= <$ **S , C , E** $>$.[3]

Central to Kant's moral philosophy is the idea that moral principles must be universal: Some particular agent is obligated, permitted, or forbidden to adopt some given maxim (if and) only if everyone is.[4]

The categorical imperative is postulated as a *necessary and suffi-*

*cient* condition for the *permissibility* of maxims. It is a necessary condition: Formula I prescribes that we "act *only* on that maxim . . . " (*G*, 421, my emphasis; *cf.* 402, 434, 437, 440). It is a sufficient condition: Kant never mentions any further condition and writes that "without far-reaching ingenuity" I need "ask myself *only* . . . " (*G*, 403, my emphasis). And it cannot be a sufficient condition for obligatoriness, as this would have the absurd consequence that every permissible maxim is also obligatory.

Taking the two preceding paragraphs together, we arrive at a somewhat atypical reading of the categorical imperative: An agent is permitted (or: can reasonably will to) adopt some given maxim just in case he can will that everyone be permitted to adopt it. Strictly speaking, it is then not his maxim that the agent must be able to will as a universal law, but the *availability* of this maxim: Other things being unchanged, can he will our world to be such that everyone feels (morally) free to—and those so inclined ("by nature") actually do—adopt his maxim? This differs from what the categorical imperative is usually taken to demand, namely that the agent must be able to will that everyone *actually* adopt his maxim.[5]

Clear traces in the text confirm that Kant appreciated this distinction, and meant to impose the former requirement. Thus he asks: "could I really say to myself that every one *may* make a false promise when . . . ?" (*G*, 403), and he speaks of "the universality of a law that every one believing himself to be in need *can* make any promise he pleases" (*G*, 422; my emphases).[6]

Moreover, this reading helps to make the categorical imperative intuitively plausible. If enough others are enjoying physical labor, then the maxim 'to lead the life of a scholar' would seem unobjectionable. If, on the other hand, the scholarly life is what most others would also be inclined to favor, then my success in leading such a life without physical work is necessarily parasitic upon the (morally motivated or coerced) sacrifice by others producing the necessities for human existence. Similarly, if enough others prefer having children, then forming the maxim 'to have no children so as to save time for my chosen projects' is perfectly reasonable. However, if my fellows were just as reluctant to raise children as I am myself, then it could be morally incumbent upon me to start a family.[7] So it makes a crucial difference in our intuitive moral reflection how others are naturally disposed toward **M** (the maxim at issue): We do not ordinarily think it wrong to adopt **M**—even if its adoption by many would be unsustainable—when those actually inclined to adopt it are so few that their adopting it would pose no problem. And just this feature of our ordinary moral thinking is captured by my reading of the categorical imperative.[8]

By contrast, suppose we consider it irrelevant that our world displays neither an abundance of scholarly ambition nor a widespread reluctance to have children. Then both maxims would presumably be classified as forbidden. And this in turn would be rather unfortunate for Kant, who, it seems, had adopted them both.

The interpretive problem now appears in this form: Suppose an agent is contemplating a maxim prompted by her inclinations, i.e. a maxim that stipulates some desired (type of) material end together with some plausible way of attaining it. How is she to decide whether she can will a universal permission to adopt this maxim? In view of Kant's adamant insistence that the categorical imperative is not a version of the Golden Rule (*G*, 430n), we cannot take literally the paraphrase in his first discussion of the promising example: "would I really be content that . . . " (*G*, 403). A real inability to will must be required to reject a maxim. In order to understand this locution, we must recapitulate in what sense Kant was using the verb "to will."

As a first step, we may suppose Kant to have thought, plausibly enough, that one cannot will (though one can wish for) what one supposes to be impossible. But even if we take this to include not just logical, but also physical impossibility, this would still not suffice to reject any maxims at all. For consider Kant's second example: In the world to be imagined, everyone would feel free to adopt the maxim 'when in need, to make deceitful promises so as to alleviate my difficulties.' Thus, people in need would (be known to) have no reason not to make deceitful promises; potential promisees would (be known to) have good reason to reject promises made by persons in need; and most people in evident need might thus not even bother to offer promises—deceitfully or otherwise. But this shows at most that, if the maxim in question were universally permitted, it would fall into disuse, as it were. It does not show that the world we are imagining is impossible.[9]

To reaffirm Kant's conclusion about the example, we must then look for a second step that strengthens the test. Such a step is suggested by his insertion into Formula I of the word *zugleich*.[10] Kant surely wants to say that, for any of one's maxims, **M**, one must be able to will **M**'s universal permission. However, this point is equally well expressed when *zugleich* (at the same time) is omitted. So the presence of the word must indicate a further point, which is, quite literally, that the agent must be able to will his maxim *together with* its universal permission: **M**'s universal availability must not make it impossible to will (to adopt) **M**. The agent must be able to will **M** even while **M** is available to everyone; he may choose a maxim only if he can (not would!) will it on that condition.

This demand—that **M** and its universal availability must be willable together—may indicate a second respect in which 'to will' differs from 'to want' or 'to wish': Willing something involves an exclusive commitment. While one may *want* to eat one's cake and have it too, it is impossible to *will* both. In our case, the agent cannot will both his maxim and its universal permission.[11]

But how might the agent, once he wills **M**'s universal availability, be unable to will (to adopt) **M**? What I think Kant has in mind is that **M**'s universal availability might subvert the material end envisaged by the maxim. We have already seen how the maxim of deceitful promising when in need would be pointless, would not alleviate one's difficulties, if universally permitted. This leads to the rejection of that maxim, because, as we can now say more precisely, its universal availability would block the agent's attainment of the material end of his conduct under the maxim. And, with the objective out of reach, the agent *cannot* will the maxim: If it cannot satisfy his interest in its material end, the agent loses his only possible (heteronomous) motive for adopting it.[12] As Kant well puts it: Such a maxim, universalized, would annihilate, or destroy itself (*CPracR*, 27f—*sich selbst vernichten/aufreiben*); "would make promising, and the end one might thereby pursue, itself impossible" (*G*, 422). In modern jargon we could say: Making this maxim morally available is collectively self-defeating.[13]

This reading has the virtue of showing how the application of the categorical imperative is not parasitic upon practices (like promising) whose moral necessity is simply presupposed.[14] Rather, adoption of a forbidden maxim brings the agent into conflict with *himself*: He both wills the practice (his objective involves taking advantage of it), and does not will the practice (he sanctions its violation).

Let me restate the general idea. Suppose you desire to attain some objective **E** attainable in circumstances **S** through conduct **C**. You may adopt the maxim **M** = < **S** , **C** , **E** > only if **E** would be attainable even while everyone felt free to adopt **M**—or, in terms of Formula Ia: even while everyone naturally inclined to adopt **M** were certain to do so. As reconstructed so far, the categorical imperative forbids then the adoption of any maxim, **M**, that engenders an inconsistency among these three items:

(1)  the ability to will **M** (in virtue of an interest in its end);

(2)  the universal availability of **M**;

(3)  natural laws (esp. those covering human dispositions).

This, I submit, is the test Kant proposes for deriving *perfect* duties from Formulas I and Ia. The test is designed to screen out maxims that "cannot even be *conceived* as a universal law of nature without contradiction" (*G*, 424), because they are collectively self-defeating, because their *raison d'etre* does not survive their universalization: Trying to imagine that world in which no one would forgo the advantage I aim for through my maxim, I see that this world is impossible. The advantage is available only because it is not realized by everyone who might enjoy it, and it becomes impossible when this condition ceases to be satisfied.

Let me confess that my reading has two consequences that may seem implausible: If the world were such that even promises given without intent to keep them are known to be normally fulfilled nevertheless—by God, perhaps—then giving such promises would not be wrong under the test developed so far, because the benefits of promising deceitfully in circumstances **S** would persist even while everyone felt free to make such false promises. One may well ask why, intuitively, Divine intervention should make a difference here.

And I must accuse Kant of having overlooked the possibility of significant historical (and cross-cultural) variations in relevant social conditions: I think Kant (wrongly) believed that the social conditions relevant for developing the content of morality (under Formulas I and Ia) are given by the laws of (especially human) nature alone. And for the sake of clarity, I am leaving this belief uncorrected, saying that the universalization requirement must be applied against the background of the laws of nature; rather than: against the background also of prevalent social conditions.

## 2. An Objection

It is high time to respond to an alternative line of interpretation, popular in the German-speaking discussion, which emphasizes the purity and *a priori* character of Kant's moral philosophy (*cf.* note 5 above). To begin with, a morality for human beings cannot be pure, i.e. without "admixture of anything empirical" (B3): In developing such a morality through the categorical imperative, Kant must (and does) draw upon rational anthropology. He clearly presupposes that human beings have needs, language, and memory, for example. Hence there is no pristine purity to be preserved by our reading. The question is then not whether, but to what extent, knowledge about human beings is presupposed.

The answer is, I think, that Kant takes for granted a general understanding of the laws of (human) nature or of the permanent conditions of human life. Thus, in illustrating Formulas I and Ia, he consistently invokes general facts: We have a need for the love and sympathy of others (*G*, 423), we have sufficient memory to learn from experience (which we are disposed to do), and we can use language to deceive one another (*G*, 403, 422). But if such knowledge (presumably analytic to the notion of humanity) is part of rational anthropology, and thus may be used in deriving the *a priori* precepts of human morality, then it seems difficult to disallow what my reading presupposes: Information about how, by and large, humans are naturally inclined—using this in a broad sense that excludes only moral motivations.[15]

Two general passages (*G*, 389, 425) deny that any anthropology is needed even for applying moral philosophy to human beings. But these passages are contradicted by others: by *G*, 410n, and by Kant's own illustrations, and most directly by *G*, 412: "ethics . . requires anthropology for its *application* to man." Thus it seems plausible to conclude that Kant is there flattening out his own conception.[16] He contrasts only two levels:

(a) pure morality, establishing the moral law that is valid for all rational beings; and

(c) the application of morality to particular situations, with the aid of (rational and) empirical anthropology.

And forgets about the intermediate level:

(b) the application of pure morality to a world of human beings for purposes of developing *human* morality, with the aid of rational anthropology.

There are further general passages stressing the purity of morality. However, I think most of these can well be read as emphasizing the purity of only the supreme principle of morality, not of particular moral precepts for human beings. For example, *G*, 425, uses the singular throughout, insisting that the practical law, this principle, etc., must not be derived from the special characteristics of human nature. Other passages (*G*, 410n, 411f, 442), it is true, emphasize the purity of moral laws and moral principles (plural); but I do not find this conclusive: Why cannot Kant be talking about the general properties of moral laws (a species), while arguing elsewhere that this species has only one member? This reading is particularly encouraged by *G*, 410n: "moral principles are not grounded on the peculiarities of human nature, but must be established *a priori* by themselves; and yet . . . from all such principles it must be possible to derive practical rules for human nature as well as for every kind of rational nature." This suggests that the practical rules need not be the same for all species of rational beings—especially since he writes, in the same footnote, that we can distinguish pure from applied moral philosophy (applied to human nature, that is). So I take Kant's considered view to be that moral philosophy—though entirely based upon its pure part—is not entirely pure. We don't need any empirical knowledge to see that the permissibility of our maxims hinges on their meeting the test of the categorical imperative. But we may need some general knowledge in order to see whether some given maxim does meet this test. Kant's question is not whether I can will my maxim to be universally available in any context, but whether I can will this in our world, against the background of the actual laws of nature.[17]

The possibility of this reading is obscured by Kant's commitment to universality. This means that the same maxims are obligatory, permissible, or forbidden for all agents interacting in the same world (and thus presumably sharing some general characteristics). Contrary to the common view, it need not mean that the same maxims are universally obligatory, permissible, or forbidden regardless of what the relevant (species of) agents and their world may be like. Formula Ia—requiring me to imagine that my maxim (atemporally) becomes a law of nature—assumes that this new law is added (as it were) to the laws of nature that are already in place. And one may therefore need to know what these other laws are, in order to assess that new (fictional) order of nature. These other laws govern what people are "naturally" inclined to do, and hence determine how they would act if their conduct in a particular matter were "de-moralized."

### 3. The Second Formula

As developed so far, the categorical imperative is still too weak to yield imperfect duties. It is quite possible, for example, to will the maxim of indifference to the needs of others together with its universal availability: The maxim's material end—to avoid trouble and expense—remains attainable even when everyone so inclined adopts the maxim. Kant's discussion of this fourth example under Formula Ia offers no convincing idea for strengthening the test. He asserts that one cannot will a universal law of open indifference to the distress of others, because "cases might often arise in which one would need the love and sympathy of others and in which one would deprive oneself, by such a law of nature springing from one's own will, of all hope of the aid one wants[!] for oneself" (*G*, 423). However, we can hardly accept this as conclusive,[18] given that an analogous argument would defeat any maxim of helping others in distress: Once again, many a situation might arise in which I would urgently want not to have to help. And Kant's point cannot be that one should ask which of the two eventualities constitutes the greater danger for oneself (or for the average agent), as this would reduce the test to a "rule egoistic" (or rule utilitarian) calculus. What Kant needs to show is that human agents *must will*, not merely that they *do want*, help in certain situations.[19]

The discussion of the third example under Formula Ia invokes the premise that "as a rational being [the agent] necessarily wills that all his powers should be developed . . . " (*G*, 423), and a little later Kant says that with maxims violating imperfect duties "we do not find this inner impossibility, but it is still impossible to will . . . " (*G*, 424). Looking at the preceding parts of the *Groundwork*, these assertions must seem quite unfounded; and so we should consider whether they might anticipate arguments yet to be made. To show that this may indeed be the case, let me extend the discussion to Formula II which, I believe, offers a textually and systematically plausible way of strengthening the categorical imperative in this regard.

The second formula demands: "So act in relation to every rational being . . . that he may at the same time count in your maxim as an end in itself" (*G*, 437)—or, as I will paraphrase, as an ultimate source of value. As Kant applies it, this is a very powerful principle. But how does he think it can be established? I can see two main readings:

A   As a rational being I consider myself an end in itself, and so cannot reasonably will the permission to treat me merely as a means. Therefore, I cannot reasonably will universal legislation permitting that any rational being be treated merely as a means, and thus (by universality) must not adopt a maxim pursuant to which any rational being may be treated merely as a means.[20]

On this reading, Kant, taking Formula I for granted, brings it to bear upon the premise that as a rational being (or person) one must consider oneself an end in itself. I believe that, while some version of this reasoning may figure in Kant's argument, this reconstruction is systematically unsatisfactory, as can be seen by considering the following analogous reasoning:

A'   As a sentient being I am sensitive to suffering and pain, and so cannot reasonably will the permission to confine or to kill me. Therefore, I cannot reasonably will universal legislation permitting that any sentient being be confined or killed, and thus (by universality) must not adopt a maxim pursuant to which any sentient being may be confined or killed.

For better or worse, this is not an argument Kant would accept. Universalizations are to range over the domain of rational beings only. But the fact that all and only rational beings can apply, and are bound by, the universalization requirement does not entail that all and only rational beings are protected by it. Formulas I and Ia, though providing the *form* of the supreme principle of morality, offer no suggestion for how the *scope* of the required universalization is to be determined.[21]

My alternative interpretation views Formula II as contributing precisely this determination, in two steps:

B$_1$   As rational beings, we recognize as ends in themselves exactly those beings who have a telos that is of absolute value.[22] However, only a good will has absolute value. Therefore, exactly those beings who have the potential for a good will qualify for the status of ends in themselves.

This argument provides what Kant needs: a way of showing just whom moral reasoning must take into account, and on what grounds. The argument singles out human beings—or rather: persons, i.e. beings who are rational, and thus capable of acting from duty.[23]

This interpretation receives some support in *G*, 427–9. Kant asserts there that persons are objective ends: The rational grounds on which I necessarily think of my own nature as an end in itself do not refer to me essentially. They are rational grounds for thinking of anyone's rational nature as an end in itself. We cannot but recognize that rational beings, and they alone, objectively are ultimate sources of value or ends in themselves. And so we must acknowledge and treat one another as such by adopting only maxims all of us can contain, endorse, consent to. Insofar as one is reasonable, one cannot will that any rational being be treated merely as a means.

On this reconstruction, it is Formula II that brings out and justifies what is implicit in the categorical imperative, namely that moral concern is due to *persons*—in virtue of our capacity to act freely and morally, to choose ends in complete independence from the ends we find ourselves inclined toward by nature.[24] So the demand that all and only persons must be able to endorse my maxims does not follow from, but rather supports and specifies the universalization requirement:

> B$_2$  Rational beings must treat one another as ends in themselves, i.e. each must choose maxims so that all can contain or endorse them (even while the maxim's end remains attainable for him). However, I may assume that all persons can endorse *my* adopting **M** (if and) only if they can endorse **M**'s adoption by any other person as well. In order to test **M**, I must therefore ask: *Can all persons endorse that* **M** *should be available to any person* (even while **M**'s end remains attainable)? I cannot reasonably will **M** if it fails this test.

Kant did think of this argument as a rationale for the universalization requirement: "Suppose, however, there were something *whose existence* has *in itself* an absolute value . . . then in it, and in it alone, would there be the ground of a possible categorical imperative. . . . But if all value were conditioned . . . then no supreme principle could be found for reason at all" (*G*, 428). "The ground of this [supreme practical] principle is: *Rational nature exists as an end in itself*" (*G*, 428f).

There is also evidence that he thought of this argument as providing a non-arbitrary way of fixing its scope: Earlier formulations of Formula I (*G*, 402, 421) merely speak of universal law, while later ones (*G*, 437f) expand this to "universal validity for every rational being" and "universal law (for all rational beings)" respectively.[25]

Through $B_1$ and $B_2$, whether *I* (the prospective agent) can will **M** to be universally available comes to depend on whether *all persons* can endorse **M**'s availability to any person. The answer is negative, if action pursuant to my maxim would fail to recognize any person as an ultimate source of value, i.e. as a being whose (permissible) ends have value simply in virtue of her free choice. Here Kant distinguishes a narrower and a wider sense in which a person could be treated merely as a means: First and most fundamentally, an agent might subvert the very conditions of free choice which, Kant says, conflicts with humanity as an end in itself. This case of treating someone merely as a means is closely related to the ordinary sense of using someone (or his actions) as a means for the furtherance of one's own ends. As examples of this sort of offense, Kant mentions deception and coercion (*G*, 430). And second, the agent might disregard the other's status as an ultimate source of value. And in order to display this failing she need not go so far as to use him—it is enough that she ignore him, be indifferent to his dignity, needs, or chosen ends.[26]

Given this distinction, there is then a narrower and a wider requirement not to treat persons merely as means: Persons cannot endorse—and therefore one cannot reasonably will maxims that envisage—the subversion of their will, or indifference toward their ends (toward *what* they will). The former is a strong inability-to-endorse/-to-will (yielding perfect duties), the latter a weak inability-to-endorse/-to-will (yielding imperfect duties).

The second, wider requirement supports the assertion that we had earlier found groundless, namely that I cannot reasonably will indifference to the permissible ends of persons (to the development of my own talents and to other persons' need for help). My maxims must positively agree, or harmonize, with humanity as an end in itself (*G*, 430). The permissible ends of persons—including those of my own (future) self (*cf. DV*, §27)—must also for me be ends,[27] or immediate (not mediated by self-interest) reasons for action.[28]

Surprisingly, Formula II also makes a contribution in the area of perfect duties. We can begin to appreciate this by observing that it offers a new rationale for the prohibition on deceitful promising. Formulas I and Ia had suggested the following thought: The agent can will to adopt the relevant maxim only if a functioning practice of promising exists. However, this practice would (among human beings) not persist, if everyone felt free to give deceitful promises. Hence the agent's success in making a deceitful promise is dependent upon the compliance of others who, restraining their inclinations, refrain from giving false promises. The agent need not give or accept promises at all; but, by giving a deceitful promise, he is (as it were) free-riding on the self-restraint of all those who, promising only in good faith, keep the practice of promising afloat.

Now Kant could easily have restated this thought in terms of Formula II: Taking advantage of a practice without accepting the burdens it stipulates uses and exploits others and thus conflicts with their status as ends in themselves; the deceitful promisor treats merely as means (in the strong sense) all those who forgo the advantages of deceit. But Kant does not do this. Instead, he contends that deceitful promising is forbidden (under Formula II) because of how it treats the *promisee*, who, if she is to accept the promise, cannot be aware of, and hence cannot endorse, the promisor's maxim (*G*, 429).

But this plainly makes the categorical imperative more powerful than a straightforward reading of Formula I would have suggested. To illustrate: Adopting the maxim 'to coerce others to serve my desires' certainly conflicts with their status as ends in themselves and thus constitutes a violation of perfect duty (under Formula II). Yet, adopting this maxim is not forbidden by Formulas I and Ia (as initially interpreted): I can will the maxim together with its universal availability. It is still possible for me to succeed (to attain the maxim's material end), even if everyone so inclined adopts the same violent policy.[29]

The sharpening of the categorical imperative through Formula II is important in yet another context, namely for the assessment of maxims that contain a reference to a subset of all persons, e.g. to women, parents, Muslims, Canadians, or the poor. When the question is merely what *the agent* can will by way of maxims available to all persons, then some outrageous maxims might seem to pass. The rich and childless husband will be quick to exclaim: "Let anyone so inclined ignore their parents, beat their wives, despise the poor, and massacre Muslims!"

The problem is resolved through (my construal of) Formula II: The agent may not adopt maxims of despising the poor, ignoring his parents, or beating his wife, because he realizes that *they*—parents, wives, the poor—cannot endorse such maxims; and, as a rational being, he recognizes them as ends in themselves, whom he cannot reasonably will to treat merely as means.

To establish the equivalence of the formulas, all this must be read back into Formula I, as throwing new light on what one cannot reasonably will as a universal permission. We pull in the new premises that, as rational agents, we are unable to will in the strong/weak sense any maxim pursuant to which persons can be treated in ways that *conflict* or *fail to harmonize* with their status as ends in themselves: We are unable-to-will (in the strong sense) maxims of coercion and wife-beating, and unable-to-will (in the weak sense) maxims of ignoring one's parents and despising the poor.

Equivalent to the Formula II requirement that a rational agent must treat every person as an end in itself, we thus get the following revised reconstruction of Formula I. The categorical imperative forbids the adoption of any maxim, **M**, that leads to an inconsistency among:

(1) the ability to will **M** (in virtue of an interest in its end);

(2) the availability of **M** to all rational beings;

(3) natural laws (esp. those governing human dispositions);

(4) the recognition of every person as an end in itself.

Such an inconsistency can take three forms: A violation of perfect duty, as the first three items are inconsistent by themselves. A violation of perfect duty, as **M** involves the use/exploitation of persons. And a violation of imperfect duty, as **M** involves indifference toward persons. While some duties (also) derivable in the latter two ways would not require appeal to general facts about human dispositions, all duties derivable without (4) will, as far as I can see, involve (3).

To sum up: Formula II represents a threefold clarification of the categorical imperative: It shows how the scope of the required universalization is determined and indicates both: the basis for the derivation of all imperfect duties as well as a further ground for the derivation of perfect duties.

### 4. The Third Formula

The third formula, discussed at *G*, 431–5, contributes two new ideas—associated with the notions of autonomy and a realm of ends.[30] Of these I shall briefly discuss only the latter (Formula IIIa), to show how it fits with my reading.

A realm of ends is a unified, harmonious whole of all ends—"both of rational beings as ends in themselves and also of the particular ends that each may set for itself" (*G*, 433). Formula IIIa builds upon the clarifications contributed by the preceding formulas: Following Formula II, membership in a realm of ends belongs to exactly those beings who are ends in themselves (*G*, 435, 437–9). And, following Formulas I/Ia and II, a realm of ends is so regulated that each member, in pursuing his material ends, will not use others, nor obstruct, or be indifferent to, their permissible pursuit of material ends.

The notion of a realm of ends is then a new way of presenting the content of the categorical imperative: In deliberating about what maxims I may adopt, I am to ask which maxims I would make universally available, if it were my task to legislate so as to guarantee unity and harmony among a plurality of (human) persons (ends in themselves) involved in the pursuit of their self-chosen ends. As a moral agent here and now I must honor the moral restrictions that, as an ideal rational legislator, I myself would enact.

This new presentation also strengthens the categorical imperative by stressing that moral reflection involves a striving for completeness. This comprises two components.

## System

All maxims to be made available must combine or fit together into [*"zu"*] a possible realm of ends.[31] This further clarifies the categorical imperative by raising a demand not apparent from the preceding formulas: My maxims must be *jointly* universalizable. As a simple example, consider someone who forms the maxim, $M_1$, of invoking some impartial arbitration mechanism in practical conflicts, so as to have honored any of her claims successful there. $M_1$ is obviously permissible, because its end can still be attained if everyone feels free to adopt it. However, suppose she also forms the maxim, $M_2$, of ignoring the verdicts of this arbitration mechanism when they are not in her favor, so as to avoid meeting the successful claims of others. She thinks, correctly, that if everyone felt free to adopt $M_2$, its end could still be attained; and that $M_2$ is therefore permissible as well. I am suggesting that the agent, though she may adopt either maxim by itself, may not commit herself to both of them, on pains of a violation of perfect duty. The reason is that if $M_2$ were universally available, $M_1$ could not be willed, because its end could not be attained: Whoever wills $M_1$ must will $M_2$ to be forbidden. Formula IIIa thus emphasizes that the categorical imperative requires the agent to bring her own commitments (to various maxims) to bear upon one another. This requirement, too, should be read back into the canonical Formula I: An agent can will *each* of her maxims to be universally available (permissible and willable) only if she can will *all* of them to be so.[32]

Applied in the area of imperfect duties, e.g. to the issue of mutual aid, this thought shows that the agent must endorse a single standard—whether she is potential helper or potentially helped. If one refuses to give help $H$ (of a certain sort, in certain circumstances in which one is not naturally, e.g. from sympathy, inclined to help), then one may not request such help for oneself. For in the world in which everyone felt free to refuse such requests, they would be refused and the end of receiving such help could thus not be attained and the maxim of requesting it could then not be willed. What this shows is that a maxim may be rejected because its universal availability would defeat— not its end, but—the material end of some other maxim to the availability of which the agent is committed. What it does not show is which of the incompatible maxims the agent must give up. As regards mutual aid, for example, the system component, though it forbids a double standard, is still compatible with the full range of attitudes left open by Formula II—from rugged self-reliance (the belief that help is called for only in genuine emergencies) to a utilitarian policy prescribing help whenever the benefit to the helped exceeds the cost to the helper.

### Extension

The requirement to construct a universalizable system of maxims becomes more demanding through the second component, which requires that the laws springing from one's legislative will must cover all aspects of human life—whether or not these play a role in one's own life. We have already seen that the agent, before adopting a maxim governing his conduct toward the poor, say, must also ask whether *they* can endorse the universal availability of his maxim. But what if our wealthy man, sufficiently distanced from the poor, is not prompted to form any maxim at all in this matter? What if the question how the rich should act toward the poor simply does not occur to him? I suggest that, by requiring the agent to conceive of himself in the role of moral legislator, the categorical imperative does not allow him to avoid such reflections: In developing a system of maxims that one can will to be available to all human beings, one must take up "the point of view . . . of every other rational being" (*G*, 438)—however remote their situations may be from one's own.

As presented in Formula IIIa, the categorical imperative requires then that the agent construct a comprehensive system of maxims-to-be-available—a system he has thought through from the various relevant points of view, including those of circumstances (of race or gender, say) that can never arise for him. To be sure, this demand need not change his mind about a particular issue. But it does render maximally effective the idea that the agent's morality can (partly) be reformed from the inside—through the realization that, if *these* maxims are to be available (permissible and willable), then *those* maxims must not be. Formula IIIa shows then how the categorical imperative is not just a filter on maxims prompted by our inclinations, on the motto "inclination proposes, reason disposes." It is a method for *constructing* a complete morality for human beings.

These remarks may help elucidate why Kant refers to a realm of ends as an *ideal* (*G*, 433) of reason. I think that this ideal corresponds to reason's central *idea* in the practical sphere: the idea of a systematic unity of rational volition, which is directly expressed by the moral law— "the only condition under which a will can never be in conflict with itself" (*G*, 437). This idea defines a regulative principle within the domain of maxims that, individually, pass the categorical imperative (as presented in Formulas I, Ia, II). This principle demands that one extend one's reflection to further and further such maxims while also eliminating maxims so as to consolidate the remainder into a unified system of maxims that one can will to be universally available together.[33] In the limit, this process of reflection converges toward a complete system of jointly universalizable maxims. Given the principle of its construction, such a system, when attained, would determine a realm of ends: a possible harmonious community of human beings pursuing their material ends under just the maxims whose availability I will have endorsed. Conversely, reason's quest in the practical sphere can then also be described as that of constructing an ideal of a realm of ends.[34]

## 5. Conclusion

The categorical imperative incorporates then the demand for unity and system in the domain of action-guiding principles. But since it contains more than this demand, Kant has—on this reading—a response to (what one might call) the content problem. My concluding summary will concentrate on this topic.

The problem concerns the fertility of the categorical imperative. Even if the maxims entertained by the agent supply the empirical concepts in terms of which a human character is to be formed (the human context to which the purely intelligible moral law must be adapted), the categorical imperative may still be thought to be useless as a guide to the assessment of maxims. In the theoretical sphere, the mere commitment to unify experience in the direction of a single system of natural law is certainly not sufficient to determine which laws hold. As Kant repeatedly objects against the rationalists: without sensible intuitions we can know nothing about the world. Yet in the practical sphere he specifically enjoins us to ignore the content of our sensibility: our inclinations (*cf. G*, 428). How then can Kant do in the practical sphere what he declared impossible in the theoretical sphere, namely squeeze substantive content out of the merely formal commitment to unity (as expressed in the moral law)?

The question must be rejected, of course, since Kant is not attempting to derive answers to all practical questions from an empty formal principle. The misreading needs correction from both ends. First, as we have seen, the categorical imperative is not purely formal. It has a form, expressed in the demand for universality. But it also contains the specification of this requirement to the domain of (rational) beings capable of moral agency, and the demand for completeness within this domain. Moreover, Kant does not leave the construction of a system of moral restrictions to unguided intuition. Rather the constructed system of maxims-to-be-available must be such that they are willable in three senses:

(A) It must be possible to attain each maxim's end within the context of the entire system of available maxims.

(B) The system of maxims must not conflict with any person's status as an end in itself.

(C) The system of maxims must harmonize with each person's status as an end in itself, must give some weight to the (permissible) ends of all persons.

In applying these requirements, we can draw upon:

(D)  The principles of empirical practical reason (to choose the most efficient means to given ends, etc.).

(E)  The general facts about the world as expressed in its natural laws, which provide information about what can be done, what are efficient means to given ends, what the relevant consequences of alternative human moralities would be, and so on.

(F)  The various material ends that particular persons freely choose, which ends help specify the two broad, imperfect duties under (C).

Even when these six elements are pulled together, the categorical imperative—though it can furnish firm moral fixed points that any construction of a unified system of maxims must accommodate—does not yield a precise determination of our duties. But then—and this is the other end from which the misreading must be corrected—Kant fully understands that we need some intuition and judgment to complete the legislative task; and that different persons with good will might yet arrive at different ideals of a realm of ends for human beings. The categorical imperative is not proposed as an algorithm for settling all moral questions with precision.[35] It greatly reduces moral indeterminacy. And beyond this, its ingenuity consists in that it facilitates a decision by transforming it from one concerning oneself in a concrete situation (where it may be quite difficult to avoid bad faith and dishonesty) to one concerning the world at large. Here the categorical imperative is, as it were, a general procedure for constructing morally relevant thought experiments. Such a thought experiment shows whether I, as a rational agent in a world of human beings, can really will the maxims I am about to adopt. In this way, the categorical imperative *amplifies* my conscience by transforming the decision from one of marginal significance into one concerning the world at large, and also *isolates* my conscience by screening out any personal considerations that might affect my choice of maxims but are irrelevant to my decisions about how through legislation to specify a realm of ends.

For Kant, conscience is not some independent faculty. It is practical reason itself, i.e. the will (*G*, 412; *CPracR*, 55), in its attempt to unify itself in accordance with elements (A)–(F). Kant writes: "Our duty with regard to conscience is only to cultivate it, to sharpen our attentiveness to the voice of the inner judge, and (an indirect duty) to utilize every means to obtain a hearing for it" (*DV*, 6:401). I assume it is this duty that we discharge by considering our contemplated maxims under the various formulas.[36]

Now the fact that not all moral issues are algorithmically resolvable by appeal to reason is not, from Kant's point of view, a terrible defect. While writing the *Groundwork* (and the *CPracR*), he is not interested in a realm of ends as a real social world to be brought about, but employs it only as a vivid image designed to secure a unified structure for the individual agent's will. Kant's focus is on the individual agent's quest for moral excellence, which is shown to require the quest for a reorganization of his will toward its complete unification. Given this emphasis, there is no need that all moral agents should arrive at precisely the same ideal of a realm of ends.[37]

Moreover, even when viewed as a concrete goal, a realm of ends is not a sophisticated political utopia, but a social world much like ours— the only difference being that all persons would act only on maxims that the agent has admitted into his system. So a realm of ends would in any case not be brought about through the success of a political party whose members have united behind a shared platform. It might be approached through the moral improvement of individuals— provided that their systems of maxims will not differ too much.

A last reason for his patent unconcern with the "content problem" is that Kant presupposes in the reader a genuine desire to understand what a morality is, and to develop one and act from it. A person attempting to minimize his moral burdens consistent with the categorical imperative will, by Kant's criteria, be identified as a bad person. What matters is the maxim from which one actually acts (perhaps: 'to take advantage of others so long as doing so can be defended under some clever description'), not the maxim one might shrewdly construct for oneself. Such a person therefore has no conceivable motive to pay attention to the categorical imperative at all.[38] We might find such an attitude naive in view of our understanding of humanity's potential for rationalization and self-deception. We might find his conception naive for the further reason that it ignores how human behavior is conditioned by social institutions. This latter objection Kant would, however, have rejected: From an empirical standpoint we may well be conditioned to the point of total determination; yet from a practical point of view we can and must view ourselves and one another as perfectly free, and hence as fully responsible for our character.

# Notes

Many thanks to Bruce Ackerman, Charles Larmore, Sidney Morgenbesser, and Jerome Schneewind for very helpful comments and suggestions. This research was supported by a grant from the Columbia University Council for Research in the Humanities and by a Rockefeller Fellowship at the University of Maryland Center for Philosophy and Public Policy.—Note added in 1997: I have made some minor changes for the reprinting and restored a few footnotes that I was forced to delete in the original version of this essay.

1. This labeling of Kant's formulas is adapted from H.J. Paton: *The Categorical Imperative* (London: Hutchinson University Library, 1947), 129. In Formulas I and Ia, the word "become" must not be understood in a temporal sense: The universal law to be imagined holds in perpetuity (at all times, not just in the future). Thus one must imagine this law to be "already" present when one acts on the maxim. *Cf.* J. Kemp: "Kant's Examples of the Categorical Imperative" in R.P. Wolff (ed.): *Kant—A Collection of Critical Essays* (Garden City: Anchor 1967), 252f.

2. Another reason for the proliferation of formulas is that through them the categorical imperative can "be brought nearer to intuition and thus to feeling" (*G*, 436). Kant considers this objective crucial to successful moral education (*G*, 410n).

3. The **S**-clause might read "in any circumstance." For a detailed discussion of Kant's concept of a maxim, see R. Bittner: "Maximen" in G. Funke (ed.): *Akten des 4. Internationalen Kant-Kongresses* (Berlin: de Gruyter 1974), and O. Höffe: "Kants kategorischer Imperativ als Kriterium des Sittlichen" in *Zeitschrift für philosophische Forschung* 31 (1977), 356–370.

4. Evidence for the last two paragraphs is omitted for reasons of space.

5. One may want to object that this distinction can make no difference to what the categorical imperative requires. Kant's morality is pure. And in asking whether we can will everyone to be permitted to adopt a given maxim, we can thus not invoke empirical information e.g. about how many would actually adopt the maxim in question if they felt free to do so. Therefore we must base our verdict on a worst-case scenario: We can will the universal availability of some maxim only if we can will its universal adoption. The next section will show that the puristic reading implicit in this objection is neither systematically promising, nor mandated by Kant's text.

6. This paragraph and the next are heavily indebted to the second of three lectures that T.M. Scanlon delivered in Baltimore in the summer of 1983 under the title "Kant's Groundwork."

7. This reading goes a long way toward blunting the force of the more telling criticisms of Kant advanced in C.D. Broad: "On the Function of False Hypotheses in Ethics" in *International Journal of Ethics* 26 (1916), esp. 378 and 392.

8. This feature is also secured, in a different and more cumbersome way, by assuming that agents adopt maxims qualified by if-clauses. Thus I could will everyone to adopt the maxim 'to have no children, if I want none and if enough others have and like to have children, so as to save time for my chosen proj-

ects.' (See B. Aune: *Kant's Theory of Morals* [Princeton: Princeton University Press 1979], 61) This device for saving the categorical imperative from implausible implications is no longer necessary, once we interpret universality as universal permission. And this is an advantage, insofar as the simpler maxim 'to have no children so as to save time for my chosen projects' is psychologically more realistic.

9. Allen Wood has suggested—"Kant on False Promises" in L. W. Beck (ed.): *Proceedings of the Third International Kant Congress* (Dordrecht: Reidel 1972)—that a world in which everyone has adopted this maxim would be impossible after all: In it our concept of promising (which implies expression of an unconditional intention to do what is promised) would not exist, and thus no one could even form the maxim of deceitful promising (in our sense of that term). This reading has problems. First, why should we be incapable of having a word for, and of expressing, a kind of intention just because no one actually has it? Second, as Wood sees clearly, such an argument can disqualify only a very broad maxim of deceitful promising. However, the maxim Kant discusses is confined to situations of distress; and if this narrower maxim were adopted by all, the notion of promising would still be anchored in many ordinary contexts not involving people in need. Third, on this reading Kant's argument becomes parasitic upon the existence of a practice whose moral necessity is simply presupposed: Not everyone can form the deceitful-promising maxim, because this would subvert a concept necessary to form(ulat)ing it. But this fact has no connection to what, intuitively, is morally offensive about deceitful promises. Compare here the maxim 'not to accept winnings from bets or gambles': If everyone adopted this maxim, then perhaps we would lack our present concept of a bet or gamble. So what? (But see J. Ebbinghaus: "Die Formeln des kategorischen Imperativs und die Ableitung inhaltlich bestimmter Pflichten" in G. Prauss [ed.]: *Kant—Zur Deutung seiner Theorie von Erkennen und Handeln* [Köln: Kiepenheuer & Witsch, 1973], 287.) Finally, it seems unlikely that Wood's reading can be extended to other cases (suicide, mutual aid, etc.).

10. See *G*, 421, 434, 436–8, 440. My reading is in accord with J. Aul: "Aspekte des Universalisierungspostulats in Kants Ethik," in *Neue Hefte für Philosophie* 22 (1983), 78f. For an alternative explanation of this word's significance, see Paton, 56 and 136.

11. Kant's as-if idiom (*G* 421, 436, 438) may be another attempt to express this point. But this idiom may also mislead by falsely suggesting a weighing of consequences as in: *Would I* adopt **M** even at the price of everyone else being free to adopt **M** as well? What the categorical imperative really directs us to ask is: *Could I will* to adopt **M** even if all others were free to adopt **M** as well?

12. *Cf. G*, 413n, where Kant claims that a non-moral interest in an action type (maxim) is always an interest in its objective (material end). We encounter here a third characteristic of Kant's term 'to will': While in ordinary English the response "I just want to (without reason, for the heck of it)" is perfectly intelligible, this reply becomes inconsistent when we substitute "will" (in Kant's sense) for "want." A heteronomously motivated agent *cannot* will what he has no inclination toward.

13. This reading assimilates ideas expressed in N. Hoerster: "Kants kategori-

scher Imperativ als Test unserer sittlichen Pflichten" (in M. Riedel (ed.): *Rehabilitierung der praktischen Philosophie Band II* (Freiburg: Rombach 1974)), 462, and also in O. Nell (O'Neill): *Acting on Principle* (New York: Columbia University Press 1975), 69f. On my understanding, however, Kant focuses on only this one case: where a maxim is rejected when its universal availability blocks the attainment of its material end. Maxims may be collectively self-defeating in other ways—for example: The maxim 'to kill to protect my property when it is in danger of being stolen' might be thought to be collectively self-defeating, because, if everyone felt free to adopt it, the maxim would have no application, let's assume, as there would be no thieves. Yet, this maxim is not collectively self-defeating in my sense, because the non-existence of thieves, far from blocking the agent's objective, ensures its attainment. The fact that, if all were (known) to feel free to kill thieves, there would be no occasions for acting on this maxim *reassures* the agent about its merits. Confining the argument in this way to the maxim's material end is then appropriate, because this end is what, in adopting the maxim, the agent himself is interested in. He seeks the protection of his property, not occasions for its defense against thieves.

14. For such readings of Kant, see G.W.F. Hegel: *Elements of the Philosophy of Right* (Cambridge: Cambridge University Press, 1991), §135 (with addition); J. Kemp: "Kant's Examples of the Categorical Imperative" in R.P. Wolff (ed.), 252; Wood; and R.P. Wolff: *The Autonomy of Reason* (New York: Harper & Row 1973), 167.

15. This understanding of the term '*a priori*' seems consistent with B3, and is supported by many passages where Kant uses the term in this vein (e.g. *Perpetual Peace*, 8:381). My view on how moral precepts for humans are to be developed through the categorical imperative can draw some general support from a study of the role of rational anthropology within Kant's project, as conducted in M. Forschner: "Reine Morallehre und Anthropologie" in *Neue Hefte für Philosophie* 22 (1983).

16. This claim is supported in Forschner, 28.

17. *Cf.* Hoerster, 460. It is undeniable that the categorical imperative is "ein reines, von empirischen Elementen freies Vernunftprinzip." But—*pace* Höffe, 372—this does not entail that the *application* of the categorical imperative to human beings must "ohne empirische Kenntnisse und deren (sozial-)pragmatische Beurteilung auskommen."

18. But see P. Dietrichson: "When is a Maxim Fully Universalizable?" in *KantStudien* 55 (1964), 161–164.

19. Consider this attempt to rescue Kant: "If men have ends they must . . . will some sufficient means to those ends. But if I will whatever means are needed to achieve whatever ends I may have, then I must will that, should I be unable to achieve my ends by my unaided efforts, I should be given assistance. I must will to be helped if in need" (Nell, 87). But then, by the same token, I would have to will the use of all other (permissible) means, such as flattery or begging, if my ends should turn out to be unattainable without them. Yet this is patently false, as I can reasonably will to get along without flattery, begging, or unpaid help. The flaw in this argument is this: Even if it is necessary that

agents have ends, it is not necessary that we have this or that *particular* end. Thus it is possible for us to renounce certain means, by resolving to pursue only ends attainable without them.

20. This sort of reconstruction is proposed in Scanlon, third lecture. I am using "rational" and "reasonable" interchangeably for the richer German "vernünftig." The qualification "reasonably" is not redundant (due to Kant's identification of the will with practical reason): I mean to stress that, when speaking in this context of what we must or cannot will, Kant is referring to a willing that reflects the proper subordination of empirical to pure practical reason. We can, *un*reasonably, will to treat others merely as means, or to adopt a maxim whose universal availability we cannot at the same time will—namely when empirical practical reason (i.e. "reason at the service of inclination"—*G*, 413n) "presumes to be the sole ground of determination of the will" (*CPracR*, 16).

21. The problem can also be illustrated through an analogous reasoning that features a *narrower* scope and thus arrives at a *less* demanding morality: "As Europeans we can reasonably will that all Europeans may colonize. . . ." This shows how the universalization requirement can convince the agent to respect another only if she *already* recognizes him as an end in itself at least to the point of including him in the scope of her universalizing. And so, again, A presupposes what it purports to achieve: the identification of all and only rational beings as ultimate sources of value.

22. Note how this phrase "absolute value"—introduced in *G*, 394—recurs at the transition to Formula II (*G*, 428).

23. On this topic, *cf.* my more recent essay "Kant on Ends and the Meaning of Life" in Barbara Herman/Christine Korsgaard/Andrews Reath (eds.): *Reclaiming the History of Ethics: Essays for John Rawls* (Cambridge: Cambridge University Press, 1997).

24. Defining the content of morality partly by reference to the capacity for morality is not circular, as Kant takes care to define this capacity independently of that content.

25. Although I am convinced that this is the argument Kant needs and intends to make, I see two gaps in it that the text does not seem to fill adequately. First, Kant would need to show that a good will really has absolute value. The opening paragraphs of Chapter I show at most that there is nothing else that might plausibly be thought to have absolute value. Second, Kant must make the transition from the absolute value of a good will to the dignity of those who merely have the *capacity* for such a good will.

26. Later, Kant confines this to indifference to another's *permissible* ends (*DV*, 6:388).

27. *G*, 430. Kant qualifies "as far as possible": The ends of different others may be incompatible; and some of their ends could not possibly be ends for me (your goals to do a good deed or to learn all by yourself how to whistle).

28. Yet it may still be possible to will that these reasons be given little weight. Thus, while I must not ignore others in distress, for example, I may still acceptably decline to help them when I believe their claims to my aid to be outweighed by my concern for the attainment of my own ends (*cf. DV*, 6:393). I will return to this point about imperfect duties below.

29. I think Kant was aware of the fact that some of his perfect duties are not derivable from Formulas I and Ia straightforwardly interpreted. He suggests that coercion would have served better than deceitful promising as an illustration of Formula II (it "leaps to the eye more obviously"—*G*, 430). So why does he not use coercion as his example? The answer may be that he wanted to use the same example of a perfect duty to others throughout and could not have used the coercion example as an illustration of Formula I at *G*, 403 and *G*, 422, i.e. *before* the introduction of Formula II. (My reading would be helped by the truth of this conjecture, but does not depend on it.)

30. *Pace* Paton, 187f, my preferred translation for "Reich" is "realm" rather than "kingdom" (for which Kant could have used "Königreich"). The central substantive reason is that a realm of ends is not governed by God as its sovereign. As Kant says often, it is not that moral imperatives hold because they are God's commandments, but, on the contrary, they can be viewed as Divine commands only because we already know ourselves as rational beings to be subject to them. If God can be viewed as the head of the realm of ends it is merely because He is not subject to the moral law—lacking any other incentives, He is necessarily in accordance with it (*G*, 434).

31. Kant says just this (*G*, 436), but unfortunately it gets mistranslated. The point is not that all my maxims must harmonize *with* a possible realm of ends—as if such a realm of ends were somehow independently given.

32. *Cf.* the second characteristic of 'to will' above.

33. The categorical imperative thus guides us toward what Rawls has called "reflective equilibrium." See J. Rawls: *A Theory of Justice* (Cambridge MA: Harvard University Press 1971), esp. § §4, 9, 87.

34. On Kant's notions of idea and ideal, see esp. A568–70 / B596–98. Kant connects the ideal of a realm of ends with the notion of a realm of nature. This connection has a twofold significance. First, the realm of ends is to be conceived in analogy to a realm of nature, which is nature regarded as teleologically unified. We must see all forces of nature as cooperating in the production of a final end—which Kant discerns to be human culture. A realm of ends, analogously, is the ideal of a world in which all human beings cooperate in the production of a reason-based, *a priori* end: the consistent attainment of freely chosen ends. Second, the realm of ends must also be consistent with the realm of nature, must harmonize with nature as we know it. Here the demand that morality be compatible with nature is expressed in the demand that my constructed realm of ends should actually come about if all rational beings were to abide by my rational legislation (*G*, 438). My realm of ends can satisfy this condition only if it recognizes and accommodates the laws of nature—mechanical and teleological. In this sense, Kant is not a utopian: The body of moral legislation I am to develop must be practicable in the world as we know it.

35. This view is elaborated in T.C. Williams: *The Concept of the Categorical Imperative* (Oxford: Oxford University Press, 1968), Chapter IX.

36. Kant may have this in mind when he advises "ein und eben dieselbe Handlung durch benannte drei Begriffe zu führen, und sie dadurch, soviel sich tun läßt, der Anschauung zu nähern" (*G*, 437). The translators think Kant is

merely repeating what he had said just before (*G*, 436), namely that the *moral law* should be brought nearer to intuition. They take the "sie" to be referring either to "das sittliche Gesetz," which is ungrammatical, or to "die allgemeine Formel," occurring five lines above. The natural reference, surely, is "die Handlung": it is the action(-type), or maxim, that is to be considered under all three formulas in order to make as plain as possible whether or not one can reasonably will it.

37. Kant does develop an elaborate political philosophy in the 1790's. This leads him to retract the claim (made at *G*, 438f.) that one ought to obey the moral law even if doing so exposes one to danger from others not disposed to act morally. For a general discussion of this shift, see my "Kant's Theory of Justice" in *Kant-Studien* 79 (1988), esp. 407–414.

38. In this regard, Kant is like the author of a book on mountain climbing, who assumes that her readers will want to climb safely and thus will not make every effort to get themselves killed without having violated any of her rules.

# 9

# The Possibility of the
# Categorical Imperative

*Paul Guyer*

## 1. The Formulations of the Categorical Imperative
## and Their Problems

In spite of two centuries of study and many fine commentaries, Kant's *Groundwork of the Metaphysics of Morals*[1] remains a deeply perplexing book. Several of its most vexing difficulties concern Kant's intentions in its Second Part. Here Kant indicates that he takes himself to be offering three different formulations of the fundamental principle of morality—a principle that we human beings call the "categorical imperative" (CI) because it presents itself as an obligatory constraint to creatures like us, whose will, because of our liability to inclination, is not necessarily determined by the pure principle of morality (413). But there are many questions about these three formulations of CI—about which ones they are, about the relationships that Kant intended to establish among them, about the basis from which he thought he could derive them and the manner in which he intended them to be derived from this basis, and about the relationship between the argument for and about the three formulations of CI in *Groundwork* II and the argument of the remainder of the book, especially the argument of *Groundwork* III.

The first difficulty is the question of just *which* statements of CI Kant takes to be its three primary formulations. In his initial enumeration of the formulations, Kant suggests that the three fundamental formulations are what have come to be known as the Principle of Universal

Law (PUL), *"Act only on that maxim through which you can at the same time will that it should become a universal law"* (421), the Principle of Humanity as an End in itself (PHE), *"Act so that you always use humanity, in your own person as well as in the person of every other, never merely as a means, but at the same time as an end"* (429), and the Principle of Autonomy (PA), which Kant does not initially state in the grammatical form of an imperative but rather in the form of "the Idea *of the will of every rational being as a universally legislating will"* (431). In introducing this third principle, Kant explicitly calls it "the third practical principle of the will, as the supreme condition of the conformity of the will with universal practical reason" (431), and on the next page he reiterates his designation of it as the "present third formulation of the principle" of morality (432). However, after next stating that "[t]he concept of every rational being, that it must consider itself as universally legislating through all the maxims of its will, . . . leads to a very fruitful concept which depends on it, namely that of *a kingdom of ends"* (433), Kant adds a review of "the three ways that have been adduced of representing the principle of morality" in which what he treats as the third formulation of CI is not the Principle of Autonomy that he originally so classified but rather a principle employing the idea of a kingdom of ends that he has just said is derived from the Principle of Autonomy, namely the principle "[t]hat all maxims from our own legislation ought to harmonize into a possible kingdom of ends, as a kingdom of nature" (436), which we can call the Principle of the Kingdom of Ends (PKE).[2] So what are the three main formulations of CI according to Kant himself—PUL, PHE, and PA, as he says at 431–32, or PUL, PHE, and PKE, as he says at 436? And is this a significant question, or is the difference between PA and PKE insignificant?[3]

The next question that arises is, whatever precisely Kant thinks that the three main formulations of CI are, how in his view are they related? Kant's own explicit statement on this issue is doubly confusing. First, he claims that PUL, PHE, and PKE are "merely so many formulations of precisely the same law," differing only in that the latter two "bring an idea of reason nearer to intuition," (436) and thus help "secure acceptance for the moral law" (437), while the first furnishes the "strict method" most useful for actual "moral *judgment"* or decision making (436). On this account, the three formulae would seem to be equivalent in their theoretical significance, although they would apparently have different roles in moral judgment—where PUL would dominate—and in moral education—where it looks as if PHE and PA and/or PKE should have the more significant role. However, Kant immediately follows this denial of a significant theoretical difference among the three formulations with the suggestion that they do play theoretically distinct and irreducible roles in the elucidation of the principle of morality: he says that PUL specifies the *"form"* of morally appropriate maxims, "which consists in their universality"; PHE specifies their *"matter—* that is, an end" to be achieved through the adoption of moral maxims; and only PKE offers "a *complete determination* of all maxims" by completing the "progression . . . through the categories of the *unity* of the form of will (its universality), of the *multiplicity* of its matter (of its objects, i.e., its ends), and of the *allness* or totality of the system thereof" (436). But since Kant uses the contrast between "form" and "matter" in so many different ways throughout his corpus, and since he makes clear elsewhere what he means by the complete determination of a *concept of an object* but not what he might mean by the complete determination of a *principle* (or even that there could be any such thing)⁴, it is not at all clear what actually is meant by this explanation of the theoretically distinct contributions of the three formulations to our understanding of the fundamental principle of morality.

But our problems in understanding the argument of *Groundwork* II only begin with this obscure statement. Further problems are raised by some of Kant's other statements about the character of his argument in *Groundwork* II and its relation to the argument of *Groundwork* III.

Early in the argument of *Groundwork* II, Kant states that he intends to ground the principle of morality in the concept of rational being in general and not in any specific features of human nature (412). Still early in his exposition, after he has introduced the contrast between hypothetical and categorical imperatives but before he begins the series of formulations of CI, Kant indicates that there are two different questions about the possibility of CI that he will need to solve. He writes:

> The question now arises: how are all these imperatives possible? This question does not demand to know how the execution of the action which the imperative commands can be conceived, but rather merely how the necessitation of the will can be conceived which the imperative expresses in the task [which it sets]. (417)

I take this to be a reference to the difference between the tasks Kant assigns to the Second and Third Parts of the *Groundwork: Ground-*

*work* III will be concerned with the question of how it is possible for *us human beings* actually to execute CI, that is, act in compliance with it; but before that question can be reached there is a more general question about how it is possible for *any rational being* to will to act in compliance with CI that must be answered—only this brief remark does not make very clear exactly what this preliminary question is.

Likewise, in the transition from discussing PUL to discussing PHE and then again in the transition from PHE to PA and PKE, Kant each time suggests that there is a question about the possibility of a categorical imperative that needs to be resolved within *Groundwork* II and its discussion of rational being in general, thus prior to the argument of *Groundwork* III that we are beings to whom this concept of rational being does apply. Kant concludes his discussion of PUL and his presentation of the four examples of the kinds of duties that arise from it by saying:

> We have thus at least shown that if duty is a concept which is to have meaning and real legislation for our actions, this can be expressed only in categorical imperatives, by no means in hypothetical ones. . . . But we have still not come so far as to prove *a priori* that there actually is an imperative of this kind. . . . (425)

Considered by itself, this might be taken as an allusion to the issue that remains to be settled in *Groundwork* III; but a page later Kant says:

> The question is therefore this: Is it a necessary law *for all rational beings* always to judge their actions in accordance with maxims which they themselves can will that they should serve as universal laws? If there is such a law, it must already by connected (entirely *a priori*) with the concept of the will of a rational being in general. But in order to discover this connection one must, however much one may bristle, take a step beyond it, namely, into metaphysics, although into a region of it which is different from speculative philosophy, namely, into the metaphysics of morals. (426)

The second remark suggests that there is a fundamental question about the possibility of *any* rational being willing to adopt PUL that must be answered within the confines of *Groundwork* II and its metaphysics of morals[5] before we reach the question of whether *we* are rational beings bound by CI. Kant then immediately proceeds to the discussion of PHE, thereby suggesting that the introduction of the idea of an end in itself is a necessary step in the demonstration of the very *possibility* of any rational agent, not just us, being bound and moved by CI. Again, however, it remains unclear just *what* question about the possibility of any rational being acting in accord with CI Kant is raising.

Similarly, Kant's transition to PA after his second discussion of his four examples following his statement of PHE also suggests that there is an outstanding question about the possibility of the principle of morality for any rational being that must be answered within *Groundwork* II rather than within *Groundwork* III. Kant's characterization of PA as the "supreme condition" of the conformity of the will with universal practical reason (431) suggests that now this third principle adds another essential condition of the *possibility* of any rational being actually willing in accord with CI that must be in hand before it can be demonstrated that we ourselves are rational beings subject to the moral law and capable of complying with it. Kant amplifies this suggestion when he says:

> Imperatives as previously represented, namely that of the universal lawfulness of actions similar to *an order of nature*,[6] [and] that of the universal *supremacy as ends* of rational beings in themselves, did, just insofar as they were represented as categorical, exclude from their proper authority every mixture of interest as an incentive;[7] they were, however, merely *assumed* to be categorical. . . . But that there were practical propositions, which commanded categorically, could not itself be proved, any more than it can be proved in this chapter generally; but one thing could have been done, namely, to show that the renunciation of all interest in willing from duty, as the specific mark distinguishing a categorical from a hypothetical imperative, was expressed in the imperative itself by means of some determination that it contains, and this is what is done in the present third formulation of the principle. (431–32)

Here Kant suggests that a critical condition for understanding the possibility of any rational being acting in accord with CI that is not addressed in either its first formulation as PUL or its second formulation as PHE, namely the possibility of any such being acting in accord with CI in spite of the renunciation of interest that CI demands, must be added as part of the metaphysics of morals of *Groundwork* II before he can proceed to the critique of practical reason and its proof of our own freedom in *Groundwork* III. Is this the question about the possibility of CI he has been referring to since 417, and is it the only such question?

Just as he suggests that there are two different questions about possibility that are to be answered in *Groundwork* II and III respectively, Kant also suggests that there are two different synthetic *a priori* propositions to be demonstrated in these two parts of the work. Thus, at the outset of *Groundwork* II, Kant suggests not only that the argument of this chapter must concern rational being in general rather than specific features of human nature, but also that this argument is to be entirely *analytical*, thus that all of the formulations of CI are to be derived from the *analysis of the concept* of a rational being in general: "since moral laws are to hold for every rational being in general, they are already to be derived from the universal concept of a rational being in general" (412). This naturally suggests that it is only in *Groundwork* III that any synthetic, let alone synthetic *a priori*, proposition is to be proved; thus, *Groundwork* II seems to be intended to derive its several formulations of CI from an analysis of a concept of a rational being, and *Groundwork* III to prove that CI in its several formulations is binding *for us* by a proof of the synthetic proposition that *we are* rational beings who instantiate the concept that was analyzed in the preceding section. Yet in spite of Kant's claims that the argument of *Groundwork* II is entirely analytical and that a *"possible synthetic use of pure practical reason"* remains to be demonstrated in *Groundwork* III in order to demonstrate that "morality is something and not merely a chimerical idea without truth" (445), there are also several passages in which he clearly suggests that there is a synthetic *a priori* proposition connected to CI that must be proved *within Groundwork* II. Thus, immediately preceding his formal introduction of PUL Kant says that "with the categorical imperative" we have "a synthetic-practical proposition *a priori*," a claim he explains by saying that in the categorical imperative, "without a presupposed condition from any inclination, I connect the deed with the will *a priori*, thus necessarily (although only objectively, i.e., under the idea of a reason which has full power over all subjective motivating causes)" (420 and 420n). This statement suggests that the connection of the categorical imperative to the will of *any* rational being is synthetic rather than analytic, and that the synthetic proposition asserting the connection of the categorical imperative to the will of any rational being is not identical to the synthetic proposition to be demonstrated in *Groundwork* III that we humans are rational beings. But how can an analysis of a concept of rational being in general yield a synthetic connection between its will and CI?

We now see that we need to answer both a substantive question of *what* conditions of the possibility of action in accord with CI Kant believes are added to PUL by PHE and PA and/or PKE, and a technical question about *how* an analysis of the concept of rational being in general can yield a synthetic *a priori* connection between that concept and the categorical imperative. I will use an analogy to the distinction between "logical" and "real" possibility in Kant's theoretical philosophy to frame my answer to these questions. According to this distinction, which Kant first used at the outset of his polemic with rationalism two decades before the publication of the *Critique of Pure Reason*,[8] the requirement that a concept satisfy the logical condition that it contain no self-contradiction is only one necessary condition for judging that it represents even a possible object; to determine that the object conceived by a concept is a real possibility also requires two other conditions: that it be conceived in accordance with the pure concepts of the understanding necessary to formulate the concept of an object of judgment (the categories), and that it be conceived in accordance with the forms of intuition through which any empirical intuition that could confirm the reality of such a concept would have to be given. As Kant puts his point in the first *Critique*'s "Postulates of Empirical Thought," where he is showing how the pure concepts of possibility, actuality, and necessity are to be schematized, or put into empirically applicable form,[9] the requirement that in a concept of anything as possible "there must be contained no contradiction is, to be sure, a necessary logical condition, but far from enough for the objective reality of the concept, i.e., the possibility of such an object as is thought through the concept" (A 220 / B 267–68); instead, if the concept of possibility "is not to have a merely logical significance and express the form of *thought* analytically, but is to concern *things* and their possibility. . . , [it] must reach possible experience and its synthetic unity, in which alone objects of cognition are given" (A 219 / B 267). Of course, the theoretical requirement that the concept of an empirically possible object must satisfy all the constraints imposed by the categories and the principles of judgment derived from them, as well as those derived from the forms of intuition, cannot be carried over without modification into practical philosophy, for it is no part of Kant's thought that we need to prove the empirical possibility of pure morality.[10] Rather, the analogy that I intend is that while Kant's initial formulation of CI as PUL states a purely formal constraint on practical reasoning, which we can compare to the logical constraint of noncontradiction in theoretical reasoning, and which may even suffice as a rule for moral judgment (as Kant suggests at 437), the further formulations of CI state conditions that are also necessary to make intelligible how the adoption of PUL by *any* rational agent can be possible in both of two different ways bearing a loose analogy to the two different ways in which the categories and the forms of intuition are conditions for the real possibility of a theoretical concept. These conditions of possibility must be specified before it is proved in *Groundwork* III that we ourselves are rational beings—a further step that would be analogous to proving the objective reality of a theoretical concept after it has been shown to define a real rather than merely logical possibility (although, of course, in theoretical philosophy that further step would consist in adducing or constructing an actual intuition for the concept, while the proof of the reality of human freedom does not involve any appeal to intuition).

The two stages in the proof of the real possibility of CI for any rational being may be conceived in the following way. First, we may take Kant to be making tacit appeal to a concept of rational being from which it follows that any action of such a being must have not only a *form* or *rule* but also an *end* or *object* and also an *incentive* or *motive*, although of course not an empirical end or motive. Thus, while PUL may be seen as being derived from an analysis of the specific concept of a *moral* or *practical law,* Kant's argument for PHE presupposes an analysis of the broader concept of a *rational being* that states that a rational being never acts without an end, or a goal to be achieved by its action, even where the action is one of adopting a principle, so that a rational being never adopts a principle without it being possible to characterize an end that is realized in or through that principle;[11] and his argument for PA turns on the need to specify a motive that can make it rational for such a being to adopt PUL. Thus, the very action of adopting PUL itself cannot be shown to be rational unless an end valid for rational being as such that can be realized both in and through compliance with PUL and a motive that can be satisfied by this compliance can be identified—a task quite distinct from showing that we human beings with all our sensuous inclinations are actually capable of complying with CI (the issue in *Groundwork* III and the *Critique of Practical Reason*). However, to make sense of Kant's claim that the connection of CI to the will of any rational being is synthetic, we need to assume that while an analysis of the concept of rational being is supposed to reveal the *need* for such an objective end and motive, Kant's designation of rationality (in the form of humanity) as the only end in itself that can give a reason for any rational being to accept PUL and his account of the dignity of autonomy as the basis of any rational being's interest in adopting PUL are intended to be seen as synthetic rather than analytic claims (even though his brief arguments for PHE and PA may leave obscure just *why* their conclusions should be synthetic rather than analytic). On this account, the synthetic *a priori* proposition demonstrated in *Groundwork* II—that any rational being has a ground to will to act in accord with PUL—would be a *different* synthetic *a priori* proposition from the proposition that is to be proved in *Groundwork* III—that we human beings *are* rational beings who are bound to act in accord with CI and are capable of doing so.

Second, I will argue that Kant's discussion of PKE makes a further contribution to establishing the real possibility of action in accord with PUL for any rational being, analogous to showing that a theoretical concept is compatible with the forms of intuition or is schematizable. While PA may provide an account of how any one rational being can have an interest in acting in accord with PUL, and thus adds to the account, begun in the discussion of PHE, of what it is that makes it rational for any being to adopt CI, it does not yet show that the formal requirement of universalizability and the end of respecting rational being as an end in itself are realizable in a domain consisting of a *manifold* of moral agents. What has to be shown here is that a multitude of agents always can find a single maxim of action acceptable to all in spite of whatever empirical interests may separate them. By postulating "the systematic combination of different rational beings through common laws," a "whole of all ends (of rational beings as ends in themselves) as well as of the individual ends that each may set for himself," which requires abstraction "from all personal differences of rational beings as well as all content of their private ends" (433), PKE expresses the further assumption that must be made in order to ensure that a multitude of agents can actually formulate a universally acceptable maxim of actions, and thus that PUL can actually be applied to a domain of multiple agents. (This is again a theoretical question distinct from the factual question of whether we human beings with our divergent inclinations can actually comply with CI.)

Thus, PHE and PA on the one hand, and PKE on the other, describe two different essential conditions for the possibility of adopting PUL. My argument will thus be that only the four formulations of CI taken together display all the conditions necessary to show that action in accord with CI is a real possibility for any rational agent, *a fortiori* a real possibility for ourselves if we are or are capable of acting as rational agents. In other words, my claim will be that while PUL alone may suffice to define the *form* of CI, only PUL, PHE, PA, and PKE taken together suffice to conceive of the possibility of a realm of rational agents acting in compliance with CI, or to conceive of a possible object for the concept of CI.

This paper is hardly intended to provide a complete assessment of Kant's arguments for his four formulations of CI and their plausibility, but only to provide an account of the relationship among these formulations that could serve as a framework for such an assessment.[12]


## 2. The Principle of Universal Law

In particular, my interpretation does not claim anything novel about PUL itself, so I will here make only two points necessary for my subsequent argument.

There is no doubt that PUL is supposed to be reached by a strictly analytical argument, but there is room for question about what concept it is that the argument is supposed to analyze. However, we should notice that although Kant begins the argument of *Groundwork* II as a whole by saying that "moral principles" must be derived from the "concept of a rational being in general" (412), he introduces his first explicit statement of PUL by stating that "the formula . . . that contains the only proposition that can be a categorical imperative" can be derived analytically from the "mere concept of a categorical imperative" (420), or of a moral law. His argument is that since the very idea of a CI excludes the possibility that the validity of its command is conditional upon any contingently occurring particular desire for an end, only the universal validity of an agent's maxim, as a purely formal feature of it, remains as that which can be commanded by the imperative:

> For since besides the law this imperative contains only the necessity of the maxim to conform to this law, but the law contains no condition to which it is limited, there is nothing left but the universality of a law in general to which the maxim ought to conform, which conformity alone the imperative properly represents as necessary. (420–21)

This analysis turns on the prior definition of a categorical imperative as "one which would represent an action as objectively necessary for itself, without relation to another end" (414). This argument itself can be seen as deriving from a prior stipulation that any genuine moral law must hold for all rational beings:

> If one does not wish to deny to the concept of morality all truth and all relation to any possible object, then one cannot dispute that its law is of such widespread significance that it must hold not merely for men but for all *rational beings in general,* not merely under contingent conditions and exceptions, but *absolutely necessarily.* (408)

This suggests that PUL is reached by a two-staged analysis: first, the concept of morality entails the validity of its fundamental principle for all rational beings; then the argument continues that a principle valid for all rational beings cannot depend upon any empirical condition, so an imperative that cannot depend upon any empirical condition can only command conformity to the idea of the universality of maxims as such.

On this account, the analysis of the concept of *morality* or *moral law* would stipulate the validity of a moral law for all rational beings, but would not itself require a complete analysis of the more complex concept of *rational being*. Thus, while Kant's argument seems simply to assume that any rational being should adopt the requirement of universality without mentioning an end that is served by so doing, this is not an objection to it, because the analysis of the concept of rational being itself that stipulates that a rational being must always have an end and a motive for its action has not yet been introduced. Only when this analysis has been broached does Kant need to introduce PHE and PA in order to explain the rationality of adopting PUL itself.

But before we can consider how PHE is introduced into Kant's argument, we need to consider whether Kant's analytical argument for PUL will *preclude* his subsequent argument for PHE. In the analysis thus far considered, Kant is clearly claiming that the idea of acting for any empirically given reason—thus, acting to bring about any *empirically given* end or objective—is incompatible with the idea of the universality of moral law. But he also seems to suggest that CI commands action without regard to *any* end at all, or that the requirement (established in *Groundwork* I) that the goodness of virtuous action lie within the action itself and its relation to CI as its principle means that its goodness is not connected to *any* end intended to be achieved by such action. The following seems to preclude a virtuous action's being a means to any end:

> All imperatives are formulae for the determination of an action which is necessary in accord with the principle of a will which is in some way good. Now if the action would be good merely *for something else* as a means, the imperative is *hypothetical*; if it is represented as good *in itself,* thus as necessary in a will which is in itself in accord with reason, as the principle thereof, then it is *categorical*. (414)

And so does this claim, that a CI

> [d]oes not concern the matter of action and that which should result from it, but rather the form and the principle from which it itself flows, and the essentially-good in it consists in the disposition, let its consequence be what it may. (416)

Such remarks seem to assert that a rational being acts without any regard to ends at all, and that the goodness of its actions is entirely independent of any end that may be achieved through them, arising instead solely from the kind of principle that is the motivation for them. In fact, however, the idea that a rational being wills in the absence of any end whatever is not only incompatible with the fuller analysis of the idea of rational agency Kant is going to introduce, but is also *not* implied by the analysis that has led to PUL.

First, the argument by which Kant reaches PUL actually excludes from the grounds for adopting a fundamental principle of morality only *empirically given* ends, not any sort of end altogether, for the obvious reason that a maxim adopted only in order to attain a particular empirically given end would be contingently rather than universally and necessarily valid.[13] What the concept of a CI excludes is not purpose as such, but any *arbitrary* purpose:

> That which it is necessary in order to do merely for the attainment of an arbitrary aim [*einer beliebigen Absicht*] can itself be considered as contingent, and we can always free ourself from the precept by giving up the aim; the unconditional command, on the contrary, leaves the will no arbitrary choice [*Belieben*] in regard to the opposite, thus it alone brings with it that necessity which we demand for a law. (420)

Kant will make exactly this point when he subsequently introduces PHE: "The ends which a rational agent arbitrarily [*nach Belieben*] sets as *effects* of his action (material ends) are all only relative; for only their relation to a faculty of desire in a subject which is determined in a particular way gives them their value" (427). Thus what needs to be excluded by CI is not all ends whatsoever, but only ends that agents arbitrarily adopt because of their contingent desires.[14]

The same pattern of argumentation is found in the *Critique of Practical Reason*, where Kant begins with the assumption that a practical principle must be universally valid (§1, 5:19), asserts that "[a]ll practical principles that presuppose an *object* (matter) of the faculty of desire as their determining ground are empirical" (§2, 5:21), and from that infers that a proper practical principle must determine the will through its form rather than its matter (§4, 5:27). Again, what is excluded is not the idea of an end as such—here Kant does not even use the word *Absicht* or *Zweck*—but only matter or object of the *faculty of desire*. In all of these passages, then, the logic of Kant's analysis entails only the independence of the principle of morality from any contingent and empirically given end, not the exclusion of any concept of end as such.

Kant's initial contrast between hypothetical and categorical imperatives may not make this point clear. Here he states that while hypothetical imperatives "represent the practical necessity of a possible action as a means to something else, whatever it may be," a CI represents "an action as objectively-necessary for itself, without relation to another end" (414), and that while a hypothetical imperative says "that an action is good for some *possible* or *actual* aim," a CI "declares the action as objectively necessary without relation to any aim, i.e., even without any other end" (414–15). These statements seem to suggest that CI commands obedience from rational beings without reference to any end at all. But even in these statements, what Kant twice excludes is relation to *another* end, an end to which the action commanded would be a *mere* means. This leaves open the possibility that there may be an end achieved *in* the adoption of CI itself.

Likewise, a number of Kant's comments after his initial introduction of PUL make it clear that he does not mean CI to be adopted without any motivation whatsoever, but only without any contingent desire for an end as the motive for its adoption. Thus, after the derivation of his four examples of duty from PUL (422–24), Kant claims to have shown only that if *duty* is a meaningful and authoritative concept, then it can be expressed only in categorical imperatives, but that it remains to be proved *a priori* "that there actually is an imperative of this kind." To prove that there actually is a CI, he says, requires showing "that there is a practical law which by itself commands absolutely and without all incentives [*Triebfedern*]" (425). In the next three paragraphs, however, he makes clear, by saying it no fewer than ten times, that what he means by requiring that the practical law command without "all incentives" is that it command without any merely *empirical* and *contingent* incentives: feelings [*Gefühle*], propensities [*Hange*], inclination [*Neigung*], subjective causes [*subjektiven Ursachen*], and so on—in a word, without reference to the *special characteristic of human nature* (425). All of these are empirical feelings directed to objects of contingent desire. What is required instead is that "if there is such" a law, it "be connected (entirely *a priori*) with the concept of a will of a rational being in general" (426). To do this requires precisely that a *nonempirical* end be supplied through which a rational being in general could be moved to adopt CI or to connect the law to its will, a noncontingent end that could be the object of a nonempirical motive. Kant states that "if *reason for itself alone* determines conduct (the possibility of which we will now investigate)" then "everything related to the empirical of itself falls away" (427). I suggest we read this to mean that all empirical ends fall away when reason supplies a nonempirical end through which PUL can be connected to the will of a rational being.

Finally, the same point emerges at the outset of Kant's introduction of PHE. Here Kant says, "Practical principles are *formal* if they abstract from all subjective ends; they are, however, *material* if they are grounded on the latter, thus on certain incentives" (427). This implies that a formal principle such as PUL does not have to be adopted without regard to all ends whatsoever, but only without regard to "subjective" ends, that is, those set by merely empirical incentives.

### 3. The Principle of Humanity As an End in Itself

My next claim is that Kant's discussion of PHE represents the first step beyond PUL into the metaphysics of morals announced at 426, or, better, a two-step, in which he first asserts that a fuller analysis of the concept of the will of a rational being in general than has yielded PUL shows the necessity of a nonempirical concept of an end for a rational being as such, produced out of the resources of reason alone, and then, in a move that is intended to yield a synthetic proposition, argues that rational being itself is the only such nonempirical end. The provision of this end thus supplies a further necessary condition for the rationality of any agent's adoption of CI, or for the real possibility of CI.

Kant makes it plain at the outset of his discussion of PHE that his analysis of rational agency is more complex than has been revealed by PUL. He first characterizes the will, "a faculty to be encountered only in rational beings," as the faculty "of determining oneself to action in accord with *the representation of certain laws*"—which may be taken to sum up PUL—but then adds that there must also be an end, "which serves the will as the objective[15] grounds of its self-determination" (427). A rational will does not act on a law without any end in sight— that would be the paradigm of irrationality. If CI were already connected to the will of a rational being, then any end *compatible* with it might suffice for rational action; but if CI itself remains to be connected to rational willing, then what is needed is an end that can itself make acceptance of this law reasonable for any rational being. Thus if there is to be a universally valid practical law, there must be an end that is universally valid, and such an end must be given by reason itself. Such an end would have "an absolute value" or be an "end in itself" in that its value would not derive from any subjective, arbitrary, or material desire. And, Kant plainly states, "in it and it alone would lie the ground of a possible categorical imperative" (428). Without the existence of such an objectively and universally valid end it would not be possible, on an analysis of a rational agent as one that both conforms its will to a law and has an objectively valid end, for such a being to adopt CI, in the sense that it would not be intelligible why such a being should do so. Thus the provision of an objectively valid end is a necessary condition of the real possibility of action on CI.

Kant characterizes in at least four different ways the objective end of reason he now introduces: "man and in general every rational being"; "rational beings which can be called *persons*" (both 428); "*rational nature*"; and "*humanity in your own person as well as in the person of everyone else.*" "Rational nature" is the fundamental characterization, and the other formulations are derivative from this: a being is a person insofar as it has rational nature, and 'humanity' here connotes not the properties essential to humans as members of a biological species but rather the rationality that makes biological humans persons.[16] Thus, Kant's claim is that rationality itself is the end for rational willing in general, objective in the two distinct senses of describing an end for action and being universally valid, which makes it possible for a rational being to adopt CI as its maxim. For the purposes of this paper, I will assume without further argument that making rational being an end in itself requires the preservation and promotion of freedom, and that the realization of this end is achieved (at least in part) through the adoption of PUL, whose requirement of universal acceptability preserves the possibility of *consent* on the part of all agents affected by any agent's proposed maxim.[17] Here the only issue I can discuss is how we are to understand the way in which Kant introduces this claim into the argument of *Groundwork* II. Kant introduces PHE by blandly stating, "Now I say: man and in general every rational being *exists* as end in itself" (427). But what is the status of this assertion?

Kant might seem to be reaching this assertion by an argument by elimination, in which case his procedure in arguing for PHE would be analogous to his method of argument for PUL. Just as there the formal requirements of universalizability was reached by the exclusion of all empirical maxims, so here the idea that reason itself is the end of reason could be seen as being reached by the exclusion of everything else as an end for universally valid willing simply on the ground that any other end would be empirically given and therefore not universally valid. This might look like another merely analytical argument, yielding a merely analytical conclusion rather than a synthetic connection between PUL and the will of any rational being. However, we must be intended to see the proposition that rational being is an end in itself as a fundamental synthetic *a priori* proposition, which could give rise to the further synthetic *a priori* proposition that the adoption of PUL is rational for any rational being, because PUL gives the form of the law that must be adhered to if the end of preserving and promoting rational being is to be attained, but that cannot itself be deduced by any antecedent argument. There are two ways in which we might be supposed to be intended to see this proposition as synthetic *a priori*. On the one hand, Kant's method in the *Groundwork* might be intended to be analogous to his method in the *Prolegomena to any future Metaphysics* of two years before, in which he assumes the synthetic *a priori* status of propositions of mathematics and pure natural science in order to prove the existence of *a priori* forms of intuition, but does not attempt to give a transcendental deduction of the former propositions themselves. On this account, we would just have to see that the proposition is synthetic *a priori*. Alternatively, in analogy with Kant's method in the "Principles of Judgment" in the first *Critique,* we may be intended to see not the proposition that rational being is the end in itself but rather the proposition that the only possible ends are empirical ends or rational being itself as a synthetic *a priori* proposition, with the elimination of the first disjunct then following from the earlier requirement that a moral law be universally valid.[18]

In any case, the assumption that there can be no direct and positive *argument* for the identification of reason as the objective end of rational willing is consistent with Kant's earliest and never retracted characterization of the methodology of moral philosophy in the essay *On the Distinctness of the Principles of Natural Theology and Morality*.[19] Here, where he already works with (though does not yet name) the distinction between hypothetical and categorical imperatives, Kant claims that a moral theory requires both a *formal* and a *material* first principle. This is because "it is impossible, by contemplating a thing or a concept of any kind whatever, to recognize or infer what one ought to do, if that which is presupposed is not an end."[20] So he holds that moral action may require a formal constraint, but also requires an end, because otherwise "no specifically determinate obligation flows from [the] rules of the good." But there cannot be a demonstration of what the fundamental end is, because such a demonstration could proceed only by showing that its candidate is a means to a further end, in which case of course it would not be the fundamental end after all. At this stage of his development, Kant concludes that the fundamental end must be recommended by feeling rather than reason, tacitly identifying the faculty of reason with the faculty of demonstration. The Kant of the *Groundwork* instead supposes that we can see that reason and only reason can be an end in itself, but still suggests no way of deducing that from any more evident premise. So we still seem to be left with the conclusion that there is no direct way to argue for PHE, although its assertion as a fundamental synthetic *a priori* proposition may be confirmed by the way it illuminates the examples of the four classes of duty that have already been derived from PUL.[21]

Even though the nature of Kant's argument for PHE remains obscure, the significance of his introduction of it into the sequence of formulae in *Groundwork* II can be further clarified by contrast to a complementary but distinct move in the introduction to the *Doctrine of Virtue* of the later *Metaphysics of Morals*. Here Kant claims that "[e]very action . . . has its end," or that "whatsoever is an act of *freedom* on the part of the acting subject, not an effect of *nature*," requires that the agent himself make "the object of his choice into an end" (6:385).[22] From this he infers that there must be ends that are also duties, and that can be universally commanded, for otherwise a CI would not be possible. "For were there no such ends, then all ends would hold for practical reason only as means to other ends; and since there can be no action without an end, a *categorical* imperative would be impossible" (6:385).[23] Kant then searches among the general classes of all our possible ends for some that could qualify as duties, excluding, for different reasons, those that cannot, namely our own happiness and the perfection of others, and leaving those that can, our own perfection and the happiness of others. These then furnish the basis of the more specific duties of virtue.

This argument can be seen as based on the assumption that a rational being cannot perform any *particular* action without a particular end, and thus that there must be ends *compatible* with the adoption of CI if the latter is itself to be a possible rule of action for rational beings. But this assumes that the necessity and therefore the possibility of adopting CI has already been established: "one can begin with the maxim of actions in conformity with duty and seek out the end that is also a duty" (6:382).[24] In the *Groundwork*, however, Kant treats the adoption of CI as something that must itself be shown to be possible for a rational being, which it can be only if there is shown to be a necessary and universal end that any rational being would hold but that can be realized only through the adoption of CI. In other words, Kant conceives of a rational being as one for whom *every* level of action must have an end, not merely particular actions that need to be compatible with CI but also the higher-order action of making CI into its fundamental maxim.[25] The *Doctrine of Virtue* requires that there be ends that are *compatible* with the adoption of CI, but this presupposes the argument of the *Groundwork* that there be a universally valid end that offers a reason for the adoption of CI itself.[26]

Before leaving the discussion of PHE, I want to return briefly to the larger question of how the idea that rational nature is itself the universally necessary end of all rational willing is to be reconciled with Kant's earlier claim that moral action is "good in *itself*" (414) rather than in relation to any "other end" (415). As is well known, in *Groundwork* I Kant argues that an action is morally praiseworthy because of the quality of its intention rather than actual outcome (394); but the considerations he appeals to there imply only that, because of the ways in which forces beyond the foresight or control of an agent can intervene between the intended and actual outcome of an action, we should praise an agent in virtue of the *intended end* of his action rather than its *actual outcome*. Understood this way, Kant's claim would not imply that the moral value of an action is independent of any end altogether, but only that it is independent from the actual realization of its intended end. In *Groundwork* II, Kant seems to have a more controversial claim in mind. As we have seen, Kant never introduced any premise from which it would follow that a virtuous action can have no end at all; rather, his requirement that the adoption of CI depend upon no arbitrarily given end will be satisfied if the adoption of CI depends on the adoption of an end that is noncontingent. However, we can now go further and see that rational being as an end in itself is in a certain sense fulfilled in any action that is performed under its aegis, and is not merely an effect of it that could in principle be attained through some other means. That is, PHE can be interpreted as presenting rational being as both the means and the end of moral action, thus as introducing an end that is neither "another" end external to moral action nor an "arbitrary" end. The relation between action performed with the intention of satisfying CI and the end that makes the adoption of CI rational can be called constitutive rather than instrumental in the sense that such an action is itself an *instance* of rational being (or of being rational), although there is also a way in which action on CI is instrumental to rational being as its end, since it is aimed at bringing about a state of affairs that goes beyond the *individual rational agent's* compliance with CI itself. That is, while there may be a kind of conceptual identity between moral action and its aim, insofar as the end of being rational is nothing other than rational being itself, and is therefore already reached in acting rationally, there is also an extensional difference between the rationality of any one action, and of any one agent, and rational nature in general, which allows rational nature to serve as an end of moral action the attainment of which goes beyond the individual agent's performance. For what is commanded by PHE is that "humanity in your own person as well as in the person of every other always be [your] end" (429), that is, that each moral agent strive to preserve and promote rational nature in all persons or all rational agents affected by his actions, not just in himself. Thus, although every moral action is already an instance of the general idea and ideal of rationality, the outcome it is aimed to produce can be the preservation and promotion of rationality in a wide range of instances other than itself. In these two ways, then, any particular exercise of rational nature is itself an instance of that which is absolutely good and yet also has an aim that is outside of and larger than itself.[27]

Kant draws on this understanding of rational nature as an end in itself in a final explanation of how PHE serves as the ground for the adoption of PUL, which without it would be fallacious:

> The ground of this principle is: *rational nature exists as an end in itself.* Man necessarily represents his own existence to himself in this way; in so far as it is therefore a *subjective* principle of human actions. But every other rational being also represents its own existence to itself in this way in accordance with the same rational ground [*Vernunftgrundes*] which is also valid for me; thus it is likewise an *objective* principle, from which as a highest practical ground all laws of the will must be able to be derived. (429)

If this were read to assert that just because I value *my* rational nature and every other human or rational being values *his* or *her* rational being, therefore *I* have a reason and an obligation to value the rational nature of *every other* human or rational being, it would be fallacious—that I love my wife and you love your husband obviously does not of itself give me a reason to love him. But I take it that what Kant means is rather that each of us values his or her own existence as a rational being because of the value of rational nature *in itself*, which however gives us the same reason to value rational nature in every one else as in ourselves. There is no fallacious inference from love of self to love of others, but rather a valid inference from a general source of value to the value of each of its exemplifications. In this way my moral action is good in itself, because it is an instance of that which is fundamentally good, but at the same time has an end lying beyond itself, namely the preservation of rational agency in general and the promotion of it wherever that is possible and reasonable for me.

PHE thus contributes an essential element to demonstrating the real possibility of CI by specifying an objective end that is realized in and through action on CI and that thereby makes it rational for a rational being to act in accord with CI. We will now consider several further contributions to the demonstration of the real possibility of CI for rational beings in general that are made by Kant's discussion of PA and PKE.

## 4. The Principles of Autonomy and of the Kingdom of Ends

At the outset of his discussion of "our third practical principle for the will" Kant states that the ideas of universal law and of rational nature as an end in itself can be combined into the complex "*idea of the will of every rational being as a universally legislating will*" (431), which idea yields the command "to do everything from the maxims of one's will as one that can at the same time regard itself as universally legislating," that is, PA (432). Then he says that "the concept of every rational being that must consider itself as universally legislating through all the maxims of its will" leads to the "fruitful concept" of a "*kingdom of ends*" (433), which in turn gives rise to PKE, the requirement "that all maxims from one's own legislating ought to harmonize into a possible kingdom of ends, as a kingdom of nature" (437). This series of assertions seems to suggest that the idea of the kingdom of ends adds nothing new to the notions of universal law and rational nature as an end in itself.

At the same time, however, Kant also claims that the first two formulations of CI "were merely *assumed* to be categorical, because one had to assume them to be something like that if one would explain the concept of duty," and that something more needs to be done in *Groundwork* II, even though the final proof that there are practical propositions that command *us* categorically still awaits the argument of *Groundwork* III. This suggests that there is an essential contribution to the analysis of the conditions of the real possibility of action on CI for rational beings in general that must precede the final proof that we ourselves are rational beings bound by the moral law. What could this be?

I will suggest that in the course of his brief discussion Kant actually introduces two distinct ideas. First, PA, or the idea of the moral agent as not merely acting in compliance with universalizable maxims but also as conceiving of himself as a universal legislator and thus as the source of these maxims, characterizes the interest we have in acting on the categorical imperative, an interest necessary to compete with the empirical interests we have in acting on hypothetical imperatives. Kant's further characterization of rational beings as having a unique dignity as makers of their own laws continues this account of the necessary conditions of the CI by exhibiting rational nature as not only an objective end but also one that can motivate us. Second, conceiving of not only oneself but of all the others who may be affected by one's actions as universal legislators, that is, as agents who have not only particular empirical interests but also the same overriding interest in universal legislation that one has oneself—that is, postulating that those whom one's actions affect can be members of a kingdom of ends—is a necessary condition of acting on CI, for only the postulation that all who are affected by one's actions are capable of universal legislation can make it reasonable to suppose that a universal law can be accepted by a manifold of agents in spite of their diverse empirical interests. Thus PKE is necessary to prove that CI is not just, as it were, intensionally noncontradictory and coherent but also extensionally realizable—the final requirement for a demonstration of the real possibility of CI, analogous to the proof that a pure concept of understanding can actually be realized in a manifold of intuition given the form of such a manifold.

Kant begins his discussion of PA by claiming that the idea of the will of a rational being as one capable of universal legislation is necessary in order to explain the possibility of "the renunciation of all interest" required for action on a categorical rather than hypothetical imperative (431). Kant's explanation of this claim is that prior efforts at moral theory have failed to see the human being "as subject *only to his own yet nevertheless universal legislating*," and thus have only been able to conceive of him "as subject to a law (whatever it might be) because it carries with it some interest as an attraction or compulsion [*Reiz oder Zwang*], since it does not arise as a law from *his* will, but the latter is necessitated in a law-like way to a certain course of action by *something else*" (432–33)—what Kant called "heteronomy" rather than "autonomy" (433). That is, on prior theories the moral agent would be capable of action in accordance with hypothetical imperatives, the adoption of which is always dependent on the presence of contingent aims or interests, but not capable of action on CI, which may require disregarding any contingent incentives. For if agents conceive of themselves as having merely empirical incentives, they may be able to conceive of themselves as using reason instrumentally in the pursuit of contingent goals, but only if they conceive of themselves as legislators or as having "a will which is itself supremely legislative" (432) will they be able to see themselves as having an interest in using their reason for universal legislation rather than for the pursuit of contingent and private aims. In other words, the idea of oneself as a universal legislator rather than as a mere subject of universal laws imposed from without allows one to conceive of oneself as having an identity that is fulfilled by universal legislating. When we so conceive of ourselves, action in accord with CI seems like the realization of our own identity rather than submission to an external constraint, and is in this way well motivated. Thus, the idea of oneself as a universal legislator essential to PA introduces a self-conception that is a condition of the possibility of being motivated to act on a categorical rather than merely hypothetical imperative.

The depiction of a motive necessary for the intelligibility of the adoption of CI is continued in Kant's account of the dignity of autonomy. The real bedrock of Kant's moral thought is his vision of the value of autonomy, the idea that an incomparable dignity attaches to freeing oneself from nature and being one's own master in the most general possible sense. Law making has dignity, as opposed to mere "market" and "fancy" price (434–35), because only through it can the will avoid being "imposed upon" or "wheedled" into doing something not of its own choice (435), and law making can determine value for other things or even transmit it to them because it itself has the incomparable dignity that attaches to self-mastery. Rational nature can be seen as an end in itself when it is interpreted as not merely subjection to but the willing of universal law because then it can be seen as the means by which agents capable of being rational free themselves from natural law and attain the dignity of self-mastery.[28]

The thought that there is an incomparable value or dignity in self-mastery over nature, which can be attained only through the willing of universal law, is what is ultimately necessary in order to explain why rational being is an end both in one's own person and in that of everyone else. The dignity of autonomy is what makes the preservation and promotion of one's own rational nature an absolute end; but it makes humanity an end in everyone else as well because one's own autonomy is not desired merely as a matter of personal preference, but as something of incomparable dignity wherever it occurs. In Kant's words, autonomy is not an object of self-love, but is rather "the ground of the dignity of human and of every rational nature" (436).

It can here be noted only in passing that this conception of the goal of morality is the ground of the constraint on what one can do for others that Kant emphasizes in all his writings on ethics from his early lectures to the late *Doctrine of Virtue*, namely that since the end of morality is self-mastery one cannot directly realize this end for others, but can at best help them in realizing it themselves. As Kant puts this point, "it is a contradiction for me to make another's *perfection* my end. . . . For the *perfection* of another human being, as a person, consists just in this: that he *himself* is able to set his end in accordance with his own concepts of duty" (6:386).[29] This overlooks the ways in which I may make it my goal to help others in realizing their own freedom, but just as clearly emphasizes that it is the rational exercise of freedom that is itself human perfection and thus the necessary and objective end of moral action.

Finally, Kant's introduction of PKE as well as PA constitutes the last step in his exhibition of the conditions of the real possibility of CI by demonstrating the assumption that is necessary in order to ensure that a universal law can be found for any manifold of agents. Kant defines a kingdom of ends thus:

> I understand, however, by a *kingdom* the systematic combination of different rational beings through common laws. Now since laws determine ends in accord with their universal validity, then, if one abstracts from personal differences of rational beings, as well as from all content of their private ends, a whole of all ends (both of rational beings as ends in themselves as well as of the individual ends which each may set for himself) in systematic connection, i.e., a kingdom of ends, can be thought, which is possible in accordance with the above principles. (433)

This passage can be interpreted as making several claims. First, if one is to conceive of rational beings as abstracting from all personal ends but still as agents, that is, as still having some reason to act, then one must also conceive of them as universal legislators, that is, as agents who see their reason and capacity for universal legislation as itself a reason to will. This reiterates the point previously made, although it applies it to all members of a kingdom of ends and not just oneself. But second, it is only if one sees both oneself and all others who may be affected by one's actions as having not only personal ends but also both the capacity for and interest in universal legislation that one can be sure that a systematic connection of ends is always possible, that is, that for any set of circumstances there is indeed some universalizable maxim that can be adopted by oneself and others. If agents have only individual ends and merely instrumental reason, there is no guarantee that in any given circumstances there will be any maxim of action that could be adopted by any single agent that will also be compatible with all those ends. But if all the agents involved have the capacity for and interest in universal legislation, they will all be able to abstract from the content of their personal ends and come up with a universally acceptable maxim, even if in some particular situations that will only be the maxim that in those circumstances everyone must refrain from seeking to fulfill any merely empirical interest. In other words, only in a community of universal legislators, where universal legislation itself is available as an end in addition to particular empirical interests, will it always be possible to formulate a universal law, and thus for any individual rational agent to comply with PUL; only in a community all of whose members see themselves as universal legislators and not just as pursuers of individual ends will there always be some maxim that is indeed not only acceptable to but well motivated for all. Thus, just as the absence of logical contradiction in the idea of a figure enclosed within two straight lines does not prove its possibility in the space permitted by our form of intuition,[30] and only figures actually constructible in that space are really possible, so too the practical concept of a universal law can be proved to be a real possibility only for a domain of agents all of whom are universal legislators capable of setting aside personal interests and acting out of their common interest in being such legislators.[31]

Thus, both PA and PKE bring out crucial features of Kant's analysis of the full conditions for the real possibility of action on CI that need to be in place before the demonstration that we are actually capable of satisfying all those conditions, to be offered in *Groundwork* III, can be contemplated. PHE took a first step towards the exhibition of these conditions in going beyond the formal requirement of the universalizability of one's maxims by introducing rational nature as an end of action; but the conceptions of the moral agent as a universal legislator and of the community of moral agents as a kingdom of ends are necessary in order to explain how an individual moral agent could possibly act apart from personal interest and how a community of moral agents could possibly arrive at a systematic union of maxims and ends. Thus, Kant was wrong when he said that the formulations of CI beyond PUL are necessary just in order to bring morality closer to intuition, and in a lesser way wrong when he suggested that three formulations of CI are necessary for a complete determination of the principle of morality: a complete account of the real possibility of action in accord with CI for any rational being requires reference to the four formulations PUL, PHE, PA, and PKE.[32]

## Notes

1. *Grundlegung der Metaphysik der Sitten* (1785), text in *Kants gesammelte Schriften*, edited by the Royal Prussian (later German) Academy of Sciences (Berlin: Walter de Gruyter [and predecessors], 1900–), at vol. 4, pp. 385–463, edited by Paul Menzer. Citations are given parenthetically by page number of this edition; translations are my own, although many are influenced

by those of H.J. Paton, *Immanuel Kant: Groundwork of the Metaphysics of Morals* (New York: Harper and Row, 1964), originally entitled *The Moral Law* (London: Hutchinson, 1948). I will comment on my divergences from Paton only where I think his version is actually misleading. I like Paton's translation of Kant's title because it preserves the sense of active effort implied by Kant's gerundive *"Grundlegung"* better than such passive translations as *Fundamental Principles of the Metaphysics of Morals* (T. K. Abbott) or *Foundations of the Metaphysics of Morals* (Lewis White Beck), without employing Ellington's neologism 'grounding'.

2. Note that here Kant does formulate his principle in something approximating the grammatical form of an imperative, which he did not do in the introduction of PA. Note that here there is also some significance to my departure in several particulars from Paton, who writes, "All maxims as proceeding from our own making of law ought to harmonize with a possible kingdom of ends as a kingdom of nature." First, in agreement with Thomas Pogge, I translate Kant's *zu* more literally as 'into' rather than as 'with' in order to convey the idea that the kingdom of ends is an ideal we strive to bring about through our actions, not a preexisting reality with which we merely attempt to comply; see his "The Categorical Imperative" in *Grundlegung der Metaphysik der Sitten: Ein kooperativer Kommentar*, ed. Ottfried Höffe (Frankfurt: Klostermann, 1989), 172–93, at 186; Second, I preserve Kant's comma between 'kingdom of ends' and 'kingdom of nature,' in order to preserve the appearance that the latter phrase is in apposition to the former, not introducing any fundamentally new requirement in addition to the idea of a kingdom of ends itself but rather suggesting that our aim from the outset is always to *realize* the ideal of a kingdom of ends in our actual actions, that is, in the kingdom of nature.

3. In suggesting that there are *four* formulations of CI the relationships among which must be understood, I would appear to be ignoring the well-known position of H.J. Paton that there are *five* different formulations: in addition to the four I have listed (which he called formulae I [PUL], II [PHE], III [PA], and IIIa [PKE]), Paton also considered as a distinct formulation (Ia) what he called the Formula of the Law of Nature, "Act as if the maxim of your action were to become through your will a *universal law of nature*" (421). Paton thought that formula Ia added an indispensably teleological conception of nature and thus of the *natural* purposes of humans to the purely formal requirement of universalizability in formula I (see *The Categorical Imperative: A Study in Kant's Moral Philosophy* (London: Hutchinson, 1947), 149–52). But Kant himself does not refer to this as a separate formulation of CI in his catalogues at 431–32 or 436. This is because, as Philip Stratton-Lake has most recently argued, on Kant's own view formula Ia does not add any teleological assumptions not included in formula I, but merely expresses the "typic" or condition of the possibility of its application: that is, in considering whether a law is universalizable, the task set for us by formula I, we do not need to refer to any ends actually set by nature, human or otherwise, but only to consider whether the world that would be defined by the universalization of the maxim being tested by PUL would actually be consistent with the realization of the end for the sake of which the adoption of that maxim is being considered. (See Strat-

ton-Lake, "Formulating Categorical Imperatives," *Kant-Studien* 84 (1993): 316–40, at 322–23; also, Bruce Aune had earlier argued (in *Kant's Theory of Morals* (Princeton: Princeton University Press, 1979), 111–16) that Ia is merely the "typic" of I.) This argument clearly holds in those cases where the universalization of a proposed maxim would lead to what Kant calls a contradiction in conception, or a self-contradiction (424); it may not hold in the case of a contradiction in willing, where the universalization of a maxim is not obviously self-contradictory but would undercut ends that every rational will is assumed to have.

4. See *Critique of Pure Reason*, A 133 / B 172.

5. Note that the "Transition from Popular Moral Philosophy to a Metaphysics of Morals" takes place in *Groundwork* II (406), whereas *Groundwork* III contains the "Transition from a Metaphysics of Morals to a Critique of Pure Practical Reason" (446). Like the subsequent *Critique of Practical Reason* of 1788 (which supersedes it), the transition to a critique of pure practical reason in *Groundwork* III concerns not the content of the principle of morality but the fact of our own freedom to act in accordance with the canon of rationality which that principle expresses. As Kant's remarks at 426–27 indicate, a metaphysics of morals is metaphysical because it shows a moral *principle* to be *a priori* rather than empirical, not because it adduces a metaphysical conception of the moral *agent*. The transition to a metaphysics of morals in *Groundwork* II thus concerns the content of the principle of morality, and the present remarks thus suggest that there is a question about the possibility of CI that needs to be answered by a synthetic proposition about rational beings in general, not the synthetic proposition about ourselves that is to be demonstrated in *Groundwork* III.

6. This sentence provides additional evidence for the view that Paton's formula Ia is not meant to be essentially distinct from formula I: the order of nature is only an analogy for the order of universal law, not anything additional to it.

7. *Triebfeder*. Paton translates it here as 'motive', although he elsewhere translates it as 'incentive', which connotes a motive based in sensuous inclination. But 'motive' should be reserved for Kant's more general term *Bewegungsgrund* (literally, moving or motivating ground), of which a sensuous inclination is only one kind, and a ground originating in reason another. If *Triebfeder* is translated as 'motive', then Kant's theory will end up implying that moral action has no motive, which he does not mean; what he means is that the motive of moral action must be rational rather than sensuous, that is, not a *Triebfeder*.

8. See *The Only Possible Argument in support of a Demonstration of the Existence of God*, 2:77–78, in Immanuel Kant, *Theoretical Philosophy 1755–1770*, ed. David Walford (Cambridge: Cambridge University Press, 1992), 122–23.

9. For an explanation of this interpretation of Kant's notion of schematism, see my *Kant and the Claims of Knowledge* (Cambridge: Cambridge University Press, 1987), 157–72.

10. Here I have in mind, of course, Kant's famous claim, "It is absolutely impossible to establish through experience a single case with complete cer-

tainty where the maxims of an otherwise dutiful action have rested solely on moral grounds and on the representation of one's duty" (407). And it is equally obvious that subjection to the universal law of causation, which is a necessary condition of the real possibility of empirical objects, is not going to be a necessary condition of the real possibility of action in accord with CI, but is instead in Kant's view incompatible with the latter.

11. The phrase 'in or through' is meant to suggest that the relationship between the adoption of the principle and the realization of an end need not be merely *instrumental*, in the sense that the adoption of the principle is merely a causally efficacious but logically independent means to the realization of the end, which might at least in principle be reached through other means; it might be *constitutive*, in the sense that the end is already attained in acting on the principle itself, and there is also no other way to attain the end. I will subsequently argue that the end connected with the formal principle of universalizability is related to it in *both* of these ways. (I owe this way of putting my point to my colleague R. Jay Wallace.)

12. This paper further develops the approach to Kant's ethics suggested in my "Kant's Morality of Law and Morality of Freedom," in R. M. Dancy, ed., *Kant and Critique: New Essays in Honor of W.H. Werkmeister*, ed. R. M. Dancy (Dordrecht: Kluwer, 1993), 43–89, while going beyond the interpretation of the relationship among the three formulations of CI sketched there (76–77). That paper was written before I had seen "Leaving Deontology Behind," the final chapter of Barbara Herman's *The Practice of Moral Judgment* (Cambridge: Harvard University Press, 1993), 208–40. Both my earlier paper and this one share Herman's views (1) that "[f]or the alignment of morality with rationality to enable us to understand the special demands of morality . . . it must reveal the sense in which rationality as a regulative norm represents a distinctive conception of value" (213), and (2) that both PHE and PA add to PUL conditions under which it is possible for CI to "'connect' substantive requirements on willings with the concept of the will of a rational being as such." Beyond my appeal to Kant's distinction between logical and real possibility for a framework for my interpretation, however, there will be another difference between Herman's account and mine. According to Herman, Kant's "successive formulations [of CI] interpret the arguments of the CI procedure in terms that reveal the aspects of rational agency that generate contradictions under universalization," thereby showing "*how* content is derived from the constraints of universal form for willing" (237–38). On this account, the several formulations of CI all analyze the same concept, but substantive information necessary for the successful use or application of the "CI procedure" is introduced only successively. I will not take a position here on whether the succession of formulations is necessary in order to derive substantive moral rules from the idea of CI. But I will argue that Kant progresses from an analysis of the concept of a moral law to an analysis of the concept of rational agency; that his argument is not exclusively analytic, but also includes a specification of the end for any rational agent that can be considered synthetic; and that both phases of this extended argument are necessary in order to explain the possibility of action in accord with CI, whatever substantive moral rules that entails, both for individual rational agents and for any community of rational agents.

13. In other words, the argument for PUL is an attack upon *empiricism* in practical philosophy, parallel to Kant's attack on empiricism in theoretical philosophy, not an argument for the rationality of action without any end.

14. Cf. Herman's remark, "Purely formal principles do not have *no* content; they have *noncontingent* content" (*The Practice of Moral Judgment*, 217).

15. Paton proposes that 'objective' be replaced by 'subjective', meaning roughly "in the subject" rather than having a ground in objects, which sense he claims is "rare" in Kant (*Groundwork*, 94 n. 63.2). But this would destroy the sense of Kant's argument, which is that if it is to be rational for any agent to determine its will in accord with an objective law such as PUL, then there must be an objectively valid end that can serve as its reason for so doing.

16. Thus, 'humanity' and 'personality', which are distinguished in the *Religion* to connote self-love and rationality respectively (6:27), are here used synonymously to connote rationality only.

17. For discussion of the normative implications of Kant's conception of rational being as an end in itself, see especially Thomas E. Hill Jr., "Humanity as an End in Itself," *Ethics* 91 (1980): 84–90, reprinted in his *Dignity and Practical Reason in Kant's Moral Theory* (Ithaca: Cornell University Press, 1992), 38–57, and also my "Kant's Morality of Law and Morality of Freedom," 63–65. In the most general terms, Kant's conception of rational being as an end in itself requires that we *preserve* rational being, both by avoiding the destruction of the *existence* of rational beings (whether ourselves or others) and by preserving the possibility of the *exercise* of rational agency in the form of *consent* to our actions (*Groundwork*, 429–30), but also that we go beyond these essentially negative duties by *promoting* the development of rational nature *in* rational beings, that is, doing what we can to advance the development of both our own and others' *capacity to act rationally* (see *Metaphysics of Morals*, 6:427)—in our own case, for example, by developing talents that will allow us to satisfy rationality's demand that we develop the means that will allow us to attain our morally permissible ends, whatever they may turn out to be.

PHE is sometimes taken to entail only that the *existence* of rational being is never to be acted against, which would furnish us with a *constraint* on our permissible actions but would not supply any positive goal that could itself be an end of rational agency instead of or in addition to ends determined by naturally occurring desires. In support of such an interpretation, H. J. Paton appeals to a passage in which Kant says, in Paton's translation (105), that "the end must here be conceived, not as an end to be produced, *but as a self-existent end*. It must therefore be conceived only negatively—that is, as an end against which we should never act" (437). Paton interprets this to mean that "[a]n objective and absolute end could not be a product of our will; for no mere product of our will can have absolute value. An end in itself must therefore be a self-existent end, not something to be produced by us" (Paton, *The Categorical Imperative*, 168; see also Bruce Aune, *Kant's Theory of Morals*, 76). What we can do with respect to such a self-existent end, however, since we cannot bring it into existence, is just to refrain from damaging or destroying its existence. Thus Paton interprets PHE as implying only a limitation on our actions, not as itself giving us a positive goal for action, and thus as not advancing Kant's argument past PUL (*The Categorical Imperative*, 178).

But this interpretation—although it explains why Paton thinks that Kant must rely on a teleological conception of natural ends in order to introduce any positive rather than merely negative duties (that is, why he thinks there is a difference between his formula Ia and formula I)—rests on a misleading translation and on taking Kant's remark out of context. First, the sentence I have quoted is preceded by this: "In the idea of a will which is absolutely good without any limiting condition (of the attainment of this or that end) there must be abstraction from all ends *to be effected* [*zu* bewirkenden *Zwecke*] (as would make every will only relatively good" (437). This should again be read to exclude only particular, contingently good ends, which would make the will to produce them merely relatively rather than absolutely good. Second, what Kant actually writes in the sentence at issue is not that the end of an absolutely good will is *self-existent* but that it is *selbstständig*, that is, *self-sufficient* or *independent*. (The latter is Lewis White Beck's translation; see *The Foundations of the Metaphysics of Morals* [Indianapolis: Bobbs-Merrill, 1959], 56.) This again suggests that Kant's claim is that the value of the good will is independent of particular, contingent ends, not that it is the kind of thing that cannot be brought into existence by our own action. Thus, Kant's remark that the end of moral action has to be conceived "negatively" as something that is not to be "acted against" has to be interpreted in the context of his aim in the whole paragraph, which is to show that PHE and PUL specify coextensive sets of duties. Kant has already clearly admitted positive duties to improve and promote the conditions of rational willing as well as negative duties not to destroy instances of rational nature. Thus he must mean here only that both the negative and positive duties entailed by PHE are negative or not to be acted against in the sense that they limit or constrain the pursuit of any merely subjective or personal ends. There is thus no suggestion that a supreme *limiting* condition consists of merely *negative* duties.

18. The analogy would be that in his proofs of the Analogies of Experience and Refutation of Idealism, Kant tacitly assumes that empirical judgments of temporal order could be made by either the perception of absolute time or inference from laws governing the behavior of objects in time, and then explicitly eliminates the first possibility. For further discussion of this as a method that is supposed to yield synthetic *a priori* principles of empirical knowledge, see my *Kant and the Claims of Knowledge* (Cambridge: Cambridge University Press, 1987), especially 418–21.

19. Submitted in the fall of 1762 for the Berlin Academy of Sciences essay competition on the question of whether the principles of theology and ethics are as certain as those of mathematics, and published in 1764. I have discussed this essay and its implications for Kant's subsequent moral philosophy in "Kant and Mendelssohn: One Source of the Critical Philosophy," *Philosophical Topics* 19 (1991): 119–52.

20. 2:299; translation by David Walford in Immanuel Kant, *Theoretical Philosophy 1755–1770*, 273.

21. Herman perhaps suggests a similar view when she writes, "The concep-

tion of value [in PHE] has no separate derivation" (*The Practice of Moral Judgment*, 240).

22. Immanuel Kant, *Metaphysics of Morals*, trans. by Mary Gregor (Cambridge: Cambridge University Press, 1991), 189–90.

23. Ibid., 190.

24. Ibid., 187.

25. *Religion within the Limits of Reason Alone* provides clear textual evidence for conceiving of the adoption of CI as itself an action—and one of, as it were, a higher order than that of adopting particular maxims. There Kant writes that a good or evil disposition, "i.e., the ultimate subjective ground of the adoption of maxims, can be one only and applies universally to the whole use of freedom. Yet this disposition itself must have been adopted by free choice [*Willkür*], for otherwise it could not be imputed" (6:25; translation by Theodore M. Greene and Hoyt H. Hudson (New York: Harper, 1960), 20).

26. Herman puts this point by describing rational agents as ones for "whom reasons go all the way down," who thus are never simply caused to act by a desire but who act for principles (whether of desire-satisfaction or of morality) that are themselves adopted for reasons. "It is for this reason," she says, "that the willings of rational agents are open to full justification" (*Practice of Moral Judgment*, 228). Of course, this should not be taken to imply that the ultimate or most fundamental decision of rational agents (to act out of self-love or the principle of duty) are open to full *explanation*; there is nothing in the present view that is incompatible with Kant's thesis of the inscrutability of the most fundamental acts of choice.

27. Here I believe there is a significant difference between my interpretation and Herman's. She holds that it "misses the point" to ask for "some other good that" willing in conformity with the principle of CI "promotes or brings about" (*Practice of Moral Judgment*, 215), and thus concludes that the task of a Kantian conception of value is to show how action in accord with the CI manifests a conception of value "in action and judgment" (ibid., 216). This could suggest that this value must be fully realized within any instance of action on CI, or, in the language I have been using, that the relation between the CI and the objective end of rational being is entirely constitutive. But it is part of my view that since action on CI is rational because it is intended to preserve and promote rational being in general, not just in the agent's own case, there is also a sense in which any individual instance of rational action is indeed instrumentally related to rational being as an end in itself.

28. In other words, the argument of the *Groundwork* reveals that the incentive of respect for the moral law, first mentioned at 435 and then so heavily emphasized in the *Critique of Practical Reason*, makes sense only because of the value we attach to that which is to be achieved through the adoption of that law, namely autonomy.

29. Translation by Gregor, 191.

30. *Critique of Pure Reason*, A 220–21 / B 268.

31. Herman's account of the function of PKE stresses that through this formula persons are seen as reasoners all the way down, but does not show how

this yields a guarantee of the possibility of universalizability itself (see *Practice of Moral Judgment*, 228–30).

32. I would like to thank R. Jay Wallace, Juliet Floyd, Samuel Freeman, and Allen Wood for comments on earlier drafts of this paper.

*Part IV*

# The Categorical Imperative and the Freedom of the Will (*Groundwork* III)

# 10

# Kant's Argument for the Rationality of Moral Conduct

*Thomas E. Hill, Jr.*

Kant is known as a champion of the idea that moral conduct is demanded by reason; but, despite a remarkable revival of interest in Kant's ethics, surprisingly little attention has been paid to Kant's explicit argument for the idea.[1] This neglect is understandable but unfortunate. The misfortune is not that we have overlooked a sound and lucid proof which could have effectively settled all contemporary controversies about whether it is rational to be moral; it is rather that we have missed, or misread, a text which is crucially important for understanding Kant's *Groundwork of the Metaphysics of Morals* and which contains ideas worth considering in their own right. The argument in question is what is summarized in the opening paragraphs of the notorious third chapter of the *Groundwork*. The usual reading not only makes Kant appear careless and unbelievably confused; it reinforces an interpretation which has Kant holding the outrageous view that immoral acts are unfree and not even willed. Moreover, common readings of the argument have Kant arguing from a forbidden empirical premise (regarding a feeling of freedom), confusing natural laws and laws of conduct, and committing an obvious non sequitur by overlooking the fact that he can only prove freedom "from a practical point of view."

In what follows I will sketch a reconstruction of the main features of Kant's argument, a reconstruction which I believe avoids these gross difficulties and yet remains (largely) faithful to the text. My discussion, however, will concentrate more heavily on the earlier stages of the argument, for two reasons. First, those early stages, in which Kant argues that rational wills have autonomy, offer an intriguing proof that

Humeans and Hobbesians are mistaken about the nature of practical reason, and the proof is quite independent of Kant's belief that he has identified the supreme moral principle. Second, though the earlier stages have drawn the heaviest ridicule, I think they are both more crucial to the interpretation of the *Groundwork* and more promising than the later stages. Though focusing upon the earlier parts of Kant's argument, I will however comment briefly on a step at the end where I believe Kant goes wrong.

## 1. Aims of the Argument and Possible Reasons for Its Neglect

The task Kant undertakes in chapter 3 of the *Groundwork* is nothing less than proving that moral constraints are requirements of reason. His argument, then, amounts to an answer to the contemporary question "Why be moral?" But Kant's aim is easily obscured by the fact that his imagined audience is not the sort of moral skeptic with which we are most familiar today. Kant does not see himself as addressing, for example, those who are indifferent to morality and demand that philosophy supply them with a motive to be moral; for Kant's own theory denies that anyone rational enough to ask the question could really be so indifferent.[2] Nor, I think, is Kant addressing an audience that doubts that common sense duties, as opposed to some revisionary standards, are genuinely moral (*G*, 403–4). He does not imagine that anyone who clearly understood his supreme moral principle would need to wait for a proof before he felt its rational force. The intended audience, I think, is rather those whose moral commitment is liable to be called into question by philosophical accounts of practical reason which imply that morality could not be grounded in reason. To these Kant argues, first, that their theories of practical reason must be mistaken and, second, that the only alternative shows moral requirements to be rational. The argument, if sound, has important implications for contemporary moral skeptics; but its focus, its style, and perhaps even the degree of care devoted to its parts are influenced by Kant's own conception of his audience. That audience may have picked up ideas of Epicurus, Hobbes, and Hume; Nietzsche comes later.

The aim of the third chapter, in Kant's terms, is to *establish* the supreme moral principle. This is the second of two main aims stated in the preface of the *Groundwork*, namely, "to seek out and establish the supreme principle of morality" (*G*, 391–92). Seeking out, or identifying the principle, is accomplished in the first two chapters, which also analyze the principle, reformulate it in various ways, and relate it to ideas of moral worth, dignity, etc. In the second chapter, using a so-called "analytical" method, Kant also argues that the concept of moral duty *presupposes* unconditional commands of reason not based on desires and hypothetical imperatives; but this only raises the stakes for the third chapter and leaves us with the possibility that there may be no genuine moral duties. That is, the argument purports to show that if there are moral duties then there must be non-desire-based requirements of practical reason (*G*, 425); but whether or not there are such rational requirements is left an open question. As Kant says, for all that has been shown, morality may be "a phantom of the brain" (*G*, 445), that is, a set of constraints falsely believed to be rational but actually having their source in imagination rather than reason. In chapter 2 the various formulations of the supreme moral principle are *labeled* "the Categorical Imperative" (*G*, 421, 428–29, 440), but it is admitted that no proof has yet been given that they *are* categorical imperatives or indeed that a categorical imperative is possible (*G*, 425, 440, 445). That task is left for chapter 3.

If my reading is right, the argument of the third chapter is obviously important; why, then, has it been so often overlooked or maligned? The most obvious explanation lies in the fact that the argument is extremely compact, unclearly stated, and deeply entangled with aspects of Kant's metaphysics that have little appeal today. A further obstacle is that Kant himself suggests that he may have been reasoning in a circle (*G*, 440–41), and though he claims to have found a way out of the circle this turns on an introduction of the "intelligible world" that is not obviously helpful (*G*, 453). One is discouraged from trying to unravel all this by the fact that in the *Critique of Practical Reason* Kant seems to abandon the project of establishing the rationality of morals. There moral obligation is simply declared a "fact of reason" and used to establish that rational wills are free (which is a crucial *premise* in the argument of the *Groundwork*).[3] Another obstacle is the fact that Kant spends so much of the third chapter of the *Groundwork* stressing the compatibility of phenomenal determinism and noumenal freedom that one is tempted to see the point of the chapter as a defense of morality against determinism. Finally, I suspect that Kant's argument has been underrated because many sympathetic commentators believe that, on Kant's own principles, it is unnecessary and perhaps even morally corrupt to ask seriously, "Why be moral?"[4] To read the third chapter of the *Groundwork* as an attempt to answer this question, then, would be to see it as misguided and bound to fail.

Although these considerations help to make the neglect of Kant's argument understandable, they are not, I think adequate to justify it. One can make some headway despite the obscurities and heavy metaphysics; the reversal of premises and conclusion in the *Critique of Practical Reason* can be explained by the different nature of its project;[5] and, despite Kant's dramatic rhetoric about circular reasoning, the argument of the third chapter is not in fact a circular one.[6] The long discussion of the compatibility of freedom and determinism (in chapter 3) cannot be the main point, because this was supposedly demonstrated earlier in the *Critique of Pure Reason* and it would not answer the question so provocatively declared open at the end of chapter 2, namely, whether alleged duties are, as they purport to be, genuine unconditional commands of reason. Again, while Kant thought it a mistake to try to give reasons for being moral in terms of desired ends contingently served by morality, this does not mean that he failed to recognize a need to demonstrate that moral requirements are rooted in reason.[7]

## II. The Structure of the Argument

The most crucial passages are the following:

> Will is a kind of casuality belonging to living beings so far as they are rational. *Freedom* would then be the property this causality has of being able to work independently of *determination* by alien causes. . . .
>
> The above definition of freedom is *negative* and consequently unfruitful as a way of grasping its essence; but there springs from it a more *positive* concept, which, as positive, is richer and more fruitful. The concept of causality carries with it that of *laws (Gesetze)* in accordance with which, because of something we call a cause, something else—namely, its effect—must be posited *(gesetz)*. Hence freedom of the will, although it is not the property of conforming to laws of nature, is not for this reason lawless: it must rather be a causality conforming to immutable laws, though of a special kind; for otherwise a free will would be self-contradictory. . . . What else then can freedom of the will be but autonomy—that is, the property which the will has of being a law to itself? The proposition 'Will is in all its actions a law to itself' expresses, however, only the principle of acting on no maxim other than one which can have

for its object itself as at the same time a universal law. This is precisely the formula of the Categorical Imperative and the principle of morality. Thus a free will and a will under moral laws are one and the same. (*G*, 446–47).

This passage argues in effect that, if free in a negative sense, every rational will is committed to morality. The following passage contains the nub of the rest of the argument, which is to show that every rational will is free (in a negative sense).

Now I assert that every being who cannot act except under the *Idea of freedom* is by this alone—from a practical point of view—really free; that is to say, for him all the laws inseparably bound up with freedom are valid just as much as if his will could be pronounced free in itself on grounds valid for theoretical philosophy. And I maintain that to every rational being possessed of a will we must also lend the Idea of freedom as the only one under which he can act.[8]

The main outline of the argument is clear enough. Reordering the parts, we have (1) an argument that any rational will is free in at least a negative sense, (2) an argument, turning on definitions of negative freedom and autonomy, that any will free in the negative sense has the property of autonomy (*G*, 446), (3) an assertion, relying on earlier arguments, that any rational will with autonomy is committed to the principle "Act only on maxims you can will as universal laws,"[9] (4) an assertion, again relying on earlier arguments, that this last principle is the supreme principle of morality.[10] From all this it follows that any rational will is committed to the supreme principle of morality. Thus we can conclude that anyone who acts immorally is acting contrary to a principle which he himself accepts. If we assume that the principle in question is an unconditional and not merely prima facie one,[11] then such immoral acts must be irrational because contrary to an unconditional commitment of the agent. If we assume further that the argument shows that rational autonomous agents are committed to the supreme moral principle *qua* rational and autonomous, then immoral acts will be irrational not only because they are contrary to the agent's commitments but also because they are contrary to a principle the agent acknowledges to be rational.[12]

Each of the major steps, of course, depends upon subsidiary arguments, some of which I shall consider shortly. But before that, a few preliminary remarks may be helpful.

First, in steps (1) and (2) Kant aims to show that any rational will has autonomy, and these stages presuppose nothing about morality. Now though these stages are parts of a larger argument that it is rational to be moral, they are of interest independently of that larger project. They are concerned not merely to affirm a freedom unthreatened by causal determinism but to argue the necessity of acknowledging rational principles of conduct other than those which prescribe efficiency in satisfying our desires or in coordinating our means and ends. The conclusion, even at this earlier stage, is that anyone who acts for reasons must acknowledge at least some reasons other than facts about what is needed to achieve his ends and to satisfy his desires. If so, then regardless of what we think of morality there must be practical reasons which are not hypothetical imperatives. Hobbesians will be wrong to construe all rational principles as rules of rational self-interest; modern decision theorists will be wrong if they suppose that all rational choice principles are relative to intrinsic preferences themselves uncriticizable by reason; and Humeans will be wrong to suppose that reason merely calculates and discovers facts rather than prescribing conduct. The conclusion is a strong and controversial one: a striking feature of the *Groundwork* is that Kant's argument for it does not depend upon claims about morality.

As a final preliminary, I must say a few words about the interpretation which I shall try to avoid.[13] According to this, the will is practical reason and so cannot will anything contrary to reason; morality is prescribed by reason and so no one wills to be immoral; the will, which is thus always good, is free negatively and wills unequivocally perfect conformity to the laws of autonomy. Thus, on this view, one who acts to satisfy desire contrary to morality, and perhaps even one who acts to satisfy a morally neutral desire, does not really will so to act and does not act freely in any sense. His behavior is a product of natural forces, like that of animals or, better, animals with complex built-in computers for calculating the best means to satisfaction. We are strange hybrids sometimes governed by freely acknowledged rational moral principles and sometimes in the grip of natural forces beyond rational control; and what switches us from the one mode to the other is inexplicable. It could not be a free choice because to be capable of free choice is to be in one mode rather than the other. When we act from desires we act heteronomously, which is to say unfreely and nonrationally; when we act from moral principle, we act autonomously, which is to say freely and rationally. And there can be no free choice between the two, for free choice is always for the rational and moral.

Kant does say things in the *Groundwork* which suggest this strange picture, but I am convinced that the textual evidence, on the whole, is opposed to it. However, in order to lay out my reconstruction of the argument under consideration even in the present sketchy form, I must leave detailed examination of particular passages for another occasion. For now I must be content to offer an alternative reading which, I hope, makes more sense of the compressed and puzzling argument in the third chapter and to call attention to the disparity between the interpretation I reject and the views Kant makes more evident in his later ethical writings. These later works,[14] with the explicit distinction between *Wille* and *Willkür*, make clear that Kant then thought the adoption of ends in general and certainly the adoption of immoral maxims were free choices of a rational agent, even though not maximally rational choices. To understand the *Groundwork* in the context of Kant's work as a whole without regarding it as a radical deviation, we must see if we can understand his argument without having to attribute to him the bizarre picture I have sketched with its consequence that immorality is unfree and unwilling.

### III. From Negative Freedom to Autonomy

Conceptual analysis, Kant suggests, should suffice to show that any rational will which is free in a negative sense is also free in the positive sense (autonomy). The crucial definitions are those of *will, negative freedom,* and *autonomy*.

*Will* is a "kind of causality," distinct from causation by prior events and natural laws, a sort of ability to make things happen peculiar to rational agents (*G*, 446). Elsewhere, importantly, Kant characterizes the will as a power to act "in accordance with (his) idea of laws—that is, in accordance with principles" (*G*, 412, 427). The idea is that to be an agent, or a rational being with a will, one must be able to make things happen in such a way that the appropriate explanation is reference to the principles, laws, or reasons on which the person acted. Principles, even laws, enter into the explanation of why a rational agent did something (as distinct from merely why the body moved) as the agent's guiding "ideas" or rationale, not as empirically observable regularities among types of events. In fact the will for Kant (in contrast, say, to

Hobbes and Hume) is not an event, a mental episode occurring prior to action, which explains that action in the ordinary empirical way.[15] Kant believed, of course, that explanations of an act by reference to the agent's reasons (and so his will) were compatible with accepting deterministic explanations of the corresponding behavior by empirical laws; but that belief is not essential to the important distinction between the two types of explanation.

This conception of the will has several important implications. First, Hume's famous *reductio ad absurdum* of indeterminism does not apply to Kant.[16] Hume, assuming that an indeterminist's "free will" was an uncaused event prior to an agent's act, argued that such an event, unconnected with the agent's character, was not something for which a person could be held morally responsible. Kant undercuts the objection by denying that "willing" is a prior event. His own metaphysical account of the will has problems enough of its own, but he may be right to suspect that, in its classic form, the dispute between determinists and indeterminists rests on a shared model of rational action that is inadequate. As many since Kant have acknowledged, those who are troubled by the picture of *desire, act of will,* and *bodily movement* as discrete physical events in a causal sequence, like falling dominos, do not obviously render responsibility less puzzling simply by denying the causal connection between the first two items (desire and will) and/or by assigning these items to an introspectible mental realm. Second, since an act of will for Kant is not an introspectible phenomenon, it is no reply to Kant's argument that the will is committed to a certain principle (e.g., the Categorical Imperative) to say, "But I don't remember deciding to follow that." An argument that the will of every rational agent is committed to morality need not be based on observations of their life histories. In at least this respect moral commitment is supposed to be like rational commitment to basic principles of logic and empirical understanding. Third, behavior cannot be attributed to the will of an agent, not even to the "free will" of an agent, unless it is supposed that the agent was acting for a reason, or guided by "the idea of a principle (or law)." Thus it is part of the concept of a will that it cannot be "lawless."[17]

Next we need to look at the *negative concept of freedom*, which is "the property (the will) has of being able to work independently of *determination* by alien causes." It is clear enough that Kant means at least to deny that there is an empirical causal account for why free wills act for the reasons they do. To attribute an act to the free will of a rational agent is not to cite its empirical causes or to refer to an empirical mechanism or power, caused or uncaused, which explains how an observed behavior came about. The *Critique of Pure Reason* is supposed to have established the *possibility* that such a will is in some sense responsible for what we do despite Kant's insistence, and supposed proof, that empirical science can in principle give causal explanations of all phenomena, mental as well as physical. The first *Critique* also makes clear the price Kant is willing to pay for this compatibility, namely, conceiving the will as something apart from the spatiotemporal order which we can "comprehend"; but that full price, I think, is not essential to the main thrust of our argument.

The preceding remarks reflect the usual (though still vague) understanding of a will's capacity "to work independently of determination by alien causes." But, importantly, there must be more than this to Kant's conception of negative freedom if the step from negative freedom to autonomy is at all plausible. For even if we conceive a negatively free will as somehow independent of causal determinism, we could still regard such wills as (causally inexplicable) capacities to act for the sake of satisfying desires and inclinations. In other words, though acting for reasons is not to be understood as being causally determined by one's given desires, nevertheless one's capacity to act for reasons might be limited, perhaps even by the concept of reasons, to policies aimed at satisfaction of some of the desires and inclinations one happens to have. We might speak of such a will as incapable of *motivation* by anything but inclination and desire, where "motivation" refers not to what causes the willing but rather to the range of things the will can count as reasons or rational objectives of its policies. Though again I must forgo detailed textual argument, I think it is evident once the distinction is made that Kant regarded a negatively free will as also capable of acting independently of motivation by desires and inclinations. There is a sense, perhaps unfortunate, in which Kant regarded even the agent's own desires as "alien," and "determination" of the will, even by "alien" factors, does not refer exclusively to having a place in a deterministic nexus of causes. On the contrary, when Kant writes of a will "determined" by reason, this is not to cite a prior event and a causal law but rather to say that the guiding idea on which the agent acted was a rational one; and, similarly, when a will is "determined" by inclination in a standard case (not a knee jerk, reflexive scratching, etc.), this means the agent's policy or guiding idea was some hypothetical imperative concerning the means to satisfy the inclination. In the latter case there is a (misleading) sense in which "alien causes" determine the will; it is not that the agent's inclination deterministically causes the agent to will what he does, but rather that the agent's chosen policy makes a certain causal connection, or strictly his belief in a certain causal connection, be a decisive (or "determining") factor for what he does. His full rationale (not a causal event) is: "I shall do whatever is necessary as a means to satisfy my inclination $B$; $A$ is a necessary means to satisfy $B$; hence I shall do $A$." The agent has let the causal law, or strictly his idea of the causal law, between that sort of means and end be the dominant or "determining" factor in his choice; but this does not mean that the willing itself was subject to causal explanation.

Notice that the interpretation I have pledged to avoid does not make this distinction between being caused to act by one's inclination and choosing to act on policies which make satisfaction of inclination the rationale for acting. Once it is made, however, it seems clear that Kant's conception of freedom, even negatively defined, encompasses not only capacity to will without the willing being explainable by causal laws and prior events; crucially, freedom also includes the ability to will, or act for reasons, where the agent's rationale is not a hypothetical imperative indicating the means to satisfy an inclination. Without this stipulation the argument that negatively free wills necessarily have autonomy would fall flat: for autonomy, as we shall see, implies a capacity/disposition to follow principles other than desire-based hypothetical imperatives.

The most difficult definition in the argument is that of *autonomy* (or freedom positively conceived). Part of the difficulty in understanding this stems from the fact that the misguided picture I am trying to avoid is rather deeply entrenched in commentaries and is encouraged both by ambiguities in Kant and by everyday (non-Kantian) talk about autonomy. On that picture autonomy is an ideal achieved by some and not others, or perhaps by some people some of the time but not always. Rather than a property of all human wills, it is seen as a property of purely conscientious wills when willing out of respect for the moral law. The misleading picture is reinforced by a facile use of the expressions, which are not Kant's, of "acting autonomously" for free/morally inspired conduct and "acting heteronomously" for causally determined or at least desire-motivated conduct.

To the contrary, Kant's view, I think, was that autonomy is a property of the will of every minimally rational agent, which includes virtually all adult sane human beings, no matter how wicked. Heteronomy is a possible property of wills which misguided moral philosophers have mistakenly attributed to human beings.[18] All rational agents, Kant argues, have negative freedom, and to have negative freedom is to have autonomy as well. This is not to say that everyone chooses to fulfill the commitments he has by virtue of having autonomy of will. The immoralist is not one who has a will characterized by heteronomy but rather one who acts as if the human will were such, i.e., one who in practice ignores the implications of having a will with autonomy and acts as if the only authoritative rational principles were hypothetical imperatives.

Kant's most explicit definition of autonomy is that it is a will's property of "being a law to itself (independently of every property belonging to the objects of volition)" (*G*, 440). Though by itself this is not so illuminating, what is meant, I think, can be plausibly reconstructed as follows: a will with autonomy is not only negatively free but is committed to at least one principle acknowledged as rational to follow but such that (a) one is not causally determined to accept or follow it, (b) it does not merely prescribe taking the necessary (or best) means to one's desired ends, (c) the rationality of accepting it does not depend upon contingent facts about what means will serve one's ends or about what ends one happens to desire, and (d) the principle is "one's own" or "given to oneself by oneself," i.e., it expresses a deep commitment from one's "true" nature as a rational and (negatively) free agent rather than, say, expressing respect for an external authority, tradition, conventions, etc. All this is simply a long way of saying what is (more vaguely) summarized by saying that a will with autonomy accepts for itself rational constraints independently of any desires and other "alien" influences.

With these preliminaries and definition in hand, we can see how that argument from negative freedom to autonomy must go. Negatively free rational wills can act for reasons without being motivated by desires and hypothetical imperatives. But, as they are not "lawless," when they so act they must be following some principle (or principles) which allows us to attribute the act to a rational agent, acting for reasons, as opposed to whimsical behavior, knee-jerk reactions, etc. So the agent must have, or be committed to, principles he acknowledges as rational even though they are not of the hypothetical imperative sort. Because the agent is negatively free, acceptance of such principles cannot be causally determined. Since principles adopted because of external authorities (e.g., God), tradition, convention, etc., would be based on hypothetical imperatives, these cannot be the rational principles in question. The only alternative, it seems, is that the principles reflect some necessary features of rational agency itself independently of its special contexts. If we assume (with Kant) that one's nature as a rational will is in some sense one's "true" self in contrast to passively "given" phenomenal desires, then we could conclude further that the rational principles in question are "one's own" or "given to oneself by oneself" in a way that desire-based principles are not.

The last step raises deep questions about personal identity which need not cloud the main point, namely, that if one can act rationally without causal determination and without following desire-based principles, then one must have some principle or principles which are rational and yet not hypothetical imperatives. If rational agents are negatively free, then, they must acknowledge rational principles of conduct beyond those recognized by followers of Hume and Hobbes. This conclusion is reached not by exhibiting an example of such a nonhypothetical rational principle but by indirect argument that there must be such if there is rational free agency.

Since the argument turns on the *capacity* to act without motivation by desire, the conclusion is not that free agents invariably follow nonhypothetical rational principles but only that they must have or acknowledge them. If they had no such commitments, they would lack the ability to act rationally without following hypothetical imperatives; but having the capacity does not mean that they will follow the principles whenever they can (or even whenever the principles prescribe for them). Thus, when later stages of the argument identify the laws of autonomy with moral constraints, it will not follow that free rational agents invariably act morally but only that they can (and must to avoid irrational conflict of will).

It may be useful to consider two objections. First, does it make sense to say (with Kant) that rational agents can act independently of desires and inclinations? This depends upon how these are conceived. Kant's idea of desires and inclinations, at least in the context of our argument, is narrower than some conceptions and wider than others. If it is confused with the narrower conceptions, Kant's idea of freedom will seem less controversial (and interesting) than it is; and if Kant's idea of desires and inclinations is confused with the wider conceptions, then his idea of freedom will seem absurd. To begin with the wider conception, there seems to be a use of "desire" and related words which refers to whatever motivates an agent, whether empirically discernable independently of his act or not. That an agent "desired" (or, better, "wanted") to do something in this sense is simply inferred from the fact that he did it, given options. Since there are no independent grounds for attributing the "desire," obviously mentioning it does not explain what was done but only characterizes it as voluntary, unlike knee jerks, etc. To say that we can freely will to act independently of desire, in this sense, is obviously absurd; and Kant did not mean this, for he held that even the purest moral acts are motivated, in some sense, by an inexplicable "interest" in the commands of reason.

Sometimes "desire" (and related words) seem to be used quite narrowly, referring to dispositions that are noticeably (and often urgently) *felt* by the agent prior to acting, involving pleasant anticipation, painful fear of loss, tendencies to search for means of fulfillment, to experience frustration when thwarted and joy when fulfilled, etc. It is tempting to suppose that this is what Kant had in mind, for it is not very controversial that we can act for reasons without being motivated by desires in this narrow sense.[19] We seem to do so often when we go about our routine business, forgo minor pleasures for health reasons, and so on. Kant does at times seem to have in mind this narrow sense, especially when dramatically depicting struggles between duty and inclination; but the argument needs more than this and Kant clearly intended more than this in his discussions of freedom. We would still be acting independently of desire in this narrow sense whenever our reasons were based simply on Hume's "calm passions," or mild preferences unaccompanied by pleasures of anticipation, or aversions we attribute to ourselves more from inference than from feeling. But, however, rational, such acts would not have the independence of empirical motivation Kant attributes to acts which manifest freedom.

What, then, is the relevant sense of "desire" and "inclination"? Fine points aside, these are virtually any empirically discernible motivations that one may happen to have so long as they are not concerns essential to all rational agents as such. They include desires in the narrow sense but also Hume's "calm passions" and any other preference, liking, aversion, love, hate, etc. which rational agents might lack and which is not attributed solely because they acted voluntarily. Negative freedom and autonomy imply capacity for rational action in which the agent's reason is not to achieve or do something desired in this intermediate sense. Since Kant repeatedly grants that any behavior may also be empirically explained (e.g., by desires, by the feelings associated with "respect," or by physical science), his point is not to deny this but to say something about reasons: namely, that the status of the rational agent's end as a reason for the agent does not always depend upon the agent having towards it an empirical disposition of the sort rational agents might or might not have. The thesis that we are free agents in this sense is controversial, of course, but not obviously absurd (as on the wide conception of desire) or uninterestingly true (as on the narrow conception of desire).

A second objection should be mentioned.[20] For all that has been said, is it not possible that a will with autonomy has for its one and only rational principle the pure Hypothetical Imperative? This is the principle that it is rational to take the necessary and available means to one's ends or else abandon those ends. I call this "the Hypothetical Imperative" because it is a version of the principle behind Kant's particular hypothetical imperatives, and I call it "pure" because it does not specify that the ends are willed because desired, or for some other reason, or indeed for any reason. It might seem that my characterization of autonomy leaves open that this is the only non-desire-based rational principle.

One problem with this suggestion is that the principle in question (as the name suggests) does not unequivocally prescribe any act even given full information about the situation, one's preferences, etc. It says only, "Take the means or drop the end," giving no standards for the rational assessment of ends. Now conceivably this principle (in a more carefully stated version) is the only necessary principle of rational agency; but then agents who followed it, selecting their ends according to their inclinations or for no reason at all, would never act for sufficient reasons, as (I believe) Kant thought a rational free will could do. Admittedly, in a sense such a will would not be "lawless," for it would have the pure Hypothetical Imperative as a necessary rational principle; but, unless we assume something further, reason would at best prescribe an option rather than a course of action.[21] Though Kant does not raise the issue explicitly, I take it that he conceived rational free wills as sometimes more definitely constrained than this.

If we could assume (as many do) that all preferences, or all preferences that survive a process of informed reflection, have some weight as reasons, then ends could be rationally assessed by the likelihood and costs of achieving coherent sets of preferences. But this would presuppose a putative principle of rationality beyond the pure Hypothetical Imperative, which is the only principle of practical reason Kant recognizes as analytic. Since that further principle assigning prima facie rational force to our empirically given preferences (or informed preferences) is nonanalytic, unless it could be given a "synthetic *a priori*" justification Kant would deny it status as a necessary principle of reason just as he denies this status to the substantive principles "Satisfy the promptings of your (supposed) moral sense" and "Do all you can to satisfy your desire to be happy." Assuming, then, that such principles are not necessarily rational and also that free wills independently of their given desires and inclinations can nonetheless have sufficient determinate reasons to act, one whose "reasons" were fixed solely by the pure Hypothetical Imperative and de facto preferences (or informed preferences) would not have a will with autonomy.

These remarks reveal a heavy burden left for the next stage of the argument, i.e., the attempt to show that rational wills necessarily have negative freedom (and so autonomy), but we should perhaps not expect the conditions for freedom to be so easily satisfied that the concept is of little use in Kant's ultimate project of showing that the basic standards of morality are necessarily rational.

## IV. From Rational Agency to Negative Freedom

Now, more briefly, we need to consider the notoriously compact argument that every rational will is (negatively) free.

First some preliminary comments. Though Kant does not explicitly refer to freedom *negatively conceived* in presenting the argument, this is what the argument requires (given that the transition from negative freedom to autonomy is argued separately). Further, we should not think of the argument as concerned with some new *sense* of freedom ("practical freedom"), as some have suggested; the qualification "from a practical point of view" which Kant attaches to the argument refers not to a sense of freedom but to the type of argument given and a restriction on the legitimate use of its conclusion. Again, we should note that the argument, strictly speaking, is not that we, or any particular individuals, are free; it is that every rational agent, as such, must be free. Later, after raising the objection that his reasoning may have been circular, Kant supplements the basic argument under consideration with the contention that even in our theoretical judgments, apart from practical questions, we must take ourselves to be members of an "intelligible world," in some sense independent of given sensuous inclinations (*G*, 448–53). This further argument seems relevant to residual doubts that *we* are rational free agents (as defined); but this goes beyond the project at hand. Finally, the standards for rational agency must not be too high. Since any being not rational in this sense will not be under moral obligation, the criteria of rationality here must be satisfied not only by the perfectly rational but also by the imperfectly rational wills that Kant thought virtually all human beings to be.

The outline of the argument for negative freedom is as follows:

(1) A rational will cannot act except under the Idea of freedom.

(2) Any being that cannot act except under the Idea of freedom is free from a practical point of view.

(3) Therefore, rational wills are free from a practical point of view.

Implicitly the argument continues:

(4) "Free from a practical point of view" is sufficient for purposes of the rest of the argument for the rationality of moral conduct; and so for the purposes of that argument the qualification can be dropped.

In order to avoid reducing the argument to obvious silliness, we need to guard against several temptations. First, the first premise cannot be read as saying that we "feel free." Whether true or not, this would be a contingent empirical premise about us incompatible with Kant's insistence on an *a priori* method; what is needed is rather a necessary truth about rational agency. It would not follow from the fact that one could not act without feeling free that one was free even for practical purposes; just as it would not follow from the fact that a professor could not lecture without feeling brilliant that he was brilliant for practical purposes. What is so "for practical purposes" is at least a reasonable assumption to make in deliberating and deciding what to do, and neither assumption is reasonable to act on just because it is an unavoidable feeling associated with the activity in question.

Second, the first premise should not be read as saying that those who sincerely believe in thorough-going determinism cannot act or, conversely, that no one who acts ever believes sincerely in thorough-going determinism. Surely many philosophers and scientists have believed in complete determinism, and it is too much to suppose that they lose that belief whenever they do anything. "Acting under the idea of freedom," then, is more plausibly construed as "seeing oneself as free" or perhaps "taking oneself to be free" for certain purposes. The point of the first premise, then, would be that rational agents, in deliberating and deciding what to do, necessarily see themselves as free, regardless of their standing convictions on the metaphysical status of determinism. It is, one might say, a necessary condition of playing the game of deliberation.

Third, an important background of the argument is Kant's belief, which he thought he had proved, that the idea of free agency is such that there can be no empirical evidence or sound metaphysical ("speculative") argument that rational agents are unfree. If there were strong reasons for believing that rational agents are not free, then one could not so convincingly argue that it is reasonable to assume the opposite for practical purposes just because that is how rational agents must see themselves in acting. By analogy, suppose (implausibly) that in acting rational agents necessarily see themselves as indestructible Cartesian souls but that there are good empirical and/or philosophical arguments that this is an illusion. Then we would naturally be reluctant to conclude that for all practical purposes they are reasonable to assume that they are indestructible Cartesian souls, for *practical purposes* include deliberation about life-risking activities and their assumption has implications for this which they should reject no matter how they unavoidably "see themselves."

Finally, we must not construe the conclusion that rational wills are free from a practical point of view as merely a repetition of the first premise that in acting rational wills necessarily see themselves as free. If construed that way, the argument would go nowhere. The conclusion is that for all purposes of deliberation and decision it is reasonable to accept all implications of the assumption that one is free and unreasonable to let one's deliberations be influenced by the contrary idea that one is, or might be, unfree.[22] We need here a distinction between merely seeing oneself as free, which is (by the first premise) unavoidable in rational deliberation, and taking full account in one's deliberation of all the implications of the assumption that one is free. This is important because, by the rest of Kant's argument, the implication of the assumption that rational wills are free is nothing less than that they are rationally bound to morality. The inevitability of rational agency (expressed in the first premise) is taking oneself to be free when deliberating and acting; the resulting prescription for all rational agents (expressed in the conclusion that we are free from a practical point of view) is that it is only rational to act on the full implications of the assumption that we are free. The latter is not inevitable but is what, according to the argument, we rationally should do.

Putting the pieces together, then, the argument runs as follows: Rational agents necessarily see themselves as (negatively) free when deliberating and acting; this means not only that they look upon themselves as choosing among options the outcome of which is not determined by prior empirical causes, but also that they see themselves as capable of reaching a decision in a way that is not a function of their given desires and their beliefs about the means to satisfy them. As in theoretical judgments guided by reason, rational agents deliberate with the view of themselves as able to reach reasoned conclusions which do not fit, or well serve, what they feel most inclined to. Given the impossibility of proof or even evidence that this view of themselves is illusory, they should accept, for all practical purposes, the idea that they are free in this sense. That is, they should accept any implication of the idea that "as a rational agent I am (negatively) free" as a reasonable assumption in all their deliberations about what to do.

This conclusion, we should note, is all that the remaining argument needs. For the argument as a whole is a practical one, addressed as it were to those deliberating about what it is rational to do and, in particular, to those wondering whether philosophical arguments concerning practical reason should be allowed to undermine their confidence that it is rational to be moral. To this audience the argument for negative freedom says, in effect, it is perfectly rational for your deliberative purposes to assume that, as a rational agent, you are negatively free: that is, you should assume that any account of practical reason is mistaken if it denies your ability to choose independently of determining causes or your ability to act for reasons other than desire-based hypothetical imperatives.

The preceding remarks are intended to reveal, or reconstruct, the initial argument for negative freedom as more coherent and plausible than it may at first appear; but two residual doubts should at least be raised. First, now that so much seems built into the first premise, what reason do we have to accept it? In particular, why suppose that rational agents must see themselves in deliberation as capable of being guided by rational standards other than maximum preference satisfaction? Kant believed that the latter standard could not be established as necessary by either the analytic or synthetic *a priori* methods he acknowledged; but has this been shown? Second, even if the sort of rational wills Kant had in mind necessarily see themselves as Kant says, why believe that *we* have rational wills of this sort? Perhaps we can form an idea of such rational agency but have to content ourselves with more mundane standards.

The argument we have been considering seems to rest the case on a thought experiment, or (more grandly) a phenomenological test: "Just try to see yourself (in acting) as lacking negative freedom and you will discover that you cannot." But this reply, as Kant apparently realized, may be unconvincing by itself. Even if we discover what Kant expects, how do we know that the test reveals anything more than a universal but contingent feature of human nature? Also since the cases in which we are most convinced of our capacity to act rationally independently of given preferences are likely to be cases of duty versus inclination, might not our conviction be due to the fact that we have presupposed the rationality of moral conduct (which is what was to be established)? These worries would lead naturally to Kant's discussion of the possibility of circular reasoning and his introduction of the "intelligible world" as the "third term" between reason and freedom. The latter idea, I suspect, stems not so much from obsessive concern with an otherworldly metaphysics as from the thought that even theoretical judgments, in science and everyday life, presuppose that we are guided (or guidable) by standards of rationality which, though applicable to experience, are not derived from experience and which are importantly different from "Find the conclusion that best suits your given preferences." That we are the sort of beings capable of being guided by such standards is supposed to be evident not only in cases of moral conflict or other practical choices but also in theoretical judgments. The reply assumes Kant's idea of the unity of theoretical and practical reason, which Kant does not try to defend in the *Groundwork;* and it raises deep questions beyond the immediate aim of this paper.

## V. From Autonomy to Morality

The preceding steps leave us with the striking conclusion that any rational agent is, as such, committed to at least some principle of conduct acknowledged as rational but not based on his desires and the imperative to take the necessary means to them. The underlying idea is that practical reason, like theoretical reason, enables us to reach conclusions on some basis other than that they get us what we most want.

The next step, of course, is to identify the rational principles acknowledged by wills with autonomy as moral principles, the supreme moral principle and (perhaps) its derivatives. Kant attempts to do this in the first and second chapters of the *Groundwork* by (a) arguing that the supreme moral principle is "Act only on maxims which you can will as universal law" and (b) arguing through successive reformulations of this principle that it is "the principle of autonomy," i.e., equivalent to saying, "follow the laws of a rational will with autonomy."[23]

Though I believe these steps to be fundamentally flawed, I must postpone the attempt to argue the point and to explore a more promising route to a later formulation of the supreme moral principle. Nevertheless I will venture one general comment on this final stage of the argument. The main problem, I suspect, is that Kant switched illegitimately between two quite different readings of his famous first formulation of the supreme moral principle. The first reading is what naturally emerges from the argument we have been considering. Ask what principle, if any, must a rational will with autonomy accept, and an obvious, though rather unhelpful answer will be "Act in such a way that you conform to laws, or rational principles of conduct, you (or any rational being) accept independently of desire." Assuming that all morally relevant acts can be construed in terms of their maxims, this can also be expressed "Act so that your maxims can be willed consistently with whatever rational constraints you (and others) are committed to as wills with autonomy." Now in his transitions to the first formula of the supreme moral principle, Kant seems to be assuming that this is just what the formula says. What it declares, he says, is "conform to universal law as such," where "universal law" has been defined to exclude rational considerations based on desires (*G*, 402, 420–21). So far, so good: that is, the formula is readily seen as one that any rational will with autonomy must accept. But now the trouble begins when Kant treats the same first formula as identical with, or as entailing, a principle that one must act only on maxims which one can will as universal laws *in the sense* that it is (rationally) acceptable that everyone act on the maxim. This moves from an undeniable formal principle to a dubious substantive principle; and despite all the brilliant aid Kant has received from sympathetic commentators, I fail to see how this transition can be made legitimately.

I conclude, however, with a more modest point. If I am right that Kant's transition to a substantive supreme moral principle is illegitimate, this would be quite in line with my main reading of his argument.

For my hypothesis has been that the task which Kant saw as most difficult and most sorely needed was not to convince anyone to accept his supreme moral principle or even to believe that if there are laws of autonomy they must be the familiar moral constraints. These matters, I suspect, he considered relatively easy, and perhaps for this reason he did not bother much about his argument for them. The harder task, and what was most needed, was what he thought he had accomplished in the earlier stages we have considered above: namely, to show that, despite philosophers' arguments to the contrary, there must be principles of rational conduct other than desire-based hypothetical imperatives. That too may be an error, but Kant's argument for it deserves more attention.

## Notes

This paper is a compressed version of ideas presented at a conference on Kant's ethics at Johns Hopkins in the summer of 1983, and an earlier version was also presented at the A.P.A., Pacific Division, meetings and at a meeting of the Triangle Ethics Group in Chapel Hill in the spring of 1985. Thanks are due to the participants at those meetings and also to Tyler Burge, Stephen Darwall, Gregory Kavka, William Lycan, Christopher Morris, and others for their helpful comments. A special thanks is due to Burge for constructive help and encouragement in long discussions on these matters.

1. There are exceptions, e.g., Dieter Henrich's "Die Deduktion des Sittengesetzes" in *Denken im Schatten des Nihilismus*, ed. Alexander Schwan (Darmstadt: Wissenschaftliche Buchgesellschaft, 1975), pp. 55–112, in this volume pp. 299–337; Karl Ameriks's *Kant's Theory of Mind*, chap. 6; and Bruce Aune's *Kant's Theory of Morals* (Princeton: Princeton University Press, 1979). Two recent important books, published after this essay, are Henry Allison's *Kant's Theory of Freedom* (Cambridge: Cambridge University Press, 1990), and Rüdiger Bittner's *What Reason Demands*, trans. Theodore Talbot (Cambridge: Cambridge University Press, 1989).

2. I assume that the person who seriously asks "Why be moral?" judges that he morally ought to do certain things but still has some sort of question. But on Kant's view, to judge that one morally ought to do something is, in part, to believe that the conduct in question is required by an unconditional "command of reason"; and surely any (even minimally) rational person who believed this could not be indifferent to the conduct. This fits with Kant's repeated suggestions that respect for moral law is, as it were, forced from us, that even murderers acknowledge the justice of their (death) sentences, etc.

3. *Critique of Practical Reason*, trans. L. W. Beck (New York: Liberal Arts Press, 1956), pp. 28–31[29–32].

4. H. J. Paton is an example; see *The Categorical Imperative* (London: Hutchinson, 1965), p. 221.

5. In *Critique of Practical Reason*, esp. pp. 29–31[30–31], Kant again argues for the mutual entailment of (a) rational beings are free and (b) rational beings are under moral law, but he says that consciousness of (b) is the grounds for knowing (a) and not the reverse. This is clearly a reversal of the order of argument in *G*, and probably represents an abandonment of that argument. But, whether Kant would want it or not, there does seem to be a way of reconciling the positions in the two works. That is, take the *Groundwork* as addressing doubts of agents deliberating about what to do, whereas the *Critique* is concerned more with completing a project on the nature of reason and which among traditional metaphysical beliefs one can reasonably accept (despite the arguments of the first *Critique*). The first, then, belongs to moral philosophy, traditionally conceived; the second to the special epistemological/metaphysical/moral undertaking involved in the new critical philosophy. Since the audience of *G* is raising a practical question, it can be presumed willing to accept for those practical purposes anything implied by what it must assume in asking the question. Thus it need not demand any theoretical demonstration or intuition ("intellectual" or otherwise) of freedom if it is made clear that freedom is presupposed in its questioning. The audience of the *Critique*, on the other hand, may be thought more concerned with the justifiability of certain metaphysical beliefs, not from sheer speculative curiosity of course but also not from a practical need to satisfy the doubts about the rationality of morals (expressed at the end of the second chapter of *G*). If so, this audience is prepared to accept what the other audience was ready to entertain doubts about (namely, that as rational agents we are really under moral obligations). And, if the *Critique*'s audience is not seen as engaged primarily in deliberation about what it ought to do, the argument of *G* from the implications of deliberation is less appropriate. In any case, it is worth noting that the argument of *G* does not commit any of the mistakes in arguing for freedom that the *Critique* condemns (e.g., supposing there is an intuition of freedom).

6. This should be clear at least in my reconstruction of the argument, for none of the premises presuppose moral obligation. As Karl Ameriks helped me to see, the suspicion of circular reasoning may arise from worry that the first premise in the argument for negative freedom (i.e., rational wills cannot act except under the Idea of freedom) might seem convincing only because it is most evident in conflicts of duty and inclination. If so, the "solution" (which emphasizes that in *all* uses of reason we view ourselves as members of an "intelligible world") would have a point without admitting that the original argument ever actually presupposed moral obligation. More needs to be said about the supposed circle and its solution, but this goes beyond the main argument I try to reconstruct here.

7. The argument reconstructed in this paper is an argument that morality is rational but it does not rely on the forbidden means-ends reasoning.

8. *G*, 448. This is the heart of (1) in the summary of my next paragraph.

9. *G*, 447. I assume that the strange formula in this passage, "the principle of acting on no maxim other than one which can have for its object itself as at

the same time a universal law," is meant to be the first formulation of the Categorical Imperative, and so have reformulated it.

10. *G*, 447. "This is precisely the formula of the Categorial Imperative and the principle of morality." This is argued twice, at *G*, 402 and *G*, 420–21.

11. Kant clearly intended the principle to be unconditional and overriding, rather than prima facie, but one may question whether the argument supports this. In fact the sort of argument he gives seems unlikely to support an overriding principle; for the idea is to show that free rational agents unmotivated by desire must nevertheless have some rational principle to follow. Why would a principle that says what one prima facie ought to do not suffice? If this is all the argument supports, then the conclusion must be more modest, i.e., that every rational agent has some reason to be moral or immorality is always opposed to some prima facie principle of the agent. I will pass over this problem here, not only from lack of time, but also because the problem concerns later stages of the argument which are not my main concern.

12. The idea here is that there are two routes to show the rationality of moral conduct. One is to show that immorality conflicts with a commitment of the agent, whether or not that commitment was independently demanded by reason. The other is to show that rational agents, as such, necessarily are committed to a principle. I suspect that Kant intended both; for he argues that all minimally rational agents have autonomy and so are committed to the supreme moral principle, and he argues that necessarily, *qua* rational and free, they must accept the supreme moral principle. It is worth noting, though, that if the argument failed for the second, stronger claim, the first, weaker claim still would need to be considered. That strategy fits with the often repeated point that immorality involves conflict of will.

13. This account is most evident in R. P. Wolff's *The Autonomy of Reason* (New York: Harper and Row, 1973).

14. The two views of *will* are discussed in John Silber's introduction to *Religion within the Limits of Reason Alone*. Silber thinks that Kant was ambivalent at least in the *Groundwork* between the later view and the dualistic picture presented by Wolff. Beck's commentary on the second *Critique* also makes much of the *Wille* vs. *Willkür* distinction. Rawls, I am told, distinguishes in lectures between the "Manichean" view and the "Augustinian" view of *will*, finding Kant ambivalent in the *Groundwork*. My concern here is not so much to deny the ambivalence, or confusion, as to see how the argument of the *Groundwork* does not rest on the more simplistic picture.

15. Strictly, the will is not even a hidden, unobservable event in time; to ascribe a will to a person is not to refer to a mysterious event or thing but merely to say, without further explanation, that the person has a capacity to make things happen in a way that makes appropriate the explanation "His reason . . . ," "He was guided by the principle . . . ," etc.

16. See the section entitled "Of Liberty and Necessity" in David Hume's *A Treatise of Human Nature*, ed. L. A. Selby-Bigge (Oxford: Clarendon, 1955), bk. II, part III, pp. 399–412.

17. Kant suggests that it is because the will is a kind of cause that it cannot be "lawless," but I take it that the point follows as well from the definition of

will as acting in accord with the idea of principles or laws. There is no doubt a play on different sense of lawful and lawless, but the main point seems clear enough, namely, that to attribute an event to a person, thing, or prior happening as its cause (source, or author) we need some appropriate connection between the event and the alleged source, something to warrant saying the event occurred in some sense because of the source. Often the connection is an observable regularity between types of events, and then the "because" is an empirical causal one; but in the case of human action, on Kant's view, the connection is between the event and a person's beliefs and policy commitments, and then the "because" must be of a different type. This leaves much unexplained, of course, but the minimal point is just that some connection must be made, that this can be of two kinds, and that both involve "laws" in some sense or other.

18. See *G*, 443–44. Note that we have *heteronomy* as (mistakenly) regarded as the "basis of morality," as a characterization of a rule or (would be) law, or as "the result" if one tries to make hypothetical imperatives the basis of morality (*G*, 441). It is significant that Kant's discussion of heteronomy concerns not the ordinary following of prudential maxims and rules of skill but wrongheaded philosophical attempts to base morality in various ways on hypothetical imperatives.

19. I owe a thanks to Gregory Kavka for alerting me when, in an earlier version, I was yielding to this temptation.

20. This objection comes from Stephen Darwall, who may still be dissatisfied with my sketchy reply.

21. There is a sense, of course, in which even the non-conditional "Always pay your debts" prescribes options, for one may pay in coins or in bills, in cash or by check, etc. I trust, however, that patience could make clear how the relevant sense differs from this.

22. Strictly speaking, I suppose, the claim that, from a practical perspective, rational wills are free implies not only (a) that one should, for purposes of deliberation, accept all the implications of assuming that one is oneself free but also (b) that one should, for purposes of deliberation, accept the implications of assuming that others one takes to be rational are also free. The latter would be of practical importance when trying to decide whether execution for murder is justified. Unfortunately, the argument for (b) has to be more complicated and raises special problems. So I shall ignore it here. Implication (a) should suffice for most practical purposes, e.g., to dispel the doubts about one's own rationality in being moral which are raised by either determinism or the thesis that all rationality is means-end calculation to maximum desire-satisfaction.

23. This culminates at *G*, 440.

# 11

## Morality and Freedom: Kant's Reciprocity Thesis

*Henry E. Allison*

At the end of the second part of the *Groundwork* Kant reflects that he has so far shown only that the autonomy of the will ("the property the will has of being a law to itself")[1] is the supreme principle of morality in the sense of being the ultimate presupposition of morality as it is commonly understood.[2] The articulation of this principle marks the culmination of an analytic of regressive argument, the aim of which is to uncover and present with philosophical precision the basic assumptions and principles of the ordinary, pre-philosophical conception of morality. Although Kant hardly minimizes this result, he also displays an awareness of the fact that, of itself, it leaves unanswered the crucial question of validation. Accordingly, he sets himself the task in the third part of the *Groundwork* of answering the moral skeptic by showing that morality is not a "chimerical Idea," a mere "phantom of the brain."[3] In Kantian terms, this requires that he provide a transcendental deduction of morality.

Unfortunately, not only has Kant's effort to accomplish this important goal been severely criticized by even his most sympathetic critics, but the purely exegetical question of what kind of argument, if any, the text supplies, has been the topic of an ongoing dispute. In fact, there seems to be no agreement as to whether the deduction is of the moral law, the categorical imperative, freedom, all three; or even whether there is properly a deduction at all.[4] Furthermore, the uncertainty about the *Groundwork* has given rise to additional questions about its relationship to the *Critique of Practical Reason*. The problem here is that while in the *Groundwork* Kant at least seems to have attempted a transcendental deduction of the moral law and/or the categorical imperative on the basis of the necessity of presupposing the Idea of freedom, in the *Critique of Practical Reason* he explicitly denies the possibility of any such deduction and claims instead that the moral law as a "fact of reason" can serve as the basis for a deduction of freedom.[5] This suggests a significant reversal in Kant's thought regarding the justification of morality; although even here the existence of such a reversal has been denied both by those who see no real deduction of the moral law in the *Groundwork* and by those who claim to find a deduction in the *Critique of Practical Reason* as well as in the *Groundwork*.[6]

Undoubtedly, most of the confusion can be traced to Kant's own confusing and sloppy formulations of both his problematic and his argument, especially in *Groundwork* III. Nevertheless, I do believe that part of the blame can be attributed to a failure on the part of Kant's critics to give proper attention to a thesis which is at least relatively clear, and which looms large in both the *Groundwork* and the *Critique of Practical Reason.* This is the claim that freedom of the will and the moral law are reciprocal concepts. Kant affirms this explicitly in both works; correlatively, he also insists in both works that, although the moral law (or, better, the bindingness of the moral law for all rational agents) expresses a synthetic *a priori* proposition, it would be analytic if freedom of the will were presupposed.[7] For convenience sake I shall henceforth refer to this as the "Reciprocity Thesis." Its significance stems from the fact that it entails that freedom of the will is not only a necessary but also a sufficient condition of the moral law.[8] Clearly, this thesis underlies Kant's attempt in the *Groundwork* to argue from freedom (or at least from the necessity of the presupposition of freedom) to the moral law, and in the *Critique of Practical Reason* from the moral law (as a putative "fact of reason") to the reality of freedom.

The goal of this paper is to provide a defense of this thesis, which lies at the very heart of Kant's moral philosophy. The defense will begin with an examination of the Kantian texts; but since his "official" arguments for the thesis are obviously inadequate, it will be necessary to go considerably beyond Kant's explicit statements on the topic. Thus, the proposed defense is also a reconstruction of Kant's argument, albeit one based largely on material which Kant himself has provided. Since the Reciprocity Thesis is only the first step in the Kantian justification of morality, a defense of this thesis will not amount to a complete defense of the Kantian "deduction." It is, however, a necessary first stage in such a project. Moreover, I hope to show that the recognition of the cogency and systematic role of the thesis is itself enough to obviate some of the standard objections to Kant's procedure. I also hope to show that, properly construed, the Reciprocity Thesis is not open to the devastating criticism which is frequently raised against it: namely, that it entails that no free action can be morally wrong.

**I**

The best known and most perplexing of Kant's formulations of the Reciprocity Thesis is at the beginning of *Groundwork* III. After defining will [*Wille*] as a "kind of causality belonging to living beings so far as they are rational," and freedom (negatively construed) as "the property this causality has of being able to work independently of determination by alien causes," Kant offers his positive conception of freedom, which presumably "springs" from this negative one:

> The concept of causality carries with it that of *laws (Gesetze)* in accordance with which, because of something we call a cause, something else—namely, its effect—must be posited *(gesetzt)*. Hence freedom of will, although it is not the property of conforming to laws of nature, is not for this reason lawless: it must rather be a causality conforming to immutable laws though of a special kind; for otherwise a free will would be self-contradictory. Natural necessity, as we have seen, is a heteronomy of efficient causes; for every effect is possible only in conformity with the law that something else determines the efficient cause to causal action. What else then can freedom of will be but autonomy—that is, the property which will has of being a law to itself? The proposition "Will is in all its actions a law to itself" expresses, however, only the principle of acting on no maxim other than one which can have for its object itself and at the same time a universal law. This is precisely the formula of the categorical imperative and the principle of morality. Thus a free will and a will under moral laws are one and the same.[9]

Kant also argues for the same thesis in §6 of the *Critique of Practical Reason*. After contending on the basis of an analysis of the concept of a practical law (§1) that such a law must be formal in the sense that it could only impose the formal condition of lawfulness on the maxims of a rational agent (§4) and that only a will that is free in the transcendental sense could have its "determining ground" in such a law (§5); he then (§6) poses the problem: "Granted that a will is free, find the law which alone is competent to determine it necessarily" [*welches ihn allein nothwendig zur bestimmen tauglich ist*]. The proposed solution exploits the dichotomy between the form (lawfulness or universality) and the matter (desired object or end) of a practical principle developed in §§2–4. Kant claims that since 1) a free will (by definition) must be independent of all "empirical conditions," which includes the "material" element of practical principles; and that 2) a free will must nonetheless be "determinable" (presumably according to some law); that 3) "the legislative form, insofar as it is contained in the maxim, is the only thing which can constitute a determining ground of the [free] will." On this basis Kant concludes at the very beginning of the Remark following the analysis that "freedom and unconditional practical law reciprocally imply each other."[10]

The argument at this point is completely hypothetical, and consequently does not involve any claims concerning the reality of either freedom or an unconditional practical law. Nevertheless, given the identification (§7) of an unconditional practical law with the moral law ("So act that the maxim of your will could always hold at the same time as a principle establishing universal law"),[11] it is but a short step to the conclusion that "It [the moral law] would be analytic if freedom of the will were presupposed." Admittedly, this last claim is somewhat strange. How, one might ask, could the presupposition of freedom convert a synthetic proposition into one that is analytic? The most reasonable reading, I take it, is that analyticity is to be attributed to the hypothetical, "If freedom then the moral law," and to its reciprocal. Kant clarifies his position near the end of the *Analytic of Pure Practical Reason* when he remarks:

> if [*per impossibile*] we saw the possibility of freedom of an efficient cause, we would see not only the possibility but also the necessity of the moral law as the supreme practical law of rational beings, to whom freedom of the causality of their will is ascribed. This is because the two concepts are so inextricably bound together that practical freedom could be defined through the will's independence of everything except the moral law.[12]

Kant does not explicitly argue for the Reciprocity Thesis in *Religion within the Limits of Reason Alone*. Nevertheless, in the course of denying that the source of moral evil can be located either in man's sensuous nature or in his "morally legislative reason" [*Wille*], he does suggest that to affirm the latter is equivalent to saying that "reason could destroy the authority of the very law which is its own, or deny the obligation arising therefrom." This, however, he claims is impossible because:

> To conceive of oneself as a freely acting being and yet as exempt from the law which is appropriate [*angemessen*] to such a being (the moral law) would be tantamount to conceiving a cause operating without any laws whatsoever (for determination according to natural laws is excluded by the fact of freedom); this is a self-contradiction.[13]

The argument in the *Groundwork*, in particular, appears to be vitiated by a gross equivocation regarding the concept of law. As even Paton, the most sympathetic of Kant interpreters, notes, it is hardly legitimate to jump (as Kant there seems to do) from the notion of a causal law, which is a law connecting causes and effects, to a "law of freedom," which, by definition, would be a law for decision itself, not one which connects decisions (as causes) with their effects in the phenomenal world.[14] Leaving this aside, however, it is possible to specify a common core of argumentation that is contained, implicitly at least, in all of the texts. The argument takes roughly the following form: 1) As a "kind of causality" the will must, in some sense, be law-governed or, in the language of the second *Critique,* "determinable" according to some law (a lawless will is an absurdity). 2) As free, it cannot be governed by laws of nature. 3) It must, therefore, be governed by laws of a different sort; that is, self-imposed ones. 4) The moral law is the required self-imposed law.

Although a compatibilist would certainly object to steps 2 and 3, the major difficulties which we need consider concern steps 1 and 4. Clearly, if a free will (in a non-compatibilist sense) is to be law-governed or "determinable," it can only be through self-imposed laws. In that minimal sense, then, the positive concept of freedom (autonomy) can be derived analytically from the negative concept (independence). However, apart from the already noted equivocation regarding the concept of law, Kant does not seem to offer any argument in support of the claim that a free will must be law-governed or "determinable" at all. On the contrary, the account in the second *Critique* suggests that this essential question is simply begged.

At first glance at least, step 4 appears to be equally problematic; for even if we assume that a free will must be governed or determinable by a self-imposed law, it does not seem at all obvious that only the moral law, as defined by Kant, can do the job. In fact, considering only the *Groundwork* account, it once again seems that Kant has begged the main question by means of his prior characterization of the principle of autonomy as the "supreme principle or morality." This characterization makes it all too easy for Kant to slide from the claim that a free will is autonomous in the sense that it is determinable only by self-imposed laws to the claim that the law which it spontaneously yet necessarily imposes upon itself is the moral law.[15]

With regard to the latter problem, it is crucial to note that Kant holds that the moral law is the only conceivable candidate for a practical law. Consequently, for Kant at least, the claims that a free will is necessarily subject to a practical law (step 1) and that it is necessarily subject to the moral law (step 4) are equivalent. According to Kant's implicit definition, a practical law is an objectively and unconditionally valid practical principle. To claim that a practical principle is *objectively* valid is to claim that it holds for all rational agents, whether or not they in fact adhere to it, that is, whether or not it holds subjectively (as a maxim). In the case of imperfectly rational beings such as ourselves, such a principle takes the form of an imperative (which is likewise objectively valid). The imperative is hypothetical if its objectivity is a function of certain ends or desires; it is categorical if this is not the case. An objectively valid practical principle is also *unconditionally* valid just in case it holds independently of any ends or desires. The imperative issuing from such a principle is always categorical, whatever its grammatical form.[16]

Given this conception, Kant claims 1) that such a law must be "formal," since it abstracts from all ends or desires (which constitute the "matter" of principle), and 2) that, as such, it can require only that rational agents select their maxims on the basis of their suitability as universal laws. This is, of course, precisely what the moral law or, better, the categorical imperative requires. Although much more work would be needed to make this line of argument fully convincing, I do find it a plausible unpacking of the implications of Kant's definitions. In any event, for the purposes of this paper, I propose to accept this claim. Thus, its goals will have been achieved if, in Kant's words, it can be shown that "freedom and unconditional practical law reciprocally imply each other."

## II

Kant's claim that the notion of a lawless will involves an absurdity places him squarely within the metaphysical tradition that rejects the conception of a "liberty of indifference." This rejection is a constant in Kant's thought; it can be found in his earliest significant discussion of freedom, where he defends the Leibnizian view.[17] It resurfaces, however, in the "critical period" in connection with a very different, radically un-Leibnizian, conception of the will and its freedom.

The gist of this new conception of the will is indicated in the famous statement in the *Groundwork* that "Everything in nature works in accordance with laws. Only a rational being has the power to act in accordance with his *Idea* of laws—in accordance with principles—and only so has he a will."[18] Kant then goes on to define the will as practical reason on the grounds that reason is required to derive actions from laws.[19] Somewhat later he defines "will" [*Wille*] as a "kind of causality belonging to rational beings so far as they are rational."[20] Rationality, construed as the capacity to form general principles, together with the power to act on the basis of these principles, thereby producing changes in the phenomenal world (if only in the psychological state of the agent), are, therefore, the defining characteristics of "will" as Kant construes it in the *Groundwork*. Only a being with both of these capacities can be said to have a will. Such a being is also one for whom reason is practical.

If one is to understand Kant's thought at this point, it is crucial to realize that "rationality" is here construed in a very broad sense. Since all that is required is the capacity to form and act upon general principles, an agent is "rational" in the relevant sense even when the principles he adopts as rules for action are morally pernicious, imprudent, or even self-defeating, that is, "irrational" in the usual sense. Kant's technical term for the "principle" or "Idea of law" on the basis of which rational agents supposedly act is 'maxim'. Consequently, it is appropriate to begin our examination of Kant's claim that a lawless will is an absurdity with a brief consideration of his account of maxims. This consideration must, of necessity, be superficial. It will concentrate solely on the presumed role of maxims in human action, thereby ignoring many of the complexities and ambiguities of Kant's account, as well as the interesting questions regarding the specification of maxims.

As is all too frequently the case, in his characterization of maxims Kant succeeds in being technical without being precise. For present purposes, however, it suffices to describe a maxim as a subjective practical principle, that is, a general rule or policy on which a rational agent actually acts in a given situation and tends to act in relevantly similar situations.[21] Expressed algebraically, maxims have the form: "To do A if B." As subjective, maxims are closely connected with the "interests"

of an agent, which are themselves never the simple result of mere impulse or sensuous desire, but always involve some conception of an
end. It is only because I consciously choose to pursue certain ends or,
equivalently, have certain interests, that I adopt certain policies of action, designed to realize these ends. A maxim thus has a purposive
component built into it; although this component need not be made
explicit in the formulation.[22] Moreover, this is true even when the interest is "pure," that is, not based on any sensuous desire for the object,
as is supposedly the case in action for the sake of the moral law.

Although there can be no quarrel with the claim that people often act
on the basis of consciously adopted maxims, it is also frequently thought
that the emphasis Kant places on maxims in his account of human action
makes human behavior appear much more rule-governed than it actually is.[23] This is particularly true if maxims are construed as relatively
fixed policies of life or *Lebensregeln,* which specify the most fundamental choices of an individual, and which, as such, are contrasted with
mere precepts or "rules of thumb."[24] So construed, maxims certainly
provide ready candidates for moral evaluation, and it is to maxims in
this sense that Kant appeals in his well known attempts to illustrate the
application of the categorical imperative. The problem is simply that
many, if not most, human actions cannot be plausibly regarded as the
result of an explicit reflection on rules of this sort; but this neither
exempts them from moral evaluation (we are justly condemned for our
"impulsive" acts), nor reduces them to mere bits of behavior, not worthy of being termed "actions."

There are, I think, two possible responses to this fairly obvious line
of objection, both of which have a basis in the Kantian texts. The first
involves a certain broadening of the notion of a maxim, making it
roughly equivalent to an intention.[25] On this interpretation, the claim
that an agent acted on the basis of a maxim does not entail either that
he acted on the basis of a principle to which he has been committed
for any determinate length of time or that he explicitly "subsumed" his
action under this principle, in the manner of someone who goes
through all of the steps of an Aristotelian practical syllogism. It entails
only that he acted with conscious intent, that there is a specifiable
reason for the action. To formulate the maxim is to describe this intent
and to give the reason. Here it will be helpful to follow Onora Nell,
who, appealing to Kant's later formulation in the *Metaphysics of Morals*
(which presupposes the *Wille-Willkür* distinction), characterizes a
maxim as a "determination of the power of choice" [*Willkür*]. As she

correctly points out in her comment on this characterization, "To say that an agent's power of choice is determined is simply to say that he intends to do a specific sort of act or pursue a specific end in some situation. If an agent has a maxim 'To do A if B', then he intends to do A if B."[26] All that needs to be added at this point is that the converse of the last claim likewise holds. If an agent really intends to do A if B, then he has a maxim "To do A if B," whether or not he is explicitly aware of it.

By construing maxims in this way it is possible to ascribe them to many actions which are performed "on the spur of the moment," without reflection or the explicit adoption of a settled policy. To borrow an example from Onora Nell: A person can suddenly decide to have an extra cup of coffee one morning without any deliberation and without the adoption of a specific policy regarding the amount of coffee to be consumed each morning. Certainly, we cannot claim plausibly that such an action involves a maxim in the sense of a *Lebensregel* (or even a "rule of thumb"). Nevertheless, we can connect it with a maxim in the broad sense insofar as we can attribute an intention to the agent, for example, to get warm or to combat the effects of a sleepless night. Moreover, as Nell notes, even if the agent himself does not reflectively formulate this maxim or intention, it can still (in principle) be discovered by determining what changes in the circumstances would have led him to decline the extra cup.[27]

This line of interpretation suggests that a Kantian maxim is very close, if not equivalent, to the "plan as it were" that J. L. Austin claims to be an essential ingredient in an intentional action. According to Austin, for an agent to act intentionally, which he is careful to distinguish from acting deliberately or purposefully, he must have a conscious idea of what he is doing, and this requires having, at least in some minimal sense, a plan of action.[28] To have such a plan, for example, "Do A if B," is precisely what it means to "know what one is doing," while the latter is a necessary condition of an intentional action. Following Austin, it can, therefore, be claimed that for any description under which an action is intentional, it must be possible to assign some "plan as it were," to the agent. But the same can be said, *mutatis mutandis,* of maxims broadly construed. Moreover, since the notion of a will without any intentions is manifestly absurd, it follows that the notion of a will without maxims (a "lawless will") is likewise absurd.

Although there are good reasons for interpreting maxims in this way (How else can one square the fact that people are deemed morally responsible for their so-called "impulsive" acts with Kant's insistence that morality is concerned with the maxims of action?), it is not necessary to insist upon it here. Even if we assume that by 'maxims' is meant something like *Lebensregeln,* which would preclude any straightforward identification of intentional action with action based on a maxim, it can still be maintained that an agent capable of intentional action at all, that is, one with the capacity for rational choice (in the broad sense of 'rational') cannot be totally without maxims. The point is simply that an agent completely bereft of maxims (in the sense of *Lebensregeln*) would also be without any self-chosen goals or interests, and this means that he would have no basis for rational choice. Consequently, his "actions" would have to be regarded either as random happenings (which is absurd) or as direct responses to stimuli, explicable in neurophysiological terms. In short, his "actions" would, like other natural occurrences, be "in accordance with laws," not, as in the case of rational agents, "in accordance with the Idea of laws."

### III

The preceding analysis may help to explain and give plausibility to Kant's claim that rational agents act in accordance with the "Idea of laws," but it obviously does not suffice to establish the thesis that a free will (the will of a rational agent) must be law-governed in any but a trivial sense of 'law'. In fact, we have seen that Kant defines maxims as subjective practical principles and explicitly contrasts them with objective practical principles or laws. Thus, given Kant's own definitions, there can be no immediate transition from being maxim-governed to being subject to an "unconditional practical law." We are still in need of an argument to bridge this gap.

The argument that comes immediately to mind at this point is a familiar one, and so is the objection to it. I do not believe that it is Kant's own argument (although it is frequently taken to be such), but I do think that it can be construed as an essential first step in an extended Kantian argument. I also think that when it is viewed merely as a first step in an extended argument rather than as a complete argument in its own right, the standard objection loses its force.

In the endeavor to sketch this argument or, more accurately, argument-segment, it will be helpful to return to the analysis of maxims in terms of intentions. This analysis strongly suggests that to stipulate an agent's maxim in performing a certain action is to give the agent's "reason" for that action, at least in one important sense of that notoriously elusive notion. (To state my intention *in* X-ing—the "plan as it were" that I have "in mind" is to give my reason *for* X-ing.) More specifically, it is to give the kind of reason in terms of which an action can be justified (or criticized) as opposed to being explained or even excused.

Such justification (or criticism) certainly includes, but is not limited to, the moral variety. A given action could be praised as morally appropriate or as prudent or, correlatively, condemned as immoral or foolish. These are obviously quite different kinds of evaluations, but the key point is that in all cases they are based upon assumptions regarding the agent's intention to act in a certain way in a given set of circumstances. Moreover, in both the moral and prudential contexts the justification takes a similar form: namely, showing that the reason (in the sense of intention) for acting in a certain way is a "good reason." Naturally, the same can be said, *mutatis mutandis,* regarding the criticism of actions, whether this be on moral or on prudential grounds.

The next step is to note that in claiming that one's reason for acting in a certain way is a "good" in the sense of justifying reason, one is, implicitly, at least, assuming its appropriateness for all rational beings. The intuition behind this is simply that if reason R justifies my X-ing in circumstances C, then it must also justify the X-ing of any other agent in such circumstances. As Marcus Singer, paraphrasing Sidgwick, remarks, "A reason in one case is a reason in all cases—or else it is not a reason at all."[29] To be sure, there is a perfectly legitimate sense in which I might claim that something is "right for me" and not for others; but this must be construed as an elliptical way of stating that there is something peculiar about my circumstances (which can include, among other things, my desires and capacities). Thus, I might claim that a course of action, say going to the race track to relax, is justifiable for me because of my superior ability as a handicapper, great wealth, or luck, etc., while it is not justifiable for others who lack these attributes. What I may not do is to claim that the possession of these attributes justifies my action but not that of other similarly inclined and endowed agents. In roughly this way, then, the universalizability of one's intention, maxim or plan of action, seems to be presupposed as a condition of the possibility of justifying one's action, even when this justification does not take an explicitly moral form.

Finally, a rational agent cannot simply refuse to play the justification game, that is, refuse to concern himself with the question of whether the reasons for his actions are "good" reasons, at least in a non-moral sense of "good." This is, of course, not to say that such an agent always acts on the basis of good and sufficient reasons or that, in retrospect, he must always believe himself to have done so. The point is rather the familiar one that an agent for whom the whole question of justification is irrelevant, who never weighs the reason for his action, who acts without at least believing at the same time that his reasons are "good" reasons, would not be regarded as rational. But since, as we have just seen, to regard one's reason for acting in a certain way as "good" is to assume its legitimacy for all rational beings in similar circumstances, it would seem, so the argument goes, that a rational agent cannot reject the universalizability test without, at the same time, denying his rationality. This, in turn, means that the universalizability test functions as the ultimate standard governing one's choice of maxims or, equivalently, that it has the status of a practical law.

This line of argument is too familiar to require further elaboration, and so, too, is the objection to it. The problem is simply that one cannot move from the claim that every rational agent must regard his principles of action as universalizable in the sense that he be willing to acknowledge that it would be reasonable for every other agent in the relevantly similar circumstances[30] to adopt the same principles, or even that such agents ought to adopt them (where the "ought" is the ought of rationality), to the desired conclusion that the agent ought to be able to will (as a universal law) that every rational agent act on the basis of the principle in question. The rational egoist might very well be willing to admit that the maxims on which he acts in pursuit of his own perceived self-interest are also those on which every other rational agent ought to act (and would act, if sufficiently enlightened). It hardly follows from this, however, that the rational egoist is committed (on pain of self-contradiction) to will that all other rational agents behave likewise.[31]

While there can be little question about the cogency of this line of objection, considered as a response to the project of somehow deducing morality, conceived in Kantian terms, from the concept of rationality, there are serious questions about its relevance to Kant's own procedure. The reason that this is generally thought to provide a decisive criticism of Kant can no doubt be attributed to Kant's misleading claim that, since moral laws hold for rational beings as such, they ought to be derived from the "general concept of a rational being as such."[32] This is intended, however, to preclude any appeal to anthropology, that is, to empirical knowledge of human nature, and not to suggest that the reality of moral obligation can be deduced from the "mere concept" of a rational being. In fact, not only does Kant himself not attempt to deduce the moral law from this concept, he explicitly rejects the possibility of doing so. We must keep in mind that the starting point of Kant's analysis is not the concept of a rational being *simpliciter,* it is rather the concept of a rational being possessing a free will (in the transcendental sense). This is because Kant realized that, for all that we can learn from its "mere concept," practical reason might involve nothing more than the capacity to determine the best possible means for the satisfaction of one's desires. Certainly many distinguished philosophers have thought as much; and there is nothing self-contradictory or otherwise absurd in the claim. Indeed, as Kant himself remarks in a highly significant but strangely neglected note in *Religion within the Limits of Reason Alone:*

> For from the fact that a being has reason it by no means follows that this reason, by the mere representing of the fitness of its maxims to be laid down as universal laws, is thereby rendered capable of determining the will unconditionally, so as to be "practical" of itself; at least, not so far as we can see. The most rational mortal being in the world might still stand in need of certain incentives, originating in objects of desire, to determine his choice. He might, indeed, bestow the most rational reflection on all that concerns not only the greatest sum of these incentives in him but also the means of attaining the end thereby determined, without ever suspecting the possibility of such a thing as the absolutely imperative moral law which proclaims that it is itself an incentive and, indeed, the highest.[33]

The conclusion to be drawn from this is that the problem with the argument "from rationality" sketched above is not that it is totally wrongheaded, but merely that it is incomplete.[34] Let us see, then, if we can meet with more success in the endeavor to establish the Reciprocity Thesis if we focus explicitly on the transcendental freedom as well as the rationality of the agent. As a first step in this process we shall take a brief look at the relevant aspects of Kant's account of freedom.

## IV

Central to Kant's conception of freedom is the contrast between practical and transcendental freedom. For present purposes, practical freedom *(freie Willkür, arbitrium liberum)* can be equated with the previously considered capacity of a rational agent to act on the basis of maxims, that is, in light of the "idea" or "representation" of a law. This involves the capacity to act independently of, and even contrary to, any particular desire. Instead of responding automatically to the strongest desire (the mark of a pathologically necessitated *Willür* or *arbitrium brutum*), a practically free agent can weigh and evaluate his desires, give priority to some and suppress others. Only *qua* conceptually determined, for example, taken up or "incorporated into a maxim," does a desire constitute a reason for acting. This does not rule out the possibility of what we normally regard as impulsive behavior, for example, an action out of anger. The point is only that in such cases the agent must be thought to give in to the emotion, to let it move him to action.[35]

Transcendental freedom, by contrast, is usually defined as absolute spontaneity or as complete independence from any determination by antecedent conditions.[36] This creates the impression that the difference between practical and transcendental freedom is between a modest conception, presumably one that a compatibilist might accept, and a radical conception, requiring indeterminism together with all of its well known difficulties. After all, independence from "pathological necessitation" is hardly equivalent to independence from all causal determination; and if practical freedom involves only the former, then it is far from obvious that it requires indeterminism. Nevertheless, Kant seems to maintain that it does. At least he claims in the *Critique of Pure Reason* that "the practical concept of freedom is based on this *transcendental* Idea," (A 533/B 561) and even that "The denial of transcendental freedom must, therefore, involve the elimination of all practical freedom" (A 534/B 56).

Largely as a result of passages such as these, Kant is frequently deemed guilty of an illicit slide from a respectable conception of practical freedom (pathological independence) to a disreputable or, at best, highly problematic transcendental conception. It is sometimes further claimed that the latter conception brings with it no discernible advantages and many significant disadvantages for Kant's moral philosophy.[37] Consequently, it is not surprising to find recent efforts to reinterpret Kant's whole theory of freedom in explicitly compatibilist terms.[38]

Although the question of whether Kant's first *Critique* conception of practical freedom requires indeterminism is quite complex, with texts pointing in both directions, I am inclined to think that it does. I cannot, however, argue the point here.[39] Similarly, I do not intend to discuss either the general issue of indeterminism or the plausibility of the Kantian version. Since we are concerned here only with the implications of transcendental freedom for Kant's moral philosophy, we can set aside these larger issues. For present purposes, the key point is that, even assuming that both practical and transcendental freedom require indeterminism, there remains a significant difference between them. Moreover, this difference is crucial for Kant's moral philosophy.

This becomes clear if we distinguish between independence from determination by any particular desire or inclination and independence from determination by desire or inclination *überhaupt*. Practical freedom involves the first and transcendental freedom the second. Given this distinction, it follows that an agent would be free in the practical (but not in the transcendental) sense if the agent's choices were ultimately governed by some fundamental drive or natural impulse, for example, self-preservation or maximization of pleasure, which can be acted upon in any number of ways but which cannot be contravened. Such an agent would be practically free, possibly even in an incompatibilist sense, because the drive or impulse serves to limit the agent's options rather than to necessitate a given choice.[40] At the same time, however, the agent's choice would be ineluctably heteronomous since it would be limited to the determination of the best means for the attainment of some end implanted in us by nature. Obviously, such a conception of agency is incompatible with the central tenets of Kant's mature moral philosophy.[41]

The situation with respect to transcendental freedom is quite different. According to this conception, the ground of the selection of a maxim can never be located in an impulse, instinct, or anything "natural"; rather, it must always be sought in a higher-order maxim and, therefore, in an act of freedom.[42] Consequently, even if one posits a natural drive such as self-preservation, it remains the case that a transcendentally free agent is, *ex hypothesi,* capable of selecting maxims that run directly counter to its dictates. Moreover, since the choices of a transcendentally free agent, including those based on desire or inclination, are grounded in a "law" (maxim) which is self-imposed, such an agent would be autonomous in a morally neutral sense. Finally, it should be clear that only an agent that is free in this sense is capable of acting out of "respect for the law," and therefore of acting autonomously in the specifically moral sense on which Kant insists.

## V

We are finally in a position to consider the implications of the presupposition of transcendental freedom for the problem of justification. The basic point is simply that without this presupposition, that is, assuming merely practical freedom, a maxim based on self-interest, happiness, or some such putatively ultimate yet non-moral end or motivational ground could be justified by an appeal to "human nature" or some given determinant of behavior. (The details are irrelevant to the argument.) With it, however, this familiar move is blocked. If self-preservation, self-interest, or happiness is the principle of my behavior, if it dictates my maxims, it is I (not nature in me) that gives it this authority. At least this is the case under the presupposition that I am free in the transcendental sense. Moreover (and this is an essential premise of the entire argument), the justification requirement is still in place. In fact, the presupposition of transcendental freedom not only blocks certain kinds of justification, it also extends this requirement to first principles or fundamental maxims. Since such maxims, like all others are, *ex hypothesi,* freely adopted, it must be possible to offer reasons in support of their adoption. Correlatively, since such principles or maxims are first or fundamental in the sense that they provide the ultimate grounds for the justification of lower order maxims, they obviously cannot be justified by deducing them from some higher order principle.[43]

How, then, is the rational egoist to deal with this problem? To be sure, the proponent of such a position can continue to assert that it would be reasonable (if not desirable for the egoist) for every rational agent to act according to that principle and, therefore, that it passes the universalizability test in the sense in which the rational egoist acknowledges it. The real question, however, is whether this claim can be justified, given the presupposition of transcendental freedom. Obviously, the claim that it is somehow in one's best interests to act according to the dictates of rational egoism is question-begging at best. (At worst it may be simply false.) But the presupposition of transcendental freedom rules out what seems to be the only alternative strategy for justification, namely, the appeal to some given determinant or ultimate fact about human nature, which somehow of itself justifies the adoption of a maxim. Presumably, the same would hold, *mutatis mutandis,* for any other "heteronomous" principle.[44]

Admittedly, the most that this line of reasoning can show is that rational egoism and similar familiar doctrines cannot be rationally justified, at least not if they are combined with the presupposition of transcendental freedom. This is not a trivial result; but it is hardly equivalent to the claim that a rational and transcendentally free agent is constrained to acknowledge the validity (as the ultimate norm) of an unconditional practical law. Consequently, even assuming that the moral law, as defined by Kant, is the only conceivable candidate for a practical law, we cannot claim to have established that such an agent is necessarily subject to that law.

Nevertheless, we are finally in possession of the materials needed for such an argument. Although Kant himself never formulated it explicitly, I believe that it is implicit in all of his major writings in moral philosophy. The argument I have in mind is from the assumption of rational and transcendentally free agency to the conditions of the possibility of the justification of the maxims (including the fundamental maxims) of such agents. It proceeds in two stages: the first contends that conformity with an unconditioned practical law is a sufficient condition for the justification of these maxims; the second contends that it is also a necessary condition.

The first point I take to be relatively unproblematic. What stronger justification could there be for one's adoption of a maxim than its conformity to an unconditionally valid practical law? If a rule of action is "right" for all rational agents whatever their interests or desires, then, clearly, it is "right" for me. Again, if my reason for X-ing is that it is dictated by such a law (in Kant's deontic terms, that it is my duty), then I have all the justification I would conceivably need for X-ing. This is not to deny that there may be grave difficulties determining exactly what such a law requires in a given instance (what my duty is), and, therefore, that Kant's moral philosophy may run into severe difficulties in this regard. The present point is only that *if* a maxim can be shown to meet this requirement then that maxim has been fully justified.

Obviously, the main difficulties concern the claim that this requirement is a necessary condition for justification. In dealing with this issue, it will be helpful to begin with the consideration of a familiar yet misguided criticism of Kant's moral theory. Couched in terms of the present discussion, the claim is that the requirement (at least as here construed) is too strong. If, so the argument goes, the only legitimate reason for adopting a maxim were its conformity to a practical law binding upon all rational agents, regardless of their interests or desires, then it would seem that no maxim to pursue one's interests or desires could ever be justified. But this is patently absurd. Thus, even if it be granted that conformity to a practical law is a sufficient condition for the justification of one's maxims, it is certainly not also a necessary condition. To claim otherwise is to commit oneself to the doctrine that only actions performed "for the sake of duty" are justifiable; and this is to conflate justifiability with moral worth.

Although there is undoubtedly a strand in Kant's moral philosophy that suggests this line of interpretation and criticism, it does not reflect his considered opinion. What this reading neglects is the centrality for Kant of the distinction between the permissible and the obligatory.[45] Not surprisingly, then, it also fails to recognize that the moral law is intended as a criterion of the former as well as of the latter.[46] This is, of course, a large topic in its own right. Indeed, it calls to mind all of the familiar difficulties concerning Kant's distinctions between positive and negative, imperfect and perfect duties. I introduce it here only because it indicates that, rather than ruling out as illegitimate all desire- or interest-based maxims, the notion of conformity to a practical law is intended by Kant as a criterion for determining which maxims of this (or any) sort are permissible. Moreover, since it seems clear that no maxim could be regarded as justified if it were not at least shown to be permissible, it follows that establishing this claim is equivalent to showing that conformity to a practical law functions as a necessary condition for the justification of maxims.

Permissibility, like other deontic notions, has both a specifically moral and a morally neutral sense. In the former case it encompasses whatever is not contrary to duty and in the latter whatever is allowable within a given context or in light of some pre-given end (in accordance with the "rules of the game").[47] Presently, however, we are concerned merely with the conditions of the justification of the desire- or interest-based maxims of transcendentally free rational agents, that is, agents for whom the choice of such maxims both requires rational justification and is attributed to an act of freedom. Given these constraints, it is apparent that permissibility cannot be construed as a function of desires or interests, even the most fundamental ones. In other words, we are not looking for a rule or set of rules which determine what is permissible within the framework of some presupposed end. On the contrary, what must be determined is the rule or set of rules governing the pursuit of any end at all, including desire- or interest-based ends. In view of the "transcendental" function of such a rule or set of rules (its function with respect to end setting *überhaupt*), it is also apparent that it must be both universal and "formal" in the specifically Kantian sense. That is, it must not only apply to all transcendentally free rational agents, it must also apply to them regardless of what desires or interests they may happen to have. But such a rule or set of rules is precisely what Kant understands by a practical law. Consequently, it must either be denied that the maxims of transcendentally free agents can be justified at all (which amounts to a denial of rationality) or it must be acknowledged that conformity to practical law is the criterion governing the selection of the maxims of such agents. Combining this result with the further claim that the moral law is the required principle, we have the Kantian argument for the "analytic" connection between transcendental freedom and the moral law.

Since the above analysis turns largely on the distinction between the rationality and the freedom of an agent, it might itself seem problematic as Kantian exegesis. Such a conclusion, however, would be erroneous. Although Kant only makes this distinction fully explicit in *Religion within the Limits of Reason Alone,*[48] it is implicit in his thought from the *Groundwork* on.[49] Admittedly, only a rational agent can be free in the transcendental (or even the practical) sense, but an agent is not free in the transcendental sense simply in virtue of being rational. At least freedom in this sense cannot be derived from rationality; and, therefore, neither can the validity of the moral law. Unfortunately, the whole point is usually missed by Kant's critics. Starting with the reasonable assumption that a Kantian justification of morality must somehow demonstrate the irrationality of rejecting the categorical imperative, these critics tend to assume that the argument to this end must proceed simply from the concept of a rational being. This is not the case, but it is only by focusing explicitly on the Reciprocity Thesis that it becomes clear why it is not.

## VI

Given the preceding analysis, we can now deal with the common objection that the Reciprocity Thesis, particularly as presented in the *Groundwork,* leads Kant to the devastating consequence that we are free only insofar as we act in obedience to the categorical imperative. This consequence is devastating not only because it entails that we are not responsible for either our immoral or our morally neutral actions, but also because it suggests that even our morally good actions (actions performed for the sake of duty) are due ultimately to a fortuitous lack of interference by nature (in the guise of sensuous inclination) with the autonomous workings of pure practical reason. After all, if a free will is defined as one governed by the moral law, and if, as Kant suggests, this is analogous to the way in which natural phenomena are governed by the laws of nature, then it would seem that a free will could no more violate the moral law than a falling body could violate the law of gravity. Correlatively, if a non-moral or heteronomous will is subject to the laws of nature, then there is no way to understand how a will that is not already moral could choose to become such. In short, by distinguishing so strongly between nature and freedom and by defining the freedom of the will in terms of its subjection to the moral law, Kant seems to have made it impossible to provide a coherent account of either immoral or moral action.[50]

The standard strategy for defending Kant against this line of objection is to admit that it applies to the *Groundwork* and to deny that it applies to the latter treatment in *Religion within the Limits of Reason Alone,* where Kant offers an account of moral evil in light of the *Wille-Willkür* distinction.[51] The basic idea is that *Willkür,* as spontaneous, is free either to determine itself to act in accordance with the dictates of *Wille* (the stern call of duty) or to subordinate these dictates to the demands of inclination. The claim, in other words, is that what the *Groundwork* presents as heteronomy and opposes to autonomy is seen in *Religion within the Limits of Reason Alone* as itself an expression of freedom.

There can be little doubt that the account of freedom in *Religion within the Limits of Reason Alone* has a subtlety and depth that are lacking in both the *Groundwork* and the *Critique of Practical Reason.* We have already seen, however, that rather than precluding this conception of freedom, the Reciprocity Thesis, as formulated in these earlier works, requires it in the sense that it is only by construing freedom in this way that the argument can be made to work. Admittedly, this does not itself prove that Kant actually held such a conception at that time, but it certainly suggests that he could have, and it puts the burden of proof on those who would deny it.

There appear to be three aspects of Kant's account in the *Groundwork* to which the critic can appeal in support of this denial. Since all three of them have already been noted, we need only recall them here. First and foremost is the language of the Reciprocity Thesis itself. By explicitly identifying a free will with a will under the moral law, Kant certainly seems to leave no room for any free action that does not conform to the law. Second, this impression is greatly reinforced by the unfortunate analogy between the moral law and a law of nature. Finally, there is the apparent identification of heteronomous action and action in accordance with (or governed by) the laws of nature. This identification suggests that a heteronomous will can be neither free nor morally responsible, and this, in turn, raises the perplexing question of how such a will could ever become either free or morally good. Although not free (because heteronomous) is it free to become free?

In dealing with the first two aspects, it is obviously crucial to determine with some precision the sense in which a free will is supposed to be subject to, or governed by, the moral law. As we have already seen, in the *Critique of Practical Reason* Kant maintains that only a formal principle (later identified with the moral law) is "competent to determine it (a free will) necessarily." This locution once again suggests the very problem currently under consideration. Being determined necessarily by the moral law seems to mean being subject to it in precisely the same sense in which a physical object is subject to the laws of nature. And this, of course, rules out the possibility of any deviation from the law. It is, however, not only unnecessary, it is also implausible to take Kant to be making any such claim. Since "determine necessarily" means simply to possess a lawlike status for a free will (to be "objectively necessary"), all that Kant is claiming here is that only a formal principle (the moral law) can serve in this capacity for a free will.

The question thus becomes what is involved in serving in this capacity and the answer is quite apparent. It can mean only that the law provides a norm or standard in terms of which the choices of a free will are justified before the bar of reason. Material practical principles cannot do the job because they presuppose an object of desire as the determining ground of the will and, as we have seen, a free will is (by definition) responsible for the selection of any such object as its ends. It hardly follows, however, from the fact that the moral law is the norm or standard for a free will that such a will is not "capable" of failing to live up to this norm. As Kant frequently insists, although "objectively necessary," the moral law is nonetheless "subjectively contingent."[52] Consequently, we are free to act heteronomously, to make the satisfaction of our desires the basis of our choice. In so doing we are, at least according to Kant's moral theory, misusing our freedom; indeed, we are misusing ourselves in that we are treating our "higher" or "proper self" [*das eigentliche Selbst*] merely as a means for the satisfaction of our "lower" or sensuous nature. Nevertheless, this misuse of freedom is still very much an act of freedom, and there is nothing in Kant's theory that requires us to think otherwise.

Perhaps the single most important Kantian text bearing on this issue is the discussion in the Introduction to the *Metaphysics of Morals*. Kant there first defines freedom (the positive concept) as "the power of pure reason to be of itself practical."[53] Then, later, after introducing the *Wille–Willkür* distinction, and claiming that *Wille* cannot be properly regarded as either free or unfree since it deals with legislation rather than action, he writes

> Freedom of choice, however, cannot be defined as the capacity for mak-
> ing a choice to act for or against the law *(libertas indifferentiae)*, as some
> people have tried to define it, even though choice as a phenomenon gives
> frequent instances of this in experience. For freedom (as it first becomes
> known to us through the moral law) is known only as a negative property
> within us, namely, the property of not being constrained to action by any
> sensible determining grounds. . . . But we can see clearly that although
> experience tells us that man as a sensible being exhibits a capacity to
> choose not only in accordance with the law but also in opposition to it,
> yet his freedom as an intelligible being cannot be thus defined, since
> appearances can never enable us to comprehend any supersensible ob-
> ject (such as free choice is). . . . For it is one thing to admit a tenet (of
> experience) and quite another to make it both the defining principle (of
> the concept of free choice) and the universal mark distinguishing free
> choice from *arbitrio bruto s. servo,* since in the first case we do not assert
> that the mark necessarily belongs to the concept, which we must do in
> the latter case. Only freedom in relation to the internal legislation of rea-
> son is properly a capacity; the possibility of deviating from it is an incapac-
> ity. How, then, can the former be explained by the latter?[54]

Already Reinhold had objected to this formulation by presenting a dilemma. According to Reinhold's analysis, if the only concept of free-dom derivable from the moral law is that of the self-activity *(Selbsttätig-keit)* of reason, then the presumed "capacity" to act immorally is not only an incapacity but an impossibility. If, on the other hand, freedom is construed as the capacity of the *person* for self-determination, then the "capacity" to act immorally is not a mere incapacity but rather the very same capacity without which moral action cannot be thought.[55] Otherwise expressed, Reinhold's complaint seems to be that the proper concept of freedom must be a morally neutral one, and that this is incompatible with Kant's insistence that our understanding of freedom is derived entirely from our consciousness of the moral law. Quite recently, Gerold Prauss has raised similar objections. Prauss, however, also claims that Kant's account of freedom in the passage currently before us marks a regression from the standpoint of *Religion within the Limits of Reason Alone,* where he at least attempted (albeit unsuccessfully) to provide an account of immoral action in terms of freedom, back to that of the *Groundwork,* where such action is seen as a product of the heteronomy of nature.[56]

We can readily accept Prauss's assertion of the agreement of the account of freedom in this passage with that of the *Groundwork,* although not his characterization of it as a "regression," and certainly not his analysis of its implications. The key term in Kant's account is obviously 'power' or 'capacity' *(Vermögen).* By the "power of reason to be of itself practical" Kant means first of all its capacity to provide a binding law for the will.[57] Reinhold is correct in suggesting that if this were all that Kant means by freedom, then the freedom to disobey the law has not been established. There is, however, no need to accept this result nor, therefore, the terms of Reinhold's dilemma. Since ought implies can (at least for Kant), the capacity of pure reason to be practical, that is, to provide a binding law, entails the capacity of a free agent to obey the dictates of this law. This is precisely the point that Kant makes when he remarks that through the moral law we are aware of freedom as a "negative property . . . of not being constrained to action by any sensible determining grounds." Thus, freedom is understood as the will's capacity to follow its own self-imposed laws, which requires an independence from constraint by any sensible determining grounds. In the preferred jargon of Kant's later moral philosophy, freedom is construed as the capacity of *Willkür* to obey the dictates of *Wille.* Once again, it should be obvious that the possession of such a capacity is perfectly compatible with the failure to actualize it. Kant acknowledges this, but he also insists that this "capacity" to fail is really an incapacity (presumably because it cannot be ascribed to perfectly rational beings) and, therefore, should not be regarded as definitional of freedom. Reinhold and Prauss to the contrary, this does not at all entail that such failure is not itself an expression of freedom.

The third and final aspect of the problem concerns Kant's tendency, particularly in the *Groundwork,* to equate heteronomy with subjection to the laws of nature. In response to this it should suffice to note that there is no need to take the claim that the heteronomous will is "sub-

ject" to the laws of nature to mean anything more than that the inclinations and desires upon which it bases its choice are themselves
products of nature. Subjection to the laws of nature in this sense is
perfectly compatible with the Kantian conception of freedom. It does
not follow from the fact that the inclinations and desires on the basis
of which one chooses to act are products of nature, that the act of
choice itself, through which they are "incorporated" into the maxim of
the will, is likewise such a product.

## VII

Even if sound, the argument offered here for the Reciprocity Thesis
hardly suffices to establish the Kantian version of morality. It shows
only that we cannot both affirm our freedom (construed in the transcendental sense) and reject the categorical imperative. In this respect
it can be said to have established the price of moral skepticism. The
problem, of course, is that this price (the rejection of transcendental
freedom) is one that the moral skeptic (or the rational egoist) is more
than willing to pay. This is particularly true in view of the notorious
difficulties in Kant's attempt to reconcile this freedom with the universal sway of the principle of causality.

Nevertheless, the question of transcendental freedom must at least
be faced by anyone who wishes to criticize the Kantian attempt at the
justification of morality. This attempt cannot be dismissed in the casual
manner of Philippa Foot, who contends that there is nothing irrational
or inconsistent in the rejection of the categorical imperative, or, at
least, that no one has ever shown that there is,[58] while also insisting
elsewhere that "a reason for acting must relate the action directly or
indirectly to something the agent wants or which it is in his interest to
have. . . ."[59] Foot is certainly consistent here, but in a way that sidesteps
the main thrust of Kant's position. Given her conception of agency, it
not only would not be irrational to reject the categorical imperative, it
would be metaphysically impossible to obey it. Perhaps it is, but simply
to assume this is the case, is to beg the whole question.

In the last analysis, then, Kant's moral theory stands or falls with the
metaphysical doctrine of transcendental freedom. As the Reciprocity
Thesis makes clear, this freedom is not only a necessary, it is also a
sufficient condition of morality as Kant conceives it. Consequently, if
this freedom be denied, nothing remains save a rather complex and

convoluted analysis of the presuppositions of a set of illusory beliefs. If, on the other hand, it be granted, then the validity of the moral law follows. This same reciprocity, however, suggests that it might very well be impossible to establish either one without presupposing the other, which would mean that Kant's attempt to justify morality is caught in a vicious circle from which there is no escape. Kant himself raises the spectre of just such a circle in the *Groundwork,* but claims to be able to avoid it. Whether he is successful, either there or in his fresh treatment of the problem in the *Critique of Practical Reason,* is a larger issue, which cannot be dealt with here.

## Notes

1. *Groundwork of the Metaphysics of Morals, Kants gesammelte Schriften,* Berlin: Königliche Preussische Akademie der Wissenschaften, 1900–, 4:440.

2. For the distinction between two senses in which Kant speaks of a "supreme principle of morality," one of which applies to the categorical imperative and the other to the principle of autonomy, see Lewis White Beck, *A Commentary on Kant's Critique of Practical Reason* (Chicago: University of Chicago Press, 1960), p. 122 and T. C. Williams, *The Concept of the Categorical Imperative* (Oxford: Clarendon Press, 1968), pp. 33–35.

3. *G,* 445.

4. The fullest and most significant discussion of this issue is by Dieter Henrich, "Die Deduktion des Sittengesetzes," in *Denken im Schatten des Nihilismus,* ed. Alexander Schwan (Darmstadt: Wissenschaftliche Buchgesellschaft, 1975), pp. 55–112; in this volume, 303–341.

5. *Critique of Practical Reason,* 5:42–50.

6. For a recent discussion of the "Reversal Thesis," which includes an excellent account of the whole debate, see Karl Ameriks, "Kant's Deduction of Freedom and Morality," *Journal of the History of Philosophy* 19 (1981), pp. 53–79.

7. *G,* 447; *CPracR,* 29–31.

8. This point is noted by Henrich, "Die Deduktion des Sittengesetzes," pp. 89–90.

9. *G,* 446. *Groundwork of the Metaphysics of Morals,* Eng. trans. H. J. Paton (New York: Harper & Row, 1956), p. 114.

10. *CPracR,* 5:29.

11. *CPracR,* 5:30.

12. *CPracR,* 5:93–94.

13. *Religion within the Limits of Reason Alone,* Eng. trans. T. M. Greene ed., Hoyt Hudson (New York: Harper & Row, 1960), p. 30. See also *Reflexion* 7202, 19:281.

14. H. J. Paton, *The Categorical Imperative* (London: Hutchinson & Co.,

1947), p. 211. A similar view is expressed by Sir David Ross, *Kant's Ethical Theory* (Oxford: Clarendon Press, 1954), pp. 70–71.

15. Rüdiger Bittner, *Moralisches Gebot oder Autonomie* (Freiburg/Munich: Verlag Karl Alber, 1983), pp. 119–134, claims that the argument of the third part of the *Groundwork*, particularly the Reciprocity Thesis, is vitiated by this slide, which is, in turn, based on a confusion of two senses of 'autonomy.' A similar line of objection is also developed by Gerold Prauss, *Kant über Freiheit als Autonomie* (Frankfurt: Vittorio Klostermann, 1983). Prauss insists upon the need for distinguishing between a morally neutral and a specifically moral sense of 'autonomy' and criticizes Kant for a failure to be clear on this point.

16. I have claimed that the above account is based on Kant's implicit definitions because his official definitions of these notions are notoriously confusing. Thus, in some places he simply identifies a practical law with an objectively valid principle (for example, *Critique of Practical Reason* §1, 5:19); while in others he seems to regard practical laws as constituting a subset of objectively valid practical principles (for example, 5:20 and *G,* 416, 420). This, in turn, is connected with Kant's equally notorious confusion of laws and imperatives. Since all imperatives are objectively valid (in contrast to maxims) I take the latter position to be the one to which Kant is committed. For a further account of some of these issues see Beck, *A Commentary,* pp. 79–84 and 121–122.

17. *A New Exposition of the First Principles of Metaphysical Knowledge,* Proposition IX, *Kants gesammelte Schriften,* 1:398–405.

18. *G,* 412.

19. Ibid.

20. *G,* 446.

21. *G,* 400n and 420n; *CPracR,* 5:19 and *MM,* 6:225.

22. For a useful discussion of this point and, indeed, of the whole topic of Kant's view of maxims see Onora Nell, *Acting on Principle* (New York and London: Columbia University Press, 1975), pp. 34–42.

23. This, again, is a fairly common line of criticism. A good formulation of it is provided by Marcus Singer, *Generalization in Ethics* (New York: Alfred A. Knopf, 1961), pp. 245–46.

24. On this point see Beck, *A Commentary,* p. 78, and Rüdiger Bittner, "Maximen," *Akten des 4. Internationalen Kant-Kongresses,* Mainz, 1974, ed. G. Funke and J. Kopper (Berlin: de Gruyter, 1974), pp. 485–98.

25. In *Eine Vorlesung über Ethik,* ed. Paul Menzer (Berlin: Rolf Hesse, 1924), pp. 52–53, Kant refers to the universalizability of the intention *(Intention)* of an action, thereby treating intentions much as he later does maxims. The problem is complicated for the English reader, however, by the fact that, in his translation of the *Critique of Practical Reason,* Beck frequently renders *'Gesinnung'* as 'intention'.

26. Onora Nell, *Acting on Principle,* p. 40.

27. Ibid., p. 41.

28. J. L. Austin, "Three Ways of Spilling Ink," *The Philosophical Review* 75 (1966), pp. 427–40, esp. 437–38.

29. Marcus Singer, *Generalizations in Ethics,* p. 57.

30. I am obviously ignoring the whole problem of specifying "relevantly sim-

ilar circumstances," which is a critical issue in its own right. I think, however, that I am here in agreement with the analysis provided by Singer, *Generalizations in Ethics,* pp. 17–33.

31. Concise versions of this criticism are given by A. W. Wood, "Kant on the Rationality of Morals," *Proceedings of the Ottawa Congress on Kant in the Anglo-American and Continental Traditions* Held October 10–14, 1974, edited by P. Laberge, F. Duchesneau, B. C. Morrisey (Ottawa: The University of Ottawa Press), 1976, p. 94–109; and by Gilbert Harman, *The Nature of Morality* (New York: Oxford University Press, 1977), pp. 76–77. In Harman's case, however, there is absolutely no attempt to connect the criticism to the Kantian texts.

32. *G,* 412.

33. *Rel,* 6:126 note. Eng. trans. p. 21.

34. One of the few recent commentators to grasp this point is Thomas E. Hill, Jr., "The Hypothetical Imperative," *The Philosophical Review* 82 (1973), pp. 429–450. In discussing the syntheticity of the principle which Kant attempts to justify in *Groundwork* III, Hill correctly notes that subjection to the moral law cannot be derived analytically from the concept of a rational person, but that the freedom of the person plays an essential role in the argument. In fact, Hill states clearly that Kant's argument rests on two poles. 1) The claim that any person that is negatively free is also positively free (which is supposed to be a matter of conceptual analysis). 2) The claim that every rational being is also negatively free (which is not a matter of conceptual analysis). I am in complete agreement with Hill regarding the structure of Kant's argument in *Groundwork* III. My concern here is to provide an argument in support of the first of these two poles, that is, to provide the required conceptual analysis, which is something that Hill does not attempt to do.

35. Admittedly, the above account of Kant's first *Critique* theory of practical freedom is grossly oversimplified. In particular, it ignores the fact that Kant explicitly connects such freedom with the capacity to act on the basis of imperatives (for example, A 534/B 562, A 547–48/B 575–76, A 802/B 830). This, in turn, has led many commentators to assume that, even here, Kant understands freedom in explicitly moral terms. In reality, however, in his first *Critique* account Kant does not focus exclusively, or even primarily, on moral imperatives. He is rather concerned with the presentation of the outlines of a general theory of rational agency. For a fuller account of my views on this topic see "Practical and Transcendental Freedom in the *Critique of Pure Reason,*" *Kant-Studien* 93 (1982): 271–290, and *Kant's Transcendental Idealism: An Interpretation and Defense* (New Haven and London: Yale University Press, 1983), Chapter 15.

36. See *Critique of Pure Reason,* A 533/B 561, A 803/B 831; *Critique of Practical Reason,* 5:97, Eng. trans. p. 100.

37. For an interesting recent formulation of this line of criticism see Terence Irwin, "Morality and Personality: Kant and Green," in *Self and Nature in Kant's Philosophy,* edited by Allen W. Wood (Ithaca and London: Cornell University Press, 1984), pp. 31–56.

38. The most detailed and scholarly of these attempts is by Ralf Meerbote,

who interprets Kant in explicitly Davidsonian terms. See his reply to Irwin, "Kant on Freedom and the Rational and Morally Good Will," *op. cit.,* pp. 57–72; and "Kant on the Nondeterminate Character of Human Actions," *Kant on Causality, Freedom, and Objectivity,* edited by William A. Harper and Ralf Meerbote (Minneapolis: University of Minnesota Press, 1984), pp. 138–163. Many other contemporary philosophers, most notably Thomas Nagel, present quasi-Kantian accounts of agency while rejecting Kant's indeterminism.

39. Although I am no longer happy with all the details of my earlier analyses of this issue in "Practical and Transcendental Freedom in the *Critique of Pure Reason*" and *Kant's Transcendental Idealism,* I still contend that, as far as the interpretation of Kant is concerned, much depends on how one construes Kant's remarks in the Canon:

> Whether reason is not, in the actions through which it prescribes laws, itself again determined by other influences, and whether that which, in relation to sensuous impulses, is entitled freedom, may not, in relation to higher and more remote operating causes, be nature again, is a question which in the practical field does not concern us (A 803/B 831).

Taken in connection with Kant's subsequent statement that "we thus know practical freedom to be one of the causes of nature, namely, to be a causality of reason with respect to the will," this suggests that, in the Canon, at least, Kant held that practical freedom would stand even if there were no transcendental freedom. Since transcendental freedom is, by definition, a non-compatibilist or indeterministic conception of freedom, the clear implication is that the detachable conception of practical freedom is not. Thus, one arrives at a compatibilist reading of practical freedom, albeit at the cost of a contradiction between the Canon and the Dialectic. Both the contradiction and the compatibilist reading of practical freedom can be avoided, however, if we keep in mind that the transcendental freedom to which Kant refers in the Canon is construed explicitly as a "causality of reason." As Kant himself states, "transcendental freedom demands the independence of this reason—in respect of its causality, in beginning a series of appearances—from all determining causes of the sensible world" (A 803/B 831). Denying the "independence" of the causality of reason in this sense would not seem to be equivalent to denying indeterminism; but it would clearly commit one to the view that the will is ineluctably heteronomous. I take Kant's position in the *Critique of Pure Reason* to be an agnosticism with respect to the latter issue, which has nothing directly to do with the determinism-indeterminism question. In order to show that Kant's conception of practical freedom requires indeterminism, it would be necessary to consider his account of "intelligible character," a task that is obviously beyond the scope of this paper.

40. The point here is simply that a fundamental drive or impulse is a "standing condition" rather than a cause in the sense of the Second Analogy. The latter, for Kant, is always an event from which another event (the effect) follows *necessarily and in accordance with an absolutely universal rule*" (A 91/B 124). For my analysis of the Second Analogy, see *Kant's Transcendental Idealism,* Chapter 10.

41. I argue, however, in "The Concept of Freedom in Kant's Semi-Critical Ethics" (*Archiv für Geschichte der Philsophie* 68 [1986]:96–115) that it is perfectly compatible with Kant's moral philosophy at the time of the first edition of the *Critique of Pure Reason.* The key point is that in 1781 Kant had not yet developed his doctrine of autonomy.

42. Kant develops this doctrine at length in *Religion within the Limits of Reason Alone* in connection with his account of "radical evil."

43. Lewis White Beck, "The Fact of Reason: An Essay on Justification in Ethics," *Studies in the Philosophy of Kant* (Indianapolis: Bobbs-Merrill, 1965), pp. 200–214, provides the best discussion, from a Kantian point of view, of the problems involved in the justification of fundamental practical principles.

44. There are obvious affinities between this line of argument and those which appeal to the is-ought distinction and the "naturalistic fallacy." For an important discussion of the relevance of such arguments to Kant's own position see Karl-Heinz Ilting, "Der naturalistische Fehlschluss bei Kant," *Rehabilitierung der praktischen Philosophie,* I, edited by Manfred Riedel (Freiburg: Rombach, 1972), pp. 79–97.

45. See *G,* 438, and *MM,* 6:422.

46. For a discussion of the issue see Paton, *The Categorical Imperative,* pp. 141–142, and Beck, *A Commentary,* p. 122.

47. Kant himself suggests such a distinction in the *CPracR,* 5:11n.

48. Kant's clearest statement on this point occurs in connection with his account of the distinction between the predisposition *(Anlage)* to *humanity* in man, "taken as a living and at the same time a *rational* being" and the predisposition to *personality* in man, "taken as a rational and at the same time accountable being," *Rel,* 6:26–28.

49. I take this distinction to be implicit in the distinction which Kant suggests in the *Groundwork* between rational beings *simpliciter* and rational beings possessed of a will, *G,* 448–459. The same distinction is also operative in the *Critique of Practical Reason,* 5:32. For a discussion of the significance of this distinction see Dieter Henrich, "Die Deduktion des Sittengesitzes," esp. pp. 91–100.

50. The most detailed and powerful formulation of this line of criticism in the recent literature is by Prauss, *Kant über Freiheit als Autonomie,* esp. pp. 60–115. Versions of it are found, however, in a large number of commentators. Indeed, as Prauss points out, it can be traced back to Kant's own contemporaries.

51. See Silber, "The Ethical Significance of Kant's Religion," 85, 127–28.

52. See *G,* 413–414.

53. *MM,* 6:214, Eng. trans. *The Metaphysical Principles of Virtue,* translated by James Ellington (Indianapolis, New York: Bobbs-Merrill), 1964, p. 12.

54. *MM,* 6:226; Eng. trans. p. 26.

55. Karl Leonhard Reinhold, "Einige Bemerkungen über die in der Einleitung zu den 'Metaphysischen Anfangsgründen der Rechtslehre' von I. Kant aufgestellten Begriffe von der Freiheit des Willens," in *Materialen zu Kants "Kritik der praktischen Vernunft,"* edited by Rüdiger Bittner and Konrad Cramer (Frankfurt am Main: Suhrkamp Verlag, 1975), pp. 310–323.

56. Prauss, *Kant über Freiheit als Autonomie*, p. 112. Prauss also offers a critique of Reinhold's own account, pp. 84–92.

57. For a similar analysis of this text and its relevance to the general problem of the possibility of free and yet non-moral action for Kant see Nelson Potter, Jr., "Does Kant have Two Concepts of Freedom?" *Akten des 4. Internationalen Kant-Kongresses,* 590–596.

58. This is the central thesis of her influential paper, "Morality as a System of Hypothetical Imperatives," *The Philosophical Review* 81 (1972), pp. 305–316. Reprinted in *Virtue and Vices and Other Essays in Moral Philosophy* (Berkeley and Los Angeles: University of California Press, 1978), pp. 157–178.

59. "A Reply to Professor Frankena," *Virtues and Vices,* p. 179. It should perhaps also be noted here that Foot defends an essentially Humean theory of agency, including a version of compatibilitism in several of the essays included in this volume. This is not, of course, to say that she is wrong in this regard, but only that the question of the cogency of Kant's analysis of morality is inseparable from the question of the cogency of his theory of agency.

# 12

# The Deduction of the Moral Law: The Reasons for the Obscurity of the Final Section of Kant's *Groundwork of the Metaphysics of Morals*

*Dieter Henrich*

## I. The Task of the *Groundwork*

In the Preface to the *Critique of Practical Judgment* Kant says that the second *Critique* presupposes the *Groundwork of the Metaphysics of Morals*. The latter makes the principle of duty known provisionally, and provides and justifies a determinate formula for the judgment of duties (*CPracR*, 13ff.)[1] The second *Critique* can therefore arrive at a derivation of the formula of the categorical imperative in a few pages. For the *Groundwork* has already shown that ordinary moral judgment itself presupposes this formula and is oriented by it, and it shows above all that this formula can actually be used for an understanding of the most important fundamental situations in which moral considerations have significance for action. The *Critique of Practical Reason* can thereby dispense with an analysis of all ordinary moral judgments—with the exception of the one, fundamental judgment that practical rules that are to be morally binding must also have objective validity, which cannot be traced back to any presupposed ends.

This account gives the impression that the *Groundwork* had been conceived as an introduction to the *Critique of Practical Reason;* and its editor Karl Vorländer described it in such a way.[2] But we have no reason to assume that in 1785 Kant had any intention at all of following the *Groundwork* with a further *Critique of Practical Reason*. Indeed, in the *Groundwork* he lays out the program for such an investigation, but also explains why he does not undertake it: It seems less important to him than a critique of pure theoretical reason. For an inquiry that investigates all of the pure cognitions of the faculty of practical reason (cf. B 869) would not have to deal with the difficulties resulting from the contradictions in which theoretical reason becomes involved in its pure judgments about objects.[3] To set those aside was a task of the first importance. A critique of pure practical reason would also be liable to claims of systematic completeness that do not need to be considered in coming to an understanding of the principle of morality (*G,* 391).

This principle, however, must be well established if a "Metaphysics of Morals" is to be written. According to Kant's conviction, which he declares more frequently than any other, the latter cannot be developed out of experience, and therefore cannot be begun immediately. It requires an investigation in which its principles are introduced and made convincing. To accomplish this is the task of the *Groundwork of the Metaphysics of Morals.* It is the introduction only to the *Metaphysics of Morals,* and that means that it is limited to what is indispensable for the solution of the task of the latter. However, as far as this task itself is concerned, it is not distinguished from that of a "Critique of pure practical reason" in any essential respect. For that too would have to provide what Kant calls in the *Groundwork* the "discovery and establishment of the supreme principle of morality" (*G,* 392). Only it would have to go beyond this central task and examine all practical cognitions that may be encountered in connection with the principle of morality and raise claims such as the postulates of pure practical reason and their foundation, the idea of the highest good.

In his Preface Kant clearly articulated that the *Groundwork* and a "Critique of pure practical reason" are parallel, not sequential, that one therefore has to read "groundwork" not as "introduction" but really as "founding": "For this reason I have used the title of a 'Groundwork for the Metaphysics of Morals' *instead* [emphasis added] of that of a 'Critique of Pure Practical Reason'" (*G,* 391).

The later remark in the preface to the *Critique of Practical Reason* should therefore not be misunderstood as if it describes the original intentions of the *Groundwork*. It refers to that in the structure of the *Groundwork* which can serve as an introduction to a *Critique of Practical Reason,* once the latter, contrary to Kant's original intention, has been published even though the *Groundwork* had already appeared.

The *Critique of Practical Reason* thus has to reckon with the existence of the *Groundwork,* and that is justified and even necessary, since the *Groundwork* had not been described as the predecessor and path-breaker for a *Critique of Practical Reason.*

The text of the *Groundwork* itself supports the false representation of its function as a path-breaker through its division into three chapters, each of which is described as a "transition," a transition among other things to a deeper investigation and insight. The final transition leads to the "Critique of pure practical reason," so that the whole text seems to end by attaining the dimensions of such a critique. The surface of its construction therefore gives the appearance that the *Groundwork,* the final chapter of which leads into the "critique of pure practical reason," can as a whole be nothing other than an introduction to this critique.

This appearance dissolves, however, as soon as one attends to the content of the third section: The part of Kant's considerations that might be counted as a transition to the *Critique of Practical Reason* ends after one page. Then Kant turns to themes that are characteristic of the type of investigation that he calls "critique." This corresponds to the fact that at the end of the second section Kant had announced that the final one would present what are "the main tendencies, *suffi-cient* [emphasis added] to our intention, of a critique of pure practical reason" (*G,* 445). This establishes that the *Groundwork,* precisely in its last part, has the same essential content as a "Critique of practical reason." Thus Kant did not write the *Groundwork* in order to make the succeeding work more readily accessible by introducing it through preparatory considerations. On the contrary, it was to spare the work that it was to precede—which was to be the *Metaphysics of Morals* and not the critique of practical reason—from a burden by freeing it from difficult investigations of the foundations of ethics, to which moral consciousness and its problems of judgment do not always have to be related. The "foundation" is separated from the theory in order not to have to "add subtleties, which are unavoidable in it, to doctrines that are more easily grasped" (*G,* 392). In this sense too the *Groundwork* replaces a critique of pure practical reason.

So have generations of students vainly sought access to Kant's ethics through a book that has unjustly been held to be the paradigmatic text for seminars? No misunderstanding without some substantive basis could have such far-reaching consequences. The contents and structure of the text of the *Groundwork* do display features that make it usable as an introduction to a certain extent: it starts out from ordinary moral cognition and grounds its argumentation initially on what is entirely evident therein. That is to be explained on theoretical grounds: at the time of the *Groundwork* Kant had already seen, and was shortly to emphasize decisively, that every understanding of moral consciousness has to proceed from its factuality. But, independently of this, Kant's conception of the structure of the *Groundwork* also took account of his experience of the reaction of contemporary philosophers to the publication of the *Critique of Pure Reason,* which had led him to follow the first critique with the *Prolegomena to Any Future Metaphysics* after just two years.

Kant conceded that the first critique suffered from a "certain obscurity" that stemmed, above all, from the "extensiveness of its plan" (*Prol,* 261). Kant had before him the entire tradition of ontology and metaphysics and at the same time the doubts and theoretical efforts of the modern empiricists. He had attempted to resolve such doubts and to develop the true theory of experience in a way that would simultaneously reveal the secret that the most worthy claims of reason had hitherto also been those which had to remain most debatable for reason itself. He wanted to explain the possibilities and boundaries of pure rational cognition in its entire scope. In his view, accomplishing this would have been a convincing criterion for the success of the critical enterprise. For if every problem of the old ontology found its solution and every concept of it found its proper place in a systematic illumination of all the activity of reason, then anyone would be convinced who had previously attempted to make contributions to ontological and metaphysical cognition without an antecedent critique. This expectation determined the conception of the first *Critique* in great measure. But it was disappointed. Kant explained the fact that the most important aims and arguments of the *Critique* initially failed to be understood and even attended to by the fact that the work as a whole required an "extensive" plan in which one "could not readily see the chief points of the inquiry" (*Prol,* 261). The critical enterprise could only enjoy general success if such a perspicuous overview could be produced.

The *Prolegomena* was to create clarity about the "chief points" of the critique and thereby remedy this defect. To this end it employs a procedure designed especially for a presentation concentrating on what is essential: the treatment of the critique by means of the analytical method. The critique really consists of knowledge that can be fully developed only by means of the synthetic method. Only thus can the doubts about certain principles of our knowledge of objects be resolved by an inquiry that goes directly to the source of all knowledge. But an argument following the analytical method is suitable for the preparation for this, because it presupposes the actuality only of knowledge the reality of which cannot be seriously doubted by anyone: Euclidean geometry and Newtonian physics. In relation to the principles by means of which these forms of knowledge are possible, we can judge and derive the possibility of all the rest of our knowledge that, like geometry and mathematical physics, does not derive exclusively from experience (*Prol,* §4). The *Prolegomena* presupposes the validity of two forms of knowledge in order with their help to reach an understanding of knowledge in its entirety. It is thereby in a position quickly to achieve fundamental clarity about a case of knowledge that is significant for the theory of knowledge, and in relation to this it can also make perspicuous the solution of the fundamental problem of the critique, that of the riddle of metaphysics.

The advantages of an analytical procedure were still clear to Kant as he composed his first critical work in moral philosophy. Thus this procedure was to be used to the extent possible in this work. In the case of moral philosophy the real question of the critical philosophy was also to be brought into the foreground with the greatest possible clarity. What Kant found lacking above all in the Göttingen review of the *Critique of Pure Reason* was that the reviewer "did not mention a single word about the real task of the *Critique.*"⁴ The groundwork of moral philosophy was to defend itself from the fate of having its real intentions misunderstood. So, in exact analogy with the procedure of the *Prolegomena,* Kant placed the chief question of the *Critique* in relation to morality, namely how categorical imperatives are possible, in the center of the *Groundwork*. Indeed, he wrote the first sketch of the *Groundwork* in connection with his preparation for the *Prolegomena.*⁵ The close connection between the two texts is also clear from the fact that in the *Prolegomena* Kant concentrates on the "chief points" of the *Critique* (*Prol,* 261), and in the *Groundwork* wants to develop the "chief tendencies" of a critique of the practical faculty of reason (*G,* 445).

But only a hasty inference can derive an identity of function from this similarity of methodological means and from the judgment of the importance of a presentation oriented toward central themes. In the critical edifice, the *Prolegomena* and the *Groundwork* fill very different roles. The *Prolegomena* is an *ex post facto* introduction, while the *Groundwork* has a significance corresponding in principle to that of the *Critique of Pure Reason.* Its task is to produce conviction about the justifiability of the claims of an imperative which, as Kant puts it, is valid for all rational beings independently of all experience and of all presupposed aims. The *Groundwork* has a part that is composed according to the synthetic method because it includes a critique of practical reason. No critical text is foreseen that would go beyond it in its chief points.

## II. Critique of Pure Practical Reason

The "critique of *pure* practical reason," the essential arguments of which are contained in the *Groundwork,* is not identical with the theory that Kant put forth in the book that appeared three years later under the title *Critique of Practical Reason.* In the introduction to the latter work Kant explicitly distinguishes between a critique of "pure" practical reason and a critique merely of practical reason. Thus the title of Kant's second work in moral philosophy cannot be understood as a short form of the name of the discipline that is treated in the last section of the *Groundwork.*

"Critique" originally means the activity of distinguishing the true from the false, what is justified from what is presumed, with regard to all possible foundations. Thus two possibilities are open to a critique: confirming something or rejecting it. But since we are overwhelmingly inclined to believe what we take as knowledge without examination, and since the wish to examine something arises from the suspicion that we have been misled, it is easy to understand that the word "critique," in spite of the neutrality of the procedure that it originally designates, comes to be used as the name for the act of well-founded *rejection* of claims to truth.

The significance of Kant's critical program also follows the tendencies of the meaning of the word "critique." From the beginning it announces an examination without the preconceived opinion that it should have the rejection of claims that were previously thought to be valid as its outcome. And just as in the word "critique" the sense of "unconstrained examination" is the fundamental component of its meaning, from which, however, the second meaning of "rejection" naturally develops, so Kant gradually gave more and more weight to the negative sense of the word "critique."

This shift can also be observed in the transformation of the meaning of the title of the second *Critique*. In 1787[6] a critique of *pure* practical reason, thus of the reason that contains principles sufficient for action, did not appear necessary to Kant, because this reason did not raise any suspicion about itself. Only that practical reason that is not pure, but instead presupposes sensibly conditioned interests for all action, has to be criticized: for it develops the opinion that all motivations are like its own, and this "presumption" is to be warded off. In a program founded in this way, "to criticize" means only to dispute and to reject. The more theoretical sense of "critique," according to which critique pertains to reason as such and thus to a whole of rational accomplishments, can no longer hold when the goal has become a critique of "empirically conditioned practical reason." For such a critique is valid for reason in a determinate use. It no longer develops an overview of rational principles of action in their entirety, even if it can be conducted only from such an overview. The procedure for attaining such an overview will still continue, to be sure, to be called "critique." But the book title *Critique of Practical Reason* is conceived entirely in the negative sense of the word "critique."

That the sense of the title of the highest inquiry in moral philosophy has changed, however, cannot be understood solely as a consequence of the development of the meaning of a word out of one of the tendencies in its original meaning. Rather, the fact that this alteration took place in just a few years must instead be explained as arising from a change in Kant's conception of the systematic possibilities for moral philosophy: it is because Kant's conception of the subject that is to be investigated in a "critique of practical reason" has been transformed that only the interpretation based on the negative sense of "critique" is left for the title which has already been put in use. In 1785, Kant did not hold the opinion that the rejection of competing claims would be sufficient to secure the ethics of pure practical reason. To establish such an ethics on a sound footing seemed to require more than developing its law and showing that doubt of its validity is not sufficiently well founded. A critique of *pure* practical reason had to be developed. In it the origin of our conviction of the validity of the law had to be investigated and our conviction justified in relation to this law.

The text of the *Groundwork* makes it obvious that Kant had difficulties in developing the arguments of a "critique of pure practical reason" in accordance with a clear and transparent conception. The nature of these difficulties is to be clarified in what follows. But we can already suspect that it was only Kant's experience with the conception of the *Groundwork* that made it possible for him to conceive of the *Critique of Practical Reason* in the unequivocalness and simplicity that distinguishes this work. In it, all moral philosophy is to be grounded on the "fact" of the consciousness of a law that makes valid the unconditional and undeniable claim on the determination of the will. One can only defend this fact, thus interpret and localise it in the nexus of all the accomplishments of reason. Kant expresses in all clarity that there is no possibility of getting behind this fact as such, thus of securing the validity of the law by beginning from premises in which this validity is not already supposed to be accepted. To be sure, the conditions of the possibility of the validity of this law may be clarified. But its validity cannot be demonstrated nor can its origin, which is beyond all rational cognition, be understood. In this sense, and in a sense that is later to be explained, Kant declares that no attempt at a *deduction* of the fact has any prospect of success (*CPracR,* 47).

Between this formulation and the foundational promise of the *Groundwork* there is a direct contrast. The central argument of the third section of the *Groundwork* is explicitly called a "deduction" three times (*G,* 447, 454, 463). It must therefore be assumed that in the two years following the publication of the *Groundwork* Kant was forced to reverse himself on a question central to his philosophy. It is important to explain how and why this happened.[7]

But with this explanation not all of the problems are solved that to this day stand in the way of a satisfactory understanding of the *Groundwork*. For it cannot and has not been overlooked that the critique of pure practical reason with which the *Groundwork* culminates does include a deduction of the principle of morality. The text of the *Groundwork* is difficult not only because it formulates a thesis that directly opposes the formulations of the *Critique of Practical Reason*. Understanding the precise sense and the foundation of this principle requires great effort, and the particular difficulty of the *Groundwork* results not primarily from the peculiarities of its position, but rather from the fact that Kant's explanations are unclear and inperspicuously intertwined, and that the decisiveness of his tone masks an exposition of his conception that is not yet fully determinate and about whose proper character Kant is not yet able to speak in a way free of theoretical obscurities and ambivalences. It must be shown what the nature of this indeterminacy is.

The indeterminacy must, among other things, be of a sort that appeared tolerable to Kant himself within the framework of the critical philosophy as already developed and that could not have held him back from the publication of the *Groundwork*. This connection too must be clarified, and it will thereby be shown that such a clarification can succeed only if at the same time some aspects of Kant's moral philosophy become visible which Kant himself was never able to make clear, even in the *Critique of Practical Reason.*[8]

### III. Logical and Transcendental Freedom

The deduction in the *Groundwork* is based on two steps, in which the principle of morality is grounded with the help of propositions that belong to the context of theoretical philosophy. In the next two sections, these will first be presented and then made as coherent as Kant's text allows.

If one could proceed from the reality of the freedom of the will, then one could derive the validity of the moral law from that. For without a determining ground independent of all matter freedom could not function as a kind of causality. But knowledge of freedom on the model of knowledge of objects is impossible. Thus the question arises whether at least the assumption of the reality of freedom can be justified purely as an assumption.

Reason, as the instrument of knowing, must already claim independence for itself. For if one were to assume that impulses and interests do not merely stimulate reason's activity, but also determine the content of its judgments—and indeed necessarily, not merely sometimes and in opposition to its own principle—then no comprehensible concept of reason could even be formulated.

Considerations that Kant adduced elsewhere suggest that this freedom of reason has two forms. On one account, reason must hold itself to be the source of its *a priori* propositions. If it were not, then these propositions would be influenced by conditions that are contingent relative to reason. But that would contradict the concept of them as *a priori* judgments (*R* 5413, 18:176; *R* 5441, 18:182–3). Second, judgments which are not apodictic, and which are in this sense contingent, also presuppose freedom in judging. For if it is possible for me either to affirm or to deny a predicate of an object, then I must assume that I am not caused to do so by any circumstances other than the actual fact of the matter to which I refer in my judgment. I must be in a position to decide about the suitability of the use of predicates in relation to the fact of the matter, without my judgment being antecedently determined. "Logical freedom" obtains "in regard to all contingent predicates" (*R,* 5442, 18:183).

The presupposition of this freedom has the advantage of deriving from reason as such. This presupposition is not made on the basis of some particular state of consciousness, but is inexorably connected with the very idea of a use of reason. As soon as it is presupposed by any rational being, it is immediately valid for all rational beings in general.

The text of the *Groundwork* does not declare explicitly that one must distinguish this freedom of reason as such from the freedom out of the reality of which the principle of morality will follow analytically. Neither does it force one to ascribe to it the assumption of the identity of the meaning of the two concepts of freedom. For it distinguishes, implicitly but clearly, between rational beings in general and those rational beings "that are equipped with a will" (*G,* 448). This distinction can only be significant if there is some difference between the concept of freedom claimed by theoretical reason and another concept of freedom which is constitutive for practical relationships. Otherwise, practical freedom would always have to be assumed whenever a being can make its reason valid in any practice at all. If the full, undifferentiated concept of reason is to be applied to all acts of thought, then every act of thought which makes action possible in any way would make this action free. Thus the distinction between rational beings in general and rational beings that will must correspond, if it is to be meaningful, to a distinction between two concepts of freedom.

In fact Kant made this distinction. The freedom that is presupposed in the principle of morality is not merely opposed to dependence on causes that bring the activity of reason into action and steer it in the form of impulses and interests. It is also incompatible with an inner determinability of reason itself. If the activity of reason were ruled from the start in an immemorial order of things, then its action would not be completely determined by the principles of which reason is conscious as the condition of its judgments. Such a consciousness would be a mere illusion. In truth, even a principle that uses this illusion would be determining things in order to carry through a universal nexus of determination. It would determine above all on what occasion reason could come into action at all and with what degree of intensity it could act. Kant calls such an hypothesis "fatalism." For him it is a position, ascribed to the Stoic philosophers, that is to be taken seriously as an historical opponent.[9]

For moral action, it is necessary that on every given occasion reason develop maxims out of itself and produce actions the determining grounds of which lie only in itself. The hypothesis of fatalism, however, would imply that it is related only to those occasions that are foreseen in the nexus of determination, and that it then derives its power of action from circumstances that are not based in reason itself. Such a fatalism may be an arbitrary hypothesis; it can never be grounded in determinate empirical knowledge. But that does not alter the fact that this hypothesis is incompatible with moral consciousness and is excluded by it. But it can be accepted, in contrast, by theoretical reason. For in thinking purely as such I am free even when I do not freely control the occasions on which I think, and when I am not in a position either adequately to motivate myself to think or to give my insight influence on my actions.

Kant had already known how to make this distinction between two concepts of freedom precise during the period of the genesis of the *Critique of Pure Reason*: "*Libertas opponitur vel necessitate brutae vel fatalitate, prior in sensu practico, posterior in sensu transcendentali*" (*R* 4684; 17:672).[10] The same distinction is also found in a period closer to the composition of the *Groundwork* (*R* 5441 and 5442, 18:182–3), and one may therefore suppose that in this work too Kant held the distinction between merely rational and rationally acting beings to be a specific difference between two sorts of rational life.

As has already been said, this distinction is not clearly marked in the *Groundwork*. Indeed, the second caption in the third section (*G*, 447) seems to force one to exclude it. For if "Freedom must be presupposed as a property of the will of all rational beings," then it seems that one must infer that there can be no rational beings without freedom of the will. But this conclusion cannot correspond to Kant's theoretical intention at all. It is one of his most fundamental premises that the faculty of desire has an independent origin from that of cognition, so that reason does not imply will. Thus even in spite of this caption the possibility must be conceded that there can be rational beings that have no will, and then the question can only be what is presupposed in the term "will" so that from the connection of the will to reason the necessity of assuming the reality of freedom follows. In the subsequent text Kant visibly makes an adequate restriction when he says that we must grant the idea of freedom to every rational being "that has a will" (*G*, 448).

But now what does it mean "to have a will"? This question is also eventually answered by Kant, at first ambiguously but in the end quite unequivocally. At first, one learns that a being has will whose reason "is practical, i.e., has causality in regard to its objects" (*G*, 448). Later this concept of practical freedom, which can also be satisfied by the freedom in pragmatic, interested action, is unequivocally limited to the transcendental freedom of moral action: will is "a faculty distinct from the mere faculty of desire, namely a faculty for determining oneself to action as an intelligence, hence in accordance with laws of reason, independent of natural instincts" (*G*, 459).

Thus Kant's text is free from the fallacious inference according to which all rational beings as such must already, merely as rational beings, be regarded as free beings in the transcendental sense. Not even all beings in whose conduct considerations of rationality play a role have a will. At least three classes of rational beings should be distinguished: 1) those who merely reflect; 2) those who act on the basis of reflection; and 3) those who have a will, who are therefore self-sufficient in their setting of ends.

But from the very absence of this fallacy another difficulty seems to arise. Namely, one can no longer see what is to be won from the fact that every rational discourse presupposes freedom of judgment. If will is a form of rational conduct, whose existence cannot be inferred merely from the fact that being has reason, then the freedom that is presupposed by the validity of moral principles can only be assumed on the basis of the reality of the will, not from the capacity for discourse alone. Thus there arises the suspicion that Kant's argument, even if it is not groundless, leads to no result.

If Kant's argument is to have a theoretically productive function, it must lie somewhere between a tautological assertion on the one hand and a logical derivation of the reality of moral principles on the other. It will turn out that it does follow something like this foundational program: to be sure, one cannot derive the possibility of action determined by reason from the structure of theoretical reason; but the presupposition of the freedom of judgment, valid for all thought, nevertheless corresponds to the presupposition of the freedom of rational willing. This correspondence gives the appeal to the freedom of judgment a certain argumentative force, which is initially weak, to be sure, but which can be strengthened in the context of more extended foundational process.

We could achieve a stronger argument if we were permitted to infer as follows: If we start out from the power of judgment, and then concede a will as well to the rational being that possesses the former, this means only that we assign rational principles immediate influence on our action. But because of the freedom of judgment that is presupposed, the conception of our principles, just like that of their application, is "free." And from this it follows (this would be the stronger argument) that the reason that is relevant to action also possesses transcendental freedom. Then one would have inferred transcendental freedom from logical freedom and the additional premise of the existence of the will. However, this conclusion is inadmissible, because of the possibility of the hypothesis of transcendental fatalism. Kant offers some ground for ascribing such a conclusion to him. The text of the *Groundwork* even seems to draw it explicitly when it says that reason "must regard itself as the author of its principles . . . *consequently* [emphasis added] as practical reason it must regard itself as free" (*G*, 448). In the text of the most important and virtually contemporaneous parallel, in his review of Schulz's *Attempt at an Introduction to the Doctrine of Morals*, Kant limits himself to a more cautious "*just as*" (emphasis added).[11] And even the *Groundwork* can at least be read so that the "consequently" that it uses is derived from the mere analogy intended by the "just as" between the two presuppositions. Something like the following foundation would then be indicated: Such a far-reaching assumption as that of the freedom of the will can never be made without any foundation. It is opposed by the conditions of all knowledge of nature and by the doubt about the possibility of assertions about the transcendent. Moral consciousness cannot convincingly validate itself against theoretical doubt entirely by itself. However, it can be shown that theoretical reason itself makes a presupposition the content of which stands in something like the same relation to discourse as the freedom of the will stands to moral consciousness. If one reminds theoretical reason that it cannot surrender this presupposition, then it suddenly becomes legitimate and even unavoidable to grant the same right to practical reason. Just as the freedom of judgment is opposed to "mechanism," transcendental freedom is opposed to fatalism. In relation to the evidence to which they are related, both are necessary hypotheses of reason. And that they really are assumed by reason is incontrovertibly revealed by the fundamental certainty that all rational creatures have that they are able to make judgments on the basis of their own insight.

Kant obviously held it to be more important to display the nature of the relation to freedom established by reason in a being that has a will than to clarify the logical relationships on the basis of which this relation can be asserted. The relation of reason to freedom is a relation to an *idea*. Theoretical reason has no knowledge of freedom as an actual state of affairs. Its certainty that it is free precedes every possible cognition, and it would be senseless and circular for it to hold itself to be authorized to think only if it has antecedently been convinced of the reality of freedom. The hypothesis of the freedom of judgment is legitimate, because without it no use of reason would be possible at all. Likewise, practical reason must regard itself as free, even if in a different sense, and on account of this parallelism to the original, legitimate hypothesis of reason its hypothesis can also be regarded as legitimated by reason. Kant was right to emphasize this aspect of his investigation strongly, for it is in fact more important than the question about the peculiarities of the logical interconnection between freedom of judgment and freedom of action. It can seem otherwise only to one who is already intimate with Kant's work in its entirety and interested above all in the problem of the connection among its parts. For the reader to whom in the *Groundwork* Kant presents his moral philosophy for the first time, the doctrine of freedom must seem more fundamental and promising in its interconnection with his doctrine of the ideas of reason. All of modern pragmatism really goes back to it.

It is certainly not to be disputed that the emphasis on the doctrine of idea offered Kant the possibility of getting past the problem of the logical connection of the hypotheses of freedom and to dispense with trying to resolve its inherent unclarity. This partially explains the confusing condition of the text.

## IV. The Intelligible and the Moral World

That Kant can have thought about the derivability of transcendental freedom, if at all, then only unclearly as well as only occasionally, can be seen from the section with the caption "On the interest that attaches to the ideas of morality" (*G,* 448–53). It initially abstracts from the questions by means of which Kant characterized the state of the problem following the investigation of the idea of freedom, and refers to the way in which he grasps the new problem that now faces the position of the moral consciousness and its exegetes, the moral philosophers.

This is the problem of circularity. It would have already been set aside if the derivation of transcendental from logical freedom had been formally compelling. The assumption of freedom of judgment is unavoidable, because without it here is no thinking. It legitimates the assumption of transcendental freedom, to be sure, but not by implying its concept. Only if this is so can it still be asked why transcendental freedom is held to be real, which assumes that this question still awaits an answer. But if this question *can* be asked, then it *must* be put. For the issue is a justification of moral consciousness, and in this connection every argument will be powerless that would only follow the interest of moral consciousness.

Kant explains the problem of a circle in a manner that already prepares the way for the solution he is striving for: It would be entirely evident that we were assuming the reality of freedom solely on account of the "already presupposed importance of moral laws" (*G,* 450) if we were to distinguish two orders and then two worlds[12] from each other exclusively for the purpose of being able to hold moral laws to be real. If the only support that one could offer in behalf of this distinction is that without it moral consciousness is imaginary, then it would already be revealed to be an *ad hoc* hypothesis. The conception of the coexistence of the two orders would not differ in any way from the mere fact that its assumption is unavoidable for moral consciousness.

To this self-generated problem Kant opposes the second of his arguments in which he constructs a connection between theoretical and practical reason. He presents this argument as the kernel of a "critique of pure practical reason." It has by now become well known, and its most important step is no longer debatable, so it may readily be evaluated.[13] It can be divided into two steps, which are closely interconnected to each other.[14] We will go into the difference between them later.[15]

1. Kant first shows that theoretical reason by itself also makes the distinction between two worlds. Through the idea of freedom we transport ourselves into the intelligible world and think of its law as immediately valid for our wills.

2. On the basis of the theoretically grounded representation of the relation of the two worlds it can also be understood how the categorical imperative can make itself valid as an imperative under the condi-

tions of the sensible world. The law is valid, especially in the form of an imperative, because we have no choice but to think of the world of the understanding as subsisting for itself and of the world of the senses as dependent on it. So if the law of freedom is the law of the world of the understanding, then we must think of this law as valid in relation to the world of the senses.

In this argument it is evident, first, that Kant is concerned, consistently even if also cautiously, to be able to ascribe the distinction between the two worlds not merely to theoretical reason, but also to theoretical reason in its *natural* use. The "commonest understanding" (G, 451), it may "well" (450) or "probably" (452) be assumed, develops a representation, "even if crude" (451), of the duality of worlds. This sort of exposition is characteristic of the systematic position of the *Groundwork*.[16]

If one compares the new argument with the first argument from the logical freedom of judgment, revealing parallels result. Again Kant aims to underline the spontaneity of reason in the distinction between the two orders. They are *standpoints* which can be adopted, thus not simply totalities of existence the reality of which we 'grasp' in pure thought. That is clearest from the fact that Kant is not satisfied to confirm that every thinking person makes this distinction. In a separate paragraph, he adds that every such person is also conscious of the capacity by means of which he makes such a distinction: his reason, as the source of all ideas (G, 452).

Similarly, the form of the inference in the new argument corresponds broadly to that of the first, even in the ambiguities of the exposition. The distinction between the two worlds, namely, is introduced exclusively by theoretical reason, and it is nowhere said that this reason is in a position to identify the world of understanding with a world of moral freedom. It is explicit only that the human being must count "his self" and "what may be pure activity in him" (G, 451) as part of the intellectual world. But of what sort the laws of the other world are is first specified only after a *will* has once again been imputed to the rational being (G, 452). The transition from the theoretical concept of reason to the completed concept of reason that is also a will occurs without comment. Where the logical status of such a decisive step for the "critique of pure practical reason" should be clarified, there reigns confusing obscurity.

If one pays attention to what is really going on here, it must be concluded that it is not possible to identify the law of the intellectual world as the moral law without assuming that the rational capacity of the will is known.[17] In the same way it was impossible immediately to interpret the presupposition of freedom in judgments as the same as transcendental freedom as opposed to fatalism. Just as little as logical freedom includes transcendental freedom can the doctrine of two worlds forcibly introduce the thought of the moral law. A rational being with only the freedom of judgment is just as conceivable as a world of the understanding that is not specified as moral. But just as the assumption of transcendental freedom is related to the possibility of a perspective of freedom that already lies in thought, likewise the assumption of a moral world is dependent upon the fact that the formal distinction between two worlds in general can be made, and it is probably also dependent on the fact that it already has been made.

Besides these correspondences, there is also a distinction between the two points of view: The freedom that reason presupposes does not require an interpretation in the thought of an interconnected world. It is indifferent to all interpretations of reality, as is demonstrated by the fact that it is compatible with fatalism. But to distinguish between two worlds means to make a distinction between two totalities of existing things. However, theoretical reason can be related to the world to which its activity belongs only indeterminately. It must think a law of this world, without being able to think it in any determinate way. It is through the existence of a will that it is enabled to complete the empty thought of a second world and an activity and for the first time to represent the determinate relation of the world of understanding to the world of appearance. Even grasped in this way, the world of understanding remains an idea. But that is to say that the thought of the world of understanding implies that this world has such a determinacy in itself. Thus the thought of the world of understanding as a world of moral freedom is an amplification of the thought of the world of understanding purely as such that is motivated by the concept of the world of understanding itself. And that means: If it is possible, then it is also unavoidable. For if an idea that is necessary for reason can be brought from an immediate but opaque consciousness to determinacy and into theoretical consistency with this consciousness, then it would be irrational to reject this picture of consistency, even if it is not an analytical relation of implication.

The second argument of the *Groundwork* thus has greater inferential force than the first, although neither of them derives moral freedom logically. Both show that freedom is not assumed arbitrarily.

Beyond that, they also show that it is unavoidable to assume freedom if the entire context within which the consciousness of a rational being exists is considered. Transcendental freedom cannot be proven by formal inferential procedures. But it has the sense of a necessary assumption that everyone who believes himself conscious of a will must make. For theoretical reason already makes a similar assumption, and, further, introduces a distinction between two worlds that demands to be made specific if that is at all possible. In this sense, thus, the assumption of the reality of freedom is *rationally* grounded. Nevertheless, freedom cannot be thought as other than an idea of reason.

## V. The Inexplicability of the Interest

In this way the argument of the "critique of pure practical reason" in the *Groundwork* is given the only form in which it can be defended. Its peculiar character will have to be treated further. But first it must be established that this interpretation nowhere oversteps the bounds of what the text permits. However, it is also to be conceded that Kant's text manifests tendencies that could suggest more far-reaching intentions—intentions for a proof that would be compelling as a formal derivation from premises. Only in 1787 did Kant definitively exclude the possibility of such a proof.

Even in the *Groundwork* there is talk of the incomprehensibility of freedom. It is the content of the final thesis of the *Groundwork* and its Socratic turn: We cannot understand under what condition freedom actually obtains. Kant indicated this "outermost boundary of all practical philosophy" (*G,* 455) in two ways, which are to be distinguished from each other.

1. First, it is impossible to find an explanation for freedom even as a principle of acting in the intelligible world. For the intelligible world is inaccessible to us, and is an object for us only on the basis of a necessary standpoint and through an idea of reason (*G,* 462). But even if this world were more than a way of considering things under an idea, freedom would still remain incomprehensible. For it is a spontaneous action on the basis of laws that hold apodictically. But we can understand the existence of something only from preceding conditions, and the validity of something only from things already presupposed to be valid (*G,* 462). However, both forms of explanation are excluded in the case of freedom and its laws.

2. The inexplicability of an action from freedom in the intelligible world corresponds to the incomprehensibility of our interest in the moral law. Kant considers both to be one and the same thing. But it is obvious that, if one considers the origin of this interest, it is the relation of the intelligible world to the sensible that one has in mind, and, considered with regard to the theory of subjectivity, the motivational aspect of the moral law, not its validity as a principle of evaluation. The two aspects are to be distinguished in this sense. It is, of course, a well-founded Kantian conviction that there can be no talk of the validity of the law if one cannot start with the assumption that an interest can be developed from it alone. Thus, without interest, freedom will be unreal, and the reality of freedom is necessarily the origin of interest.

This interest too cannot be explained, but only confirmed. At the time of the *Groundwork* Kant had long since given up the attempt to make the interconnection between reason and sensibility in the moral consciousness theoretically comprehensible. A decade earlier this problem had seemed to him the deepest and most important in all of philosophy and the mediating point between theoretical and practical reason.[18] Now, however, he has traced the impossibility of a derivation of motives and interests of the good will back to the inexplicability of freedom. He has even identified the two to the extent that the underivability of a "satisfaction" directly from the consciousness of the law is an expression for the opacity of freedom, insofar as this is the principle of action of a rational sensible being. The validity of the law, to be sure, this most general expression of freedom, is already presupposed where a motivational force incomprehensibly arises from the consciousness of the law.[19]

The inexplicability of freedom as a manner of action and as the ground of interest follows immediately from the explanation that the "critique of pure practical reason" has given of the ground of our conviction of the validity of the law: Its ground lies in ideas of reason. This interconnection between the two parts of the last section of the *Groundwork* stood clearly before Kant's eyes. He saw in it the greatest strength of his whole argument: One can show that it is legitimate and necessary to presuppose the idea of freedom. But then it is also already said that no knowledge of the principle of morality can be expected that could be measured against the standard of knowledge of objects. Thus the justification and the limitation of practical knowledge are of a piece.

## VI. Deduction or Proof?

We have now interpreted the sequence of the three steps in Kant's argument. It is characteristic of the peculiar difficulty of the third section of the *Groundwork,* however, that even with a complete clarification of the arguments actually given by Kant the text is still not fully transparent. The most difficult problems of interpretation always arise when an argument that is in principle clear or at least capable of clarity is so presented that this clarity is never attained, and not merely accidentally, say because of insufficient effort or the absence of sufficient conceptual means, but because further considerations are in play that could only be developed if entirely different theoretical problems were solved. To overcome such difficulties in the comprehension of a text is particularly worthwhile, because only in this way can the interpretation be made convincing even against subsequent reservations that originate from renewed reading of the test. It is also only in this way—and this is the more important reason—that the most general methodological interconnection in which the text's solutions of problems develops can be made into the theme of philosophical consideration. To transform the unclear into clarity is always easier, but usually also more trivial, than making unclarity as such transparent.

From the beginning it has proven difficult to know with certainty what sort of "proof" is really aimed at in the third section of the *Groundwork* and what sort is actually given. It is appropriate to the function of this book as a particular form of a "critique of pure practical reason" that its proof-program is a subject of reflection throughout. Kant is always concerned to instruct the reader about the stage of insight he has reached. Thus it is always clear that the first two sections provide an analysis of moral consciousness and that in them it may not yet be presupposed that this analysis is valid for anything that really exists beyond any possibility of doubt. It is only the significance of talk about the good will and duty, about the categorical imperative and an autonomy of the will, that is being investigated. Kant repeatedly emphasizes that moral philosophy must be concerned to advance to knowledge of the validity of the law. This step is to be made possible by the "critique of pure practical reason" the chief points of which are presented in the third section.

It has already been shown that in truth Kant cannot and does not offer a strong proof of the validity of the law, nor does he seriously attempt to offer such a proof. Nevertheless, in the course of the

*Groundwork* he expresses himself several times in a way that can hardly be taken as other than an announcement of a proof-program. Here are several instances: "We have not yet advanced as far as *to prove a priori* that such an imperative really holds. . . . For the purpose of achieving this . . ." (*G,* 425); "But that there are practical propositions, that command categorically, could not be *proved* in itself" (*G,* 431); what is to be avoided is a *petitio principii* in the case of a principle "which we could never put forth as a *demonstrable* proposition" (*G,* 453) (emphases added). Kant calls the foundation that is provided in the third section a "deduction" three times (*G,* 447; 454; 463).

It is advisable to concentrate first on this talk of a deduction, for it seems to be the strongest expression of Kant's claim to a proof. The opposition between the *Groundwork* and the *Critique of Practical Reason* of 1788 also is clearest here. For the second *Critique* declares entirely unequivocally: "Thus the objective reality of the moral law cannot be proven through any deduction, through any effort of theoretical, speculative or empirically supported reason" (*CPracR,* 47).

"Deduction" is a word that usually designates the strongest proof-procedure of all, that of truth-functional inferential logic. This was also true in Kant's time. But one must note that Kant gave this technical term "deduction" a new meaning, specific to his theory, out of the necessity of having to find a designation for the form of transcendental derivation that is peculiar to the critical philosophy. It is well known that to this end he drew upon the special usage of the word "deduction" in the language of jurisprudence. But it has not previously been seen how far-reaching the influence of the juridical usage on the transcendental usage is and how well the peculiarity of transcendental derivation is captured by it. The *quaestio juris* (B 116; see among other places *Ak* 28:399) is contrasted to the determination of facts on the basis of the "consensus of witnesses" (*R* 454, 15:187). But one will miss the decisive point of the analogy if one supposes that every weighing of legal grounds is as such a *quaestio juris.* This question is to be seen in contrast to the weighing of facts, and in such a way that with regard to the same facts it can be asked both whether they really obtain and whether it is right that they obtain. The *quaestio juris* always pertains to the legal title to *possession,* whether of things, of entitlements, or of functions or privileges.

The weighing of rights which are decided by the *quaestio juris* are always of a very special sort. In the case of disputes concerning such rights a proof[20] is to be provided that a claim or possessions has *come to be* rightfully, that it derives from legitimate acquisition, a valid contract, or from an inheritance. Kant's conception of transcendental foundation corresponds to this so completely that new light is shed on it by the analogy of the proof of a legal title. For a transcendental derivation is also related to the *origin* of a cognition. A claim to cognition can be justified by providing insight into its origin. To be able to make a claim to a cognition, however, means to be justified in asserting that one really possesses this cognition. The examination of such a claim, like the examination of a title to a right, does not concentrate on the factual conditions that held during the origin and temporal development of a possession, but on those aspects by means of which it could and had to arise as a possession at all. In this sense the answer to a *quaestio juris* concerning knowledge is a deduction from the origin of a cognition as the condition of its possibility.

A deduction justifies, by recourse to its origin, the lawfulness of a claim, whether it is a claim to cognition or to possession. A deduction is called for, whether in cognition or in court, when the title to a right is in dispute. If the doubt is not explicit there is no basis for the deduction. The deduction is not undertaken for the sake of amplifying cognition, but for justifying it.

From this far-reaching formal analogy it may be understood why Kant almost stereotypically expounds the methods of the critical philosophy by means of metaphors from jurisprudence. This habit is grounded in insight into a structure. One should not understand it merely as an expression of Kant's baroque rhetoric, although that too certainly had some influence on it.

It is particularly useful to make clear that in the case of claims to entitlements *justification* can really be nothing other than clarifying their origin and showing that the claims were acquired and not usurped. A transcendental theory proceeds in entirely the same way. Its procedure it thus different from that of derivation from true premises antecedently presupposed. Kant says several times that even where no proof is possible a deduction may be carried out (B 286; *MM*, 6:238)—a deduction of the "lawfulness of an assertion." Early in his philosophical development he had already discovered the question, how can one argue in behalf of propositions that cannot be secured by direct proof-procedures? This question also applied to the propositions related to Hume's doubts. Kant found that such a procedure could consist only in the "critique of the subject," and he saw this form of argument prefigured in the civil trial. The justification of propositions that cannot be proven like theorems can only come about through the clarification of their origin.[21]

Now the formulations with which Kant expounds his deduction programs, and which must otherwise always remain vague and ambiguous, become comprehensible. In the procedure of a deduction the primary task is always to trace a cognition back to its origin. This task can be described as that of clarifying the conditions of its possibility in the subject of knowledge. If it is solved, then this cognition is also thereby *immediately justified.* Then, however, it can also be said that the deduction has accomplished something that at least corresponds to a proof. Claims to rights are grounded by being derived and successfully defended against the suspicion of usurpation. Thus a deduction is just as compelling for a claim to a right as a proof is for a proposition. The proposition accomplishes what the proof also has to accomplish: Through both it is established that the assumption of propositions is irrefutable.

These considerations can easily be applied to the text of the *Groundwork.* In it Kant says predominantly that the "critique of pure practical reason" has to make the *possibility* of a categorical imperative comprehensible. In normal theoretical circumstances, one can hold something to be possible without thereby having to accept it. "Critique," however, investigates origins. It proceeds from the methodological postulate that the possibility of a cognition is always to be admitted only in view of its origin. Once the origin of a cognition has been clarified, then as a rule its reality is also secured as an indisputable claim with title to a legitimate origin and which holds within the boundaries that follow from this origin. It is for this reason that Kant so frequently speaks in the same breath of both the possibility and the necessity of a cognition. It is for this reason that he supposes that the validity of a cognition is understood as soon as its possibility is illuminated.

If the cognition the origin of which is displayed is an *a priori* cognition, then the deduction as a form of argumentation is the clearest interpretation of the philosophical program that Kant called "transcendental philosophy." Transcendental philosophy illuminates the conditions of the possibility of an *a priori* cognition in a way that simultaneously justifies this cognition and determines the boundaries of its use. It works with "transcendental deductions."

This clear and elegant presentation of the actual accomplishment of a deduction, however, cannot be used without modification in the interpretation of all the arguments that Kant himself designated as "deductions." Two such modifications must be mentioned here, since we need to consider whether they may have played a role in the variants of "deduction" in practical philosophy.

In the *Prolegomena,* Kant distinguished between an analytic and a synthetic method of presenting the critique (*Prol,* §4). In contrast to the *Critique of Pure Reason,* the *Prolegomena* presupposes the validity of the synthetic propositions of mathematics and mathematical physics, and asks only how, not whether they are possible. One could explain this procedure as dispensation from a dispute about rights in a matter in which there is hardly a skeptic ready to come before the court of critique. Thus it can proceed without an extensive critique of the subject and thus without justification, which could lie only in the origin of such cognition. The legitimacy of other claims to knowledge is subsequently to be investigated in relation to these, and it is this further investigation that would first be called "deduction." But Kant's language does not univocally restrict the usage of the term "deduction" to this sense.[22] He also calls designates as "deductions" arguments that specify an origin for a cognition that is already accepted as valid. Thus what the *Prolegomena* achieves under the name of a deduction is not limited to what can be determined about the origin and status of cognitions beyond but in relation to mathematics and physics—especially the ideas on which metaphysical claims to knowledge rest. This is clear from the fact that the investigation into the origins of our knowledge of space and time is called a transcendental deduction several times (*Prol,* §12; B 121). In this usage, the argumentation that is called a "deduction" can no longer be described as "the legitimation of a pretension," in accordance with the definition of "deduction" which the *Critique of Judgment* provides (*CJ,* § 30, 279). It only makes comprehensible what is already beyond doubt. Thus it merely secures what is already beyond doubt against misuse and allows for the clarification of the origins of knowledge in its entirety.

It is obvious that the *Groundwork* cannot have been interested in a "deduction" which proceeds simply by assuming the validity of the principle that is up for a deduction in the "critique of pure practical reason." It has been assigned the task of "establishing" this principle. This task is not undertaken for the sake of clarifying the origin of other, dubious knowledge, but solely for the sake of the foundation of the principle of morality itself.

Nevertheless, this as it were moderate sense of "deduction" may have influenced the self-presentation of the *Groundwork.* In the *Prole-*

*gomena,* the knowledge the possibility of which is to be made intelligible is elevated above all doubt. However, other principles, for which that is not the case and for which there is therefore good reason to raise the *quaestio juris* in the full original sense of "deduction," are also justified in a certain way, insofar as one discovers a connection which allows their legitimate derivation to be at least assumed. Whoever produces a title for such a connection and makes it perspicuous and credible in principle, in any case, silences all the objections that would prosecute them with the argument that the claim of those principles is incomprehensible and without any imaginable basis.

One must therefore not merely distinguish deductions in general from proofs. Deductions themselves are divided into two fundamental forms, a strong one and a weak one. And there are further variants of the weak form. Deductions of the strong form derive principles of cognition from their origins in reason, without these principles and cognitions themselves already having to be credible or even known in some form or other. A weak deduction proceeds from a given cognition that one can adduce either as already known or even as undisputed. It represents it as having its origin in reason itself. If the cognition is antecedently known but not credible, then it gains legitimation through the reference to its origin. Cognitions can thus be defended in the strong as well as the weak form of deduction, so it would therefore be possible to use either form in the "establishment" of the principle of morality in the *Groundwork.* Every deduction, however, whether it defends the deduced cognition or seeks its origin only for the defense of other cognitions, as in the *Prologomena,* must lead to the principle that is deduced from an investigation of the inner constitution of reason. This method of investigation defines the Kantian sense of the word "deduction."

There is in Kant's work yet another variant of the talk of a "deduction" with a meaning departing from its original sense. It is an essential part of every program for a deduction that it answer the question *how* a cognition is possible. In the case of the transcendental deduction of the categories, however, Kant explicitly declared it to be permissible to relieve the argument of the deduction from the burden of the question "how" the categories are applied to given appearances (A xvi; see also *MFNS,* 4:474–6n.) That could imply that the foundational argument of a deduction in which no reference is made to the genesis of cognition must be distinguished from another form of deduction, which searches exclusively for an answer to the question "how." However, the contradiction between these suggestions and the restriction of all deductions, through the very definition of "deduction," to the task of illuminating conditions of possibility, is only apparent. For the question "how" that is here separated from the kernel of a deduction is not the question about the conditions of possibility which first makes an argument a transcendental one in Kant's sense. One can decline to reconstruct the precise path of an acquisition or an inheritance and yet indicate the origin of an acquisition in a way that is sufficient for the legitimation of a legal title. That a cognition is not merely imaginary, that certain categories are applicable to given representations, can be established if I know where they originate and what they do. A deduction that does not investigate the process of application itself is a deduction in the full sense of a proof of origin, which is merely limited to the minimum for a compelling derivation.[23]

The transcendental deduction of the categories, of course, also has aspects in which it goes beyond the claims of a transcendental deduction in general. According to the mere concept of a deduction, however, it would already have accomplished enough if it merely displayed the categories as conditions of the possibility of experience. But it also wants to communicate the scope of the relation of our understanding to our sensibility and, further, to clarify the possibility of the understanding itself. It therefore goes back to the innermost interconnection of all cognition in its origin and yields several results that are fundamental for any convincing critique of the subject. Its program thus stands under even stricter methodological constraints than other transcendental deductions do. These further claims, and methods with whose help they might be sustained, cannot be investigated here. In the *Groundwork* the term "deduction" is used in its normal sense, thus without the special implications of a transcendental deduction of the categories. In it, therefore, one only needs to proceed in accordance with the normal understanding of the justification of cognitive claims from a cognition of origins.

However, it has been seen that such a deduction could succeed in accordance with the original, strong conception of a deduction as well as with a weaker sense of deduction. We must still investigate further which of the two Kant had in mind in the *Groundwork* and which he really accomplished.

It is already evident from the fundamental tendencies of the work how far Kant could have believed that he had really accomplished a deduction of the principles of morality. He has shown that the assumption of the reality of freedom is not made arbitrarily. It follows from the nature of the understanding, under the further presupposition that one has a will. It is also supported by the natural distinction between two worlds, which keeps the distinction between two orders of being from appearing as a groundless and arbitrary assumption. However, freedom in the practical use of reason cannot be more than the hypothesis of an idea. The presupposition of freedom, which is necessary for the defense of moral propositions, is thereby really traced back to its origin in reason itself. But if the idea of freedom is shown to be necessary, then a transcendental justification for the moral law has thereby been attained *eo ipso*.

### VII. Deduction of the Law or Deduction of Freedom?

Kant's usage of the term "deduction" has now been made perspicuous. With that, the clarification of Kant's program for a proof in the *Groundwork* has also begun. In what sense an argument back to the rational origin of freedom can be called a deduction without being a proof in the strong sense has been indicated.

However, the interpretation of the *Groundwork* is still far from its conclusion. For now all difference between the *Groundwork* and the *Critique of Practical Reason* seems to disappear. Suddenly one thinks one understands why Kant never gives even a hint that there has been any change in his position since the publication of the *Groundwork*.

But such a conclusion is irremediably opposed by the direct contrast between the formulations of the *Groundwork* and of the *Critique:* The former lays claim to a deduction of the moral law, the latter excludes it from the domain of sensible tasks. The question remains, then, how this contrast is to be explained. It can only be answered when we have uncovered further conceptual connections in the field of forces within which Kant's text was formed.

First it must be recalled that it was only with considerable effort that the *Groundwork* succeeded in getting a sense of "deduction" that would be identical with formal proof. As has been shown, for a long time Kant experimented with derivations that would not merely have secured an origin in reason for the principles of morality. They would instead have shown that these principles are nothing other than antecedently deduced principles of reason, only in a particular application, which would, however, have been compelled by these principles.[24]

Such a foundation would have been part of a transcendental deduction, namely the most fundamental deduction of the transcendental philosophy in general. In this deduction the principles of unity would have been founded to which theoretical reason would subject everything given. From them it would then have been shown that they are likewise immediately valid as principles of the unity of rational conduct, by which they would have obtained the function of practical principles— the same function yielded by the analysis of moral consciousness. These principles would thereby have been justified. Such a deduction would not be a self-standing deduction, rather only an argument in a chain of argumentation that is itself identical with the fundamental transcendental deduction.

Only later, certainly after the publication of the *Critique of Pure Reason,* did Kant free himself from this program. Yet the *Groundwork* was still affected by it. That is also clear where Kant lays claim to the presupposition of freedom for all rational beings without any differentiation in the sense of the talk of "freedom." Only in the course of the exposition of the third section does Kant make the premise of his argument, namely that a rational being ascribes a will to itself, visible in its full weight. In contrast to the *Critique of Pure Reason,* further, Kant never distinguishes in the *Groundwork* between a proof and a deduction. He frequently announces the deduction of the categorical imperative as a proof of its validity and declares that this imperative will be revealed to be a "demonstrable proposition."

Nevertheless, all of the arguments already lie ready *de facto* in the *Groundwork* that will ground the position of the second *Critique.* "Deduction" means derivation from an origin, and the origin is the inner constitution of the cognizing subject. The two steps in the argument of the *Groundwork* show which are the principles of reason by means of which that idea of freedom can be developed which must be presupposed by the principles of morality. In its judgments, reason already presupposes its independence; it is also the ground for the projection of ideas and for the idea of a world that is not that of natural objects. The conditions of the origin of the idea of freedom are discovered in the critique of the subject.

It has also been shown that the *Groundwork,* first obscurely but finally in all its clarity, makes a concession that reduces the prospects not merely for a proof, but even for a deduction of moral principles: Reason generates the idea of moral freedom only in relation to a point of reference that itself already logically implies the conviction of reality of the energy of the moral will—the deduction must necessarily make reference to the consciousness that a rational being has of its will. Thus the assumption of the reality of freedom can indeed by defended against the objection that it is arbitrary. But it cannot be derived purely from the self-consciousness of a rational being that does not already in some way understand itself as a moral being. In what way this understanding is included in the argumentation of the *Groundwork* has still to be indicated. But it can already be said, quite generally, that even in the *Groundwork* all deduction is in the end referred to the factual self-certainty of the moral being. It can develop this certainty, but never fully comprehend it from anything else, not even the constitution of reason, however much this constitution can make it comprehensible how the idea of freedom evolves in relation to the rational will.

The deduction of the *Groundwork* is thus not only not a proof; it cannot even be a deduction in the original and strong sense of this term. As a deduction, it can only be understood through the weaker concept of a deduction that was used in the *Prolegomena* and that made it possible to call even the analyses of the origins of space and time transcendental deductions. It is distinguished from these deductions, to be sure, by the fact that it is carried out in such a way that it can at the same time serve for the legitimation of moral principles.[25]

The foundational course of the *Groundwork* thus really does move in a "sort of circle" (*G,* 450). However, this circle is not exactly the one which was to be avoided by means of the most important steps of the "critique of pure practical reason" in the *Groundwork*. That circle was vicious because in it freedom was assumed merely as an *ad hoc* hypothesis. As such, it cannot find any justification through reason. It is presupposed without any reference to the general interconnection of all rational ideas. Finally, it is even presupposed in a way that makes it impossible to avoid the contradiction between it and the most fundamental conditions for the use of the cognitive faculty in the cognition of objects in nature, those of natural causality. Without a critique of reason, neither the rationality nor even the possibility of this hypothesis could be secured.[26] What is shown in the deduction of the *Groundwork* is that the conviction of the reality of the moral law does not depend merely on postulates without context and comprehensibility. In that and in that alone does its accomplishment consist.

In what way the deduction of the *Groundwork* comes about has not yet been investigated. It is clear that it has a premise in moral consciousness. But what exactly does the claim that the deduction is valid for beings "who believe themselves to be conscious of a will" mean? And what can count as being deduced from this premise? The second of these questions is taken up first, and it is assumed that the deduction of the *Groundwork* must in any case start from an aspect of moral consciousness that is not identical with the consciousness of freedom. This is legitimate, among other reasons, because freedom is continually described as a presupposition for moral principles, which we are always of conscious *as* a presupposition, and of which we are therefore never immediately conscious.

If freedom itself is not the moral-practical starting-point of the deduction, then this starting-point can properly lie only in the consciousness of obligation itself. If Kant had decided on this starting-point, then his deduction would have defended the conviction of the reality of this obligation by producing general grounds in the system of ideas of reason on the basis of which the inexorable presupposition for the reality of moral principles, the reality of freedom, could be asserted. And it is really only the origin of this idea in reason as a whole that the deduction of the *Groundwork* makes intelligible. For it is this task that the two arguments from the parallel between the presupposition of the freedom of the good will and the freedom of judgment, and from the natural distinction of reason between two totalities of existence, fulfill. *The deduction of the* Groundwork *is thus primarily a deduction of the consciousness of freedom.*

Following this result, the question necessarily arises, how is the form of such a deduction of freedom to be described? Given everything that has been said, one can proceed from the assumption that it will yield a legitimation of the moral law that remains basically within the framework of the weak form of deduction. However, the deduction of the idea of freedom also exhibits tendencies that bring it closer to a deduction of the strong form, for this deduction really seeks the origin of the idea of freedom in the "structure" of reason itself. It is reason in its natural use that puts forth the idea of freedom as a cosmological idea and as the principle of a world, without depending upon antecedent moral evidence. The conviction, however, that freedom possess *reality* and that I myself am a member of a world to which real freedom belongs, has a ground in moral consciousness, and indeed in the evidence that we have a will, the vagueness of which is to be cleared up in the next section. If one were to assume that this evidence is identical with the conviction of the reality of freedom, that would be to say that the deduction of freedom, purely as an idea, follows the strong form of deduction, while the deduction of the reality of freedom is the weak type of deduction. But Kant comes close to distinguishing the evidence that we have a will from the consciousness of freedom. Then it follows that the strong deduction of the idea of freedom on the basis of an additional premise, which establishes a fact, would become a deduction of the reality of freedom, which is in any case no longer a strong deduction, because I cannot completely derive the consciousness of freedom from origins in reason that are exposed by a "critique of the subject." The deduction of freedom would then proceed in accordance with a variant of the weak form of deduction that is peculiar to it: A deduction in the strong form, which, however, must remain incomplete, would be supplemented by a simple logical inference, yielded by a fact presumed to be evident. From the first part of this deduction it would follow that the whole deduction can serve as a legitimation.

In the *Critique of Practical Reason,* Kant held the deduction of the concept of freedom but not that of the moral law to be possible (*CPracR,* 47). He described the deduction of freedom in a way that does not essentially differ from the deduction that has now been determined to be that which the *Groundwork* brings off *de facto.*[27] In the *Groundwork,* however, Kant had spoken of a deduction of the moral law, which is excluded by the *Critique of Practical Reason.* So it must be asked, on what could Kant's assertions in the *Groundwork* be based, and how are the negative claims about a deduction of the moral law in the *Critique of Practical Reason* related to them?

The principles of morality can only be acknowledged as valid if the idea of freedom can be held to be more than a mere fiction or a regulative principle of cognition. The reality of this idea is thus a necessary condition for the reality of the moral law. But it is at the same time a *sufficient* condition for this reality. One can therefore conclude not merely that if moral consciousness is real then freedom must be possible, and in this way initiate a deduction of freedom; one can also fully ground the reality of moral consciousness in the reality of freedom. If a deduction of freedom is attained, then a foundation of the moral law is also given *eo ipso.* This logical relation can mislead one into taking the deduction of freedom as a deduction of the moral law.

If one could also call the transition from the deduction of freedom to the justification of the reality of the moral law a deduction, then in the context of the *Groundwork* it would certainly be a deduction on the weak model. For we had to start from the fact that a premise from moral consciousness was a already present in the deduction of freedom, and that this could really be none other than the experience of the obligatoriness of the moral law. Then, however, the deduction of the reality of freedom by recourse back to the reality of the moral law would only justify one of its own premises (even if not in a vicious circle).

But the meaning of "deduction" in both its strong and weak senses offers reasons against regarding the transition from the deduction of freedom to the justification of the moral law as a deduction in any of its variants that could still be distinguished from the deduction of freedom as such. For a deduction is given only where origins for principles in the constitution of reason can be made manifest by a critique of the subject. The reality of the moral law, however, follows from the deduced reality of freedom on the basis of simple formal implication, thus without all the further steps that would constitute a "deduction" in the sense of an explanation of possibility.

Thus if Kant speaks of a deduction of the moral law, this is a deduction in the specific sense only insofar as the deductions of the possibility and of the legitimacy of the consciousness of freedom are *identical*. To be sure, in the *Groundwork* Kant speaks of a deduction of the "supreme principle of morality" (*G,* 463) but also of a deduction of "the concept of freedom" (447). This second way of talking must be regarded as the more precise.

In the same way, we can understand why in the *Critique of Practical Reason* Kant excludes a deduction of the moral law. To give a deduction of it would mean that one can make its origin in reason comprehensible. But one can only comprehend how the condition of the moral law, freedom, proceeds from reason, but only as an idea. But just because of that the moral law, which cannot itself be deduced, is the premise for a deduction of the objective reality of the idea of freedom. In functioning as this premise, it at the same time earns a "credential" for itself.

The logical relations that have been clarified result from a presupposition that has been made from the start in Kant's moral philosophy, even if its consequences have not always been respected: The consciousness of the moral law and the idea of freedom mutually imply each other. Moral experience, however, includes immediate certainty only of the validity of the law. The reality of freedom, which can be inferred from the obligatoriness of the law, is for its part beyond any immediate certainty. In the realm of the critique of the subject, however, which yields deductions, the relation is reversed. Only the idea of freedom can be derived from the organization of reason. Here the moral law is as it were opaque. Once Kant had given up the attempts to discover its origin in reason itself, its interpretation and justification could only come about through a justification of the idea of freedom. The *Groundwork* has already swung towards this theoretical position. Only Kant was not yet in a position to reckon with this fully and clearly in the construction of his arguments and in his self-presentation. Under such conditions obscurities in his program for a deduction could hardly be avoided.

Such obscurities were made even more probable by the fact that Kant had not clearly enough drawn the boundaries within which talk of a deduction is still legitimate. His original thought of a procedure that answers *quaestiones juris,* that accomplishes a critique of the subject, and that legitimizes claims to validity by displaying conditions of possibility, is ingenious and clearly conceived. However, Kant never properly described the various procedures by means of which one or another sort of justification of *a priori* principles could be accomplished. We have no reason to suspect that he somewhere produced an overview of them and that he had investigated and classified them in a methodology of critique. He introduced new variants of deduction as he needed them. Thus he could even add a further variant to the weak form of deduction in the conception of a deduction of the idea of freedom first described in the *Critique of Practical Reason*. If one keeps this in mind, then one will not expect any clarity about the way in which a justification of the moral law could really be brought about through a deduction of freedom from the *Groundwork,* which had not even established the difference between proof and deduction.

## VIII. The Presupposition of the Will

In order to reach such clarity we have thus far held to the assumption that Kant's deduction of freedom has its presupposition in moral consciousness, in the consciousness of the moral law itself and its binding obligatoriness. For the Kantian position, this presupposition is the only alternative to an immediate consciousness of freedom, which in turn Kant could not allow. It is also the presupposition of the argumentation in the *Critique of Practical Reason*. The text of the *Groundwork,* however, contains no suggestion that Kant wanted to admit such a presupposition at least indirectly and after the fact. In the end, and *de facto,* the *Groundwork* really took back its promise of a proof by means of a deduction in the weaker form, which could not be conducted without a premise coming from moral consciousness itself. It was not possible for Kant even to suggest or implicitly concede that this premise itself has its ground in the consciousness of obligation. For he had previously presented the prospect for establishing the principles of morality in a way that would not allow such a concession without thereby destroying the whole text of the *Groundwork* itself. This text is therefore logically compelled to use a presupposition in moral consciousness for the deduction of the principles of morality which is distinct from both the consciousness of the moral law and the consciousness of freedom. But since the Kantian position does not really permit any alternative to these two thoughts, this further presupposition can only be introduced as a vague, indeterminate, and necessarily indeterminable thought. Kant's talk of the human being "claiming a will for himself" (*G,* 457) plays this role in the text of the *Groundwork*.

It has already been shown that in the third section Kant initially speaks of the will in a way that comes close to holding it to be that faculty by means of which we can set any ends at all for ourselves and by means of which rational considerations of any sort whatever can gain influence on our actions. Only gradually does it emerge that "will" is only "a faculty different from any faculty for desire" (*G,* 459), a faculty by means of which we can consider ourselves as self-sufficient citizens of an intelligible world.

But what sort of consciousness is that in which I know, and know immediately, that by means of my will I stand under the law of the intelligible world as a self-sufficient being? There is no unequivocal information about this question to be found in Kant's text. In the transition from the still entirely unspecific thought of beings that "are endowed with a will" (*G,* 448, 449) to later formulations, which already lodge the will in the intelligible world, Kant merely indicates one consideration: Common sense distinguishes appearances from things in themselves, and does that in such a way that it must allow that there is something that corresponds to "the constitution of its own subject composed of mere appearances"—"namely its self, as it may be constituted in itself," "in regard to that in it which my be pure activity (which comes to consciousness not through the affection of the senses but immediately)" (*G,* 451). It seems that Kant is here really preparing the way for the thesis that our will comes to consciousness immediately and that by means of this consciousness we also have the basis for a deduction of the moral law.

But this thought is not carried through or maintained. In what follows (*G*, 452 ff.), the pure activity of the self is first identified as the activity of the will that brings forth ideas. This activity is not the activity of the will. Now it is, to be sure, on the basis of the projection of the ideas that the distinction between two worlds is established. The *Critique of Pure Reason* had already shown that one of these ideas is the idea of freedom. But it had also shown that in the mere fact that I must think of freedom I have no ground and no occasion for ascribing freedom to myself. Likewise the self-sufficiency of the activity of my reason, of which I really have immediate consciousness, gives me no ground for inferring my status in the intelligible world, the idea of which I have brought forth by this very activity of reason. It is, to be sure, correct that the activity of reason in bringing forth ideas, and its product, the distinction between two worlds, is the necessary presupposition for my ascribing a will to myself in the intelligible world and understanding myself as a moral being. But both of these presuppositions taken together do not give me sufficient ground for ascribing a will to myself and considering myself as a self-sufficient member of the intelligible world, not merely as a dependent chain of events. A human being in fact puts himself into that world *if* he thinks of himself as an intelligence endowed with a will (*G*, 457). The self-sufficiency of his reason as a faculty for bringing forth ideas is a presupposition of his being able to do this. But the further condition, namely *that* he ascribe a will to himself, must also be fulfilled. And it is independent from the condition that is already fulfilled insofar as reason can reach beyond appearances by means of ideas in general. One can thus say that the fact that the human being claims to have a will "comes from" (*G*, 457) the fact that he glimpses beyond appearances. But since this second standpoint in regard to an intelligible world cannot be a *sufficient* ground for the claim to possess a will, a further ground for this claim must be established. This can be nothing other than the consciousness of the moral law's claim to validity, the elementary and only immediate moral consciousness.

But this conclusion escapes Kant because of the ambiguity of his talk about the grounds that make it possible for us to ascribe a will to ourselves. By tracing the ascription of the will back to its necessary condition in reason's production of ideas, he at least apparently avoids the assumption, which is untenable for him, that we are immediately conscious of a will. Nevertheless, he must finally decide on formulations from which it follows that the consciousness of the will is not as compellingly grounded in reason as such as is the consciousness of the distinction between the two worlds. The idea of freedom is valid for a being "that *believes itself to be conscious* of a will" (*G,* 459; emphasis added). It is thereby conceded in a way that can be tolerated in the text of the *Groundwork* that the consciousness of freedom has a presupposition in moral consciousness. But at the same time the question about how the presupposition of a will is produced in *moral* consciousness is cut off. Only after it has begun to seem as if the presupposition of the will results from the doctrine of two worlds is the will spoken of in a way that must raise a new question—precisely the question of the origin of the consciousness of the will in the elementary moral principles of reason. Since the *Groundwork* could give no answer at all to this question without fundamentally modifying its promise of a deduction and explicitly having recourse to the weak form of the legitimation of morality, it makes the concession by means of which the character of the deduction that it has accomplished can first be determined only at the conclusion and in the misleading disguise of a mere summary.

Kant's broad tolerance in what he means by "deduction" and his own unclarity about the constitution of the deduction he has actually given undercut all possibility of understanding the third section of the *Groundwork* by itself and without effort. These difficulties, which must have been palpable to Kant himself, made it necessary for him to use a premise in the argument of the section which allowed him to avoid at least verbally several undesired positions and consequences. But since this premise itself could not have been made sufficiently precise without bringing up the very problems that it was supposed to avoid, the potential for obscurity in this premise was realized, and the premise was made virtually inscrutable.

[In the original, there are three further sections that are here omitted for reasons of space, though all of the points they make are important points that have been touched upon in the Introduction to this volume. In Section IX, "The Deduction of the Imperative," Henrich discusses Kant's further attempt to derive the imperatival character of the moral law as it appears to us by showing that it is necessary for us to consider ourselves as members of the sensible as well as intelligible world. In Section X, "The 'Importance' of Moral Laws," Henrich discusses Kant's tendency to interpret wrong-doing only as making an exception for ourselves to moral laws the general validity of which is not denied, an analysis that Kant must give in order to preserve the universal validity of consciousness of the moral law as the premise for any inference to our freedom. In the final Section XI, "Structural Consequences of Missing Distinctions," Henrich argues that Kant's determination to set up the argument of the *Groundwork* as beginning from an analysis of common moral consciousness causes him to miss the opportunity for a more abstract argument that human autonomy requires more than merely instrumental reasoning, which he might have been able to give on the basis of a more general theory of reason. These important points do not alter Henrich's basic analysis of the failure of the *Groundwork* to provide a strong deduction of the validity of the moral law itself.—PG][28]

## Notes

1. Following the format of the present collection, Henrich's references to the original pagination of the second and third *Critiques* have been replaced with references to the pagination of the *Akademie* edition. The *Reflexionen* have been cited with the numbers given to them in the *Akademie* edition.

2. In the edition in the *Philosophische Bibliothek* (Hamburg: Felix Meiner, 1906), p. xvii: "The *Groundwork* forms the preparation and introduction for the work that appeared in 1788 under the title of [the *Critique of Practical Reason*]."

3. [I.e., the illusory inferences that Kant analyses in the "Dialectic of Pure Reason" in the first *Critique.*—Ed.]

4. Kant says this in a draft of the *Prolegomena;* see 23:62. [The "Göttingen review" is the review of the *Critique of Pure Reason* published in the *Göttinger Anzeigen von gelehrten Sachen,* Supplementary Vol. I, 1782. This hostile review, produced by the Göttingen professor and editor J.G.H. Feder from a longer and more sympathetic draft by the better-known philosopher Christian Garve, angered Kant and played some part in his decision to write the *Prolegomena.* A translation of the Göttingen review as well as of Garve's original version may be found in: Johann Schultz, *Exposition of Kant's Critique of Pure Reason,* ed. and tr. James C. Morrison (Ottawa. University of Ottawa Press, 1995).—Ed.]

5. See 23:60.

6. [Here Henrich is referring to the date of the composition of the second *Critique* rather than to the date of its publication in the spring of 1788.—Ed.]

7. The author's 1960 essay "The Concept of Moral Insight and Kant's Doctrine of the Fact of Reason" (in Dieter Henrich, *The Unity of Reason: Essays on Kant's Philosophy,* ed. Richard Velkley [Cambridge, Mass.: Harvard Univer-

sity Press, 1994], pp. 55–87) has already shown that Kant came to exclude a deduction for the fundamental principle of morality solely on the basis of a self-critique of his attempt to derive the origin of moral consciousness from other principles. But there the ambivalent position of the *Groundwork* in connection with this problem had not yet been clarified.

8. The number of publications in which noteworthy contributions to the interpretation of the *text* of the third section of the *Groundwork* are provided is almost vanishingly small. Besides Paton (see note 13), there may be mentioned the essay by Margot Fleischer, "Das Problem der Begründung des kategorischen Imperatives bei Kant," in *Walberger Studien I: Sein und Ethos* (Mainz: 1963), pp. 387 ff. Unfortunately, after some acute considerations, this author retreats to a global diagnosis for which Heidegger's unarticulated and arbitrary interpretation of Kant is responsible. [Remember that Henrich wrote this note in 1975!—Ed.]

9. See, e.g., *CPracR*, 98; see note 11 below.

10. "Freedom can be opposed to brute necessity or fatalism, the former in a practical sense, the latter in a transcendental sense."

11. This refers to Kant's review of Johann Heinrich Schulz, *Attempt at an introduction to a doctrine of morals for all human beings regardless of different religions* (Berlin: Stahlbaum, 1783), printed in the *Akademie* edition at 8:10–14 and translated in Kant, *Practical Philosophy,* ed. Mary J. Gregor (Cambridge: Cambridge University Press, 1996), pp. 3–10.

12. Kant first distinguishes the order of purposes from that of efficient causes (*G,* 450). But it is not that, but only the distinction between two worlds (451) that first breaks the vicious circle of the *ad hoc* presupposition of freedom.

13. See Henrich, "Das Prinzip der Kantischen Ethik," in *Philosophische Rundschau,* Vol. 2 (1954–55), and H.J. Paton, *The Categorical Imperative* (London: Hutchinson, 1947), Ch. XXIV, Appendix.

14. Henrich will add details about the distinction between them in a later part of the paper not translated here.

15. See section IX below.

16. Again Henrich elaborates on this claim in a part of the original paper that is omitted here.

17. Cp. the criticism in Paton, *The Categorical Imperative,* Ch. XXIV, § 4 (pp. 244–5). It should also be noted that in Kant there are analyses of categories that make it necessary to assume freedom in the intellectual world in any case. For one must conceive of this world through the unschematized category of substance. And Kant frequently argues that substantiality includes freedom (*R* 5653, 18:306–12); see "On the Unity of Subjectivity" (originally published in 1955), in Dieter Henrich, *The Unity of Reason: Essays on Kant's Philosophy* (Cambridge, Mass.: Harvard University Press, 1994), pp. 17–54, at p. 28. But abstracting from the fact that freedom cannot be thought in relation to willing through pure categories, it must in any case remain open whether the self-conscious subject belongs to the intellectual world as a self-sufficient member and as substance at all. According to the thesis of the paralogisms [in the *Critique of Pure Reason*], it could also be an appearance of mere conditions of intelligible entities.

18. See "The Concept of Moral Insight," pp. 73–82.

19. See Henrich, "Ethics of Autonomy," in *The Unity of Reason*, pp. 89–121.

20. Ed.: *Nachweis*, not *Beweis*, the term connoting truth-functional proof.

21. See Henrich, "Kants Denken 1762/1763," in Henrich, Kaulbach and Tonelli, eds., *Studien zu Kants philosophischer Entwicklung* (Hildesheim: Georg Olms, 1967), and "Kant's Notion of a Deduction and the Methodological Background of the first *Critique*," in Eckart Förster, ed., *Kant's Transcendental Deductions* (Stanford: Stanford University Press, 1989), pp. 29–46.

22. Other transcendental deductions concern the ideas of reason (B 697–8), pure aesthetic judgment (*CJ*, §§ 30–39), the idea of purposiveness in nature (*CJ*, Introduction § V, 182), acquisition through contract (*MM*, 6:272), etc.

23. See Henrich, "The Proof-Structure of Kant's Transcendental Deduction, in *Review of Metaphysics* 22 (1968–69): 640–59, at p. 651.

24. See "The Concept of Moral Insight. . ." (note 5).

25. Weak deductions, which are nevertheless legitimations, lead to the conclusion that the principle that is deduced can now provide "a credential" (*CPracR*, 48; *Prol*, § 5).

26. If Kant speaks of a "circle" in the transition from the order of efficient causes to the order of ends, surely he conceives of it as a consequence of the contradiction between the principles of the two orders that exist as long as the orders are not though of as real, distinct worlds.

27. The deduction of the idea of freedom which the *Groundwork* achieves and the objective reality of the concept of freedom of which the *Critique of Practical Reason* speaks are not undermined by the thesis of the *Metaphysics of Morals* that given "the concept of freedom . . . no theoretical deduction of its possibility is possible" (*MM*, 6:252). This "theoretical deduction" would be either insight into the real conditions of freedom or a strong deduction from the principles of pure reason alone. The *Groundwork*, however, accomplishes only a weak deduction of the idea of freedom. Insofar as it presumes the idea of freedom to be valid, it is not a real explanation; insofar as it has a premise in moral consciousness, it is identical with the concept of freedom that the *Critique of Practical Reason* develops from the moral law as a fact.

28. The editor thanks Curtis Bowman for his careful scrutiny of this translation.

# Bibliography

This is a selective bibliography of work on Kant's *Groundwork* and related issues in his ethical theory, giving special emphasis to work published in the last ten to fifteen years. Apart from the references to Kant's own texts, it includes only books and articles in English or books including material in English. All works on Kant in English that are cited in the essays reprinted in this volume are included, but other works cited are not. The list of articles (section 6) cites separately some of the articles collected in several of the books included in sections 4 and 5, but by no means all of them. For a more general bibliography on Kant's philosophy, see Paul Guyer, ed., *The Cambridge Companion to Kant* (Cambridge: Cambridge University Press, 1992), pp. 451-71.

## 1. German Texts

*Original Edition*

Kant, Immanuel. *Grundlegung zur Metaphysik der Sitten.* Riga: Johann Friedrich Hartknoch, 1785.

*Standard Modern Edition*

*Grundlegung der Metaphysik der Sitten,* edited by Paul Menzer, in Volume 4 (1911), pp. 385–463, of *Kant's gesammelte Schriften.* Edited by the Royal Prussian (later German) Academy of Sciences. Berlin: Georg Reimer (later Walter de Gruyter & Co.), 1900–.

## 2. English Translations

Abbott, Thomas Kingsmill, tr. *Kant's Critique of Practical Reason and Other Works on the Theory of Ethics.* Third Edition. London: Longmans, Green and Co., 1883.

343

Beck, Lewis White, tr. *Kant's Critique of Practical Reason and Other Writings in Moral Philosophy.* Chicago: University of Chicago Press, 1949.

Kant, Immanuel. *Foundations of the Metaphysics of Morals.* Lewis White Beck, tr. Indianapolis: Bobbs-Merrill Co., Inc., 1959.

———. *Grounding for the Metaphysics of Morals.* James W. Ellington, tr. Indianapolis: Hackett Publishing Co., 1981.

———. *Groundwork of the Metaphysics of Morals.* Translated and analyzed by H[erbert] J[ames] Paton. London: Hutchinson University Library, 1948.

———. *Practical Philosophy.* Translated and edited by Mary J. Gregor, general introduction by Allen W. Wood. Cambridge, U.K.: Cambridge University Press, 1996. (The first single volume translation of all of Kant's writings in moral and political philosophy; the *Groundwork* is on pp. 37–108.)

### 3. Historical Background and the Development of Kant's Ethics

Beck, Lewis White. *Early German Philosophy: Kant and His Predecessors.* Cambridge, Mass.: Harvard University Press, 1969.

Beiser, Frederick C. *The Fate of Reason: German Philosophy from Kant to Fichte.* Cambridge, Mass.: Harvard University Press, 1987.

Broad, C. D. *Five Types of Ethical Theory.* London: Routledge & Kegan Paul, 1930.

Schilpp, Paul Arthur. *Kant's Pre-Critical Ethics.* Second edition. Evanston: Northwestern University Press, 1960.

Schneewind, J. B., ed. *Moral Philosophy from Montaigne to Kant.* Two volumes. Cambridge, U.K.: Cambridge University Press, 1990.

Schneewind, J. B. *The Invention of Autonomy.* Cambridge, U.K.: Cambridge University Press, 1998.

Velkley, Richard L. *Freedom and the End of Reason: On the Moral Foundations of Kant's Critical Philosophy.* Chicago: University of Chicago Press, 1989.

Ward, Keith. *The Development of Kant's View of Ethics.* Oxford: Basil Blackwell, 1972.

### 4. Commentaries on the *Groundwork of Metaphysics of Morals*

Aune, Bruce. *Kant's Theory of Morals.* Princeton, N.J.: Princeton University Press, 1979.

Duncan, A. R. C. *Practical Reason and Morality: A Study of Immanuel Kant's 'Foundations for the Metaphysics of Morals.'* London: Thomas Nelson & Sons, 1957.

Höffe, Ottfried, ed. *Grundlegung der Metaphysik der Sitten: Ein kooperativer Kommentar.* Frankfurt am Main: Vittorio Klostermann, 1989. (In addition to the essay by Thomas Pogge included in the present volume, this book also contains chapters in English by Karl Ameriks, Ralph Walker, Viggo Rossvaer, Onora O'Neill, and Henry E. Allison.)

Hutchings, Patrick Æ. *Kant on Absolute Value: A Critical Examination of Certain Key Concepts in Kant's* Groundwork of the Metaphysics of Morals *and of His Ontology of Personal Values.* London: George Allen & Unwin, 1972.

Paton, H. J. *The Categorical Imperative: A Study in Kant's Moral Philosophy.* London: Hutchinson University Library, 1947.

Ross, Sir David. *Kant's Ethical Theory: A Commentary on the Groundwork of the Metaphysics of Morals.* Oxford: Clarendon Press, 1954.

Sullivan, Roger J. *An Introduction to Kant's Ethics.* Cambridge, U.K.: Cambridge University Press, 1994.

Wolff, Robert Paul, ed. *Foundations of the Metaphysics of Morals with Critical Essays.* Indianapolis: Bobbs-Merrill Co., Inc., 1969.

Wolff, Robert Paul. *The Autonomy of Reason: A Commentary on Kant's Groundwork of the Metaphysics of Morals.* New York: Harper & Row, 1973.

## 5. More General Books and Essay Collections on Kant's Ethics

Acton, H. B. *Kant's Moral Philosophy.* London: Macmillan, 1970.

Allison, Henry E. *Kant's Theory of Freedom.* Cambridge, U.K.: Cambridge University Press, 1990.

———. *Idealism and Freedom: Essays on Kant's Theoretical and Practical Philosophy.* Cambridge: Cambridge University Press, 1996.

Atwell, John E. *Ends and Principles in Kant's Moral Thought.* Dordrecht: Martinus Nijhoff, 1986.

Auxter, Thomas. *Kant's Moral Teleology.* Macon, Ga.: Mercer University Press, 1982.

Baron, Marcia W. *Kantian Ethics Almost without Apology.* Ithaca, N.Y.: Cornell University Press, 1995.

Beck, Lewis White. *A Commentary on Kant's Critique of Practical Reason.* Chicago: University of Chicago Press, 1960.

———. *Studies in the Philosophy of Kant.* Indianapolis: Bobbs-Merrill Co., Inc., 1965.

Bittner, Rüdiger. *What Reason Demands.* Translated by Theodore Talbot. Cambridge, U.K.: Cambridge University Press, 1989.

Carnois, Bernard. *The Coherence of Kant's Doctrine of Freedom.* Translated by David Booth. Chicago: University of Chicago Press, 1987.

Chadwick, Ruth, ed. *Immanuel Kant: Critical Assessments.* Volume III: *Kant's Moral and Political Philosophy.* London: Routledge, 1992. (Includes essays not included in the present volume by John Rawls, Mary J. Gregor, Nelson Potter, Barbara Herman, Christine Korsgaard, John Atwell, John Silber, Andrews Reath, Ralph Walker, Robert Louden, Thomas E. Hill, Jr., and others.)

Cox, J. Gray. *The Will at the Crossroads: A Reconstruction of Kant's Moral Philosophy.* Washington, D.C.: University Press of America, 1984.

Cummiskey, David. *Kantian Consequentialism.* New York: Oxford University Press, 1996.

Engstrom, Stephen, and Jennifer Whiting, eds. *Aristotle, Kant, and the Stoics: Rethinking Happiness and Duty.* Cambridge, U.K.: Cambridge University Press, 1996. (Includes essays wholly or partly on Kant by Barbara Herman, T. H. Irwin, Stephen Engstrom, Allen W. Wood, Christine M. Korsgaard, Julia Annas, and J. B. Schneewind.)

Gregor, Mary J. *Laws of Freedom: A Study of Kant's Method of Applying the Categorical Imperative in the* Metaphysik der Sitten. Oxford: Basil Blackwell, 1963.

Henrich, Dieter. *The Unity of Reason: Essays on Kant's Philosophy.* Edited by Richard Velkley. Cambridge, Mass.: Harvard University Press, 1994.

———. *Aesthetic Judgment and the Moral Image of the World: Studies in Kant.* Stanford, Calif.: Stanford University Press, 1992.

Herman, Barbara. *The Practice of Moral Judgment.* Cambridge, Mass.: Harvard University Press, 1993.

Hill, Thomas E., Jr. *Dignity and Practical Reason in Kant's Moral Theory.* Ithaca, N.Y.: Cornell University Press, 1992.

Hudson, Hud. *Kant's Compatibilism.* Ithaca, N.Y.: Cornell University Press, 1994.

Jones, Hardy E. *Kant's Principle of Personality.* Madison: University of Wisconsin Press, 1971.

Jones, W. T. *Morality and Freedom in the Philosophy of Kant.* Oxford: Oxford University Press, 1940.

Korsgaard, Christine M. *Creating the Kingdom of Ends.* Cambridge, U.K.: Cambridge University Press, 1996.

Mulholland, Leslie A. *Kant's System of Rights.* New York: Columbia University Press, 1990.

Murphy, Jeffrie G. *Kant: The Philosophy of Right.* London: Macmillan, 1970.

Nell, Onora [O'Neill]. *Acting on Principle: An Essay on Kantian Ethics.* New York: Columbia University Press, 1975.

O'Neill, Onora. *Constructions of Reason: Explorations of Kant's Practical Philosophy.* Cambridge, U.K.: Cambridge University Press, 1989.

Paton, H. J. *In Defense of Reason.* London: Hutchinson's University Library, 1951.

Potter, Nelson T., and Mark Timmons. *Morality and Universality: Essays on Ethical Universalizability.* Dordrecht: D. Reidel, 1985.

Reath, Andrews, Barbara Herman, and Christine Korsgaard, eds. *Reclaiming the History of Ethics: Essays for John Rawls.* Cambridge, U.K.: Cambridge University Press, 1997. (Includes essays by the editors and others, including Thomas Hill, Onora O'Neill, and Thomas Pogge.)

Reiner, Hans. *Duty and Inclination: The Fundamentals of Morality Discussed and Redefined with Special Regard to Kant and Schiller.* Translated by Mark Santos. The Hague: Martinus Nijhoff, 1983.

Rossvaer, Viggo. *Kant's Moral Philosophy: An Interpretation of the Categorical Imperative.* Oslo: Universitetsforlaget, 1979.

Shell, Susan Meld. *The Rights of Reason: A Study of Kant's Philosophy and Politics.* Toronto: University of Toronto Press, 1980.

Sherman, Nancy. *Making Necessity of Virtue: Aristotle and Kant on Virtue.* Cambridge: Cambridge University Press, 1997.

Singer, Marcus J. *Generalization in Ethics.* New York: Alfred A. Knopf, 1961.

Stevens, Rex P. *Kant on Moral Practice.* Macon, Ga.: Mercer University Press, 1981.

Sullivan, Roger J. *Immanuel Kant's Moral Theory.* Cambridge: Cambridge University Press, 1989.

van der Linden, Harry. *Kantian Ethics and Socialism.* Indianapolis: Hackett Publishing Co., 1988.

Whitney, George Tapley, and David F. Bowers, eds. *The Heritage of Kant.* Princeton, N.J.: Princeton University Press, 1939.

Wike, Victoria S. *Kant on Happiness in Ethics.* Albany: State University of New York Press, 1994.

Williams, T. C. *The Concept of the Categorical Imperative: A Study of the Place of the Categorical Imperative in Kant's Ethical Theory.* Oxford: Clarendon Press, 1968.

Wolff, Robert Paul, ed. *Kant: A Collection of Critical Essays.* Garden City, N.Y.: Doubleday, 1967. (Includes essays on Kant's ethics by Julius Ebbinghaus, Jonathan Harrison, John Silber, and others.)

Wood, Allen W. *Kant's Moral Religion.* Ithaca, N.Y.: Cornell University Press, 1970.

———, ed. *Self and Nature in Kant's Philosophy.* Ithaca, N.Y.: Cornell University Press, 1984. (Includes essays on Kant's ethics by T. H. Irwin, Ralf Meerbote, Wood, and Jonathan Bennett.)

Yovel, Yirmiahu, ed. *Kant's Practical Philosophy Reconsidered.* Dordrecht: Kluwer, 1989. (Includes essays in English by Henry E. Allison, Christine M. Korsgaard, Onora O'Neill, Ottfried Höffe, and others.)

Zeldin, Mary Barbara. *Freedom and the Critical Undertaking: Essays on Kant's Later Critiques.* Ann Arbor, Mich.: UMI Monographs, 1980.

## 6. Essays

This list includes essays cited in the present collection, some but by no means all further articles by authors represented in this collection (in some cases included in their books listed in the previous section), and other important articles, with a few exceptions from the last three decades and with special emphasis on the last fifteen years. The bibliographical data for books already listed in the previous sections are abbreviated.

Allison, Henry E. "The Concept of Freedom in Kant's 'Semi-Critical' Ethics." *Archiv für Geschichte der Philosophie* 68 (1986): 96–115.

———. "Justification and Freedom in the *Critique of Practical Reason.*" In *Kant's Transcendental Deductions in the Three 'Critiques' and the 'Opus postumum,'* edited by Eckhart Förster, pp. 114–30. Stanford, Calif.: Stanford University Press, 1989.

Ameriks, Karl. "Kant's Deduction of Freedom and Morality." *Journal of the History of Philosophy* 19 (1981): 53–79.

———. "The Hegelian Critique of Kantian Morality." In *New Essays on*

*Kant,* edited by Bernard den Ouden and Marcia Moen, pp. 179–212. New York: Peter Lang, 1987.

Atkinson, R. F. "Kant's Moral and Political Rigorism." In *Essays on Kant's Political Philosophy,* edited by Howard Williams, pp. 228–48. Chicago: University of Chicago Press, 1992.

Atwell, John. "The Uniqueness of the Good Will." In *Akten des 4. Internationalen Kant-Kongresses,* Vol. II, edited by Gerhard Funke, pp. 479–84. Berlin: Walter de Gruyter, 1974.

———. "Kant's Moral Model and Moral Universe." *History of Philosophy Quarterly* 3 (1983): 423–36.

Baier, Annette. "Moralism and Cruelty: Reflections on Hume and Kant." *Ethics* 103 (1993): 436–47.

Baker, Judith. "Do One's Motives Have to be Pure?" In *Philosophical Grounds of Rationality,* edited by Richard Grandy and Richard Warner, pp. 457–74. Oxford: Oxford University Press, 1986.

———. "Counting Categorical Imperatives." *Kant-Studien* 79 (1988): 389–406.

Bamford, Paul. "The Ambiguity of the Categorical Imperative." *Journal of the History of Philosophy* 17 (1979): 135–41.

Baron, Marcia: "The Alleged Moral Repugnance of Acting from Duty." *Journal of Philosophy* 81 (1984): 197–220; revised in her *Kantian Ethics Almost without Apology,* pp. 117–45.

———. "Kantian Ethics and Supererogation." *Journal of Philosophy* 84 (1987): 237–62; reprinted in her *Kantian Ethics Almost without Apology,* pp. 21–58.

Beck, Lewis White. "Apodictic Imperatives." *Kant-Studien* 49 (1957–58): 7–24; reprinted in his *Studies in the Philosophy of Kant,* pp. 177–99.

———. "The Fact of Reason: An Essay on Justification in Ethics." In *Studies in the Philosophy of Kant,* pp. 200–214. Indianapolis: Bobbs-Merrill Co., Inc., 1965.

———. "Five Concepts of Freedom in Kant." In *Philosophical Analysis and Reconstruction,* edited by J. T. J. Szrednicki, pp. 35–51. Dordrecht: Martinus Nijhoff, 1987.

Benson, Paul. "Moral Worth." *Philosophical Studies* 51 (1987): 365–82.

Benton, Robert J. "Kant's Categories of Practical Reason as Such." *Kant-Studien* 71 (1980): 181–201.

Broadie, Alexander, and Elizabeth M. Pybus. "Kant's Concept of Respect." *Kant-Studien* 66 (1975): 58–64.

———. "Kant and Direct Duties." *Dialogue* 20 (1981): 60–67.

————. "Kant and Weakness of Will." *Kant-Studien* 73 (1982): 406–12.

Buchanan, Allen. "Categorical Imperatives and Moral Principles." *Philosophical Studies* 31 (1977): 249–60.

Campbell, John. "Kantian Conceptions of Moral Goodness." *Canadian Journal of Philosophy* 13 (1983): 527–50.

Cummiskey, David. "Kantian Consequentialism." *Ethics* 100 (1990): 586–615.

Dietrichson, Paul. "When Is a Maxim Fully Universalizable?" *Kant-Studien* 55 (1964): 143–70.

Donagan, Alan. "The Structure of Kant's Metaphysics of Morals." *Topoi* 4 (1985): 61–72.

————. "The Relation of Moral Theory to Moral Judgments: A Kantian Review." In *Moral Theory and Moral Judgments in Medical Ethics,* edited by Baruch A. Brody, pp. 171–92. Dordrecht: Kluwer, 1988. Reprinted in *The Philosophical Papers of Alan Donagan,* Volume II, edited by J. E. Malpas, pp. 194–216. Chicago: University of Chicago Press, 1994.

————. "The Moral Theory Almost Nobody Knows: Kant's." In *The Philosophical Papers of Alan Donagan,* Volume II, edited by J. E. Malpas, pp. 144–52. Chicago: University of Chicago Press, 1994.

Engstrom, Stephen. "Herman on Mutual Aid." *Ethics* 96 (1986): 346–94.

————. "Conditioned Autonomy." *Philosophy and Phenomenological Research* 48 (1988): 435–53.

————. "The Concept of the Highest Good in Kant's Moral Theory." *Philosophy and Phenomenological Research* 52 (1992): 747–80.

Flynn, James R. "The Logic of Kant's Derivation of Freedom from Reason." *Kant-Studien* 77 (1986): 441–64.

Foot, Philippa. "Morality As a System of Hypothetical Imperatives." *Philosophical Review* 81 (1972): 305–16.

Friedman, R. Z. "The Importance and Function of Kant's Highest Good." *Journal of the History of Philosophy* 22 (1984): 325–42.

Galvin, Richard F. "Does Kant's Psychology of Morality Need Basic Revision?" *Mind* 100 (1991): 221–36.

————. "Ethical Formalism: The Contradiction in Conception Test." *History of Philosophy Quarterly* 8 (1991): 387–408.

Genova, Anthony C. "Kant's Transcendental Deduction of the Moral Law." *Kant-Studien* 69 (1978): 299–313.

Green, Michael K. "Kant and Moral Self-Deception." *Kant-Studien* 83 (1992): 148–69.

Green, Ronald M. "The First Formulation of the Categorical Imperative As Literally a 'Legislative' Metaphor." *History of Philosophy Quarterly* 8 (1991): 163–79.

Guyer, Paul. "The Unity of Reason: Pure Reason As Practical Reason in Kant's Early Conception of the Transcendental Dialectic." *Monist* 72 (1989): 139–67.

———. "Mendelssohn and Kant: One Source of the Critical Philosophy." *Philosophical Topics* 19 (1991): 119–52.

———. "Kant's Morality of Law and Morality of Freedom." In *Kant and Critique: New Essays in Honor of W. H. Werkmeister,* edited by R. M. Dancy, pp. 43–89. Dordrecht: Kluwer, 1993.

———. "Duty and Inclination." In *Kant and the Experience of Freedom: Essays on Aesthetics and Morality,* pp. 335–93. Cambridge, U.K.: Cambridge University Press, 1993.

———. "The Value of Agency: Review Article of Barbara Herman, *The Practice of Moral Judgment." Ethics* 106 (1996): 404–23.

Harbison, Warren G. "The Good Will." *Kant-Studien* 71 (1980): 47–59.

Harris, Nigel. "Kantian Duties and Immoral Agents." *Kant-Studien* 83 (1992): 336–43.

Harrison, Jonathan. "Kant's Examples of the First Formulation of the Categorical Imperative." *Philosophical Quarterly* 7 (1957): 50–62. Reprinted in *Kant: A Collection of Critical Essays,* edited by Robert Paul Wolff, pp. 228–45, and in *Foundations of the Metaphysics of Morals with Critical Essays,* edited by Robert Paul Wolff, 208–29.

Henson, Richard. "What Kant Might Have Said: Moral Worth and the Overdetermination of Dutiful Action." *Philosophical Review* 88 (1979): 39–54.

Herman, Barbara. "On the Value of Acting from the Motive of Duty." *Philosophical Review* 90 (1981): 359–82; reprinted in her *The Practice of Moral Judgment,* pp. 1–22.

———. "The Practice of Moral Judgment," *Journal of Philosophy* 82 (1985): 414–36; reprinted in her *The Practice of Moral Judgment,* pp. 73–92.

Heyd, David. "Beyond the Call of Duty in Kant's Ethics." *Kant-Studien* 71 (1980): 308–24.

Hill, Thomas E., Jr. "The Hypothetical Imperative." *Philosophical Review* 82 (1973): 429–50; reprinted in his *Dignity and Practical Reason in Kant's Moral Philosophy,* pp. 17–37. Ithaca, N.Y.: Cornell University Press, 1992.

———. "Humanity As an End in Itself." *Ethics* 91 (1980): 84–99; re-

printed in his *Dignity and Practical Reason in Kant's Moral Theory,*
pp. 38–57.

————. "Donagan's Kant." *Ethics* 104 (1993): 22–52.

Hinman, Lawrence M. "On the Purity of Our Moral Motives: A Critique
of Kant's Account of the Emotions and Acting for the Sake of Duty."
*Monist* 66 (1983): 251–67.

Hudson, Hud. "*Wille, Willkür* and the Imputability of Immoral Actions." *Kant-Studien* 82 (1991): 179–96.

Jensen, Henning. "Kant and Moral Integrity." *Philosophical Studies* 57
(1989): 193–205.

Kemp, John. "Kant's Examples of the Categorical Imperative." In *Kant:
A Collection of Critical Essays,* edited by Robert Paul Wolff, pp. 246–
58, and in *Foundations of the Metaphysics of Morals with Critical
Essays,* edited by Robert Paul Wolff, pp. 230–44.

Korsgaard, Christine M. "Two Distinctions in Goodness." *Philosophical Review* 92 (1983): 169–95; reprinted in her *Creating the Kingdom of Ends,* pp. 249–74.

————. "Kant's Formula of Universal Law." *Pacific Philosophical
Quarterly* 66 (1985): 24–27; reprinted in her *Creating the Kingdom
of Ends,* pp. 77–105.

————. "Aristotle and Kant on the Source of Value." *Ethics* 96 (1986):
486–505; reprinted in her *Creating the Kingdom of Ends,* 225–48.

————. "Kant's Formula of Humanity." *Kant-Studien* 77 (1986): 183–
202; reprinted in her *Creating the Kingdom of Ends,* pp. 106–32.

————. "The Right to Lie: Kant on Dealing with Evil." *Philosophy and
Public Affairs* 15 (1986): 325–49; reprinted in her *Creating the Kingdom of Ends,* pp. 133–58.

————. "Morality as Freedom." In *Kant's Practical Philosophy Reconsidered,* edited by Yirmiahu Yovel, pp. 23–48; reprinted in her *Creating the Kingdom of Ends,* pp. 159–87.

Louden, Robert. "Kant's Virtue Ethics." *Philosophy* 61 (1986): 473–89.

Lukow, Pawel. "The Fact of Reason: Kant's Passage to Ordinary Moral
Knowledge." *Kant-Studien* 84 (1993): 204–21.

MacBeath, A. Murray. "Kant on Moral Feeling." *Kant-Studien* 64
(1973): 283–314.

Massey, Stephen J. "Kant on Self-Respect." *Journal of the History of
Philosophy* 21 (1983): 57–74.

McCarthy, Michael. "Kant's Application of the Analytic/Synthetic Distinction to Imperatives." *Dialogue* 18 (1979): 373–91.

————. "Kant's Rejection of the Argument of *Groundwork* III." *Kant-Studien* 73 (1982): 169–90.

————. "The Objection of Circularity in *Groundwork* III." *Kant-Studien* 76 (1985): 28–42.

McCarty, Richard. "The Limits of Kantian Duty, and Beyond." *American Philosophical Quarterly* 26 (1989): 43–52.

————. "Moral Conflicts in Kantian Ethics." *History of Philosophy Quarterly* 8 (1991): 65–79.

————. "Kantian Moral Motivation and the Feeling of Respect." *Journal of the History of Philosophy* 31 (1993): 421–35.

————. "Motivation and Moral Choice in Kant's Theory of Rational Agency." *Kant-Studien* 85 (1994): 15–31.

Mulholland, Leslie A. "Kant: On Willing Maxims to Become Laws of Nature." *Dialogue* 17 (1978): 95–105.

Nakhnikian, George. "Kantian Universalizability and the Objectivity of Moral Judgments." In *Morality and Universality,* edited by Nelson Potter and Mark Timmons, pp. 187–233. Dordrecht: D. Reidel, 1985.

————. "Kant's Theory of Hypothetical Imperatives." *Kant-Studien* 83 (1992): 21–49.

Nesbitt, Winston. "Categorical Imperatives—A Defense." *Philosophical Review* 86 (1977): 217–25.

Nuyen, A. T. "Sense, Passions and Morals in Hume and Kant." *Kant-Studien* 82 (1991): 42–62.

————. "Counting the Formulas of the Categorical Imperative: One Plus Three Makes Four." *History of Philosophy Quarterly* 10 (1993): 37–48.

O'Connor, Daniel. "Good and Evil Disposition." *Kant-Studien* 76 (1985): 288–302.

O'Neill, Onora. "Universal Laws and Ends in Themselves." *Monist* 72 (1989): 341–61; reprinted in her *Constructions of Reason,* pp. 126–44.

————. "Vindicating Reason." In *The Cambridge Companion to Kant,* edited by Paul Guyer, pp. 288–308. Cambridge: Cambridge University Press, 1992.

————. "Kant's Virtues." In *How Should One Live? Essays on the Virtues,* edited by Roger Crisp, pp. 77–97. Oxford: Oxford University Press, 1996.

Packer, Mark. "Kant on Desire and Moral Pleasure." *Journal of the History of Ideas* (1989): 429–42.

Paton, H. J. "Conscience and Kant." *Kant-Studien* 70 (1979): 329–51.

Potter, Nelson. "Does Kant Have Two Concepts of Freedom? In *Akten des 4. Internationalen Kant-Kongresses,* edited by Gerhard Funke, pp. 590–96. Berlin: Walter de Gruyter, 1974.

———. "How to Apply the Categorical Imperative." *Philosophia* 5 (1975): 395–416.

———. "Kant on Ends That Are at the Same Time Duties." *Pacific Philosophical Quarterly* 66 (1985): 78–92.

———. "What Is Wrong with Kant's Four Examples." *Philosophy Research Archives* 18 (1993): 213–29.

———. "Kant and the Moral Worth of Actions." *Southern Journal of Philosophy* 34 (1996): 225–41.

Rauscher, Frederick. "Pure Reason and the Moral Law: A Source of Kant's Critical Philosophy." *History of Philosophy Quarterly* 13 (1996): 255–71.

Rawls, John. "Themes in Kant's Moral Philosophy." In *Kant's Transcendental Deductions: The Three 'Critiques' and the Opus postumum,* edited by Eckhard Förster, pp. 81–113. Stanford: Stanford University Press, 1989.

Reath, Andrews. "Two Conceptions of the Highest Good in Kant." *Journal of the History of Philosophy* 26 (1988): 593–619.

———. "The Categorical Imperative and Kant's Conception of Practical Rationality." *Monist* 72 (1989): 384–410.

———. "Kant's Theory of Moral Sensibility: Respect for the Law and the Influence of Inclination." *Kant-Studien* 80 (1989): 284–302.

———. "Hedonism, Heteronomy, and Kant's Principle of Happiness." *Pacific Philosophical Quarterly* 70 (1989): 42–72.

———. "Legislating the Moral Law." *Nous* 28 (1994): 435–64.

Reich, Klaus. "Kant and Greek Ethics." *Mind* 48 (1939): 338–54, 446–63.

Riley, Patrick. "Kant on Persons as 'Ends in Themselves'." *Modern Schoolman* 59 (1979): 45–56.

Rollin, Bernard. "There Is Only One Categorical Imperative." *Kant-Studien* 67 (1976): 60–72.

———. "Beasts and Men: The Scope of Moral Concern." *Modern Schoolman* 55 (1978): 241–60.

Rumsey, Jean. "The Development of Character in Kantian Moral Theory." *Journal of the History of Philosophy* 27 (1989): 247–65.

Schaller, Walter B. "Kant on Virtue and Moral Worth." *Southern Journal of Philosophy* 25 (1987): 559–73.

————. "The Relation of Moral Worth to the Good Will in Kant's Ethics." *Journal of Philosophical Research* 17 (1992): 351–82.

————. "Should Kantians Care about Moral Worth?" *Dialogue* 32 (1993): 25–40.

Schoeman, Ferdinand. "Are Kantian Duties Categorical?" *History of Philosophy Quarterly* 8 (1991): 59–63.

Schneewind, J. B. "The Misfortunes of Virtue." *Ethics* 101 (1990): 42–63.

————. "Autonomy, Obligation and Virtue: An Overview of Kant's Moral Philosophy." In *The Cambridge Companion to Kant*, edited by Paul Guyer, pp. 309–41. Cambridge: Cambridge University Press, 1992.

————. "Kant and Natural Law Ethics." *Ethics* 104 (1993): 53–74.

Sedgwick, Sally. "On the Relation of Pure Reason to Content: A Reply to Hegel's Critique of Formalism in Kant's Ethics." *Philosophy and Phenomenological Research* 49 (1988): 59–80.

————. "Can Kant's Ethics Survive the Feminist Critique?" *Pacific Philosophical Quarterly* 71 (1990): 60–79.

————. "On Lying and the Role of Content in Kant's Ethics." *Kant-Studien* 82 (1991): 42–62.

Seidler, Michael. "Kant and the Stoics on the Emotional Life." *Philosophy Research Archives* 7 (1981): 1–56.

Sherman, Nancy. "The Place of Emotions in Kantian Morality." In *Identity, Character and Morality*, edited by Owen Flanagan and Amélie Rorty, pp. 149–70. Cambridge, Mass.: MIT Press, 1990.

Shope, Robert. "Kant's Use and Derivation of the Categorical Imperative." In *Foundations for the Metaphysics of Morals with Critical Essays*, edited by Robert Paul Wolff, pp. 253–91. Indianapolis: Bobbs-Merrill Co., Inc., 1969.

Sidgwick, Henry. "The Kantian Conception of Free Will." *Mind* 13 (1888); reprinted in his *Methods of Ethics*, seventh edition, pp. 511–16. London: Macmillan, 1907.

Silber, John. "The Copernican Revolution in Ethics: The Good Reexamined." *Kant-Studien* 51 (1959): 85–101.

————. "Kant's Conception of the Highest Good as Immanent and Transcendent." *Philosophical Review* 58 (1959): 469–92.

————. "The Context of Kant's Ethical Thought." *Philosophical Quarterly* 9 (1959): 193–207, 309–18.

————. "The Importance of the Highest Good in Kant's Ethics." *Ethics* 73 (1962–3): 179–97.

————. "Procedural Formalism in Kant's Ethics." *Review of Metaphysics* 28 (1974): 197–236.

————. "The Moral Good and the Natural Good in Kant's Ethics." *Review of Metaphysics* 36 (1982): 397–438.

Simmons, Keith. "Kant on Moral Worth." *History of Philosophy Quarterly* 6 (1989): 85–100.

Singer, Marcus G. "The Categorical Imperative." *Philosophical Review* 63 (1954): 577–91.

————. "Reconstructing the *Groundwork.*" *Ethics* 93 (1983): 566–78.

Skorpen, Erling. "Making Sense of Kant's Third Example from the *Groundwork of the Metaphysics of Morals,*" *Kant-Studien* 72 (1981): 415–29.

Stern, Paul. "The Problem of History and Temporality in Kantian Ethics." *Kant-Studien* 78 (1986): 504–45.

Stratton-Lake, Philip. "Formulating Categorical Imperatives." *Kant-Studien* 83 (1993): 317–40.

Swoyer, Chris. "Kantian Derivations." *Canadian Journal of Philosophy* 13 (1983): 409–31.

Timmons, Mark. "Contradictions and the Categorical Imperative." *Archiv für Geschichte der Philosophie* 66 (1984): 294–312.

————. "Kant on the Possibility of Moral Motivation." *Southern Journal of Philosophy* 23 (1985): 377–98.

Ward, Andrew. "On Kant's Defence of Moral Freedom." *History of Philosophy Quarterly* 8 (1991): 373–86.

Watson, Gary. "Kant on Happiness in the Moral Life." *Philosophy Research Archives* 9 (1983): 79–108.

Westphal, Kenneth. "Hegel's Criticism of Kant's Moral World View," *Philosophical Topics* 19 (1991): 137–76.

Wiggins, David. "Categorical Requirements: Kant and Hume on the Idea of Duty." *Monist* 74 (1991): 83–106.

Wike, Victoria S. "Metaphysical Foundations of Morality in Kant." *Journal of Value Inquiry* 17 (1983): 225–34.

————. "Does Kant's Ethics Require That the Moral Law Be the Sole Determining Ground of the Will?" *Journal of Value Inquiry* 27 (1993): 85–92.

Wood, Allen W. "Kant on False Promises." In *Proceedings of the Third International Kant Congress,* edited by Lewis White Beck, pp. 614–19. Dordrecht: D. Reidel, 1972.

————. "Kant on the Rationality of Morals." In *Actes du Congrès d'Ottawa sur Kant/Proceedings of the Ottawa Congress on Kant,* edited by Pierre Laberge, Francois Duchesneau, and Bryan E. Morrisey, pp. 94–109. Ottawa: University of Ottawa Press, 1976.

———. "The Emptiness of the Moral Will." *Monist* 72 (1989): 454–83.

———. "Unsocial Sociability: The Anthropological Basis of Kantian Ethics." *Philosophical Topics* 19 (1991): 325–51.

Young, Julian. "Schopenhauer's Critique of Kant's Ethics." *Kant-Studien* 75 (1984): 191–212.

# Index

agency: circumstances affecting, 139, 160n11; and inclination, 92; for Kant and Crusius, 20–21; for Kant and moral skeptics, 15, 17–18; true needs of human agents, 142, 157. *See also* rational agency; right action; will, the

analytical method: for determining supreme principle of morality, xviii–xxi, 43, 60, 273; in *Groundwork* Section II, xxxix, 220, 251; in *Prolegomena,* 306–7, 326

animals, 149, 171

appearances: and reality in human action, xli; skeptics moved by, 8, 14–15; and things in themselves, 336

Aristotle, 58, 93, 94–95, 99n15, 99n26

autonomy: in categorical imperative's derivation, 41–42; and categorical imperatives first formulation, xxxvii–xxxviii; in categorical imperative's third formulation, xxxvi, 216; and consistency, 104; definition of, 258–59; freedom of the will as, 252, 253–54; and the good will, 81; and humanity as an end in itself, 170, 171; and morality, 267–69; from negative freedom to, 255–63; and possibility of categorical imperative, 234–39; as source of obligation, 70; universality tests for autonomous agents, 111

beneficence: contradiction in nonbeneficence, 122–23, 125, 135–36; as a duty, 64, 133–64, 184n2

benevolence: Butler on self-love and, 77n41; and good will, 81–100; Hutcheson on, 11–12, 18; mutual aid contrasted with, 158–59; Price on, 78n43

blame, 75n24

Butler, Joseph: on benevolence and self-love, 77n41; on conscience, 5, 6, 23n14, 76n33; on method in ethics, 22n11, 24n26; on morality and religious skepticism, 24n37; on moral precepts, 22n10; and natural law theory, 7

categorical imperative, 101–246; as condition of rational action, xxxi–xxxii; content problem, 205–7; as criterion of right action, 43, 44–45; deduction of, 330; defined, xxvi; ends in themselves as grounded in, 172–73; examples in argument for, 134–35; first formulation, xxvi, xxxii–xxxiv, xxxv, 36, 103–29, 189–93, 216–28, 268; formal character of, 128; formulations of, xxxii, xxxvi–xxxviii, 208n2, 215–24, 240n3, 242n12; for Kant and moral skeptics, 16–17; Kant's justification of, 40–42, 49n23; as necessary and sufficient condition of permissibil-

# About the Authors

**Henry E. Allison** is professor of philosophy at Boston University and was previously professor of philosophy at the University of California, San Diego, for many years. His numerous books include *Lessing and the Enlightenment* (1966), *The Kant-Eberhard Controversy* (1973), *Kant's Transcendental Idealism* (1983), *Kant's Theory of Freedom* (1990), and *Idealism and Freedom: Essays on Kant's Theoretical and Practical Philosophy* (1996).

**Paul Guyer** is the Florence R. C. Murray Professor in the Humanities at the University of Pennsylvania. His books include *Kant and the Claims of Taste* (1979, 1997), *Kant and the Claims of Knowledge* (1987), and *Kant and the Experience of Freedom* (1993). He is also the editor of *The Cambridge Companion to Kant* (1992). With Allen W. Wood, he is the editor and translator of Kant's *Critique of Pure Reason* in the Cambridge Edition of the Works of Immanuel Kant (1998). He has also edited *Essays in Kant's Aesthetics* with Ted Cohen (1982) and *Pursuits of Reason* with Ted Cohen and Hilary Putnam (1993).

**Dieter Henrich** is professor of philosophy, emeritus, at the Ludwig-Maximilians Universität, Munich. Two collections of his essays have been translated into English: *The Unity of Reason: Essays on Kant's Philosophy* (1994) and *Aesthetic Judgment and the Moral Image of the World: Studies in Kant* (1992). Among his numerous books in German, some of the most important are *Der Ontologische Gottesbeweis* (second edition, 1960), *Hegel im Kontext* (1971), *Identität und Objektivität* (1976), *Selbstverhältnisse* (1982), *Der Gang des Andenkens* (1986), and *Konstellationen: Probleme und Debatten am Ursprung der idealistischen Philosophie* (1991).

**Barbara Herman** is Griffin Chair of Philosophy at the University of California, Los Angeles. She is the author of *The Practice of Moral Judgment* (1993) and the editor, along with Christine M. Korsgaard and Andrews Reath, of *Reclaiming the History of Ethics: Essays in Honor of John Rawls* (1997).

**Thomas E. Hill, Jr.,** is Kenan Professor of Philosophy at the University of North Carolina at Chapel Hill. His many papers on both Kantian and contemporary ethics have been collected in *Dignity and Practical Reason in Kant's Moral Theory* (1992) and *Autonomy and Self-Respect* (1991).

**Christine M. Korsgaard** is professor of philosophy at Harvard University. She is the author of *Creating the Kingdom of Ends* (1996) and *The Sources of Normativity* (1996), and, along with Barbara Herman and Andrews Reath, editor of *Reclaiming the History of Ethics: Essays in Honor of John Rawls* (1997).

**Onora O'Neill** is professor of philosophy and principal of Newnham College, Cambridge University. She has written widely on moral and political philosophy. Her books include *Acting on Principle* (1975), *The Faces of Hunger* (1986), *Constructions of Reason: Explorations of Kant's Practical Philosophy* (1989), and *Towards Justice and Virtue* (1996).

**Thomas W. Pogge** is associate professor of philosophy at Columbia University. In addition to many articles on ethics and political philosophy, he has published *Realizing Rawls* (1989) and *John Rawls* (1994, in German).

**Nelson Potter** is associate professor of philosophy at the University of Nebraska. In addition to his numerous articles on Kant's moral and political philosophy, he has edited, with Mark Timmons, *Morality and Universality: Essays on Ethical Universalizability* (1985).

**J. B. Schneewind** is professor of philosophy at Johns Hopkins University. His many publications include *Background of Victorian English Literature* (1970), *Sidgwick's Ethics and Victorian Moral Philosophy* (1975), the two-volume anthology *Moral Philosophy from Montaigne to Kant* (1990), and *The Invention of Autonomy* (1998). With Peter

Heath, he is editor of Kant's *Lectures on Ethics* for the Cambridge Edition of the Works of Immanuel Kant (1997).

**Tom Sorell** is professor of philosophy at the University of Essex (England). His publications include *Hobbes* in "The Arguments of the Philosophers" (1986), *Descartes* (1987), *Moral Theory and Capital Punishment* (1987), and *Scientism: Philosophy and the Infatuation with Science* (1991); he has also edited *The Rise of Modern Philosophy: The Tension between the New and Traditional Philosophies from Machiavelli to Leibniz* (1993) and *The Cambridge Companion to Hobbes* (1996).

**Allen Wood** is professor of philosophy at Yale University, having been for many years previously professor of philosophy at Cornell. His many publications include *Kant's Moral Religion* (1970), *Kant's Rational Theology* (1978), *Karl Marx* in "The Arguments of the Philosophers" (1981), and *Hegel's Ethical Thought* (1990). As editor and translator, he has produced, with Gertrude Clark, *Kant's Lectures on Rational Theology* (1978); with H. B. Nisbet, Hegel's *Elements of the Philosophy of Right* (1991); with George De Giovanni, Kant's *Religion and Rational Theology* in the Cambridge Edition of the Works of Immanuel Kant (1996); and with Paul Guyer, Kant's *Critique of Pure Reason* in the same series (1998). He has also edited *Self and Nature in Kant's Philosophy* (1984).